LP Clerc's PHOTOGRAPHY
THEORY AND PRACTICE

Edited by **DA** Spencer PhD, DIC, FRIC, Hon. FIIP, Hon. FRPS

PHOTOGRAPHY
THEORY AND PRACTICE

Monochrome
Processing

Revised by RE Jacobson MSc, PhD, ARIC

AMPHOTO
American Photographic Book
Publishing Company, Inc.
New York, N.Y. 10010

Completely revised and enlarged edition.

Originally published by Sir Isaac Pitman & Sons Ltd.

First Edition 1930
Second Edition 1937
Reprinted 1940
Reprinted 1942
Reprinted 1944
Reprinted 1946
Reprinted 1947
Third Edition 1954
Completely revised Edition 1970/71

© 1971 FOCAL PRESS LIMITED

ISBN 0-8174-0780-4

Library of Congress Catalog Card No. 73-106378

Printed and bound in Great Britain at the Pitman Press, Bath

Preface

There have been few really classical textbooks in photography. One of these, Louis Philippe Clerc's *La Technique Photographique,* was first published in 1926, and went through six French editions. The last of these was published just after the author's death in 1959. It was as unique a work as L. P. Clerc's personality was as a man. For *La Technique Photographique* was the first comprehensive treatise on photographic theory and practice, covering the whole field concisely yet precisely, scientifically yet in clearly understandable form.

The key to these qualities is that L. P. Clerc was probably the last photographic scientist to be able to keep an overall view over a discipline which – since his death in 1959 – has expanded far beyond the scope of any single man or mind.

L. P. Clerc himself devoted a long life to photographic research and writing. He accumulated the leading honours awarded in photographic activities – from membership of the Council of the *Société Française de Photographie et de Cinématographie* and honorary professorship at the *Institut d'Optique* to the progress medal of the *Royal Photographic Society* and the honorary Fellowships of the *R.P.S.* and the *Photographic Society of America.* At the same time he gained some of the highest distinctions in public service – including the *Croix de Guerre* and *Chevalier de la Legion d'Honneur.*

His qualification for the unique coverage of *La Technique Photographique* was his encyclopaedic and versatile knowledge of photographic science and technology which ensured his leading position in the French photographic industry as scientific consultant, research leader, teacher, lecturer and author. In this connection he read for over fifty years almost everything published on photography in the majority of international technical journals. The worthwhile and significant parts of this information appeared in the journal *Le procédé* which he started in 1898, and later in *Science et Industries Photographique,* which he founded in 1921 and which is still being continued by one of his close collaborators.

Three English editions of *La Technique Photographique* – with a number of intermediate reprints – appeared as *Photography: Theory and Practice* between 1930 and 1954. The last of these had to face the problem that one man could no longer span the whole photographic field, and it became the joint work of a number of expert photographic scientists and writers who brought their specialized knowledge to the sections they covered. The present edition necessarily continues this principle. It also has two specific purposes.

The first is to make *Photography: Theory and Practice* once more the exhaustive current textbook which *La Technique Photographique* was in its day. It has therefore been very extensively rewritten. But even with this radical revision the express aim remained to follow Clerc's original style and presentation as far as possible. Inevitably the work has grown to just over double the size of the third English edition, even though certain very marginal sections have been dropped.

The second purpose is to make *Photography: Theory and Practice* easily accessible to students of scientific as well as professional photography at photographic schools and courses – for whom such a comprehensive text and reference book should prove particularly valuable. To this end the book is being published in separate sections which the student can buy at an economic price and handle more easily. Eventually, the complete work will be issued in a hardbound version.

The present volume is the fourth in this series, and concerns itself with the handling of monochrome materials before, during and after processing as well as basic information on developing agents, theories of development and after-treatment procedures.

Two points of detail remain to be made:

(1) The sections, though part of a whole, are self-contained. Their sequence is logical, but not a compulsory order of study, especially for students with a certain basic knowledge of the subject. Even the paragraphs – though following a rational progression within each section – present essentially distinct aspects, steps of exposition or items of information. They are of course cross-referenced where necessary. For this reason the paragraphs are numbered; this numbering is also the form of reference in the index at the end.

(2) As in previous editions, no bibliographical references are included. The reason is that such references would have added enormously to the bulk of the book – with comparatively little advantage to most readers, in view of the limited accessibility of original literature sources in other than specialized libraries. The references have therefore been confined to a mention of the names of authors (and dates) of various discoveries, improvements, etc. This will serve to narrow down the scope of any bibliographic search which some readers may wish to carry out.

PUBLISHER'S NOTE

Please note that the pagination of this volume is arranged as follows:
Section V pages 427–608.

Volume I contained: Section I pages 1–60
Section II pages 61–176

Volume II contained: Section III pages 177–300.

Volume III contained: Section IV pages 301–426.

Contents

SECTION V
MONOCHROME PROCESSING

CHAPTER XXVII

DARKROOM EQUIPMENT

485. Illumination. The choice of illumination to be used when handling sensitive material, either during manufacture or during the various operations prior to and including fixation, depends on two factors, firstly on the distribution of the spectral sensitivity of the emulsion under consideration, and secondly on the colour sensitivity of the eye.

It may be laid down that there is no really *non-actinic illumination* in the true sense of the word ; that is to say, that there is no light, whatever may be its spectral distribution and however weak in intensity it may be, which will not fog a photographic emulsion if allowed to act for long enough.

It is seen that in choosing suitable illumination for a darkroom a compromise has to be made between somewhat incompatible conditions. Sufficient light must be available, when needed, for the effective control of operations being carried out, but this must not appreciably fog the sensitive material during the normal time required for the necessary manipulations.

In order to make the practical application of these ideas clear, the optimum conditions for handling a panchromatic emulsion equally sensitive to all the colours of the spectrum will be considered. Three filters, coloured respectively blue-violet, green, and red, each transmitting a third of the range of the visible spectrum and in the same proportions, could be used indifferently as filters for the darkroom lamp if only the actinic values of the light thus transmitted were being considered. An emulsion, given the same exposure time, would give the same fog-density to each of the three illuminants. But, if the physiological response to the three illuminations is considered, the blue-violet becomes a poor illuminator, the red little better, while the best visibility is obtained by the use of the green. This is in agreement with what has already been stated with regard to the spectral sensitivity of the human eye (§ 4, Fig. 1.3). If, by suitable regulation of their respective intensities, two filters, coloured red and green, were prepared to have the same visual intensity, it will be found that if the source of light common to both be reduced in intensity, the red will appear less intensely illuminated than the green (Purkinje phenomenon).

By means of the aperture of the iris and the sensitivity of the retina, the eye adapts itself automatically to low levels of illumination after a period of time. While the opening and shutting of the iris is very rapid, the adjustment of the retina is slow. From bright sunlight to darkness about half an hour is required for adaptation while approximately ten minutes is necessary when passing from normal illumination to that of the photographic darkroom. The rate of adaptation from light to dark is very much slower than the reverse action. When coming into the light for a short time, after dark adaptation, in order to avoid the loss of time of a fresh adaptation, black spectacles (density 2, approximately) with a fitting excluding all light except that passing the glasses may be worn. The presence in the field of view of a spot more strongly illuminated than the objects that are being looked at reduces the sensitivity of the eye and is a cause of fatigue. This is found in its worst form if the lamp, or its reflection from some bright object, is in the field of view when the illumination in the darkroom is extremely low (P. G. Nutting, 1916).

The same physiological considerations still apply even when the emulsion under consideration is not equally sensitive to the whole of the spectrum. For example, an emulsion sensitized with pinachrome may be regarded as insensitive to the extreme red (beyond 680 n.m.) but a coloured filter transmitting only these radiations would appear so feebly luminous that a green filter, transmitting much less luminous energy but giving the same visibility, would give, as a rule, an equal degree of safety. For the same reason, although an orange filter usually transmits all the red, there is often less risk of fog with an orange light than with a red one, since, for the same visibility, less total luminous energy is necessary. The advantage of an orange light is particularly noticeable when working with very rapid emulsions which, are often slightly sensitive to the extreme red, as the proportion of these feebly active radiations is much less than it would be in the case of a red light.

The source of light and filter combined must not transmit ultra-violet which is very active on all sensitive emulsions. (This condition is satisfied when the usual artificial illuminants are used, but it must be borne in mind if daylight is employed or electric lamps with metallic gases or vapours of neon, mercury, sodium, thallium, etc.).

486. Choice of Darkroom Illumination. In practice, the following lighting is used for various types of sensitive material—

Slow positive silver chloride emulsions (for development) . . .	Yellow
Rapid positive silver bromide emulsions	Yellow or Orange
Rapid negative emulsions (blue sensitive)	Orange-red or yellow-green
Orthochromatic emulsions (green sensitive)	Ruby-red
Panchromatic and colour emulsions .	Bluish-green or amber of low intensity
Emulsions sensitive to infra-red, but not to green	Pure green

It should be remembered that red light increases the apparent contrast of images and induces one to curtail the development; where

there is a choice of illumination, orange or green should be chosen.

From the fact that a certain red and a certain green are complementary, inventors have attempted to get a colourless non-actinic light for ordinary plates by blending red and green lights, which separately are non-actinic. As it is possible to produce only a yellow in this manner, it is much simpler to use a plain yellow filter in all cases where the sensitivity of the emulsion permits.

Special filters for the illumination of photographic darkrooms are usually described as safelight screens. The safelight screen is generally made by coating a gelatine layer, containing suitable dyes, on glass. One or more of these elements (together with some form of diffuser) may be combined to make the safelight.

Safelights applicable to each case are worked out by taking into consideration the colour sensitivity of the eye and the particular photographic material, and then suitable tests are made to determine the density required for the filter. This may be determined by the time taken to give a certain fog density on the material, the intensity of the light source and distance of safelight from the photographic material being fixed. The minimum safety time is chosen and the density of the safelight screen adjusted to give this safety factor. A darkroom may be well illuminated in its entirety by use of suitable direct and indirect safelights, without the sensitive material being too strongly illuminated. Whereas in earlier times when the traditional deep-red glass safelights were used, only a small area immediately next to the safelight was illuminated and the rest of the room was completely dark.

Although badly illuminated darkrooms hinder work, it is interesting to note that, as a result of many clinical observations on workers in photographic plate and film factories who have worked for many years in darkness or in feebly actinic light, Drs. F. Heim and E. Aglasse-Lafont (1912) have concluded that *occupational anaemia,* caused by working in darkness, *does not exist.*

To ensure good general illumination of the darkroom, the walls and ceiling should be light in colour; the diffused light from the walls cannot be more dangerous than the light which issues directly from the darkroom lamp. Since red light is so frequently used, red ink and pencils which give marks totally illegible in red and faintly legible in yellow light, should not be used for labels, notes, or for any memoranda used in darkrooms.

The use of a desensitizer, either as a preliminary bath or in the developer itself, allows a very bright light to be used from the moment the emulsion has been effectively desensitized, so that the remaining operations may be carried out in a yellow or white light without the slightest risk of fog whatever the original sensitivity of the materials in use.

487. Light Sources. Safelight screens supplied by a reliable photographic manufacturer are recommended for use with a particular wattage lamp, usually a 15- or 25-watt lamp, and provided the lamp is run at the correct voltage, it should be possible to obtain the maximum illumination permissible with any particular emulsion.

Failure in the domestic electricity supply may be guarded against by having an emergency lighting outfit, thus avoiding being interrupted in the course of work. Also an electric pocket lamp may be converted into a darkroom lamp by fixing a safelight in front of the lens, which acts as a filter for the light.

Particular care should be taken in a darkroom to ensure that all electrical fittings are sufficiently insulated and guarded. Fatal accidents have happened following contact of wet fingers with poorly insulated connexions and earthed fittings, especially when the floor is damp or the other hand is dipped in a liquid connected to earth.

Despite the considerable progress which has been made in electric lighting, most of the energy consumed is converted into heat, and so the ventilation of electric lamps is just as necessary as it is for other types of lamp. The life of an electric lamp is always shortened if the lamp is used at a higher temperature than would be attained if it were not enclosed.

Neon pilot lamps which emit a very feeble orange glow (about 1 candle-power) may be used with advantage where only a very faint light is required (e.g. for reading a darkroom watch or clock placed on the work bench, or for illuminating passages between several darkrooms). Whenever these lamps are used on the work bench a yellow safelight should be employed to cut off the small proportion of violet rays emitted.

For large darkrooms (greater than about 20 × 30 ft.) sodium safelamps may be used. They provide a good general illumination equivalent to about ten conventional safelights but may be used only for low speed non-colour sensitive materials. For smaller darkrooms diffusers are required to reduce the illumination to a safe level.

The reader should be cautioned against the use of lamps with red bulbs (red glass or glass covered with red varnish), which are more useful for decorative lighting at fêtes than for photographic purposes. The few lamps specially manufactured to transmit the correct part of the spectrum are very much higher priced than ordinary lamps, and the difference in price, after several replacements, amounts to more than the cost of a good darkroom safelight fitting.

488. Safelight Fittings. The chief quality demanded of a safelight is that it shall stop all light other than that which passes through the safelight screen or filter. It must be sufficiently well ventilated not to cause damage through over-heating of the filters of paper or gelatine (charring, melting, etc.), which are obviously more susceptible to injury of this kind than the coloured glass which, at one time, was the only material used. In some safelights the screens are separated from the lamp itself by a sheet of glass, and the two compartments thus formed are separately ventilated.

From every point of view work is considerably facilitated if the lamp gives only a diffused light. This may be achieved either by the safelight screen itself being a diffuser, or by arranging the source of light so that the light which falls on the screen comes from the mat-white surface of the interior of the safelight box which can be regarded as a source of diffused light. In addition to the safelight which illuminates the work bench, it is useful to have one illuminating the ceiling. This gives a general indirect illumination, the value of which has already been emphasized for other purposes. The screens for this safelight may pass more light than those for bench use. This method of illumination is the only one used in the emulsion-coating rooms of some factories.

It is preferable that the luminous surface of the safelight should not be visible to the operator in his normal working position. This may be achieved by careful positioning of the safelights or by using a hinged shutter or opaque screen to eliminate illumination falling directly into the operator's eyes but which can be removed when required to allow a negative to be examined by transmitted light in the course of its development.

Mention may be made for the sake of reference of an arrangement which has often been commended, namely a plate of glass, illuminated from beneath, on which a glass developing dish is placed. The negative can then be examined by transmitted light when necessary, without it being necessary to remove it from the dish.

It is not necessary to describe the innumerable types of safelight, more or less satisfactory in design and construction, which have been manufactured; description of those at present available will be found in the dealers' catalogues.

489. Testing of Safelights. The spectroscopic examination of safelights, which is sometimes recommended and possibly used as a guarantee of these goods, is entirely illusory. The harmful rays, for example the violet rays transmitted by many red glasses, when dispersed by the spectroscope, affect our eyes so little that they are often unnoticed even when the source of light is the sun or a strong electric arc. A spectrographic examination can only be of use when the eye is replaced by a photographic plate of the same kind as that for which the safelight is intended. It has been suggested (H. Arens and J. Eggert, 1929) that the spectrograph should be illuminated through a filter to give an equal visual intensity throughout the spectrum obtained. A spectrogram on the emulsion to be used indicates by its least dense areas at what wavelengths the safelight may be designed to give the maximum transmission. A second test with the safelight under test interposed indicates whether the active spectral areas have been absorbed. The only visual examination capable of giving any safe indication as to the quality of a safelight is that in which various filters transmitting only one portion of the spectrum (*monochromatic filters*) are superposed on to the safelight to be examined; in these circumstances the combination should in no case appear to transmit rays which should be absorbed by the safelight.

The best, and, incidentally, the simplest, method of testing a safelight is to make a practical test under reasonable conditions. Taking into consideration a number of factors, such as the time normally required for loading the photographic material into a dark-slide, length of time for development and whether the plate or film will be covered or exposed to the safelight during the development, a period of time is chosen to be the maximum that the material will be exposed to the safelight. During this time it should not receive an exposure sufficient to give any sign of fog on development. Supposing 4 minutes is decided to be the required safety time. Then, to make the test, a plate (or film) is placed in a printing frame, and about a third of it is covered with black paper. A piece of cardboard, which at the start covers the whole of the sensitive surface, is moved back after fixed periods of time, so that successive strips of the material are exposed to the light; for example these strips may receive exposures of 1, 2, 4, 8, etc. minutes respectively. After development, the plate is examined, and if the 4-minute strip and the portion which has not been exposed at all do not appear to differ in density, then the safelight may be regarded as suitable for the material in question. If on the other hand, fog appears on the 1- or 2-minute strip, it is necessary either to use a lamp of lower intensity or to decrease the transmission of the safelight: this might be done by adding one or more sheets of paper, or some similar diffusing material. If, however, the first appearance of fog on the test strips indicates that a much longer exposure than 4 minutes is safe, then it is possible to increase the intensity of the lamp. In either case a test should be made after the alteration considered to be necessary has been carried out.

An exposed piece of photographic material is much more sensitive to the light from darkroom lamps than unexposed material. The reason is the existence of a non-developable kind of latent image (the sub-image), which is strongly intensified by the weak light emitted from a darkroom lamp. This has the effect of raising preferentially the low densities in the negative, i.e. of lowering the contrast. In the case of negatives for direct inspection, such as radiographs, or in prints, this effect may lead to a considerable deterioration in quality. Thus it is essential to test a safelight with an exposed piece of photographic material; the best method is to print on the material a step wedge or perhaps an ordinary picture, and to expose one-half of it to the safelight. The two halves are then processed together and a comparison will reveal the effect of the safelight.

490. Darkroom Design and Construction. A specially equipped darkroom is not essential for the production of good photographs. Any room (preferably kitchen or bathroom containing a sink and running water) may be used *after dark* as a photographic "darkroom" without alteration. Care must, of course, be taken to avoid staining the floor, furniture, and wall hangings. They may be protected by linoleum, oil cloth, American cloth or modern plastic materials. Work may also be done in a large dish, fitted to serve the purpose of a sink. If the room faces a lighted window or if there is a light outside (e.g. a street lamp), some dark fabric must be hung so that it fits tightly over the window; any light that filters through the cracks will not matter as long as the sensitive films are not exposed directly to it.

The amateur who has sufficient leisure and opportunity to work during the daytime requires a safelight and can fit up, according to his resources, a darkroom similar to that of a professional photographer. Directions are given for this in the following sections.

491. Construction of the Ideal Professional Darkroom. The first consideration is the health and safety of the worker. Do not let the darkroom be so large as to lead to its subsequent conversion into a lumber-room. On the other hand, no room should be smaller than about 6 × 8 ft., with adequate height; 400 cubic feet is usually the minimum space allowed for each worker in a darkroom. The closed rooms used for work are to be well ventilated and comfortably heated in winter. During intervals of work the air in the rooms is to be completely renewed. The floor is to be cleaned at least once a day either *before* or *after* work by washing with a damp cloth. The walls and ceiling are to be frequently cleaned.

Most solutions of salts, particularly the concentrated solutions of hypo used for fixing, cause disintegration of cement. The floor of the darkroom, at least in the working space, should preferably be paved (earthenware tiles, *not* cement, jointed with bitumen), asphalted, or covered with some impermeable composition such as *PVC* sheet or tiles. When asphalt and some composition floorings are used, heavy objects resting on the material indent it. Benches and supports for sinks, etc., should therefore be bedded on the floor below.

At the bottom of each wall, the waterproofing on the floor can usefully be swept up the corner to a height of 8 in. or more, thus preventing moisture seeping down the wall. It is particularly desirable to waterproof the floor thoroughly if there are other rooms below.

It is convenient to provide a drain in the floor to enable it to be thoroughly washed.

The interior walls, and, if possible, the ceiling, should be covered with a washable paint, preferably mat (many water paints withstand water after complete drying) of a light colour—but not white, as it gets dirty so easily, and occasions reflections, which may cause trouble when the darkroom is used for enlarging. Yellow and cream are the most suitable. They remain light whatever illuminant is used (red or green). It is well to cover the wall at the back of the sink with earthenware tiles or thin sheet lead to protect the wall from splashes. Ceilings should preferably be between 9 ft and 11 ft in height and should never be whitened with ordinary distemper as this powders and is a common cause of "pinholes" in negatives. Enamel or oil-bound distemper is satisfactory. Ducts and conduits should be kept away from the ceiling when possible.

If possible, the darkroom should have a window for ventilation when the room is not in use. The easiest way of excluding light is to replace the panes of glass by tin plate or plywood or to paste black paper over them; or a blind may be fitted between two frames, forming a trap for the light; or a detachable shutter may be constructed of plywood or by gluing opaque paper on cloth stretched on a framework, which, in turn, may be wedged in the window frame or secured by screws and bushes.

492. Passages. Where there is ample room, it is a great convenience to provide means for entering and leaving the darkroom without admitting light. One method is the *revolving door*, as shown in Fig. 27.1, the vanes closing on one another for ventilation when the darkroom is not in use. Revolving doors are not advisable unless the darkroom has an emergency exit freely accessible for use in case of danger. Another plan is a series of partitions represented in Fig. 27.2, the centre partition, at least, being preferably movable to admit large objects. If neither of these means is possible, one must be content with an ordinary door (Fig. 27.3) opening into an enclosure, covered with a large opaque black cloth, hanging in folds and arranged if possible against a frame which forms a rebate. Room can be saved by the use of two sets of such curtains, one in place of the door (Fig. 27.4). Curtains should be hung well above the level of the top of the entrance, to ensure easy entry, and should be made of thick, limp, opaque material, preferably weighted at the bottom. Whatever the means adopted, the walls of the " passage " must be painted mat black to absorb as completely as possible any light that may reach them.

If entrances and exits cannot be made

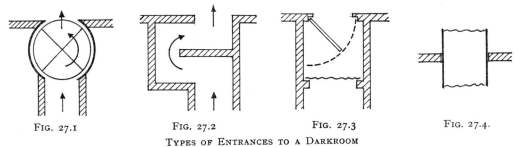

FIG. 27.1   FIG. 27.2   FIG. 27.3   FIG. 27.4.

TYPES OF ENTRANCES TO A DARKROOM

without admission of extraneous light to the darkroom, it is convenient to be able to pass slides containing exposed plates from the studio to the darkroom, or re-loaded slides from the darkroom to the studio, without having to admit white light to the darkroom. An arrangement as shown in Fig. 27.5 can be built in the partition for this purpose. It consists of a wooden box with a false bottom and

bolt has been fitted into a hollow in the other door, which is thus locked. When one door is open the bolt cannot be disengaged from the other, since it is flush with the inside wall of the open door.

Use has been made for the same purpose of a drawer opening from either side of the partition, and sliding in a sheath long enough to cover it entirely.

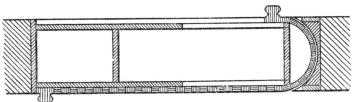

FIG. 27.5. BOX FOR LIGHT-TIGHT DELIVERY TO A DARKROOM

two openings opposite each other; a flexible curtain of strips of wood mounted on cloth is arranged so that one opening cannot be uncovered until the other has been completely closed.

Another device for the same purpose is shown in Fig. 27.6. Within the thickness of a partition wall a kind of cupboard is arranged, closed on each side by a guillotine or sliding door. A cylindrical iron rod, sliding in grooves, forms a common bolt between the two doors, one of the latter being able to slide only after a peg in the

493. **Ventilation.** Except in the case of darkrooms having permanent entrances by "passages," the exclusion of all light obviously necessitates the closing of all the means of ventilation usually found in a room. It is therefore necessary to arrange a system of ventilation which does not allow the passage of light, by air-ways to another room, or preferably to the open air.

In the more elaborate premises proper air-conditioning may be installed and this is ideal provided the plant is of sufficient size and properly fitted. In other cases, two systems are required, one for the entrance of fresh air, and the other for the removal of the contaminated air, the former near the floor of the darkroom and the latter near the ceiling.

When the ventilation is taken from a corridor or from another room, the partition is provided with a wooden frame similar to that shown in section in Fig. 27.7. The passages are formed by thin sheets of wood or metal mounted in the frame. When the ventilation is taken from the

FIG. 27.6. BOLT FOR SELF-LOCKING DARKROOM
DOOR

open, the wall is fitted with hollow bricks (Fig. 27.8), the passage being made on the outside by a zinc baffle plate, and, on the inside, by a wooden frame with a wood or iron panel. In both cases all inside walls of the passages are

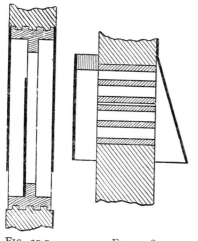

FIG. 27.7   FIG. 27.8
DARKROOM VENTILATORS

painted mat black to avoid successive reflections of light.

Ventilation to the open may also be made by shafts or wide tubes of wood or sheet iron with bends, so as to exclude the light.

Apart from providing entry and egress for air, it is desirable to ensure that a constant flow through the room is maintained. Suitably designed ventilators will do this to some extent but the use of an electric exhaust fan in a ventilator in or near the ceiling is more efficient. A six-inch fan is sufficient for small rooms but a nine-inch or larger fan should be used for bigger rooms so that the air flow is sufficient to change the air of the darkroom at least eight times in one hour. Each fan should be light-trapped by baffles similar to those in Fig. 27.8.

494. Heating. The temperature of the baths used in photography considerably affects the speed of the reactions and the quality of the images. The use of time methods of working requires the temperature of the developer to remain practically constant from one operation to another, or at least during a single operation. It is useless to try to use a warm developer in a cold darkroom, or vice versa, except by employing a water-bath of large capacity.

The best way is to keep the temperature of the darkroom constant within narrow limits (about 68°F 20°C). If full air-conditioning or central heating is not available, electric heaters may be used; special types of portable electric heaters are available which give out no light and tubular heaters or radiators can be used round the walls. Thermostatic control of the room temperature is advisable when using fixed heaters. Electric immersion heaters are very useful when one wishes to warm up rapidly a very cold bath to the temperature of the darkroom. They are heated interally by resistances, and are plunged into the liquid to be heated, and used as a stirrer.

495. Sinks. It is best to conduct all operations with liquids in a large sink. This can be made, for example, of wood, lined inside with lead (all joints must be welded, not made with tin solder), bitumastic paint, epoxy resin, polyurethane or PVC. It is possible to use sinks of bare pine, the boards being held firmly together by bolts passing the full width of the sink. It is sometimes advisable to use a jointing of thick tar in the grooves of the joints. Cement sinks are to be avoided; they are cheap but do not last long; earthenware sinks are usually too small. Chemical stoneware sinks of adequate size are made. Stainless-steel sinks are satisfactory provided chemically-resistant steels (such as type EN 58J) are used and that the sinks are entirely seamless or at least welded and polished. Rigid PVC reinforced with glass-fibre is also suitable and if damaged can be easily repaired. The bottom of the sink should always be on a slope, to allow all the water to flow away through the waste pipe (Fig. 27.9).

The sink is provided with a wooden rack from one end to the other, fitted with triangular rods,

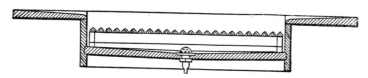

FIG. 27.9. DARKROOM SINK

so that it makes very little contact with the bottoms of dishes, and consequently does not wet them appreciably.

The internal dimensions of the sink should be such that it will hold side by side the dishes used in the various operations. It should be 6 to 9 in. deep and should not be less than 2 ft 6 in. from the floor. The sink may be extended on one side or the other by draining-boards where stock solutions can be mixed. These should have grooves draining into the sink to prevent water collecting on them.

Cold water should be laid on, if possible, from two taps; one supplies the washing tank and is arranged at one end of the sink, while the other, near the centre, is used for mixing solutions, rinsing, etc. In a darkroom often used for the handling of large plates it is an advantage to be able to operate one of the taps by foot to give the operator free use of both hands. A hot-water tap, while not essential, is often useful. It is well to choose taps of a long-neck pattern, and to fix them so that they project from the wall to about the middle point of the sink, placing them at a height such that they allow the passage under them of the tallest vessels used when standing in the bottom of the sink or on the grid. The water supply being usually at a lower temperature than that best for the various baths, it is convenient, for diluting stock solutions at the time of use, to have a separate container of about two gallons capacity, in which the water can come to the temperature of the darkroom and give up at least a part of the gases dissolved in it.

The waste pipe should preferably be covered with a perforated dome-shaped cap, to prevent its stoppage by odd pieces of film or paper. If it is wished to wash large prints in the same sink, it is useful to fit a support for a vertical tube in the waste pipe, the arrangement serving the purposes of an overflow. The waste pipe should also be provided with a trap, with an inspection plug at each bend, in case the pipe becomes stopped up.

Lead pipes should be used for the smaller waste channels and earthenware pipes for the larger drains. Other materials suitable for waste pipes and traps include: polythene, rigid PVC, stainless steel and iron. But iron corrodes quickly especially in the presence of acidic solutions and stainless steel is attacked by ferricyanide bleach, so the modern plastics are most suitable and are generally easier and cheaper to install than metal fittings. On no account should brass or copper be used for waste pipes because photographic solutions corrode them very rapidly indeed. Open, glazed gullies between the lead pipes and the main drains are convenient for cleaning and inspection. Photographic solutions can, in general, be discharged into the normal drain system unless very large volumes are involved, in which case the local authority should be consulted.

496. White Light in the Darkroom. Apart from the safelights for the darkroom, which we have studied previously, there must obviously be ordinary lighting, chiefly for cleaning, getting things ready, and examining negatives, etc., after fixation. Where electric light is used, steps must be taken to avoid confusion, during working, between the switches operating the white light and those operating the safelights. The switches for the white light may be boxed in or operated by removable keys, or may be placed higher than the others, or be of a different design and material. It is possible, for example, to use a foot-switch to light up momentarily a lamp with a white or bluish ground glass window used for examining negatives and prints immediately after fixing.

To avoid dazzling the eyes and rendering them slow in getting accustomed to the safelight, any white lights in the darkroom should be provided with ground glass or opal diffusers, so as to render the filaments or flame indistinguishable. The lamps should be arranged as high as possible so as to be out of the direct field of view.

497. General Considerations. It is a good rule that the darkroom be used only for operations which cannot be performed except in safelight. An extra "work-room" should be provided, with a sink and one or two tables and cupboards, for any work which can be done in white light, e.g. weighing chemicals, preparing baths, intensification and reduction of negatives, toning, and washing prints, and drying. If the darkroom and workroom are next to each other, the sink may be extended through the partition by making a passage through the partition. This should be of a size to allow space for a dish between the grid and the top of the aperture. The amount of light which can thus enter the darkroom will not be serious if the communication with the workroom is made in the darkest corner of the latter; a movable trapdoor or a blind of rubber cloth may be used as a safeguard. But let it be borne in mind that neither of these rooms, where the atmosphere is always somewhat damp, is suitable for keeping stocks of plates, papers, etc. There should, however, be one or two drawers in the table, for use when loading slides, for opened packets, and sufficient material to last the day only.

The table used for loading and unloading slides should be far enough from the sink to be out of the range of any splashes, and not in the direct rays of the lamp. In a very small room, a folding table with a cloth cover can be used, being erected only when required.

Bench tops should be covered with a protective material such as Formica, stainless steel or at least painted with a polyurethane paint. Polyurethane paint is also suitable for protection of exposed woodwork such as bench supports and cupboard fronts. A convenient height for tables is 2 ft 6 in. to 3 ft. Cupboards may be placed underneath provided space is left for the toes. Benches used for solutions and those for dry operations should be carefully segregated.

The darkroom should contain only what is absolutely necessary in order to facilitate working in the dim light. All useless shelves and cupboards should be vetoed; they only encumber a darkroom and make it difficult to keep it clean. A rack suitable for draining dishes under the sink, a shelf above the sink for bottles of solutions, and under this shelf a rack with notches to hold measuring and other glasses upside down, form, with the table for loading dark slides, the only necessary equipment of a darkroom used for negative-making.

If printing is to be done in the same room, there must obviously be provided a printing box and a cupboard for the printing frames and opened packets of papers. If no other room is available, there is also the enlarger to be included which may, however, be of the vertical type, and thus save space.

For ease in cleaning, avoid securing to the walls any fittings which can remain unattached. For the same reason, tables and shelves should be painted with some washable preparation, or covered with linoleum, so that they can from time to time be sponged with a wet rag. It is advisable to get rid of sharp corners in the room by nailing into them strips of wood of triangular cross-section. Sheets of fibro-cement form excellent darkroom tables if painted with bitumen or other waterproof paint. Sheets of rubber cemented on to tables of hard material greatly reduce the risk of breaking glassware.

A soap dish above the sink and a roller towel on one of the walls should not be forgotten.

It is absolutely essential to rinse the hands in clean water before drying on the towel after contact with any chemical substance, dry or in solution. This precaution is particularly necessary in the case of the fixing bath, which by contamination of the towel is the cause of many failures through handling sensitive films with fingers which are supposed to have been wiped clean.

498. Small Scale Processing Equipment. If only one or a very few negatives are treated at a time, the plates or cut films may be laid flat in a shallow dish, but when large numbers are often treated at once much time is saved if they are placed in a deep tank holding several plates vertically.

Dishes are made with the sides splayed outwards, and with a lip at one of the corners for pouring the liquid out. The sides of dishes are often made too much splayed out, to facilitate the packing of one inside the other for transport and storing. It is thus very difficult to move a dish half full of liquid or to rock it even gently without spilling some of the liquid. The fluting on the sides of glass dishes concentrates locally on the sensitive emulsion the light reaching them obliquely, thus sometimes giving rise to fogging restricted to narrow black shaded bands along one edge of the plate or film. The dishes most frequently used are not deep enough, especially in large sizes; the depth being usually the same for a dish 20 × 24 in. as for one 5 × 4 in.

For many years it was usual to make projecting ridges on the inside of the bottom of the dish to facilitate the removal of the plates. This practice was a nuisance in the use of papers and is now almost entirely abandoned. In its place we have a depression in one corner of the dish, which allows for the introduction of a finger nail or a hook under the plate to lift it.

Dish or tray development is, however, suitable only for single plates or flat films. For the handling of both plates and films in larger quantities tanks must be used. These tanks can also accommodate roll films (§ 499).

The plates or films are placed singly in metal frames or hangers (Fig. 27.18), where plates are held during all the operations until drying, or even including drying, in the case of films. The frame shown in plan and elevation in Fig. 27.18 is of the type used for plates. To assure a better hold on a film after it has been softened by wetting, curved frames may be used, or, for large films, frames with a deep rebate (which can then be perforated to allow free circulation of the liquids) or frames with spring clips at the four corners. If curved frames are used the emulsion side of the film must be the concave one. The frames, once filled, are introduced one by one, and left for the time necessary in the different baths and in the washing tank. Hangers are supported by their crosspieces on the top edge of the tank or on an internal ledge (Fig. 27.11), the latter arrangement facilitating the fitting of a light-tight lid, which enables white light to be turned on in the darkroom during development, if need be. To avoid air-bells both plate and film hangers can be introduced at an angle (not vertically). As soon as the whole emulsion is wetted the hanger is lifted up and down a few times.

The tanks should always be of such size that the plates are covered by at least $\frac{3}{4}$ in. of liquid and allow $\frac{3}{4}$ in. of liquid below them, for the accumulation of used developer or the deposition of sediment and insoluble matter.

The capacity of these vertical tanks is considerable (about 3 gallons for 12 × 10 in.), and it would be ridiculous to pour the by no means exhausted developer into a bottle every time it is used, to protect it from spontaneous oxidation. A very ingenious way of protecting the developer consists in placing in the tank, when not being used, a *floating lid* (shown in position on the tank in Fig. 27.10). This lid fits in the vessel with as little play as possible, thus reducing the surface of liquid in contact with the air. A floating lid can be improvised by cutting a piece of polythene or perspex of size about 1/16 of an inch smaller than the internal dimensions of the vessel.

The temperature of the processing solutions may be accurately controlled by placing the tanks in a water bath maintained at the required

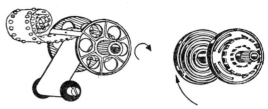

FIG. 27.12   FIG. 27.13

ROLL FILM SPOOLS

temperature by a heater and thermostat. If the water supply or the ambient temperature is above the operating temperature a refrigeration unit is required. Such systems are commercially available as temperature controlled darkroom sinks.

For development of roll films, cylindrical tanks with light-tight lids are available. These tanks are manufactured from plastic or stainless steel in various sizes which can hold from one to about six films wound in a spiral. In the *apron or band type* (Fig. 27.12) the film and the apron are wound together on the centre spool. The apron is generally made of celluloid and has projections along its edges to support the film and provide space for access of the processing solutions to the film. This type of tank has largely been superseded by the *spiral guide type* (Fig. 27.13) which has no cumbersome apron. The spool has spiral guides on its flanges which lead in to the centre and support the film with a gap between the turns. After loading the tank with the film wound on the spool, in the darkroom, all processing operations may be conducted in the light.

Daylight loading tanks are also available which eliminate the need for a darkroom. Where a large number of films are processed, a number of spirals may be loaded into a specially designed basket and processed in the rectangular tanks described previously.

A very simple procedure for the rapid development of 35 mm. films in daylight uses a monobath solution (§621), the processing being carried out with the film remaining in the cassette. The only additional apparatus required is a small beaker and a stirring rod which fits into the cassette spool. The tongue of the film is cut off and the first few inches of the film are folded back and secured with a rubber band (Figs. 27.14 and 27.15). The stirring rod is then inserted in the cassette spool (Fig.

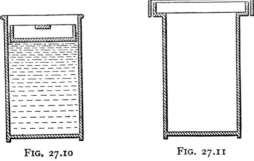

FIG. 27.10   FIG. 27.11

DEVELOPING TANKS

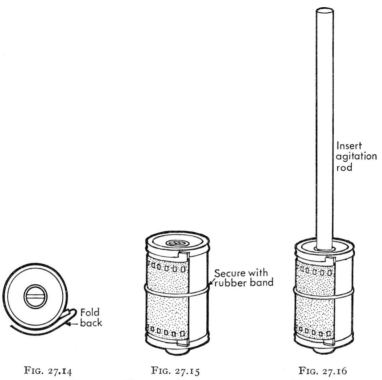

FIG. 27.14   FIG. 27.15   FIG. 27.16

DAYLIGHT MONOBATH PROCESSING OF 35 MM. FILM

27.16) and the cassette is immersed in approximately 40 mls. of the monobath solution while slowly winding and unwinding the film until processing is complete. Further details of this simple method are given in a Kodak publication: *Record Photography in the Classroom* and a small tank complete with stirrer is commercially available (Tokyo Kako Co., Ltd.).

However, with the exception of the monobath method, the above methods of development require a relatively large volume of developer for each film. *Tube processors* are available which use only small volumes of processing solutions for development of a number of films. This type of processing is generally termed the *one-shot system* because the small volume of solution is used only once and then discarded. Tube processors use tanks or tubes containing spools of film, similar to the cylindrical tanks described above, except that they are placed on rollers in the horizontal position, agitation being effected by an electric motor rotating the rollers. The tubes may also be used for the development of paper or cut film.

Another type of one-shot processor develops roll film by wrapping the film, emulsion side outwards, around the circumference of a rotating drum which dips in a shallow trough of developer.

These systems have advantages for the small to medium scale user, but they are small batch processors which require a fairly intricate loading operation and, therefore, are unsuitable for commercial photofinishers.

499. Large Scale Processing Equipment. For large scale production, deep tanks are used, big enough to accommodate all sizes of roll film fully extended. Developer tanks are usually equipped with a circulating pump unit which is mounted on the side of the tank: this includes the motor and pump as well as the heating and cooling units. In this way the space in the tank itself is reserved entirely for the films. The heating elements and the cooling coil are located in the path of the circulating developer so that an even temperature is maintained throughout the tank. Plain tanks without pump units are used for processing solutions in which agitation and temperature control are not so important. For washing films, tanks with a water inlet at the bottom and an exit at the top are used.

The films are loaded into frames which have clips at the top and bottom to prevent their touching or movement. The frames are transferred manually from tank to tank during the processing sequence. For large scale production the transfer of frames by hand would be too costly and time consuming and automatic processing machines are used.

In these machines, timing, temperature control, agitation, filtration, and replenishment are carried out automatically. The films are placed in clips and hung on bars or carriers with weights at the bottom. The bars holding the films are automatically moved up and down, and moved forward in each tank by a rack. After washing they are passed through a drying tunnel and then taken out for printing.

Output from these machines is limited by the depth of the tank and because it is a batch process, but a higher output may be obtained from a continuous process such as a *self-threading roller processor*, in which individual sheets or rolls of film are transported through the various processing and drying stages by powered transport rollers. The basic arrangement of the rollers in a typical self-threading roller processor is shown in Fig. 27.17.

Advantages of this type of processor are that clips or racks are not required and long lengths of film may be handled, because the process

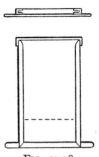

FIG. 27.18
FILM OR PLATE HANGER FOR DEVELOPING TANK

is continuous and not limited by the depth of the tank.

500. Materials for Tanks, Hangers, and Dishes. Material for photographic equipment has to be chosen for its resistance to the chemical solutions to be used with it, any effect it may have on such solutions and the cost and ease of fabrication of the material itself. Owing to its absolute impermeability and resistance to nearly all chemical reagents, *glass* is certainly a good material for the manufacture of tanks and dishes, at least in the smaller sizes required by the amateur. After proper cleaning, a glass dish can retain none of the products it previously held, and can therefore be used alternately for very different operations without risk of contamination; it is, however, somewhat fragile. Transparent glass dishes are sometimes used in order to be able to illuminate the negatives from below in the course of development or fixing in order to follow the progress of the operation without touching the plates.

Porcelain (white *translucent* ware) has the same properties, but is no longer used for dishes and tanks. Dishes sometimes described as " porcelain " are nearly always made of some variety of earthenware (opaque porous ware) with the surface protected by a glaze, which is fragile and easily chips off. This glaze readily cracks, allowing the products to penetrate into the porous substance, whence they can only be partially removed by washing, or even by the action of powerful reagents. Not only should an earthenware dish be kept as far as possible for the same bath, but one should avoid leaving the solution in it longer than is necessary for the operation; for if a solution of a salt is left in such a dish it tends to crystallize out in the earthenware, breaking up the glaze and sometimes even the earthenware itself. This does

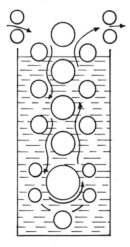

FIG. 27.17
SELF-THREADING ROLLER PROCESSOR

not apply, however, to the special stoneware made for the chemical industry and used for the manufacture of vertical tanks for handling numbers of roll-films at a time. These are excellent for use with most photographic solutions but they should not be used with caustic alkalis.

Vessels of *enamelled steel* made by manufacturers for the chemical industry resist the usual photographic reagents well. The steel does not usually become deformed, and the enamel, having the same coefficient of expansion as the steel does not tend to crack. Unfortunately, the enamel is slowly etched by alkaline solutions, even developers, and is easily chipped by careless handling. Once the metal underneath is bare its corrosion is rapid, and the enamel soon comes off in flakes on both sides of the cracks. Cheap dishes of thin metal, especially if welded, instead of being cast or pressed, are particularly prone to show such troubles.

Ebonite-covered steel, which is sometimes used for medium-sized tanks, is not open to the same objections, as ebonite is sufficiently elastic not to crack in case of slight temporary or permanent distortion of the metal. Other suitable coverings include soft rubber sheeting, asphalt paint, either alone or mixed with rubber solution, hard asphalt (applied hot), halogenated rubber paints and polyvinylchloride. None of these materials is completely impervious to any solution upon prolonged exposure, however. The outsides as well as the insides of tanks should be protected.

Pure, hard rubber, free from sulphur compounds, is an excellent material for dishes and tanks. The following *plastics* are generally suitable for the construction of processing equipment: *Perspex, nylon, polythene, polypropylene, polystyrene, polyvinylchloride (PVC), polytetrafluoroethylene (PTFE)*, and *epoxy resin* reinforced with glass fibre. The reader is recommended to consult the manufacturers of the above materials as to their suitability for the proposed use. Some plastics such as Perspex may be distorted by hot water and many of the plastics contain plasticizers which may diffuse into the processing solution with harmful results. Also plastics such as Perspex or polystyrene are somewhat brittle and may be suitable for the construction of dishes but not large tanks.

When bare metal is employed, the action of the metal on the bath, as well as that of the bath on the metal, has to be considered. In particular, *copper* and *tin*, with their *alloys* (with the exception of the copper-nickel alloy to be mentioned), *bronze, brass,* and *solder*, should *never come into contact with a developer*, since they are certain to produce an intense chemical fog (J. I. Crabtree, 1918). Rubber of ordinary quality (tubing, stoppers, etc.), which contains antimony sulphide (always present in the red variety) and sulphur, also causes fog if allowed to contaminate the developer. Pure rubber (English sheet) does not give rise to this trouble.

In considering the choice of a metal, a distinction must be drawn between a material suitable for amateurs, which is not likely to be exposed for long periods to chemical action, and one used on a commercial scale, which may be almost continually in contact with the solutions used.

Stainless steel for chemical industries containing not more than 0·08 per cent carbon (J. I. Crabtree, 1936) and about 18 per cent chromium and 8 per cent nickel, pure nickel and nickel alloys rich in nickel (Monel, Inconel) are suitable for development, fixation and washing; copper or brass thickly and evenly nickel-plated, are suitable for vessels used for development and washing; they may also be used for fixation, but the time of exposure to hypo must be strictly limited to the time necessary for fixation, and the vessels must be washed immediately afterwards. Chromium, cadmium, and silver are not suitable for plating photographic equipment as the layer is not fully resistant to solutions. Plated metals should not be used for apparatus likely to be cut or abraded; in the event of such damage, electrolytic action occurs and the plating is quickly removed. If absolutely necessary, the tanks may be soldered *externally*; developing hangers should never be soldered.

Tanks of cast iron and of mild steel have been used with advantage for developers with a strong content of caustic alkalis.

Lead is only very slowly attacked by developing or fixing solutions (the latter may contain acid, alum, or silver salts), and does not affect the solutions. In general any metal when placed in used fixing baths, as in solutions of silver salts, becomes covered with a weakly adhering film of silver, which gives only very incomplete protection against the action between the metal and the solutions in which it is immersed. Wooden tanks lined with lead (the joins must be made by welding and not with a tin solder) are very satisfactory, as are small lead-lined steel tanks. Type metal has similar properties, and may be used, particularly for taps in photographic tanks.

Zinc is not affected by pure water, but it is rapidly attacked by photographic solutions, even when very dilute. When tanks for washing are made of or lined with zinc, it is essential to restrict the corrosion of the metal by at least rinsing plates or prints before putting them into the tank. The tank should always be emptied and drained after use. Aluminium should also never be allowed to come into contact with developers or fixing baths, as a chemical reaction may take place which leads to stains on the gelatine.

In general, all metal vessels which come into contact with developing or fixing solutions should be made of one homogeneous metal. Of two metals in contact with each other and with the solution, one is always more quickly corroded than it would be alone, owing to electrolytic action. Most alloys thus suffer greater corrosion in contact with solutions than would either of the constituents separately.[1]

In general, metals should not be used for photographic work unless tests show them to be suitable for the specific purpose in mind. Non-porous, non-metallic substances should be the first choice, provided they are chemically stable and do not contain sulphur or metallic sulphides.

501. Accessories. The photographic outfit comprises a number of glass articles, notably graduated glasses (measuring glasses, conical glasses, and measuring cylinders), the graduations of which are often marked with a pleasing disregard of exactness (the graduation of measuring cylinders is generally less crude than that of the conical measures, and is, at any rate, fairly uniform), stirrers (glass rods rounded at the two ends by heating), and a dropping bottle. The volume of the drop varies with the nature of the liquid and with the temperature, but it varies most with the *outside diameter* of the dropping tube. The drops given in some formulae are, as in pharmacy, the drops delivered by a *standard dropping bottle* with capillary tube of external diameter 3 mm. In a darkroom of any size funnels for filtrations are essential, and a funnel stand of wood is a useful thing; the "notch" type is preferable to the "ring" pattern.

_____
[1] Many of the data given in this section are taken from the papers of J. I. Crabtree and G. E. Mathews, published in 1923, 1924, and 1936.

The risk of breaking measuring glasses is greatly reduced by fitting a projecting band of rubber round the top edge. For measuring large volumes (500 or 1000 c.c.) it is better to use unbreakable measuring cylinders made of polythene or graduated stainless steel jugs.

At its upper surface a solution ascends the walls of a vessel (capillarity). The observer must read the lower surface of the meniscus thus formed, the eye being on the same level.

When using a stirrer in a vessel of thin glass it is well to cover the ends of the stirrer with a small piece of rubber tube. For mixing large quantities of liquids, a large spatula or paddle of soft wood is best, but each of these must be kept strictly for a particular bath, the purpose being marked on the handle.

For the preparation of baths it is useful to have some pots or pans of enamel ware or aluminium in which water may be heated (if hot water is not laid on), the dissolution of the chemicals being done in a bottle or in some vessel of a material resistant to the substances used. For warming-up any solutions, chemical glass-ware or stainless-steel jugs should be used exclusively.

As regards *balances*, it is best to choose the Roberval type, such as is commonly used as shop scales, thus permitting the weighing of substances in a weighed vessel without interference of the usual stirrups supporting the pans. The sensitiveness of a balance being about a two-thousandth of the maximum weight it will carry, it is well not to buy a balance which is capable of dealing with greater weights than are necessary. If, in a large establishment, it is necessary to have balances for heavy weights, it will be best to provide a separate balance for light weights. A Roberval balance, having a very long needle, will weigh 3 oz. to 7 oz. to the nearest grain. A very practical type of balance, since it avoids the use of the very small weights, often lost, consists of a graduated beam along which a small mass can be moved as in the steelyard. More convenient single-pan balances with digital read-out scales are available in various sizes, do not require any weights and are extremely easy to read.

An essential accessory in the photographic darkroom is a small clock having only a minute and second hand, both being visible in the semi-darkness of the darkroom. Excellent spring-driven and synchronous electric clocks are available with large second hands coated with phosphorescent material. These should be of sufficient size to be easily seen in the dark and ideally should have a mechanism for presetting for given time intervals and an audible ring or buzz at the end of the time interval.

A final item of equipment is a thermometer, fixed at some distance from the wall, to indicate the temperature of the darkroom; also a small thermometer, graduated on the stem, for placing in tanks or dishes to ascertain the temperature of the baths. Alcohol thermometers for photographers should not have the liquid coloured red, but deep purple blue, in order that it may be easily seen in non-actinic light. Dial thermometers, with the bulb at the end of a flexible pipe, are available for use in tanks. Thermostatic controls can be fitted if electrical warming devices are used.

For washing, a syphon is a useful accessory. A small type can be fitted to the side of a large dish to maintain the level of water at a predetermined height. Another sort can be used in the drain-hole of the sink, for the same purpose.

502. Cleaning of Utensils. Dishes, tanks, and all vessels or utensils of glass or earthenware which have become stained are best cleaned by running a little strong hydrochloric acid all over. The acid can be used a great number of times. With a hard brush or a rubber sponge it is then very easy to remove all adherent deposits, and the cleaning is finished by rinsing in pure water and draining.[1] It is better not to wipe; the cloth used is generally dirtier than the vessel to be cleaned.

If a point is made of cleaning vessels immediately after use, it is usually sufficient to rinse

[1] Although the acid decolorizes all stains, thorough scrubbing and washing is necessary to remove the contamination, which will otherwise reappear as soon as developer is used in the vessel.

them in water to be sure they are perfectly clean.

Adherent deposits on the inside of bottles can often be removed by shaking up with lead shot and a solution of sodium carbonate.

Wooden developing frames or racks placed successively in developing and fixing baths must be cleared of all traces of the hypo which has penetrated into the wood before being used again. This can be done by allowing them to remain for some time in a solution of about 80 gr. to the gallon of potassium permanganate (followed by a rinse in pure water). The same precaution can be taken with metal frames, but they need not remain so long in the bath. The silver which is deposited on the metal frames forms an uneven layer liable to stick to the gelatine of the negatives. It is best to remove the large deposit of silver from time to time by means of a steel brush. After this, proceed with the treatment indicated above, and then brush with a tooth brush, rinse in water, and put to dry.

Metal tanks can, if cleaning with water is insufficient, be rinsed occasionally with hydrochloric acid diluted with about ten times its volume of water, but the vessel must not be allowed to remain in contact with this acid bath too long. For stainless steel use fairly dilute nitric acid.

Too great emphasis cannot be laid on the necessity of carefully cleaning every new vessel before taking it into use. For the first cleaning of metal goods (except for aluminium, which can be cleaned with soap or with a solution of trisodium phosphate) hot soda solution should be used to remove the greasy material which has been employed for polishing or for the protection of the surface.

CHAPTER XXVIII

CHEMICALS: PREPARATION OF SOLUTIONS, WATER SOFTENING, INDICATORS, pH

503. Choice of Chemicals. Substances which are entirely free from chemical impurities cannot be obtained as ordinary commercial products, and are only necessary for certain scientific investigations, for which purposes they are specially prepared by elaborate processes of purification. Intermediate between the purest chemical products and the raw materials, there are a large number of grades, which differ from one another in the amount of active constituent they contain, as well as in the nature and proportion of the various impurities. Certain impurities, according to the use for which the substance is needed, are not injurious. For instance, impurities which merely lower the amount of active substance present may be permitted, but others, which would retard or interfere with the intended reaction, should be excluded.

For this reason, chemical substances to be used in pharmacy must comply with the standards of purity laid down in the *British Pharmacopoeia*. There are no equivalent standard specifications for all photographic chemicals but many common photographic chemicals are specified in British and American Standards published by *The British Standards Institution* and *The American Standards Association* respectively. Many firms issue certain specifications to their suppliers of chemicals, which state the limits of admissible impurities in each product, and fix the price according to the actual content of active substance. It may be gathered from these remarks that care should be exercised in buying photographic chemicals,

and that a comparison of prices is not the only consideration to be taken into account.

In his own interests, therefore, the photographer should purchase his chemicals from reputable specialized firms, who, from their knowledge of the ultimate uses of the materials, can supply the required qualities.

504. Anhydrous, Crystalline, Efflorescent, and Deliquescent Substances. The amount of active substance contained in a product varies considerably with the chemical form in which it is obtained, and also with the extent to which it may have been changed by the action of the air.

Many salts exist in two forms, *anhydrous* and *hydrated*, the latter appearing most usually in the form of crystals. Anhydrous sodium sulphite (Na_2SO_3) for example, is equivalent to exactly twice its own weight of the crystalline sulphite ($Na_2SO_3.7H_2O$) the difference (assuming both substances to be pure) representing the *water of crystallization* contained in the crystalline salt. The fact that this numerical relationship is fortuitous and applies only to the case of sodium sulphite, is often overlooked. Thus, anhydrous sodium carbonate (Na_2CO_3) is equivalent to 2·7 times its own weight of the crystalline carbonate ($Na_2CO_3.10H_2O$) and anhydrous sodium thiosulphate ($Na_2S_2O_3$) ("hypo") to approximately 1·5 time its own weight of the crystalline salt ($Na_2S_2O_3.5H_2O$)

The water, which constitutes an integral part of hydrated salts, is not always firmly retained, and, in a very dry atmosphere, certain of these salts such as crystalline sodium carbonate (washing-soda)*effloresce*, the outer coating of the crystal being converted to the powdery anhydrous compound.

Substances, such as sodium hydroxide, which can absorb sufficient water from the atmosphere to form saturated solutions are *deliquescent* compounds. Substances like gelatine which absorb water from the atmosphere without dissolving are said to be *hygroscopic*. These *deliquescent* or *hygroscopic* salts, are very difficult to keep in good condition, and their weighing-out becomes so uncertain that it is often advisable to prepare from these substances, immediately they are received, a stock solution of known concentration, from which, at any future time, the various mixtures may be prepared.

505. Unstable Substances. Many other substances change very rapidly, either spontaneously or due to the influence of atmospheric oxygen. These changes are usually accelerated by the presence of moisture. In this manner sodium sulphite, particularly as the crystalline salt or in solution (in which case the weaker the solution the more rapid the change), is gradually converted into a mixture of sulphate and dithionate by absorption of oxygen. Similarly, developing agents turn brown or black, in time, by oxidation, especially if they have been transferred to a damp vessel; cyanides and sodium or potassium hydroxide are gradually converted into carbonates by the carbon dioxide in the air. In a manner similar to the loss of gas from soda-water, ammonium hydroxide constantly loses ammonia gas, which, dissolved in water, forms the active constituent. Solutions of formalin, or formaldehyde, deposit a white insoluble mass (trioxymethylene) produced, without external interference by a transformation of the original gaseous product.

These examples, which could be multiplied indefinitely, indicate, in the first place, that every precaution should be taken to store the substances as carefully as possible, and also that, for the majority of chemicals which are used, the actual amount of active substance present is very uncertain.

Fortunately, the ordinary photographic processes do not require great precision. A considerable variation of an active substance in a photographic bath would often pass unnoticed. It is therefore useless to discuss the relative merits of formulae differing from one another in a small degree, since the variations which occur unknown to the operator are in many cases much larger.

506. Solutions, Concentration, Solubility, Saturation. A solid, liquid, or gaseous substance dissolves in a liquid when it disappears into the liquid, giving a homogeneous *solution*; the dissolved substance is called the *solute*, and the liquid in which it is dissolved the *solvent*; evaporation of the solvent leaves the solute unchanged.

For practical purposes the *concentration* or *strength* of a solution may be taken as the weight in grammes of the solute in 100 ml of the solution. For example, if 20 g of hypo are dissolved in a certain quantity of water and, after solution, made up to 100 ml, then this solution is said to be 20 per cent, or a 20 per cent "hypo" solution. (When the solvent is water, the fact is not usually stated.) To be correct such a solution should be labelled "20 per cent solution of hypo, hydrated" because it contains less than 20 per cent of anhydrous hypo.

At any one temperature, a solvent will dissolve only a fixed amount of a salt, and when the solution has attained its maximum concentration it is said to be *saturated*. This concentration is known as the *solubility* at the temperature in question.

Except in very rare cases the solubility of a salt increases with rise in temperature. On cooling a saturated solution, the excess of the solute over the solubility at the lower temperature separates out in the form of crystals, which are generally much purer than the original substance (purification by crystallization), since the impurities present have not been able to reach their saturation point as long as the amount present in the salt is not considerable.

In certain cases, however, a carefully cooled saturated solution will not deposit crystals, but will remain in unstable equilibrium. Such a solution, called *supersaturated*, will deposit the excess of salt in solution immediately, if a speck of the same salt is brought into contact with it.

The speed of solution depends on various factors. A porous or very finely divided substance will dissolve much more readily than one in the form of large compact lumps. Nevertheless, water should not be poured on to a powdered anhydrous substance, but the latter should be dropped into the water in small quantities to prevent the formation of a large compact mass of the hydrated salt. Solution takes place more rapidly in hot than in cold water, and is accelerated by agitation. Since the solution is denser than the solvent, there is a tendency for a saturated solution to be formed in the neighbourhood of the salt unless it is efficiently stirred.

507. Expression of Formulae. In a formula the quantities are expressed in weights of solid substances, or volumes (at 68°F or 20°C) for liquids. The arithmetic of compounding solutions is greatly simplified by the use of the metric (grammes, litres, millilitres) system. The use of this system is especially valuable in avoiding confusion between Imperial and U.S. ounces, pints, and gallons. In both of these systems the ounce[1] is the same, but the U.S. pint = 16 fluid oz and the U.S. gallon = 128 oz, instead of 20 oz and 160 oz as in the Imperial (British) system. Above all, it is worse than useless to compromise, as is sometimes done, and to work with a mixed system of grammes and fluid ounces. Accordingly all the formulae in the following chapters are given in the metric system.

The weights or volumes are arranged to give a total volume of 1,000 ml. (1 litre). The volume of the principal solvent need not be expressly stated, but may be indicated by the instruction, "Sufficient quantity to make 1,000 ml" or some such equivalent term.

When a formula denotes that a certain number of drops of a solution are to be measured, to avoid confusion the number is usually given in roman figures. It is, however, better to prescribe the quantity in millilitres of a more diluted solution.

508. Water used in the Preparation of Processing Solutions. With the exception of distilled or de-ionized water, the water usually at our disposal (tap, river, and well water) contains dissolved salts (chiefly bicarbonate and sulphate of lime), suspended matter (dust, rust particles from the iron pipes), organic substances of animal and vegetable origin, which in colloidal form escape the most perfect filters, and after coagulation deposit in the baths as a fine mud, and, lastly, dissolved gases, notably oxygen and carbon dioxide.

Business establishments, possessing a water supply of poor quality, but which are able to obtain distilled water quite cheaply (condensed water from boilers) should certainly use the distilled water for the preparation of all baths, since the only impurities it contains are small quantities of dissolved gas.

Amateurs and professionals, who would have

---

[1] Note that this refers to the ounce weight. The *fluid* ounces differ, the U.S. ounce being slightly larger than the Imperial.

to purchase their distilled water from outside sources, but who are supplied with ordinary drinking water, should use freshly boiled water for the preparation of the baths.

A few substances form traces of precipitate in presence of the calcium sulphate which exists in boiled water, but if the baths are made up in relatively small quantities it is quite easy to filter them before use.

As a general rule, therefore, distilled water is not necessary for the preparation of photographic baths, in spite of the instructions to the contrary which are given in various formulae. The only exceptions to the use of tap water are in the preparation of the stock solutions of the salts derived from the precious metals (silver, gold, platinum).

509. Methods of Purification. The *filtration* of the water does not remove dissolved substances but, if the filter is sufficiently fine, will remove all suspended matter, and thus constitutes a useful precaution in the case of water used for all photographic treatments, including washing. It should be considered as indispensable when working with miniature negatives and, in all other cases, for the final wash.

Boiling the water drives off dissolved gases and decomposes calcium bicarbonate, liberating carbon dioxide and precipitating calcium carbonate which, with calcium sulphate, forms the furry lining inside kettles and boilers. Boiling often causes the coagulation of certain organic substances. On cooling the boiled water, air will redissolve in it.

Various processes enable the calcium and magnesium salts that are dissolved in the water to be replaced by harmless sodium salts. By other processes all the dissolved salts can be removed, the treated water then being practically identical with distilled water.

For quite a long time, boiler-feed waters and laundry waters have been *softened* by running them through a filter of *artificial zeolites* (base or ion exchangers, *Permutites*) consisting of coarse particles of sodium aluminosilicate (R. Gans, 1906) which becomes progressively transformed into calcium and magnesium aluminosilicates when in contact with hard water. The Permutite may be regenerated by bringing it into contact with a 12 per cent solution of sodium chloride (common salt) when the sodium ions enter the Permutite, displacing the calcium and magnesium ions.

Modern synthetic ion-exchangers are based on the original invention of Adams and Holmes

(1935). These resins are available in two common forms: an acidic or *cation-exchange* resin such as sulphonated polystyrene ($R-SO_3^-$ H^+) which exchanges protons (H^+) for metal ions such as calcium (Ca^{2+}) and a basic or *anion-exchange* resin such as a quaternary ammonium polystyrene ($R-N^+X_3$ OH^-) which exchanges hydroxyl ions (OH^-) for anions such as chloride (Cl^-). The protons and hydroxyl ions displaced from the resin then combine to form water. Thus on passing tap water through these resins all cations and anions, other than protons and hydroxyl ions are removed and *de-ionized* water is obtained.

Many commercial units are available which employ a mixture of these cation and anion exchange resins termed *mixed-bed ion-exchangers*. These units generally include a conductivity meter which indicates when the resins are exhausted.

510. The Sequestration of Calcium Salts. The calcium salts in ordinary waters can be transformed into soluble complexes that cannot be precipitated by the sulphite and carbonate in developers and which do not give rise to a calcium scum on drying, by adding a small quantity of sodium hexametaphosphate $(NaPO_3)_6$, "Calgon" or Grahams' salt (R. E. Hall, 1934), or tetra sodium pyrophosphate $Na_4P_2O_7$, $10H_2O$, or tetraphosphate $Na_6P_4O_{13}$ (R. W. Henn and J. I. Crabtree, 1944) and sodium tripolyphosphate $Na_5P_3O_{10}$. To sequester a given quantity of calcium salts it is necessary to use rather more of the pyrophosphate than of the other three.

These salts, which are stable in the solid state when they are stored in dry air, hydrolyse slowly in aqueous solution with the formation of orthophosphates which give a precipitate of calcium phosphate or of aluminium phosphate with the alum in hardening fixers. The hydrolysis is more rapid in warm solutions or in very alkaline or acid solutions.

The feebly acid hexametaphosphate hydrolyses to the acidic monosodium phosphate. The feebly basic pyrophosphate hydrolyses to the basic disodium phosphate. The tetraphosphate, whose solutions have a pH (§ 512–514) of about the same value as that of the low-activity developers, gives an equimolecular mixture of the mono- and disodium phosphates (pH = 6·5). The tetraphosphate is thus the only one of these three products which, in itself, or in the form of its hydrolysis products, does not affect the activity of developers. Therefore, the

tetraphosphate is the only product considered in the following discussion.

In the developers made alkaline with borax (the fine-grain developers), and prepared from waters which should not be too *hard* (i.e. they should contain less than 0·2 g of calcium salts per litre; if the content is as high as this, the water needs softening) the optimum concentration of the tetraphosphate is 0·05 per cent in terms of the working strength solution. In the carbonate developers the concentration of tetraphosphate should be increased to 0·2 per cent. In developers containing caustic alkalis, the calcium salts do not generally precipitate and there is no need to add tetraphosphate.

The hydrolysis of $\frac{1}{4}$ of the tetraphosphate, at 20°C, requires 3 years in feebly alkaline developers and 18 months in carbonate developer, these periods being much longer than the normal storage times. In warm climates these periods are considerably shortened (at 32°C) to 9 and 3 months respectively, but the hydrolysis can be retarded by adding to the developer some sodium citrate (from 2 to 4 times the weight of the tetraphosphate) which, in this low concentration, has no harmful effects on the hardening properties of the fixing bath.

The concentration of tetraphosphate should be about 0·05 per cent in the final rinse, applied after washing in hard water.

A large number of sequestering agents similar in structure to ethylenediaminetetraacetic acid or EDTA ($HOOC.CH_2)_2N.CH_2.CH_2.N$ $(CH_2.COOH)_2$ are available and used in developers. Less EDTA than any of the above phosphates is required for a similar softening effect on hard water. These quantities are shown in the following table:

Compound	Parts required for a similar softening effect
EDTA .	1
Sodium hexametaphosphate .	5
Sodium tripolyphostate .	14
Tetra sodium pyrophosphate .	20

However compounds such as EDTA are known to enhance the catalytic effect of trace amounts of ferric ions on the aerial oxidation of developing agents. Another disadvantage of this type of compound is its tendency to form complexes with silver ions and thereby afford a source of silver ions in solution (physical developments § 523) which may cause dichroic fog.

511. The Control of the Alkalinity or the Acidity of Solutions. For a long time the various substances in nature have been classed as acid, neutral, or basic (alkaline). Even with the qualifying terms "strong" and "weak," these expressions do not suffice to define precisely the state of a solution nor are they specific enough to allow solutions of equal activity to be prepared when the degree of acidity or alkalinity has a considerable influence on their behaviour, as is the case in some photographic processes.

The usual *indicator papers*, a typical one being *litmus paper* which turns red on being moistened by an acid solution and blue when made alkaline, give no idea of the degree of alkalinity or acidity. Acidimetric and alkalimetric titrations determine the concentration of an acid or alkali in solution without differentiating between substances, e.g. hydrochloric and acetic acids, which give very different results in practice.

A simple experiment reveals a phenomenon which cannot be explained on the basis of the traditional notions of acids and alkalis. When acetic acid is added to a solution of sodium thiosulphate (hypo), the hypo is instantly decomposed with the precipitation of sulphur. If, before adding the acid, a quantity of sodium acetate is dissolved in the hypo solution, the mixture will remain perfectly clear. Yet a sodium acetate solution is neutral to litmus and an acidimetric determination shows that all the acetic acid that was used is available in the hypo solution. Under similar conditions the addition of a chloride would not protect the hypo against the adverse effect of an addition of hydrochloric acid.

512. The Concentration of Hydrogen Ions. When an acid, a salt, or an alkali is dissolved in water, it dissociates, at least partially, into *ions*. These ions consist of atoms, or groups of atoms having negative or positive charges which greatly modify their properties, for example—

$$HCl \quad \rightleftharpoons \quad H^+ \quad + \quad Cl^-$$
hydrochloric acid　　hydrogen ion　　chloride ion

$$NaOH \quad \rightleftharpoons \quad Na^+ \quad + \quad (OH)^-$$
sodium hydroxide　　sodium ion　　hydroxyl ion

In this way, all acids liberate hydrogen ions and all alkalis liberate hydroxyl (OH) ions. It is the concentration of the ions thus liberated that determines the true alkalinity or acidity of the solution. All acids and all alkalis do not dissociate into ions to the same degree. For example, the "strong" hydrochloric acid, and the "weak" acetic acid, dissolved in equivalent concentrations in water at 18°C, are *ionized* to the extent of 91·4 per cent and 1·34 per cent respectively.

Pure water dissociates into hydrogen and hydroxyl ions, but to an extremely small degree. Only one gram-molecule of water, i.e. nearly 18 g, would be dissociated at 20°C in 10,000,000 litres of water. This can be expressed in another way by saying that pure water contains, per litre, $\frac{1}{10}^7$ or 10^{-7} g ions of hydrogen ions and hydroxyl ions.

The equilibrium conditions for water require that the product of these concentrations, if some circumstance causes a change in either of them, should remain constant at nearly 10^{-14} (from 10^{-12} to 10^{-15} as the temperature changes from 0°C to 100°C).

A liquid is regarded as acid or alkaline according to whether the concentration of hydrogen ions or hydroxyl ions exceeds 10^{-7} g ions per litre. The product of these two concentrations being always 10^{-14}, it is possible, instead of referring to the concentration of hydroxyl ions in an alkaline solution, to refer instead to its hydrogen ion concentration, as in the case of an acid solution. In this way it is possible to measure all degrees of alkalinity and acidity on one common scale (Fig. 28.1).

513. Acidity Index (pH) and Buffer Solutions. Because of the smallness of these ion concentrations and the very wide range between the extreme values, it is convenient to use a more compact means of expressing them. For this purpose the term *p*H (introduced by Sørensen) is used where

$$p\mathrm{H} = \log_{10}\left(\frac{1}{\text{Hydrogen ion concentration}}\right)$$

Neutrality is then represented by 7, the various degrees of acidity by numbers less than 7, and the various degrees of alkalinity are represented by numbers greater than 7.

The difference between the activity in solution of a strong and a weak acid is considerably increased if the sodium or potassium salt of each acid is added to its solution. A salt of a strong base and a weak acid will ionize in solution. The acid ions thus liberated restrict the degree of ionization, already small, of the weak acid. On the other hand, a salt of a strong acid and a

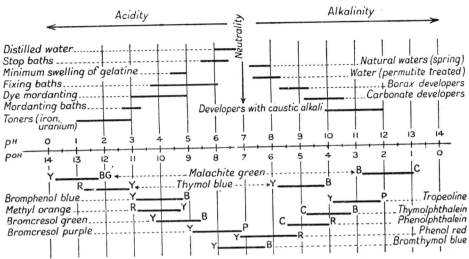

FIG. 28.1. THE pH RANGES OF VARIOUS PHOTOGRAPHIC BATHS AND SOLUTIONS OF CHEMICALS AND INDICATOR DYES

strong base, though it ionizes freely, has little or no effect on the very highly dissociated strong acid. The results of the experiment described above (§ 511), where the sodium acetate acts as the buffer, can be explained in this way.

In general, the term *buffer solution* is applied to solutions in which a small variation in composition results only in a negligible change in the pH.

Developers are generally buffered at an alkali pH value by the inclusion of a buffer mixture in the formulation. The buffer mixture consists of a weak acid and its sodium or potassium salt. The ionization of a weak acid is given by the following equation:

$$HA \rightleftharpoons H^+ + A^-$$

and the ionization constant (K_a) of the acid is given by:

$$K_a = \frac{[H^+][A^-]}{[HA]}$$

in which the square brackets represent concentrations which are generally expressed in moles per litre. If the above equation for the ionization constant is rearranged and logs are taken, the following equation is obtained:

$$\log_{10} \frac{1}{[H^+]} = \log \frac{1}{K_a} + \log_{10} \frac{[A^-]}{[HA]}$$

or

$$p\text{H} = p\text{K}_a + \log_{10} \frac{[\text{salt}]}{[\text{acid}]}$$

This is the well known *Henderson-Hasselbalch* equation from which the quantities of acid and its salt may be calculated to obtain a buffer solution of a particular pH value (see Fig. 28.2). The value of pK$_a$ for a particular acid may be found in tables of physico-chemical constants. Generally the acid is chosen such that pH = pK$_a \pm$1 for maximum stability of the buffer solution. The capacity of a buffer solution increases with increase in concentration of the constituents.

In photographic developers frequently only a single salt such as sodium carbonate is added as the buffer. This is because sodium carbonate is hydrolysed, in solution, to form sodium bicarbonate and sodium hydroxide:

$$Na_2CO_3 + H_2O \rightleftharpoons NaHCO_3 + NaOH$$

It is the bicarbonate anion (HCO$_3^-$) that acts as the acid in this system:

$$HCO_3^- \rightleftharpoons H^+ + CO_3^-$$

Accordingly it is the pKa for this ionization that should be used in the Henderson-Hasselbalch equation.

514. The Measurement of pH. The pH can be determined precisely only by electrometric means, and in the case of solutions containing sulphite it is necessary to use a glass electrode in conjunction with a valve electrometer and a reference electrode. Such instruments are marketed under the name "pH meters."

The glass electrode (Fig. 28.3) consists of a glass membrane sealed to the stem of high resistance glass containing an inner silver/silver chloride electrode and liquid filling, which provides electrical contact with the pH sensitive membrane. This electrode together with the reference electrode is immersed in the solution under test. The reference electrode (Fig. 28.3) consists of an inner glass tube containing a mixture of mercury, mercurous chloride (calomel) and potassium chloride solution closed at one end by cotton wool plug, a wire at the other end makes electrical contact with the mercury. This inner tube is surrounded by another tube, containing saturated potassium chloride solution, termed the salt bridge, with a porous plug at the bottom. Thus the circuit between the glass electrode, the solution, the reference electrode and the pH meter is completed.

For measuring a pH value in practice, the scale of the meter must be calibrated by dipping the electrodes in one or more buffer solutions of known pH and adjusting the instrument so that the reading on the scale corresponds to the actual pH of the buffer solution. This procedure must be carried out before measuring the pH of test solutions.

The use of coloured indicators serves to give only an approximate indication of the pH in photographic solutions. The effective range of a number of such indicators is shown in Fig. 28.1. The colour changes are indicated by the letters C (colourless), P (purple), R (red), Y (yellow), O (orange), BG (blue-green), and G (green). It will be seen that two of these indicators have two ranges of colour change.

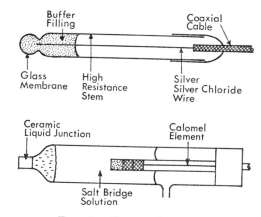

FIG. 28.3. TYPICAL GLASS AND REFERENCE ELECTRODES

515. Preparation of Photographic Baths. For the weighing-out of small quantities, the balance pans are covered with small sheets of paper, which are renewed for each fresh substance. To avoid the formation of dust, each sheet is wetted under the tap before being thrown away. For large quantities the substance is gradually introduced into a weighed and counterbalanced receptacle. Where a substance is obtained regularly in crystals of approximately the same dimensions it is possible to replace weighing by the more rapid method of a measurement of volume. Metal or strong cardboard boxes are cut down until they will just contain the required weight or sub-multiple of the weight of substance when filled level with the sides.

A bottle large enough to contain the total volume of the bath is half or two-thirds filled with freshly-boiled warm water, into which the substances are introduced in the prescribed order with constant stirring, taking care that each substance is fully dissolved before the next is added. After the complete solution of all the constituents, the bottle is filled with boiled water and, if necessary, the solution filtered or decanted off.

Never pour water on to a powdered anhydrous salt as this, in becoming superficially hydrated, is covered with a compact crust, dissolving then being extremely slow. To dissolve such products (such as sodium sulphite and carbonate) quickly, add them to the water a little at a time with constant stirring.

For the preparation of baths in large quantities, the work is carried out in a large vessel or tank, in which the final volume is adjusted

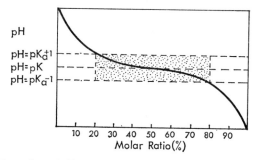

FIG. 28.2. A TYPICAL BUFFER CURVE SHOWING THE RANGE OVER WHICH THE BUFFER MAY BE USED.

either to a mark on the inside of one of the walls or to a notch on the handle of a wooden stirrer placed in contact with the bottom. Having introduced a certain quantity of water, the substances, contained in a linen net fixed on a wooden frame, are successively dissolved by sprinkling them with water. When all the constituents are dissolved, the level is brought up to the mark by the addition of the requisite amount of water.

In addition to the developing agent, developers generally contain a preservative and an alkali. A correctly stated formula gives these substances in the order in which they are to be dissolved and, unless otherwise stated, the other should be: 1. the preservative (e.g. sodium sulphite), 2. the developing agent and, 3. the alkali (e.g. sodium carbonate.) Each constituent should be allowed to dissolve before adding the next. One of the main functions of a preservative such as sulphite, is to prevent aerial oxidation of the developing agent; it is therefore dissolved first because many developing agents are readily oxidized in aqueous solutions in the absence of sulphite. An exception to this order is the developing agent metol which is dissolved first because it is not readily soluble in sulphite solutions. As alkalis increase the rate of aerial oxidation of aqueous solutions of developing agents, they are added to the solution of the developing agent containing the preservative.

A more detailed decription of the functions of these, and other, developer constituents is given in the following chapter.

516. Filtration. Filtration through paper is usually much slower and more costly than through either fabric or absorbent pads. The process is best carried out in a wide funnel (cone 60°) with a cylindrical stem, which is plugged with a piece of cotton wool or a lightly compressed piece of sponge, or, alternatively, the cone of the funnel may be fitted with a flannel or chamois leather bag. The three last-mentioned materials may be used repeatedly, if washed in running water and set to dry immediately after each filtration.

With large bulks of liquid, filtration is usually done through felt pads, each pad being kept for a special solution. In such cases, however, it is often preferable to stand the solution in a reservoir with a tap fitted at a little distance from the bottom. After the solution has cleared by sedimentation the top layer is drawn off, and it is then only necessary to filter the small quantity at the bottom, which contains the sediment and any surface scum. The decantation may also be carried out by a siphon.

517. Stock Solutions. Stock solutions may be used with advantage for all substances which are as stable in solution as in the dry state, and which are constantly being used in small quantities at a time. Weighing is then replaced by a measurement of volume, calculated from the concentration of the solution.

It has often been proposed to use saturated solutions for stock solutions, but their concentration, although well defined if maintained at a constant temperature, is liable to considerable variations. The salt, which crystallizes out on cooling, is often deposited in a difficultly soluble mass, so that when the temperature rises again the solution is no longer saturated. All concentrations which exceed the saturation value at 40°F (4°C) the lowest temperature usually reached in any commercial establishment, even during the interruption of work at the week-end, should therefore be avoided in the preparation of stock solutions.

Stock solutions may also be prepared for unstable substances, but sufficient only for one week should be made up, bearing in mind the fact that concentrated solutions keep much better than dilute solutions (this is the case with sodium sulphite and sodium sulphide).

To avoid the necessity of handling a large bottle when only a small quantity of liquid is required, the stock solutions may be stored in

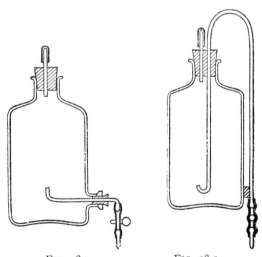

FIG. 28.4   FIG. 28.5
CONTAINERS FOR STOCK SOLUTIONS

bottles fitted with either a glass tube outlet at the bottom or a piece of glass tubing, which, after passing the neck of the bottle, is bent round to form a siphon (see Figs. 28.4 and 28.5). In either case, the outlet is connected to a glass jet by means of a length of rubber tubing, which is closed by a spring clip or by the insertion of a glass bead. In the latter method, the liquid is delivered by pinching the rubber tubing round the bead.

When baths are prepared immediately before use by the admixture of stock solutions, insufficient care is often taken to secure a perfectly homogeneous mixture. This cannot be obtained merely by pouring out the solutions (which have been measured together in a graduated measure) into another receptacle, for the mutual penetration of many solutions is much slower than is often realized. The mixing should be carried out in a measure which is closed securely with the palm of the hand, and then inverted several times, or the liquid decanted several times from one container to another.

518. Commercial Preparations. There are two main methods of packaging developers: as concentrated solutions or as powders.

Highly concentrated liquid developers are available which require dilutions of the order of $1 + 9$ for films and $1 + 19$ for papers. Far greater dilutions are used for the "one-shot" system of processing (§ 498). The manufacturer has in general, selected the constituents of these concentrated solutions so that they do not form saturated solutions at low temperatures and on dilution with water the optimum pH value for the developer is obtained. However, these solutions should not be stored at very low temperatures or crystallization may occur. Also they should not be stored at high temperatures because hydrolysis of constituents such as calgon (§ 510) can occur.

The main disadvantages of these concentrated solutions are relatively high price, susceptibility to undesirable side reactions, and bulky packaging.

Powders are generally supplied in pre-weighed packets or tins for making either stock or working solutions. Each packet or tin usually contains a separate smaller packet (sachet, plastic or glass phial) which holds the developing agent and some of the preservative.

The larger bulk consists of the preservative, alkali etc. For preparing the developer the contents of the smaller packet are completely dissolved in somewhat less than the total quantity of water. The contents of the larger packet are then dissolved and the solution is made up to the stated volume.

More recent developments in the packaging of developers include tablets and the use of soluble plastic sachets or phials which only require dissolving in the appropriate quantity of water.

519. Storage and Labelling. Solutions are stored best in bottles of capacity such that they fill them completely. This is especially important for developers, because aerial oxidation is reduced by prevention of the surface of the solution from coming into contact with a large volume of air. Dark-brown glass bottles are recommended for the storage of developers because they minimize any chemical changes induced or catalysed by light. Polythene bottles are, however, not suitable for the storage of developers because they have a porous structure which is susceptible to penetration by oxygen. Also some colour developers contain solvents that are able to remove the plasticizer from the polythene and make it brittle. Both solids and solutions should be stored at a reasonably even temperature that is neither very warm nor very cold.

For solid substances bought in small amounts it is best to rely on the manufacturer's packaging. Where chemicals are bought in bulk the manufacturer's advice on storage should be sought, especially if the chemicals are in paper bags or sacks which are easily torn and affected by moisture.

The necessity for labelling very clearly the containers of all substances and solutions immediately they are bottled cannot be over emphasized. Neglect of this elementary precaution, especially in the darkroom to which several people have access, leads to annoying mistakes and to loss of materials which cannot be identified.

Labels written in indian ink on white paper can be made waterproof by painting them with clear varnish or melted paraffin wax, after the gum has dried. Bottles may also be labelled by using felt tipped pens containing waterproof ink that adheres to glass.

CHAPTER XXIX

DEVELOPMENT OF THE NEGATIVE IMAGE

520. Development—selective reduction. 521. Microscopy of the developing grain—induction period—development centres—grain growth. 522. Effect of exposure on the developing grain— exposure level—mean grain size and concentration. 523. Physical and chemical development— definitions. 524. The structure of the developed silver—filamentary silver—effect of developer constitution and exposure—particulate silver. 525. Reduction-oxidation (Redox) potentials— model system. 526. Redox potential and development— limiting values. 527. Variations in Redox potentials—reducing agents—effect of bromide, pH and emulsion type. 528. Redox potential and physical development. 529. Inorganic developing agents—non-metallic—metal ions. 530. Organic developing agents—structural rules—developing function. 531. Kendall's rule. 532. Pelz's rule. 533. Oxidation reactions of inorganic developing agents. 534. Sodium hydrosulphite developer—preparation and properties. 535. Ferrous oxalate developer—preparation—redox potential. 536. Development by metal ions. 537. Oxidation reactions of organic developing agents—proton loss—electron loss—semiquinones. 538. Oxidation products of organic develop- ing agents—intermediate and final products from common developing agents. 539. Mechanism of development—general requirements. 540. Charge barrier theory. 541. The induction period— effect of charge of the developing agent. 542. Adsorption or catalytic theory—evidence for ad- sorption—activation energy. 543. Electrode theory—experimental evidence—mechanism. 544. Mechanism of the growth of the silver image—chemical development—physical development. 545. Quantitative laws of development—relationship of development rate with density and con- trast—determination of the rate constant. 546. The Elvegard equation. 547. The arithmetic coefficient of a developer: the Watkins factor (W)—determination—values for developing agents. 548. Superadditivity; Synergism—definition—examples—mechanism. 549. Monobaths —constitution—mechanism—control of processing—covering power—edge effects. 550. The various causes of fog—emulsion fog—chemical fog—aerial fog. 551. Emulsion fog—distinction between emulsion fog and development fog. 552. Development fog—selectivity. 553. Aerial fog— mechanisms. 554. The distribution of fog in the image. 555. Removal of fog. 556. Antifogging agents—bromide—organic antifoggants—mechanisms. 557. The distribution of the image in the thickness of the emulsion layer—exposure—development time and concentration—exposure through support. 558. Effect of dilution of the developer—contrast-time relationships—ex- haustion—sulphite concentration. 559. Depth development. 560. The Sterry effect. 561. The effect of waste products of development—streamers. 562. Defects in machine processing—rack marks—directional effects—perforation modulations. 563. Border effects—Mackie lines— Eberhard effect—Kostinsky effect. 564. Infectious development—mechanisms—contagious development. 565. The effect of agitation. 566. The influence of temperature—coefficients—time- temperature charts. 567. Normal constituents of a developer—developing agent—preservative- alkali—restrainer. 568. The role of alkalis in development—activity of developing agents— buffer solutions—optimum pH ranges—formaldehyde-bisulphite. 569. The role of sulphite— quantity—silver halide solvent. 570. Reactions of sulphite with organic developing agents. 571. The effect of soluble bromide on development—characteristic curves and bromide concentration— regression of inertia. 572. The formation of sulphite in used developers. 573. Oxidation products of developers—tanning—secondary images—colour and intensity of images. 574. Tanning developers. 575. Applications of secondary images—intensification—dye mordant—dye formation. 576. Colour development—chromogenic development—azomethine, indophenol, indoaniline and indamine dyes. 577. The effects of various substances added to developers— iodides—thiourea—urea—alcohols—neutral salts—silver bromide solvents—sugar—poly- ethylene glycols—cationic dyes—wetting agents.

The Usual Components of Developers

578. Organic developing agents. 579. Hydroxyphenols—hydroquinone—chlorohydroquinone—catechol—pyrogallol. 580. Aminophenols—p-aminophenol—metol—glycin. 581. Diaminophenols—2, 4-diaminophenol (Amidol). 582. Phenylenediamines—p-phenylenediamine—p-aminodimethylaniline—o-phenylenediamine. 583. Phenidone. 584. Summary of the properties of developing agents. 585. Developer dermatitis. 586. Alkalis—sodium hydroxide—potassium hydroxide—lithium hydroxide—ammonium hydroxide—triethanolamine. 587. Alkaline carbonates—sodium carbonate—potassium carbonate—ammonium carbonate. 588. Various alkaline salts—sodium phosphates—sodium borates—Kodalk. 589. Practical equivalents of the usual alkalis. 590. Sulphites—sodium sulphite. 591. Bisulphites—sodium bisulphite—sodium metabisulphite—potassium metabisulphite. 592. Alkali bromides—potassium bromide—sodium bromide—ammonium bromide.

Practical Notes

593. Qualities desirable in a developer—formulae for developers. 594. The swelling of gelatine—effect of pH and temperature—reticulation—salt concentration. 595. Methods of agitation—rocking the dish—mechanical devices—scraper blades—nitrogen burst. 596. Exhaustion of the developer—solution carry-over—consumption of developing agents by oxidation. 597. Replenishment; maintaining a developer at constant activity—automatic replenishment—replenisher constitution. 598. Electrolytic maintenance of a developer at constant actinity. 599. Method for the comparative testing of two developers—use of simple step wedges. 600. Quality control—maintaining emulsion speed and contrast—characteristic curves—process control charts. 601. Interrupting the course of development—developing in several baths. 602. Factors influencing the time of development—type of emulsion—composition, concentration and temperature of the developer. 603. Judging the end of development. 604. Rinsing after development—stop baths—provisional fixing. 605. Critical examination of finished negatives—negative viewers—underexposed and overexposed negatives—classification of negatives.

Working Procedure

606. Preliminaries—arrangement of equipment—dilution of stock solutions—removal of sediments. 607. Wetting of plates and films before development. 608. Hardening the emulsion before development in warm solutions. 609. Air bubbles—formation and prevention. 610. Immersion in the developing bath.

Developer Formulae

611. Introduction—classification of formulae. 612. General purpose developers—M-Q: ID3, D61a, ID2—P-Q: ID 67. 613. Fine grain developers—granularity—classification. 614. Medium fine grain developers—D76 (ID11)—D76 replenisher—D76d. 615. Ultra fine grain developers—solvent type—DK 20—p-phenylenediamine type. 616. High contrast developers—ID 13—D153—ID 19—D19G—D85. 617. High acutance developers—metol type. 618. Two-bath developers—advantages and examples based on D76. 619. Tropical developers—prevention of swelling of gelatine—use of sodium sulphate—prehardening bath (IH5). 620. Ultra-rapid development—use of high temperatures and active developers—cell processors—viscous layer application—porous plate applicators—spray applicators—roller applicators—saturated web applicators. 621. Monobath—universal monobath—ultra-rapid monobath. 622. Tanning developers—D 175. 623. Chromogenic developers—development of magenta, cyan, yellow and blue images. 624. Metol ion developers—titanous chloride EDTA developer. 625. Physical developers—classical physical developers—stabilised physical developers.

520. Development. A developing agent is a reducing agent and development involves the *selective* reduction of only the exposed grains of a photographic emulsion.

$$Ag^+ + \text{reducing agent} \rightarrow Ag + \text{oxidized}$$
$$(e) \qquad \text{reducing agent}$$

The reducing agent transfers an electron (e) to a silver ion and forms metallic silver. As a consequence of this electron transfer the reducing agent is oxidized. However, not all reducing agents can be used as developers because some indiscriminately convert all the silver halide grains to metallic silver (fogging) while others are insufficiently powerful to act even on the exposed grains. Within the limits of the *reduction or redox potential* (§ 525) between which a reducer may be used as a developer, the degree of exposure of the grain has an influence. Grains which received only a small exposure can be developed only by the more energetic developers of lower redox potential. It is now generally accepted that the latent image must consist of a minimum of four silver atoms for development to take place (G. C. Farnell and J. B. Chanter, 1961, A. Marriage, 1961) although a lower size of three atoms had been proposed previously (W. Reinders and L. Hamburger, 1933).

521. Microscopy of The Developing Grain. A number of experimenters (notably K. Schaum and V. Bellach, 1901, S. E. Sheppard and C. E. K. Mees, 1906, W. Scheffer, 1907, M. B. Hodgson, 1917, T. Svedberg, 1922, L. F. Davidson, 1925, W. Meidinger, 1935, J. W. Mitchell, 1954, W. F. Berg and H. Ueda, 1963) have attempted to follow, under the microscope, the course of the chemical development of emulsion grains (§ 523). Cinephotomicrographs of developing grains have also been made (C. Tuttle, E. P. Wightman, and A. P. H. Trivelli, 1927, and H. Frieser, 1939). More recently the electron microscope has been used for investigations of the development of emulsion grains (M. Von Ardenne, 1940, F. A. Hamm and J. J. Comer, 1953, I. M. Ratner, 1966).

A delay occurs between the instant that the developer reaches the grain and the time that the development sets in. This delay is known as the *induction period*. The grain darkens at a few points (latent image silver specks or *development centres*, corresponding generally to the location of the sensitivity specks) on the surface of the grain. Development spreads from these points until the whole grain becomes blackened. Development is, in effect, an amplification of the very small latent image to large visible masses of metallic silver. An amplification factor of approximately 10^9 has been reported for the development

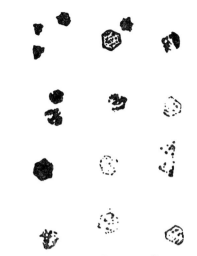

FIG. 29.1. SILVER BROMIDE GRAINS AT VARIOUS STAGES OF DEVELOPMENT

reaction (T. H. James and J. F. Hamilton, 1965). Fig. 29.1 after Hodgson, shows the appearance of some grains at various stages of their development. The magnification is about ×1,350 diameters. Some grains would not develop, whatever the exposure. Any one grain could either be entirely developable or entirely non-developable. However, the entirely developable grains were not always completely developed at the instant of stopping the development.

522. Effect of Exposure and Development time on the Developing Grain. The grains all develop in approximately the same time once development has set in. But the development starts only after an induction period that is greater for smaller exposures to light. However, the induction period is also considerable in the region of solarization. The average time of development of the individual grains increases as the developer is diluted.

As a result of the existence of this variation in the initial phase of development between grains belonging to different parts of the image, the size of the grains, when development is stopped at a low gamma, represents a fraction of the size of the parent silver halide grain; the size of the fraction depends upon the degree of exposure. For example, in an experiment of Sheppard and Mees on a step-wedge developed in dilute ferrous oxalate developer, the mean diameter of the grains was $1 \cdot 01 \mu$ in the step that had received an exposure of 1 metre-candle-second, and was $1 \cdot 82 \mu$ in the step that received

22 metre-candle-seconds. This difference decreased as development was more prolonged. The mean diameter of the developed grains becomes independent of exposure when development is carried out until gamma infinity is reached.

When development is stopped at an intermediate value of gamma the grains are finer in the depths of the emulsion layer than on the surface, these lower grains having been reached by the developer having to diffuse to the greater depth. When the gamma value is a maximum, i.e. at gamma infinity, no difference is found between grains on the surface or in depth.

The number of grains developed per unit area of the emulsion layer increases with the exposure (except in the region of solarization) and is approximately proportional to the resulting density.

523. Physical and Chemical Development. The two pathways to the reduction of silver ions are physical and chemical development. In physical development, which involves a homogeneous chemical reaction, the developing agent reduces a soluble silver salt that is added to the developer, and the silver that is formed is deposited on the latent image nuclei, usually in a light grey form. The silver halide grains of the emulsion play no important part in the development which can be carried out after fixation (*postfixation physical development*), i.e. after the removal of the silver halide.

Physical development was used exclusively for wet collodion plates, but rarely for gelatine-bromide emulsions. It is however, used for obtaining negatives of low granularity, and occurs in monobaths (§ 549).

In chemical or direct development, which involves a heterogeneous chemical reaction, the silver halide of the grains that are affected by the light is reduced *in situ*. The developers used for chemical development usually contain a silver halide solvent (e.g. sulphite) so that some of the silver halide of the emulsion dissolves in the developer with the result that the image is formed partly by physical development. The silver that is reduced by physical development is deposited on the walls of the tank or dish and forms a fine sludge that settles slowly on the bottom. It can also lead to dichroic fog (§ 553, 668).

524. The Structure of the Developed Silver. The structure of the developed silver varies markedly with the nature of the developer and the type of development occurring. Thus in *prefixation physical development*, i.e. development before fixation, long coarse ribbons of

silver approximately $0 \cdot 1\mu$ wide, extending from the grain, are produced (A. Küster, 1948). But in postfixation physical development, the silver grains grow at approximately equal rates in all directions and round particles of silver are formed.

Photomicrographs, made with the aid of the electron microscope (C. E. Hall and A. L. Schoen, 1941), have shown that the chemically developed grain consists of a tangled mass of fine silver filaments often referred to as "seaweed." In normal development the filamentary particle is confined within the mould that the original silver halide formed within the gelatine and when viewed at the ordinary resolving power of the optical microscope the developed grain usually appears to preserve approximately the shape of the undeveloped grain.

If silver halide solvents are present in a chemical developer, such as potassium thiocyanate in a solution of metol-ascorbic acid, the filaments are shorter and thicker than those formed in the "pure" chemical development of a metol-ascorbic acid solution (E. Klein, 1958), i.e. they approach the form found in physical development. When the activity of a chemical developer is decreased, plates rather than filaments are formed (G. I. P. Levenson and J. H. Tabor, 1952). Physical development results when development is carried out in a solution of p-phenylenediamine at pH value below 11 and compact round particles of silver are formed because of the marked solvent action of this compound for silver bromide, but at pH values greater than 12, filamentary silver characteristic of chemical development is produced (T. H. James and W. Vanselow, 1958).

It has also been shown that the shape of the developed grain is influenced by the exposure (G. C. Farnell and J. B. Chanter, 1961). Thus high exposure leads to compact grains which resemble the shape of the unexposed grains while low exposures give irregularly shaped grains of high covering power when developed in a metol-hydroquinone developer.

The shape and size of the silver grains that make up a physically developed image bear no relation to the shape and size of the parent silver halide crystals. The induction period is negligible when compared with the total developing time, and the final size of the silver grains depends only upon the time of deposition of silver, this size being the same for both fine- and coarse-grained emulsions (A. and L. Lumière and A. Seyewetz, 1924). At the start of development the silver particles are so small that neither their shape nor their size can be determined. Later, they are found to consist of hexagonal crystalline tablets. On extending development up to 48 hours, the diameter of the crystals can reach 2·5 μ in paraphenylenediamine (the bath changed every hour) used after fixation.

From the foregoing discussion it can be seen that the structure of the developed silver grains varies with the constitution of the developer, its activity, the nature of the developing agent, and the exposure. As a broad generalization filamentary silver is formed in chemical development and rounded particles of silver are formed in physical development.

525. Reduction-oxidation (Redox) Potentials. In the most general sense of the term, the *oxidation* of an ion means the increase of its positive charge, while *reduction* refers to the inverse phenomenon. For example, the oxidation of ferrous to ferric ions involves the transfer of an electric charge of 96,490 coulombs for each gramme equivalent. This oxidation may be effected by oxygen or by a substance that can act as a source of oxygen, but it can also be effected without the intervention of oxygen, the requisite charge being accepted by silver ions which are then converted into neutral atoms of silver. This last reaction is reversible, in the sense that an atom of silver can give up an electron (negative charge) to a ferric ion, becoming a silver ion in the process—

$$Fe^{++} + Ag^+ \rightleftharpoons Fe^{+++} + Ag$$

Ferrous ion Silver ion Ferric ion Silver atom

Readers who are not acquainted with the terminology of electro-chemistry should note that in equations of this type the positive signs indicate, according to their number, the *lack* of negative charges (i.e. electrons). Positive charges cannot be transferred from one ion to another because they belong to the atomic nuclei. It is the electrons, or negative charges, that are transferred leaving behind a greater net positive charge on the oxidized ion.

Imagine that a voltaic cell is set up using two liquids, a partially oxidized ferrous solution and a dilute solution of potassium bromide saturated with silver bromide, these being separated by a porous membrane. A platinum electrode is placed in the iron solution and a silver electrode is placed in the other. The electro-motive force, EMF, of this cell would be the difference between the electrical potentials that exist between each electrode and its electrolyte, that is, between the silver and the solution of silver bromide on the one hand (E_{Ag}) and between the platinum electrode and the solution of the reducer (E_{Red}) on the other. If E_{Ag} is greater than E_{Red} a current would flow from the platinum electrode to the silver electrode if they were connected by a wire and silver ions would be reduced to silver in one compartment and some of the ferrous salt would be oxidized to ferric salt in the other.

Such a cell is never set up in reality. The two half-cells are compared, separately and in turn, with a standard reference half-cell to which is arbitrarily assigned a zero potential in much the same way as one refers to the temperature of melting ice as being zero degrees on the Centigrade scale. The standard reference electrode, to which the potentials of other electrodes are referred, is the hydrogen electrode, consisting of platinum in contact with hydrogen gas. The potential of any real or imaginary cell would be the difference, therefore, between the potentials (referred to the hydrogen electrode) of its two electrodes.

The value of E_{Ag} thus measured at 18°C in a 0·01 N solution of potassium bromide, i.e. 0·119 per cent which is about the concentration usually found in developers, is 0·202 volts.

In order that in this case the silver bromide should become reduced to silver it is necessary that the potential E_{Ag} should be greater than E_{Red}, or in other words the redox potential E_{Red} of the platinum electrode in the solution of the reducer should be lower (more negative) than 0·202 volt. The reduction-oxidation potential of a solution depends upon the relative concentrations of the reduced and oxidized forms according to the following equation—

$$E_{Red} = E_0 - \frac{0·058}{n} \log_{10} \frac{[Red.]}{[Ox.]}$$

which is valid at 18°C. [Red.] and [Ox.] represent approximately the concentrations of the reduced and oxidized forms and n represents the number of electrons transferred on oxidation or reduction. In the case of the ferrous-ferric solution $n = 1$. Finally, this equation given for the reduction-oxidation potential holds only when the system is not affected by a change in pH.

526. Redox Potential and Development. Using mixtures of ferrous and ferric citrates and malonates, in the presence of 0·01 N potassium bromide, whose reduction-oxidation potentials (E_{Red}) were at various values between 0·10 to 0·60 volt, W. Reinders (1934) found that a partially developed photographic image continued to develop in a solution for which E_{Red} was less than 0·2 volt, the difference $E_{Ag} - E_{Red}$ (ΔE) being, of course, positive. When E_{Ag} was equal to E_{Red} the partially developed image was unaffected. However, when E_{Red} was greater than E_{Ag} the partially developed silver image was partly reconverted to silver bromide.

Those parts of the test strips which had not received any preliminary development were bathed in the ferrous-ferric solutions and only developed in those solutions whose reduction-oxidation potentials were below 0·110 volts, at which value $\Delta E = 0.090$ volt.

The curves of Fig. 29.2 show the results obtained. Some pieces of the same film had been uniformly exposed so that under normal conditions the developed density would have been about 3·0. The pieces of film were developed for a short time in an energetic developer so as to obtain a density of 0·82. The strips were bathed for 20 hours in the experimental ferrous-ferric solutions, after which they were fixed. The curves show (I) the densities of the areas of the pieces which had received the preliminary development and (II) the density of the area, on each strip, that was treated only with the ferrous-ferric solutions.

This illustrates that for chemical development to occur ΔE must have a value of at least 0.090 volts (curve II in Fig. 29.2) but once development has started it is only necessary for ΔE to be slightly positive (curve I in Fig. 29.2). It has, however, recently been shown that physical development can be initiated at ΔE values at or very close to zero (R. Pontius et al., 1968, H. Jonker et al., 1969).

527. Variations in Redox Potentials. In order to start development of a latent image on normally exposed silver bromide, the EMF, represented by ΔE must be positive and greater

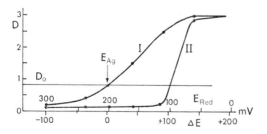

FIG. 29.2. EFFECT OF THE REDUCTION-OXIDATION POTENTIAL OF THE DEVELOPER ON PARTLY DEVELOPED IMAGE (I) AND ON EXPOSED BUT UNDEVELOPED EMULSION (II)

than a certain critical value of approximately 0·09 volt, or greater when the exposure was very small. The solubility of small particles of silver increases when the dimensions of the particles decrease and a solution which is in equilibrium with large silver grains can attack agglomerates of only a few atoms. In order that silver may be deposited upon the latent image it is necessary to increase the value of ΔE considerably beyond the level for which the solution is in equilibrium with the relatively large grains of the developed image.

M. Abribat (1935) found experimental evidence that solutions of all organic and inorganic reducers whose reduction-oxidation potentials were below this limit (0·1 volt) were developers. He was thus able to develop images, though often of poor quality, in such widely diverse solutions as; culture of anaerobic bacilli, old red Burgundy wine, resorcinol partially oxidized by ferricyanide, leuco-bases of various dyes, and other substances mentioned in the literature as having suitable reduction potentials.

A consideration of reduction potentials provides an explanation why silver iodide emulsions are not developable in normal developers and why these developers must be restrained, by decreasing their effective reduction potential by the addition of potassium bromide, when they are to be used with silver chloride emulsions. The potential E_{Ag} of silver metal in contact with a 0·01 N solution of soluble halide saturated with silver ions is − 0·023 volt in the case of potassium iodide and 0·34 volt in the case of potassium chloride. A ferrous developer that could just develop a latent image on silver bromide in the presence of 0·01 N potassium bromide would, as was mentioned above, have a reduction-oxidation potential of 0·1 volt. Since this potential is greater than the E_{Ag} for the iodide system, such a developer could not develop silver iodide under the conditions stated because its potential would be too high. On the other hand its potential would be rather low for the development of a silver chloride emulsion and in this case an increased concentration of potassium bromide acts as a restrainer, limiting the indiscriminate reduction of silver chloride grains by decreasing E_{Ag} according to the equation (18°C)—

$$E_{Ag} = (0.086 - 0.058 \log_{10} [Br^-])$$

where $[Br^-]$ represents the concentration of bromide in the solution.

J. Rzymkowski (1943) found that a solution of

sodium anthraquinone-2-sulphonate at $pH = 5$ would act as a developer for silver iodide emulsions but that it indiscriminately reduced both exposed and unexposed silver bromide grains unless the pH was further lowered.

These ideas are only rigorously applicable to oxidation-reduction systems that are reversible and in equilibrium, conditions which were closely approached in the work of Reinders that was described above. These conditions are not usually met with in the case of developers compounded from organic developing agents. The direct measurement of the reduction-oxidation potentials of such developers is difficult (A. E. Cameron, 1939). In these cases it is necessary to take account of the effect on the system of the pH of the solution.

If an organic developing agent acts as a bivalent ion, as is most common, and supposing that the concentration of the ions remains constant during the action, the EMF of the system may be approximately given by the equation—

$$E_{Ag} - E_{Red} = \Delta E = 0.086 - 0.058 \log_{10} [Br^-]$$
$$- E_0 + 0.029 \log_{10} \frac{[Red.]}{[Ox.]} + 0.058\, pH$$

where the value of the constant term E_0 depends upon the developer used.

It will be seen that, as in the preceding case, the EMF is decreased when the concentration of bromide in the developer is increased. The EMF is increased by an increase in the pH value. It should be noted that the EMF depends not upon the absolute concentrations of the components of the solution, but upon the relative concentrations. Thus there is no direct correlation between its value and the speed of development in practice.

At equal reduction potentials, the ability of a developing solution to reveal details in the shadows of the image is independent of the developing agent used. V. Veidenbach (1934) established the equivalence of metol and paraminophenol in this respect in developers also containing hydroquinone, by suitable adjustment of the alkalinity; he used metol at $pH = 9.6$ and paraminophenol at $pH = 10.15$.

At equal values of pH, two alkalis may be interchanged in a negative developer without affecting the properties of the fresh solution (H. Faerman and N. N. Schischkina, 1933). In positive developers, or in contrasty developers, at high pH values, a close relationship is not always found between the pH and the activity of the bath (J. G. Stott, 1942).

528. Redox Potential and Physical Development. Similar considerations have been applied to physical development by W. Reinders and M. C. F. Beukers (1939). The supersaturation of a developer with nascent silver is proportional to the difference $E_{Ag} - E_{Red}$ between the potentials of the silver and the developer. If Ag represents the concentration of silver in the supersaturated solution and Ag_0 the normal solubility of silver—

$$\Delta E = E_{Ag} - E_{Red} = 0.058 \log_{10} \frac{Ag}{Ag_0}$$

It should be noted that when the silver salt dissolved in the developer is not in the form of a complex, and the concentrations of bromide ions $[Br^-]$ is extremely small, the potential E_{Ag} is then much greater than in the case of chemical development.

In order to ensure that the reduced silver is deposited smoothly the value $E_{Ag} - E_{Red}$ should not be too high. This value may be decreased by adding a substance that will form a complex with the silver ions thus reducing Ag and E_{Ag}, or by adding an acid to the solution, thus increasing E_{Red}.

529. Inorganic Developing Agents. Inorganic developing agents may conveniently be divided into two groups: non-metallic inorganic reducing agents and metal ions. Non-metallic inorganic reducing agents such as hydrogen peroxide, H_2O_2 (M. Andresen, 1889), hydroxylamine, NH_2OH (C. Elgi and A. Spiller, 1884), hydrazine, N_2H_4 (M. Andresen, 1891), and sodium dithionite, $Na_2S_2O_4$ (J. Eder, 1890) are rarely used other than for academic studies.

Metal ions are increasing in their importance as developing agents because they may be used in the manufacture of printed circuits by a physical development technique (Philips PD process) and as intensifiers of silver images (§ 689) or of latent images in non-silver processes such as systems based on titanium dioxide (H. Jonker et al., 1969). The oxidized metal ion may be regenerated electrolytically (A. Rasch and J. Crabtree, 1954).

The basic requirement for development by metal ions is that they must be of variable valency i.e. exist in a reduced and an oxidised form such as the ferrous ferric ion system quoted previously (§ 526). In addition to ferrous oxalate (M. Carey Lea, 1877) and various other ferrous complexes (fluoride, citrate,

3

ETDA), the following have been suggested as developers: Titanous oxalate (A. Stahler, 1905), titanous chloride/ETDA (G. Haist *et al.*, 1956), and vanadous sulphate (A. Rasch and J. Crabtree, 1954).

At the present time none of these developing agents receive the extensive use which is made of the organic developing agents.

530. Organic Developing Agents. It has been pointed out that any solution whose redox potential falls within certain limits can be used to develop a latent image (§ 526). However a large number of the substances that would qualify in this way as developing agents are eliminated by practical considerations. For a reducing agent to be a successful developing agent it must be able to develop images of very low exposures, without tendency to fog. It must be sufficiently soluble in water and the resulting solution must be stable and non-toxic. Its cost per unit area of film developed must not be excessive. Except in a few specialized applications, the developing agent should give a neutral grey image.

The earliest organic developing agents known were derivatives of benzene (Fig. 29.3) and naphthalene (Fig. 29.4), and their homologues (aromatic compounds). In 1891 M. Andresen and L. Lumière independently formulated a rule by which it was possible to predict whether a substance of known chemical structure would act as a developing agent.

The essential requirement of this rule is that for a compound to act as a developing agent, two carbon atoms in the nucleus (the same nucleus in multi-ringed compounds) must each carry an hydroxy group (—OH) or an amino

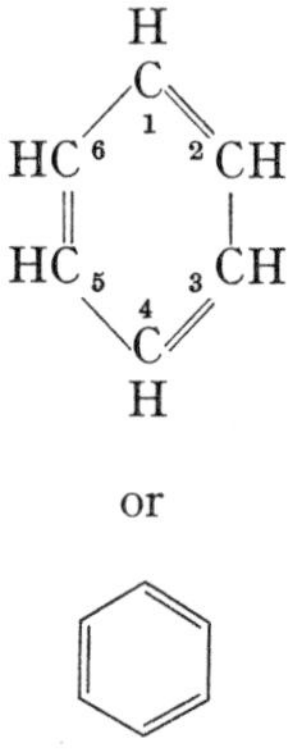

group (—NH$_2$) in the *ortho* (*o*) or *para* (*p*) positions. The *ortho* position signifies that the hydrogen atoms in positions 1 and 2 in the benzene or naphthalene nuclei are substituted by the —OH or —NH$_2$ groups. Similarly the *para* positions are represented by positions 1 and 4. A substance possessing a structure such that it satisfies this rule is said to possess a *developing function*. Thus of the three di-hydroxybenzenes, $C_6H_4(OH)_2$, the *ortho* isomer (catechol) and the *para* isomer (hydroquinone) are developing agents, whereas the *meta* or 1,3 isomer (resorcinol) is only a very poor developing agent and its weak developing function is thought to be due to its oxidation to 1,2,4-trihydroxybenzene in alkaline solution (J. D. Kendall, H. Staude and J. Eggers, 1962). This oxidation product acts as a developing agent because it is both *ortho* and *para* substituted.

The hydrogen atoms of the amino group or groups may be substituted by other groups without losing the developing function of the parent compound, e.g. glycin (*p*-hydroxyphenyl-aminoacetic acid) or metol (*N*-methyl-*p*-amino-phenol). Also the developing function can be modified or removed by the presence of other substituents in the nucleus. Thus chloro-hydroquinone is more active than hydroquinone.

531. Kendall's Rule. The above rule of Andresen and Lumière was revised by Kendall (1935) who stated that compounds of the general formula α-(C=C)$_n$-α' can act as developing agents, when n is zero or any integer and α and α' are —OH, —NH$_2$, —NHR, or —NRR'.

Thus when n is zero the compounds are the known non-metallic inorganic developing agents: hydrogen peroxide (HO—OH), hydroxylamine (HO—NH$_2$), or hydrazine (H$_2$N—NH$_2$) (§ 529). When n is one we have catechol (Fig. 29.5), *o*-aminophenol (Fig. 29.6), or *o*-phenylene-diamine (Fig. 29.7) as representative examples. It should be emphasized that Kendall's rule does not exclude the linking of α and α' groups. Thus the compound 1,2,3,4-tetrahydroquin-oxaline (Fig. 29.8) has been patented as a developing agent. In this compound the α and α' groups have the structure —NHR in which the R group (—CH$_2$—CH$_2$—) is common to both nitrogen atoms

When n is two we have examples of the most commonly used developing agents such as, hydroquinone (Fig. 29.9), *p*-aminophenol (Fig. 29.10), N-methyl-*p*-aminophenol (metol, Elon) (Fig. 29.11), and *p*-phenylenediamine

FIG. 29.3. STRUCTURAL FORMULAE FOR BENZENE

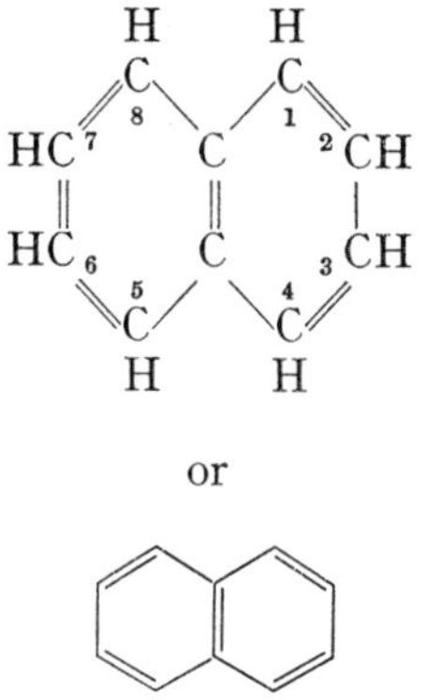

FIG. 29.4. STRUCTURAL FORMULAE FOR NAPHTHALENE

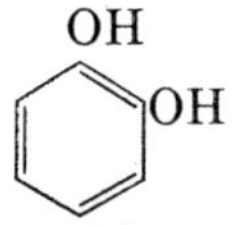

OH

catechol
(pyrocatechin)
FIG. 29.5

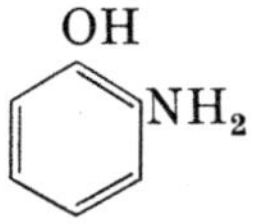

OH

o-aminophenol
FIG. 29.6

NH₂

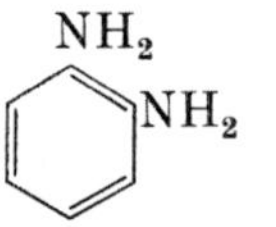

o-phenylendiamine
FIG. 29.7

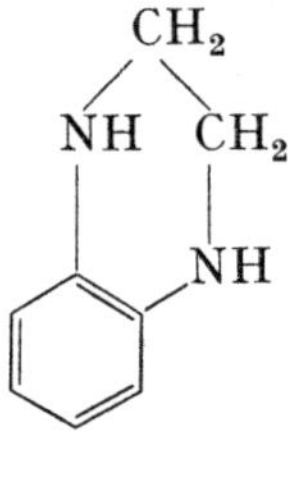

CH₂

1,2,3,4-tetrahydroquinoxaline
FIG. 29.8

OH

hydroquinone
(quinol)
FIG. 29.9

OH

p-aminophenol
FIG. 29.10

OH

metol
(Elon, or N-methyl-p-aminophenol)
FIG. 29.11

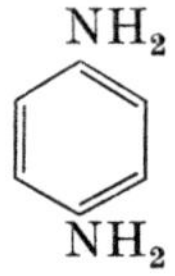

NH₂

p-phenylenediamine
FIG. 29.12

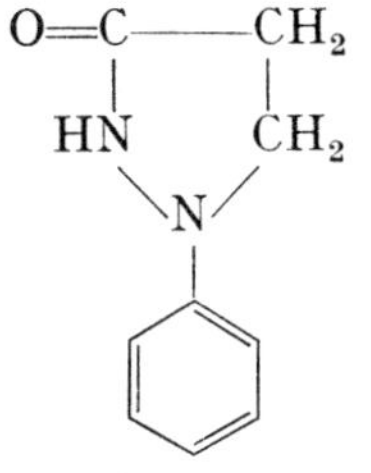

FIG. 29.13. PHENIDONE
keto FORM

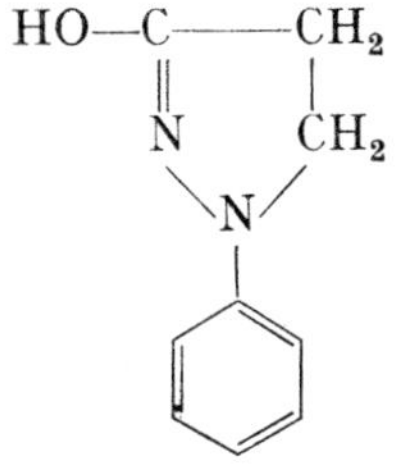

FIG. 29.14. PHENIDONE
enol FORM

was discovered as a developing agent by Kendall (1941) and in doing so he broke his own rule. Pelz's rule is a more generalized form of Kendall's rule which includes *heterocyclic* compounds, i.e. ring compounds containing carbon and atoms other than carbon in the ring system. This rule states that compounds of the general formula $\alpha(A{=}B)_n{-}\alpha'$ are developing agents where A is a carbon atom and B is either a carbon atom or a nitrogen atom; n, α, and α' are defined as in Kendall's rule.

Thus from the formula of Phenidone (Figs. 29.13, 14) written in the enolic form, it can be seen that this compound obeys Pelz's rule in which A is a carbon atom, B is a nitrogen atom, n is one, α is —OH, and α' is a substituted amino group.

The above rules are empirical and many exceptions are known. They are, however, extremely useful for classifying the known developing agents. It should be emphasized that the converse of the rules are not true i.e. if the rules are not obeyed the compound cannot act as a developing agent. Nowadays classifications of the developing properties of particular compounds are based more on physico-chemical properties such as redox potential, charge, or adsorption by silver halide or silver rather than on structural formulae alone.

Among the developers not provided for by these rules are various derivatives of N-heterocyclic compounds (Fig. 29.15) such as 5-amino-2, 6-dihydroxy pyrimidine, 5-amino-4,6-dihydroxy pyrimidine, and 2-amino-4,5-dihydroxy-6-methyl pyrimidine (R. W. Henn and S. V. Carpenter, 1959). Mason (1966) has suggested that the rule of Pelz can be applied to these compounds if the central section of the general formula can contain both —(C=N)— and —(C=C)— groups in the same compound.

533. Oxidation Reactions of Inorganic Developing Agents. Non-metallic inorganic reducing agents are rarely used as developing agents,

(Fig. 29.12) and its derivatives which are used as colour developing agents (§623).

532. Pelz's Rule. The above rule of Kendall, like that of Andresen and Lumière, does not exclude nuclear substituted derivatives of the above compounds, such as chloroquinone, acting as developing agents. However, with respect to cyclic compounds, both these rules apply only to *homocyclic* carbon compounds, i.e. compounds having only carbon in the ring system. Therefore the rules were revised by Pelz (1954) to include compounds such as Phenidone (1-phenyl-3-pyrazolidnone). Interestingly this compound

FIG. 29.15. STRUCTURAL FORMULA OF THE PYRIMIDINE NUCLEUS

but their reactions may be summarised in the following chemical equations.

Hydrogen peroxide is active as a developer only in strongly alkaline solutions (J. Weiss 1935) when

$$H_2O_2 + OH^- + Ag^+ \rightarrow H_2O + H\dot{O}_2 + Ag.$$

The $H\dot{O}_2$ radical is extremely reactive and capable of undergoing further complex reactions. Similarly hydroxylamine acts as a weak developer in alkaline solution but nitrogen is liberated as an oxidation product and forms bubbles in the emulsion:

$$2NH_2OH + 2OH^- + 2Ag^+ \rightarrow 4H_2O + N_2 + 2Ag$$

Hydrazine also acts as developer in alkaline solution with the liberation of nitrogen:

$$N_2H_4 + 4Ag^+ \rightarrow 4H^+ + N_2 + 4Ag$$

Sodium dithionite is oxidized to bisulphite in neutral or acidic solutions during the development of silver ions according to the following reaction:

$$Na_2S_2O_4 + 2H_2O + 2Ag^+ \rightarrow 2H^+ + 2NaHSO_3 + 2Ag$$

The above equations represent the simple chemical reactions which occur during development by some inorganic non-metallic reducing agents. However, under certain conditions other oxidation products may be formed. For example, nitrous oxide and nitrogen are formed from the reduction of silver bromide by an excess of hydroxylamine by an unknown mechanism (S. E. Sheppard and C. E. K. Mees, 1907).

534. Sodium Hydrosulphite Developer. Few of these reducing agents have received extensive use as developing agents but the use of sodium hydrosulphite as a developer was proposed by W. B. Bolton (1893). Sodium hydrosulphite, more systematically known as sodium dithionite, is a white powder which when pure has the molecular formula $Na_2S_2O_4 . 2H_2O$. Its neutral solution can be used to develop positive emulsions, but it needs to be acidified by sodium

bisulphite, or by an acid, organic buffer, in order for it to be able to develop negative emulsions. On being exposed to air, a solution of sodium hydrosulphite loses its developing power without losing its reducing properties. The partly oxidized solution produces warm-toned images on chloride papers.

A "developer-desensitizer" for non-colour-sensitized emulsions was suggested by A. Seyewetz (1931). To prepare it, dissolve immediately before use 12 g of an intimate mixture of—

Sodium hydrosulphite	.	. 100 g
Potassium bromide	.	. 35 g
Sodium bisulphite	.	. 165 g

The appearance of the image is much delayed, but once it has appeared the gamma increases rapidly. The emulsion speed of a material developed in this way to $\gamma = 2\cdot6$ is less than 10 per cent of that obtained by developing the same material to $\gamma = 1\cdot0$ in a metol-hydroquinone developer. The energy of the developer can be somewhat increased by the cautious addition of acid, but this procedure involves the risk of causing fog. The dry, powdered mixture will keep well in a tightly stoppered bottle, but the solution is unstable, evolving a sulphurous gas which makes its use very unpleasant in a confined space.

After one minute's immersion in the developer, the speed of the emulsion is reduced to about 5 per cent of normal and a very bright safelight can be used.

If colour-sensitized materials are developed in this solution an intense fogging results. In order to develop transparencies, or paper prints, the concentration of the solution should be reduced. After 30 seconds' immersion a bright yellow safelight may be used.

535. Ferrous Oxalate Developer. The ferrous oxalate developer, of which the present method of preparation was indicated by J. M. Eder (1879), is now scarcely ever used by either amateur or professional photographers. Its very low reduction potential does not enable it to develop satisfactorily any but well exposed negatives. Its preparation and use demand more care than is required for organic developers, and afford no material economic compensation for these practical drawbacks. But for various scientific uses of photography this developer possesses the distinct advantage of containing no solvent of silver bromide, and of thus avoiding various disturbing factors which sometimes occur in the use of ordinary developers, but noticeable only in exact localization of

points, and in photometric measurements of a high order of accuracy. This developer is the only one with which chemical fog is completely avoided (F. Hurter and V. C. Driffield, 1890) and which produces a perfectly neutral grey image, completely free from all coloured oxidation products.

The ferrous oxalate developer is prepared *at the time of use* by pouring slowly, with constant stirring, 1 volume of a 25 per cent solution of ferrous sulphate into 3 volumes of a 25 per cent solution of neutral potassium oxalate $(K_2C_2O_4 . H_2O)$. This produces a limpid reddish mixture (potassium ferro-oxalate), which can be used as a developer without any addition of potassium bromide.

The reduction potential $(E_{Ag} - E_{Red})$ of the ferro-oxalate developer, which acts according to the equation—

$$3 \, Fe \, C_2O_4 + 3 \, Ag \, Br \rightleftharpoons 3 \, Ag \\ + Fe_2 (C_2O_4)_3 + Fe \, Br_3$$

is 44 mV when fresh (W. Reinders, 1935. See § 527).

Over-exposure can be corrected to a certain extent by adding potassium bromide. Being a developer with a low reduction potential, the iron developer is very susceptible to the action of bromides. For correction of over-exposure it suffices to add a relatively small quantity of potassium bromide to the developing bath (e.g. not more than 1 g per litre of bath).

Sodium thiosulphate (hypo) in very minute quantities (a few drops of a 1 : 1,000 solution) has a marked accelerating effect on the ferrous oxalate developer (it decomposes the ferric salts formed), the image then appearing much more rapidly. An excess of hypo produces heavy fog, and, finally, reversal of the image, the fog being then denser than the image proper.

On the negative impregnated with the oxalate solution being placed in the wash-water or the fixing bath, a uniform precipitation of calcium oxalate takes place in the upper layers of the gelatine, forming a white deposit. During washing, after fixing, this deposit is readily removed by placing the negative for a few moments in a very weak solution of hydrochloric acid, e.g. 1 : 200 solution (= about 5 ml in 1 litre).

536. Development by Metal Ions. The reduction of silver ions to metallic silver by metal ion developers may conveniently be summarized in the following single general equation.

$$M^{n+} + Ag^+ \rightleftharpoons M^{(n+1)+} + Ag$$

metal ion   oxidized metal ion

The reaction is reversible and some oxidized metal ions are capable of oxidizing the silver back to silver ions unless they are made innocuous by the addition of a substance with which they form complexes. Oxalate or fluoride ions are added to ferrous/ferric system so that a stable complex is formed with ferric ions which is less capable of causing the reverse reaction to occur than are uncomplexed or free ferric ions.

537. Oxidation Reactions of Organic Developing Agents. Because of the diversity in the structures of organic developing agents they are capable of undergoing a number of different reactions which are specific to the particular compound. Fortunately some generalizations are possible especially in their oxidation reactions. From the following equations it will become clear that the oxidation of organic developing agents involves two electrons and it has been shown by physico-chemical experiments that the transfer of electrons takes place in two single electron transfers. Transfer of the first electron to a silver ion results in the formation of an atom of silver and an unstable *free radical* or *semiquinone* (L. Michaelis, 1935) which rapidly transfers another electron to a second silver ion to form the stable developer oxidation product and a second atom of silver. A second generalization is that if a developing agent contains an acidic group, such as the

semiquinone
unstable free radical

benzoquinone

Structure of Oxidation Products

Developing agent	Structure in alkaline solution	Unstable intermediate product	Stable oxidation product

phenolic —OH groups in hydroquinone, then *proton loss precedes electron loss.* This is because development is normally carried out in alkaline solution and the acidic developer is usually in the form of a salt. Thus the oxidation reactions of hydroquinone may be represented by the equations given on the previous page.

This reaction scheme is a simplified form of the scheme proposed by Eggers (1961) and occurs in strongly alkaline solutions ($pH > 11$). In these high pH solutions other products such as hydroxyhydroquinone and hydroxyquinone are also formed by further complex reactions of benzoquinone (J. E. Luvalle, 1958).

538. Oxidation Products of Organic Developing Agents. Many other developing agents react in an analogous manner to hydroquinone. The structures of the products of oxidation of some of the more common developing agents are given in the above table together with their structures in alkaline solution.

Although the fourth column in the above table has been headed "stable oxidation product", it should be emphasized that all these products are not necessarily stable under the conditions of high pH normally used in developers and may undergo further reactions.

The intermediate unstable products, being "half-way" products between the developing agent and its first stable oxidation product are termed semiquinone in the case of hydroquinone and semiquinonediamines in the case of p-phenylenediamine etc.

539. Mechanism of Development. In previous sections (§§ 520, 523, 524) the development reaction and the structure of the developed silver were discussed but no explanations of the mechanisms were given. In this section we will consider some of the currently accepted mechanisms by which silver ions are reduced to silver in the development reaction.

Any mechanism of the development reaction

must be able to explain experimental observations. The more important experimental observations which require explanation by a theoretical mechanism of development may be summarized as follows:

1. The selectivity of the reaction.
2. Development centres.
3. The kinetics of the reaction (autocatalytic nature, rate dependence on concentrations of various developer constituents and the structure of the developing agent, the induction period etc.).
4. The form of the developed silver.
5. Superadditivity.

At the present time no single theory of development can explain all the above phenomena and there is still much controversy on the proposed mechanisms. Some of the more recent theories of development which may explain some of the experimental observations are as follows.

540. Charge Barrier Theory. This theory assumes that the surface charge on the emulsion grain plays a dominant role. The approach of developing agents which act in the form of negatively charged ions, to the silver bromide grains would be hindered by the excess of

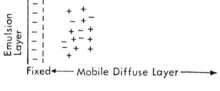

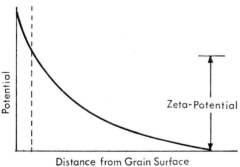

FIG. 29.16. THE ELECTRICAL DOUBLE LAYER CONSISTING OF A FIXED MONOLAYER OF NEGATIVELY CHARGED IONS NEXT TO WHICH IS A THICKER MOBILE DIFFUSE LAYER CONTAINING SLIGHTLY MORE POSITIVE IONS THAN NEGATIVE IONS. THE EXCESS OF POSITIVE IONS DECREASES WITH INCREASE OF DISTANCE FROM THE GRAIN SURFACE.

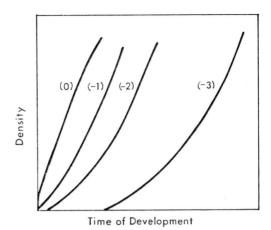

FIG. 29.17. EFFECT OF IONIC CHANGE OF THE DEVELOPING AGENT ON THE DEVELOPMENT RATE (JAMES, 1940)

bromide ions that are adsorbed to the grain during the preparation of the emulsion, since these bromide ions form a continuous negatively charged sheath around the grain. There is thus an electrostatic potential difference between the grain surface and the solution. Any species similar in charge to the adsorbed ions on the grain surface must do work against this potential gradient (zeta potential) on their approach to the grain. The electrical double layer surrounding the emulsion grain is illustrated in Fig. 29.16.

Explanations for the induction period and the mechanism of development according to the charge barriers theory are given in § 541.

541. The Induction Period. The curves that show the growth of density as a function of the time of development (Fig. 29.17) of a batch of emulsion that has received a given exposure can be classified into four types. The shape of the curves in each type depends not upon the chemical nature of the developing agent, but on the electrical charge on the active species which may be either a neutral molecule or a single-, double-, or treble-charged ion (T. H. James, 1939).

In the case of the phenylenediamines, which act as the neutral molecule, the rate of development is a maximum at the start of development and decreases as the time of development is extended. The curve is always concave towards the time axis.

In development by the aminophenol developers (metol, p-aminophenol, p-aminophenylglycine) and by hydroxylamine, all of which act in the form of single-charged ions, the rate of development rapidly increases to a maximum and then remains constant for a considerable period before ultimately decreasing.

In the case of development by agents that act in the form of double-charged ions, e.g. hydroquinone, pyrogallol, ferrous oxalate, glycin, and metolsulphonate, the rate of development is extremely small at the outset, and increases rapidly only after a considerable delay.

Hydroquinonesulphonate, which gives a treble-charged developing ion, acts similarly to the hydroquinone group, but gives a much greater induction period.

The absence of an induction period in development by the phenylenediamines is unaffected by the addition of soluble bromide to the developer. However, in the case of the other developers the induction period is increased by the addition of bromide, the increase being more marked as the negativity of the active species is greater. The appearance of the induction period is due to the negative charge barrier, the magnitude of which has been estimated as 0·1 volt, that surrounds each silver bromide grain as the result of the adsorption of excess bromide ions to the crystal surface. This negative barrier tends to repel negatively charged developer ions with a force proportional to the charge on the ion. Only those ions whose energy is sufficiently in excess of the average value can penetrate the barrier, which is smaller in the vicinity of the latent-image speck, at the start of development. As development proceeds the latent-image speck grows, thus locally reducing the potential of the barrier and admitting a greater number of developer ions. Thus development will be an auto-accelerating or auto-catalytic process for negatively charged developer ions and an induction period will appear.

Another negatively charged zone surrounds each grain by virtue of the fact that the gelatine layer that is adsorbed to the grain carries a net negative charge when immersed in solutions of pH greater than the *isoelectric point*, which is the usual case in practical development.

The induction period becomes shorter as the exposure, and the size of the latent image, is increased.

If two parts of the same emulsion layer are exposed, part A at low intensity for a long time and part B at high intensity for a short time, so that they give equal densities on development to γ_∞, it is found (J. Cabannes, 1928, and P. O. Hoffmann, 1935) that part A develops more rapidly than part B.

Although the above theory gives an explanation for the effects of the charge on the developing agent and the influence of cationic wetting agents and adsorbed sensitizing dyes, antifoggants etc., on the induction period, it cannot explain the development rates after the induction period. Nor can the charge barrier theory explain how neutral developing agents discriminate between exposed and unexposed grains, (L. F. A. Mason, 1966). Moreover, in order for the charge barrier to have an effect on the approach of a developing agent, its influence must extend some distance from the grain surface. A recent calculation by Mason (1969) has shown that its influence is short-range (0·175 nm., which is the thickness of a single layer of adsorbed ions). Mason concluded that since the charge barrier did not extend far from the grain surface under normal development conditions, the approach of the developer ions to the grain was unaffected by their ionic charge. Charge barrier effects are now thought to be due to the influence of a negatively charged sheath surrounding the grain, on adsorption rather than on a long-range influence of the negative charge on the approach of the developing agent.

542. Adsorption or Catalytic Theory. The basis of this theory is that the development reaction is catalysed by an adsorption complex formed between the developing agent, a silver ion and the development centre. In its modern form which was proposed by James (1939) this theory is an extension of an earlier similar theory of Sheppard and Meyer (1920) and is supported by much experimental data.

From the studies on the rates of reduction of silver ions in solution by a variety of developing agents in the presence of metallic silver (i.e. in model systems resembling physical development) James found that the rate of formation of silver was directly proportional to the concentration of the developing agent (such as hydroquinone or catechol) and proportional to a fractional power of the silver ion concentration i.e.

$$dAg/dt \propto [Ag^+]^n \, [\text{developing agent}] \, .$$

In the above equation the square brackets represent concentrations and n is less than one. The fractional power for the silver ion concentration is indicative of a reaction occurring in the adsorbed state. Thus the above equation implies that silver ions are adsorbed to metallic silver. Direct measurements have shown that developing agents such as *p*-phenylenediamine are adsorbed to metallic silver (R. J. Newmiller and R. B. Pontius, 1960) and further experiments by James on the reduction of precipitated silver halides (i.e. chemical development) have shown that developing agents are adsorbed to silver specks. In addition to these experiments which have shown that both silver ions and certain developing agents may be adsorbed to metallic silver, in systems similar to chemical and physical development, the exact nature of the adsorption complex is further complicated by more recent experiments which have shown that developing agents are adsorbed to silver bromide (T. H. James and W. Vanselow, 1951). Thus the adsorption theory may be visualized as a general adsorption of the developing agent to the grain surface and the formation of an activated triple complex at the latent image speck (developing agent —Ag+—Ag). The formation of this complex leads to strong catalysis of the reduction because the activation energy for this heterogoneous reaction is significantly lower than for a homogeneous reaction in solution involving a silver ion—developer complex. This is illustrated in Fig. 29.18.

For a chemical reaction to take place the reactants must be raised to a higher state of potential energy i.e. they have to overcome the potential energy barrier (the activation energy in the above diagram). This is generally achieved by warming the reactants but any reaction conditions which bring about a lowering of the potential energy barrier will cause the reaction to proceed more readily at the same temperature.

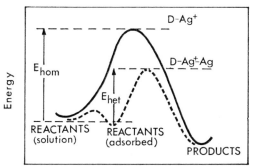

FIG. 29.18. THE ACTIVATION ENERGIES FOR THE HOMOGENEOUS (—) AND THE HETEROGENEOUS REACTION (---), E_{hom} AND E_{het} RESPECTIVELY. D REPRESENTS THE DEVELOPING AGENT

The adsorption theory explains the selectivity of the development reaction, the kinetics of the reaction and its autocatalytic nature i.e. as more silver is formed there is greater tendency to form the activated complex. The inhibition of development by substances adsorbed to the silver halide (e.g. gelatin) is also explained by this theory. Further support has come from experiments which show that increasing the hydrophobic character i.e. the ability of hydroquinone derivatives to salt-out from aqueous solutions and become adsorbed onto the silver halide leads to an enhancement of developer activity (J. F. Williams and G. F. Van Veelen, 1966).

543. Electrode Theory. It has been demonstrated by a number of workers that development can occur without direct contact of the silver halide with the developing agent (H. Baines, 1954, H. D. Keith and J. W. Mitchell, 1953, W. Jaenicke *et al.*, 1951–59). The model experiment used by Baines to show that silver bromide could be reduced to silver without contact with the developing agent is illustrated in Fig. 29.19. The circuit between the developing agent, silver and silver bromide is completed by the solutions and the salt bridge. After one to two hours the silver bromide was reduced to silver.

This theory is an extension of the Gurney-Mott theory of latent image formation and requires an electron transfer from the developing agent to a silver ion through the development centre. The developing agent is adsorbed to the silver of the development centre which acquires a negative charge by electron transfer. The negatively charged development centre then attracts a silver ion from the emulsion grain which is reduced to silver. Thus on the surface of the latent image an anodic reaction takes place and at the inter-face between the silver ion and the latent image a cathodic reaction takes place.

However, the electrode theory also requires adsorption of the developing agent for electron transfer to occur and therefore closely resembles the adsorption theory. The main difference is that the silver is assumed to form at or around the surface of the latent image in the adsorption theory whereas in the electrode theory the silver would be formed underneath the latent image (see Figs. 29.20 and 29.21.)

At the present time there is much controversy concerning the relative merits of the adsorption and electrode theories of development. Both give adequate explanations for most of the

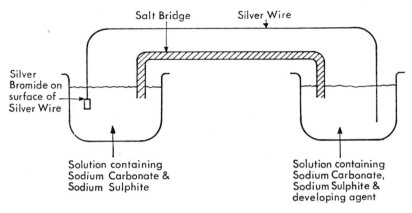

FIG. 29.19. MODEL EXPERIMENT TO DEMONSTRATE THE ELECTRODE THEORY

requirements of the development theory outlined in the first paragraph of this section. It is possible that the adsorption theory explains the start of development when the silver speck is small, i.e. when the developer, silver ions and silver are almost co-incident, and the electrode theory then explains development when the distance between the silver ions and developer increases owing to enlargement of the silver speck (L. F. A. Mason, 1969).

544. Mechanism of the Growth of the Silver Image. In the preceding sections no mention was made of the mechanism by which filaments of silver are formed in chemical development and rounded particles of silver are formed in physical development. A pictorial summary of these processes as explained by the adsorption theory is given in Figs. 29.21 and 29.22 (T.H. James and J. F. Hamilton, 1965).

In chemical development silver ions are reduced to silver at the interface between the grain and the latent image. Filaments of silver are formed because the newly formed silver atoms are mobile and the nucleus grows preferentially in one direction. However filamentary growth could be better explained as resulting from the formation of silver at the underside of the latent image by the electrode theory (Fig. 29.20) and thus exuding a filament of silver from the surface of the grain.

In physical development silver ions first pass into solution and are then reduced to silver on the surface of the latent image. The reduced silver ions cause the latent image to to increase in size (Fig. 29.22).

545. Quantitative Laws of Development. The total rate of development is influenced by the rates of diffusion and adsorption of the developer to the developing grains, the opposite diffusion and desorption of the oxidized developer, the rate of reduction of silver ions, the swelling of the gelatine layer and the diffusion of the halide ions of the silver halide.

At any instant the rate of development (the rate of growth of the density) in the usual developers is approximately proportional to the number of undeveloped grains remaining in the area of the emulsion under consideration. It is thus proportional to the difference between the maximum density $D\infty$ that would be reached after a very long development, and the actual density D (F. Hurter and V. C. Driffield,

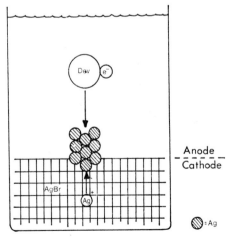

FIG. 29.20. THE ELECTRODE MECHANISM

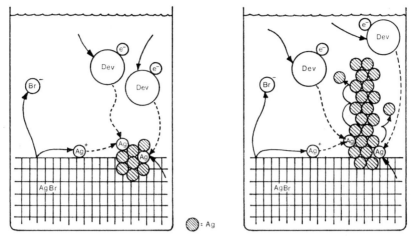

FIG. 29.21. THE GROWTH OF SILVER DURING CHEMICAL DEVELOPMENT

1890, S. E. Sheppard and C. E. K. Mees, 1907, K. V. Chibisov, 1935).

$$V = \mathrm{d}D/\mathrm{d}t = K(D\infty - D).$$

The coefficient K, called the *rate constant*, depends on both the emulsion and the developer. An essentially similar equation to that given above has been used to relate the rate of development to the rate of growth of contrast ($\mathrm{d}\gamma/\mathrm{d}t$).

$$V' = \mathrm{d}\gamma/\mathrm{d}t = K'(\gamma\infty - \gamma).$$

Other things being equal the rate constant decreases slowly in proportion to the age of the sensitive material, S. E. Sheppard and C. E. K. Mees (1907) found that, in the course of a series of experiments for plates of the same batch, K decreased in six months from 0·293 to 0·0100. K varies from one brand to another, and from one batch to another of the same brand. Finally the rate constant varies from one developer to another and, for the same developer, it is proportional to the concentration of the active ions.

In the course of experiments on ferrous oxalate at different concentrations, and on glycin developers with varying potassium carbonate content, A. von Hübl (1901) noted that the rate of development is proportional to the conductivity of the developer. This finding is in agreement with the fact, already mentioned,

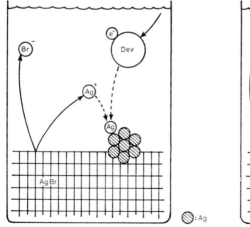
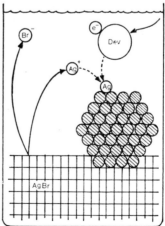

FIG. 29.22. THE GROWTH OF SILVER DURING PHYSICAL DEVELOPMENT

that alkalies may be interchanged at equal pH values.

The equations given above may be stated in the following forms—

$$\log (D_\infty - D) = \log D_\infty - 0.4343\, K\, (t - t_0)$$

$$\log (\gamma_\infty - \gamma) = \log \gamma_\infty - 0.4343\, K\, (t - t_0)$$

where t represents the duration of development and t_0 the length of the induction period.

When the induction period is negligible, as when the *Arithmetic Coefficient* (§ 547) of the developer is at least equal to 15, one can, using the second formula, calculate the values of K and γ_∞ if the values of the gammas (γ_1 and γ_2) that are reached after times of development t_1 and t_2 such that $t_2 = 2t_1$, are known (S. E. Sheppard and C. E. K. Mees, 1907). Starting from these values for K and γ_∞ the time of development required to reach any intermediate γ value can be calculated for the same developer and for the same temperature from the following equations—

$$K = \frac{1}{t_1}\log_e \frac{\gamma_\infty}{\gamma_\infty - \gamma_1}$$

$$= \frac{\gamma_1}{1 - e^{-Kt_1}}$$

$$t_2 - t_1 = \frac{\log_e (\gamma_\infty - \gamma_1) - \log_e (\gamma_\infty - \gamma_2)}{K}$$

The same results may be obtained more simply by a graphical construction (W. Heydecker, 1925).

Finding γ_∞. Mark off on a straight horizontal line a length AB (say 10·0 cm for convenience). At B erect a perpendicular and mark off lengths BC and BD proportional to γ_1 and γ_2. Draw

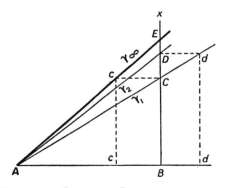

FIG. 29.23. GRAPHICAL CONSTRUCTION FOR γ_∞

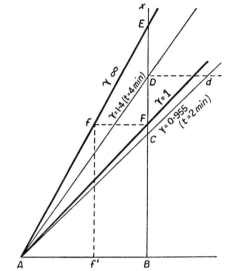

FIG. 29.24. GRAPHICAL DETERMINATION OF THE TIME OF DEVELOPMENT REQUIRED TO REACH A DESIRED GAMMA VALUE.

straight lines from A through C and D. From D draw a line parallel to AB to cut AC in d. Draw from C towards A a line Cc parallel to AB and equal in length to Dd. Draw a straight line from A through c to cut the gamma ordinate at E. The length BE gives the value of γ_∞ according to the scale adopted.

To find K. The value of K is given by the equation—

$$K = -2.302 \times \frac{\log_{10} (Bd/AB)}{t_1}$$

To find the time required to reach a given gamma. On the graph already used to find γ_∞ draw the line AF in which F fixes the desired value of γ. In the example in Fig. 29.24 the desired value of γ is taken as 1·0. Draw from F a line parallel to BA to meet AE at f. The desired time of development is given by the equation.

$$t = -2.302\, \frac{\log_{10} (fF/AB)}{K}$$

It must be emphasized that these relationships are only approximate. The most certain way to develop a plate or film to a given gamma is to find experimentally the curve relating γ and t for the particular batch of films or plates by developing them in the chosen developer at the temperature at which it is proposed to operate.

546. The Elvegard Equation. A simple empirical equation relating contrast with the time of development has been put forward by E. Elvegard (1943): equations (b) and (c)—

$$\frac{d\gamma}{dt} = K(\gamma\infty - \gamma) \tag{a}$$

$$\gamma = A \log t + B \tag{b}$$

or

$$\frac{d\gamma}{dt} = \frac{A}{t} \log e \tag{c}$$

A and B are constants which depend on the system and conditions used, γ is the contrast and t is the time of development. This equation is valid only for intermediate development times i.e. at very short or very long development times a plot of γ against $\log t$ deviates from a straight line as shown in Fig. 29.25.

Recently Brand and Farthing (1968) have shown that the rate constant K can be evaluated from a combination of the Sheppard and Mees equation (a) and the differentiated form of the Elvegard equation (c):

$$t = \frac{A \log e}{K\gamma\infty} + \frac{\gamma t}{\gamma\infty}$$

Thus if γt is plotted against t a straight line results of slope equal to $1/\gamma\infty$ and the intercept on the t axis gives a value for $A \log e/K\gamma\infty$. In this relationship the only unknowns are K and A. Hence K may be evaluated because A may be found from the slope of the Elvegard plot (Fig. 29.25). Analogous equations using D-max in place of γ may also be used to find K and D-max∞ but a different value of the rate constant is obtained. This procedure was adopted for studies on development where D-max∞ or $\gamma\infty$ occurred after a very long development time and would not be found experimentally with any degree of accuracy.

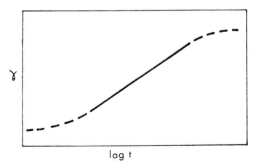

FIG. 29.25. A TYPICAL ELVEGARD PLOT

547. The Arithmetic Coefficient of a Developer; the Watkins Factor (W). The following rule was formulated by A. Watkins (1894) to provide a relationship between the time of appearance (ta) of the first details of the image (excepting the images of the sky and other obviously overexposed highlights) and the total time of development (td) that is required to give a desired gamma value. For the rule to be applied it is essential that the negative should have been properly exposed within reasonable limits and that the composition of the developer remains constant throughout the entire time of development. This last conditions excludes developers containing ammonia or other volatile ingredients, and plates or films that have been soaked in water or desensitizer prior to immersion in the developer.

The development time required to obtain a negative of a given gamma value is obtained by multiplying the time of appearance of the image by a number which is practically constant and characteristic of each developer. This number, or *arithmetic coefficient*, is usually known as the *Watkins Factor (W)*.

$$td = Wta$$

Although the Watkins factor is affected by the emulsion, by the temperature, and by the composition of the developer, it depends chiefly upon the developing agent used. Some inaccuracies are inevitable in its determination. Different observers assess the time of appearance of the image differently, and one observer repeating the experiment under other conditions of safelighting often obtains somewhat different results.

This method of development control is obviously applicable only to emulsions that can be developed by a bright safe-light, such as non-colour sensitive and orthochromatic materials.

The Watkins factor always has a greater value for developers for which the induction period is short or nil, than for developers that give a long induction period. Any circumstance

Developing agent	Watkins Factor
Hydroquinone (with sodium carbonate)	from 5 to 7
(the lower value applies to a strongly bromided solution)	
Pyrogallol	from 4 to 18
(the lower value corresponds to solutions having a high concentration of pyrogallol and bromide)	
Catechol (pyrocatechol) . . .	10
Glycin (with potassium carbonate) .	12
p-Aminophenol	16
Amidol	18
Metol (with sodium carbonate) . .	30

that reduces the induction period, such as the addition of basic dyes or traces of iodide, increases the Watkins factor.

The values quoted for the Watkins factor relate usually to a gamma value of about 0·8.

For developers containing several developing agents, the Watkins factor may be approximately arrived at by taking an average per unit weight of the developing agent. For example if a developer contains, per litre, x grammes of metol and y grammes of glycin, the Watkins Factor for the compound developer would be roughly—

$$W. = \frac{(x \times 30) + (y \times 12)}{x + y}$$

This rule will not apply to developers that behave non-additively, for example metol-hydroquinone.

From the above (§ 545–547) it can be seen that there is no single universal equation that can quantitatively account for the rate of development under all conditions. The rate equations in the previous sections are of some use in academic studies of rates of development. In practice more simple relationships are used for making comparisons between rates of development under varying conditions. These methods require that graphs of a photographic parameter, such as contrast, D-max, or density at a given exposure, against time be drawn. From these graphs the rate of development may be arbitarily defined. The rate may be defined by any of the following parameters: the time to reach a given density or contrast value, the time to change the density or contrast from one value to another value, or the slope of the curve at a certain density or contrast.

548. Superadditivity; Synergism.
Super-additivity was first recognized by Lupo–Cramer (1900) who found that a mixture of gallic acid and metol would develop an emulsion faster than metol alone, under conditions where gallic acid was almost inactive. A super-additive or synergistic mixture of two developing agents results when the rate of development (such as time to reach a given density) is greater than the sum of the individual rates obtained from developers containing only one of the developing agents in the same concentrations as in the mixture. This effect is illustrated in Fig. 29.26. (W. Lee and T. H. James, 1962).

The maximum in the dotted curve of the diagram represents the optimum concentration for the superadditive mixture. A large number

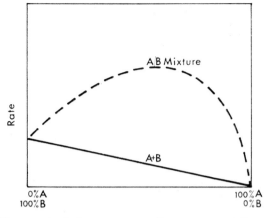

FIG. 29.26. A SUPERADDITIVE COMBINATION OF TWO DEVELOPING AGENTS A AND B

of superadditive developer combinations are known but the mixtures in current popular use are those based on metol-hydroquinone or Phenidone-hydroquinone. Similar results are obtained when the exposed material is first bathed in a solution of amidol (H. Frötschner, 1937) or metol (T. H. James, 1940) followed immediately by development in a hydro-quinone developer.

On the basis of the available evidence, the following steps are involved in superadditivity (W. Lee and T. H. James, 1962, J. F. Willems and G. F. Veelen, 1962, 1963, 1968, L. F. A. Mason, 1963, 1966, 1969, G. I. P. Levenson, 1949, A. J. Axford and J. D. Kendall, 1954).

1. Adsorption of the *primary* developing agent to the grain surface, where the primary developing agent is a nitrogen containing compound such as metol, Phenidone or *p*-phenylenediamine.

2. Reduction of silver ions to silver by the primary developing and oxidation of this compound to a free radical intermediate (a semiquinone) which remains adsorbed.

3. Regeneration of the primary developing agent (reduction of the semiquinone) by the *secondary* developing agent (hydroquinone) at the grain surface.

4. Removal of the oxidized secondary developing agent generally by reaction with sulphite.

According to this scheme the primary developing agent is continually being regenerated at the grain surface and steps 2 and 3 are repeated until the reaction is finished.

1. Adsorption of Phenidone

2.

(adsorbed)   (adsorbed)

3.

(adsorbed)   (adsorbed)

4. (i)

$+$ sodium sulphite $+$ water $\rightarrow$

or (ii)

$+ Na_2SO_3 + H_2O \rightarrow$ $+ NaOH$

This explains why the mixture of the two developing agents is more efficient than a single developing agent where no regeneration of the oxidized product is possible and this product has to diffuse away from the grain surface and a fresh developer molecule approach and react.

The above chemical reactions illustrate these steps in a Phenidone-hydroquinone developer.

The reaction (4) is complex and it is not known whether the sulphonated hydroquinone is formed by direct reaction of the semiquinone with sodium sulphite or the semiquinone is first oxidized to benzoquinone either by reaction with silver ions or by transfer of a second electron to regenerate Phenidone.

No regeneration of Phenidone occurs in a Phenidone-hydroquinone developer in the absence of sulphite (G. F. Van Veelen and H. Ruysschaert, 1960) and reaction 4 is therefore of the utmost importance in superadditivity. Moreover the primary developing agent or its oxidiation products must sulphonate less readily than the secondary developing agent or its oxidation products because otherwise the primary developing agent would be removed from the grain surface and the regeneration step 3 would not readily occur. This condition is fulfilled by Phenidone and explains in part why Phenidone-hydroquinone developers are more efficient than metol-hydroquinone because the oxidation product of Phenidone does not react with sulphite, whereas the oxidation product of metol can be sulphonated (§ 570).

A second contributing factor to the higher activity of Phenidone-hydroquinone developer than metol-hydroquinone developers is that hydroquinone monosulphonate (formed in step 4) can itself form a superadditive developer with Phenidone (W. E. Lee and T. H. James, 1962) but is not superadditive with metol.

Although the above equations give a plausible explanation for superadditivity, charge barrier effects may also be involved (W. E. Lee and T. H. James, 1962). Lee and James suggested that a positively charged radical is formed from the oxidation of Phenidone, which reduced the negative charge barrier and so aided the approach of the secondary developing agent for step 3. There is, however, much conflicting experimental evidence concerning the sign of the charge on the oxidation product of Phenidone. Mason (1969) has recently reviewed the evidence and has concluded that in developers the neutral product is formed, as given previously (§ 537) and in the above reaction scheme.

It follows that in Phenidone-hydroquinone developers charge barrier effects are unlikely to be important, whereas in p-phenylenediamine-hydroquinone developers charge barrier effects are probably involved because the semiquinone of p-phenylenediamine is certainly positively charged (§ 538).

549. Monobaths. The combined developing and fixing of photographic materials in a single solution has been known since 1889 (W. D. Richmond) but monobaths have only relatively recently become a general technique of processing. Monobaths require an active developer of short induction period which is provided by the Phenidone-hydroquinone system described in the previous section and was first used in monobaths by H. S. Keelan (1957). Most monobaths contain sodium thiosulphate as the fixing agent but thiocyanates (A. Sasai and N. Mii, 1964) and many organic thio-compounds have been used as silver solvents (Kodak, U.S.P. 2,875,084/1959; Agfa, B.P. 909,492/1962). Monobaths contain a relatively high concentration of developing agents and are used at high pH values to increase the activity of development. Because of the high pH, swelling of the gelatine and reticulation will occur unless a hardening agent such as potash alum (H. S. Keelan, 1957) or formalin (M. Levy, 1958) is used. As a consequence of the high activity of the developing agents excessive fogging results and an antifoggant is, therefore, usually included in the formula.

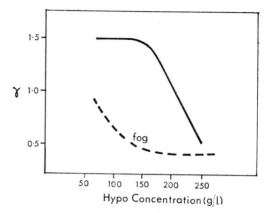

FIG. 29.27. VARIATION OF CONTRAST WITH HYPO CONCENTRATION

Far less control of processing is possible with monobaths than with conventional processing solutions because the contrast and speed obtained from material processed is fixed by the composition of the monobath and cannot be varied appreciably by change in dilution or time of processing. It is however, possible to obtain a wide contrast range by the simple method of varying the thiosulphate content (Fig. 29.27, M. Levy, 1958).

The effect of temperature variation in monobath processing is complex because it depends on the relative temperature coefficients of development and fixation which in turn depend on the material being processed and the composition of the monobath. M. Levy (1958) has shown that fog, speed and gamma rise with increase in temperature, because developer activity increases with rise in temperature at a greater rate than fixer activity.

The effect of agitation in monobath processing is relatively unimportant because increase in agitation increases the rate of development and fixation by approximately the same amount (D. A. Kazen and M. F. Wolnick, 1962) but may decrease the clearing time.

G. Haist (1966) has summarized the variations in monobath formulation and processing conditions which may be used to modify the result obtained.

To increase contrast and emulsion speed

1. Raise the pH.
2. Increase the concentration or activity of the developing agents.

3. Reduce the concentration of the fixing agents.

4. Raise the processing temperature.

5. For more contrast increase the concentration of hydroquinone (or secondary developing agent). For more emulsion speed increase the concentration of Phenidone (or primary developing agent).

To reduce contrast or emulsion speed.

1. Lower the *p*H.

2. Increase the concentration or activity of the fixing agents.

3. Increase the salt content or viscosity.

4. Use more vigorous agitation.

The most important requirement in monobath processing is the use of a very active developer of short induction period so that development can start before fixation. It has been shown that initial chemical development process forms filaments of silver which subsequently act as nuclei for deposition of silver from solution by a physical development reaction (T. H. James and W. Vanselow, 1955, J. C. Barnes, 1961).

The silver image formed in monobath processing contains at least twice the quantity of silver as an image formed in conventional processing i.e. it has a low *photometric equivalent* or *covering power*. This low covering power is ascribed to the physically developed silver filling the gaps between (i.e. thickening) the mass of filamentary silver of high covering power formed in the initial stage of development. Thus the area or light-stopping power of the chemically developed grain will not be increased by subsequent physical development and the density will be very little different from that obtained by chemical development alone (T. H. James and W. Vanselow, 1955).

Edge effects similar to those obtained from a high acutance developer (§ 565) are also obtained in monobath processing (J. C. Barnes, G. J. Johnston and W. J. Moretti, 1964). These edge effects are shown diagrammatically in Fig. 29.28 and the enhancement of edge densities is thought to result from deposition of more silver from adjacent unexposed grains on the silver of the developed grain i.e. more silver-fixer complexes are present in the unexposed region and these can diffuse across the boundary from the low density region to the high density region where they are reduced to silver and deposited on the silver filaments at the boundary between the two regions.

Monobaths are of obvious importance in the rapid access field and processing times as low

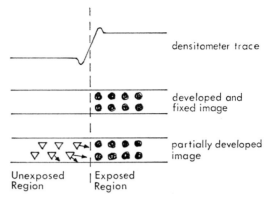

FIG. 29.28. EDGE ENHANCEMENT IN MONOBATHS

as 2·5 seconds at 120°F have been achieved in an ultra-rapid monobath which used α-thioglycerol as the fixing agent and antimony potassium tartrate as a stabilizer (L. Corben, C. Bloom, D. Willoughby and A. Shepp, 1966). Monobaths may be used for processing microfilm, X-ray film, motion picture film and in silver diffusion transfer processes (§§ 672—3), as well as in the various ingenious applicators used in rapid access systems such as spray, saturated web, roller, viscous layer etc. (§ 620).

550. The Various Causes of Fog. Negatives are never entirely free from fog. The fog, or veil, may be caused by exposure to light, by the storing of the sensitized materials under bad conditions, by the presence in the emulsion of spontaneously developable grains (*emulsion fog*), or by the action of atmospheric oxygen on a developer-wetted emulsion (*aerial fog*). *Chemical fog* is the general term applied to all types of fog caused by side reactions in the developer or fixer and includes *aerial fog*, chemical stains and fog due to silver deposition resulting from the presence of a silver halide solvent in the developer e.g. thiocyanates.

The density in the shadows of the image that is found as a result of flare from the lens or in an amply exposed negative, is not counted as fog. An attempt to obtain almost zero density in the shadows of the image leads invariably to a loss of shadow detail because of the low gradient of the characteristic curve on the extreme toe.

551. Emulsion Fog. All rapid emulsions contain a small proportion of developable grains (*latent fog*), which develop to a greater or less extent according to the composition of the developer. Examination under the microscope reveals some developed grains even in slow negative or positive emulsions that seem entirely free from fog.

It is often impossible to distinguish between development fog and latent fog because the latter appears only on development and both are likewise restrained by the same agencies.

It should be emphasized that rapid emulsions do not necessarily give the most dense fog, but the growth of fog on ageing (a fog which some authors have attributed to a very slow after-ripening) is often shown sooner on rapid than on slower emulsions.

The fog density is greatest in those areas of the emulsion that bear the least amount of image. Sometimes, in the case of an under-exposed emulsion that is also slightly fogged, the density of the shadow detail can be slightly lower than the fog density. It is well known that an unexposed plate always gives a greater degree of fog on development than a similar plate that has been exposed to light save on the area where the fog density is measured. These apparent anomalies are caused, as will be explained below in the section on development fog, by the soluble bromide, formed in the course of development of the image, retarding the growth of fog.

In order to reduce the tendency of old negative materials to give chemical fog, J. Traill Taylor (1891) recommended prolonged immersion in a dilute dichromate-sulphuric solution. This solution dissolves latent-image and sensitivity specks on the grain surfaces and the speed of the material is considerably reduced, even after rinsing, bathing in dilute bisulphite, washing and drying. Lüppo-Cramer (1923) found that all surface nuclei were destroyed on immersing foggy plates and films for 3 minutes in a solution containing

p-Phenylenediamine		
hydrochloride .	.	1 g
Ammonium bromide .	.	25 g
Acetic acid, glacial	.	12·5 ml
Water to .	.	1 litre

After washing and drying, the speed is much less reduced than by the dichromate treatment. The colour sensitivity is destroyed. This treatment does not destroy the internal latent image on exposed plates, which may be developed physically after iodizing or after fixing.

R. W. Swenson (1958) has carried out experiments to differentiate between emulsion fog and development fog. In Fig. 29.29 curve 1 represents an emulsion showing emulsion fog produced by accelerated ageing, curve 2 represents a fresh emulsion and curve 3 represents

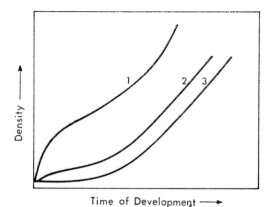

FIG. 29.29. VARIATION OF EMULSION FOG AND DEVELOPMENT FOG WITH DEVELOPMENT TIME

the aged emulsion of curve 1 after treatment with a ferricyanide bleach prior to development. Thus curve 3 is showing development fog as the emulsion fog-centres have been removed by the bleach and curves 1 and 2 are showing both emulsion fog and development fog. The aged emulsion of curve 1 show considerably more emulsion fog than the fresh emulsion of curve 2. These density *vs.* time curves show definite sections corresponding to the rapidly developing emulsion fog and the less rapidly developing development fog.

552. Development Fog. For each emulsion there is a critical time of development in a given developer, after which the unexposed grains start to develop. This critical time is reduced at higher temperatures and is increased by the addition of an anti-fogging agent. It is generally quite short for rapid negative emulsions though the rate of growth of fog is slow. On the other hand in the case of slow, contrasty emulsions, the fog appears only after a high gamma value has been reached, and then grows rapidly. In all cases this growth of fog makes it necessary to limit the time of development and often adversely affects the correct rendering of shadow detail.

The comparison of the tendencies of various emulsions to fog in a given developer, or the tendencies of the same emulsion to fog in various developers must always be made at equal values of gamma. It is generally found that the most energetic developers give the least fog. Thus there is no proportionality between the tendency to fog and the reduction potential. The ratio between the rates of growth of the image and the rate of growth of the fog has been called the *selectivity* (V. I. Sheberstov and Y. A. I. Bukin, 1932) of the developer under consideration. This ratio varies from one sensitive material to another and with the temperature of the developer. Bromide in the developer reduces the tendency for fog formation to a greater extent than for image formation. Thus an increase in bromide concentration increases the selectivity of the developer.

For each developer there is an optimum pH value at which its fogging tendency is least. Dilution retards the growth of fog much less than the growth of the image; thus the image is cleaner after development in a developer of moderate concentration than after development in a very dilute solution.

When an exposed emulsion has received prolonged development, the *covering power* of the silver is found to be lower for the fog than for the image. When development is extremely prolonged, there is formed in the non-image parts of the emulsion a *dichroic* fog which, intensified by the deposition of silver by physical development, can become sufficiently dense to transform the negative into a positive (A. P. H. Trivelli and W. F. Smith, 1940).

Diverse observations indicate that the reduction of silver ions from solution in the developer plays a major role in the formation of fog. Among other factors the addition of a silver bromide solvent to the developer often increases the fog.

The presence in the developer of a number of impurities, particularly traces of tin salts (§ 500) or of sulphides (§ 572) will give rise to fog. The fogging influence of copper salts is reduced when the developer contains a relatively high concentration of sulphite. The very dense fog sometimes found in development by hydroquinone has been attributed by Rzymkowski (1928) to the action of an intermediate oxidation product.

553. Aerial Fog. When a film or plate saturated with a developer containing hydroquinone is allowed to come into contact with air for some time during the course of development a dense fog may appear especially when the sulphite content is low. This fogging was a particular nuisance in the development of roll-films and of cinematograph films that were wound on drums which dipped into a shallow trough of developer. It was suggested by E. Fuchs (1924) that this fog was caused by chemi-luminescence occurring during the oxidation of hydroquinone and for this reason could be overcome by desensitization.

The work of T. H. James established that this fog could not be attributed to chemi-luminescence because in this case the effect would be most marked on rapid emulsions, which was not the case. Neither could the fog be due to the formation of hydrogen peroxide (see the following equation) in the course of the oxidation of

$$\text{OH}\text{-}C_6H_4\text{-}\text{OH} + O_2 \longrightarrow \text{O}\text{=}C_6H_4\text{=}\text{O} + H_2O_2$$

the developing agent, another source which had been claimed. In order to obtain the same effect as that produced by the action of the air, the concentration of hydrogen peroxide in the developer would need to be many thousands of times greater than could be produced by the oxidation of the developer. The aerial fog appears to be caused by the formation of an unstable peroxy-radical (such as HO_2) as an intermediate in the oxidation of hydroquinone. The formation of this fog is inhibited by desensitizers, the oxidation products of pyrogallol, and especially by ethylenediamine at a concentration of 0·03 per cent. The aerial fog is more severe when the developer is more alkaline. Its density varies with the sulphite concentration and is a maximum when the sulphite concentration is equal to that of the hydroquinone. It increases with the bromide concentration, and is considerably enhanced by thiocyanates and by traces of copper salts.

554. The Distribution of Fog in the Image. In many cases where it is desired to know the photographic density that has resulted from an exposure, e.g. to the image of a star, it is important to be able to differentiate between the density corresponding to the image proper and the fog density. The fog density is not uniform over all the densities of the image. The fact that on prolonging development the gamma passes through a maximum (γ_∞) and then decreases shows that the rate of growth of fog is greater in regions where the image density is lower. The rate of growth of fog is decreased in the higher image densities because of the greater concentration of exhausted developer, containing bromide and iodide and having a lower pH, that is formed in the vicinity of the already developed image grains. As a rough approximation the fog density at a given point in the image may be considered to decrease in proportion as the image density increases.

Various formulae have been proposed (R. B. Wilsey, 1925; S. E. Sheppard, 1926; H. A. Pritchard, 1928) in order to calculate what the densities of an image would have been in the complete absence of fog. The application of these methods of correction is somewhat involved and their validity has never been strictly established.

555. Removal of Fog. Chemical fog formed by oxidation may be removed if the image is bleached by permanganate and then redeveloped in a non-staining developer (see chapter XXXV). If the fog is due to silver deposits it may be removed by a weak reducer but a uniform weak fog in negatives is not usually harmful.

556. Anti-fogging Agents. The presence of a soluble bromide in the developer inhibits the growth of fog more than that of the image. In fact, the bromide inhibits the formation of development nuclei on the unexposed grains. Once the nuclei of reduced silver are formed on the unexposed grains, their development, as fog, proceeds at the same rate as the development of the exposed grains (T. H. James, 1942). The fog-inhibiting influence of bromide is particularly effective in the case of developing agents of high reduction potential. However, large concentrations of bromide can increase the fog density, expecially in pyrogallol developer. Above 10 g/litre of potassium bromide the solvent effect of bromide occurs and physical development will take place with formation of a somewhat yellow image.

Because of the fact that all emulsions are stabilized by potassium bromide which is imparted to the developer (except when a pre-bath is used), and that a soluble bromide results from the reduction of silver bromide ($Ag^+Br^- + e \rightarrow Ag + Br^-$) a used developer always contains more bromide than it did when fresh. The used developer also contains a trace of iodide, resulting from the simultaneous reduction of the silver iodide that is usually present in bromide emulsions. Most of the soluble iodide created in this way reacts at once with the undeveloped silver bromide forming silver iodide, while a very small proportion diffuses into the developer (M. L. Dundon and A. E. Ballard, 1930). This provides an explanation

why a used developer gives less fog than a fresh developer containing the same, or a slightly greater, concentration of bromide.

Since the addition of bromide to a developer causes a loss in emulsion speed, especially in the case of developers having a low reduction potential, there has been some attempt to replace it by other agents that do not decrease the sensitivity so much. Of the numerous agents that have been suggested, the following heterocyclic nuclei are the basis of most modern antifoggants:

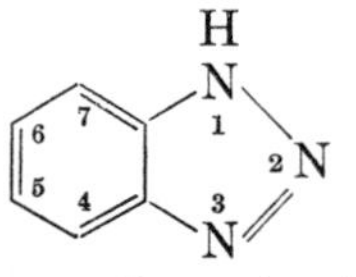

FIG. 29.30. Benzotriazole 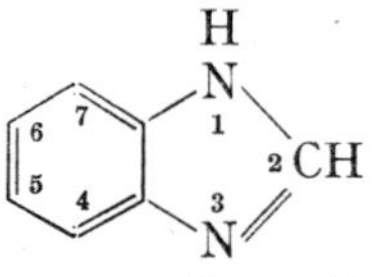   FIG. 29.31. Benzimidazole

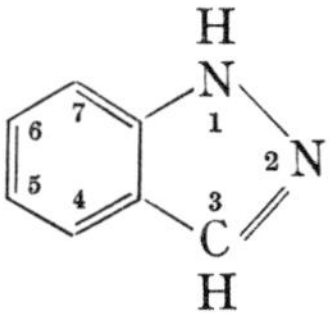

FIG. 29.32.   FIG. 29.33.   FIG. 29.34.
Indazole   Benzothiazole   Tetrazole

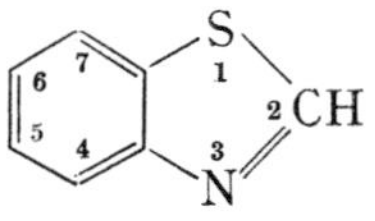

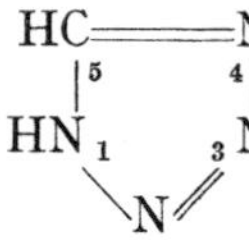

Examples of specific compounds containing these heterocyclic nuclei, which have been used as antifoggants are: benzotriazole, 5-methylbenzotriazole, 6-nitrobenzimidazole nitrate, 5-nitroindazole, 2-mercaptobenzothiazole, and 1-phenyl-5-mercaptotetrazole. These compounds vary widely in their activity, benzotriazole is one of the least active and 1-phenyl-5-mercaptotetrazole is one of the most active. The concentration required depends not only on the activity of the antifoggant itself, but also on the activity of the developer and the type of emulsion being developed. Thus in a typical Phenidone-hydroquinone developer such as ID 67 (§ 612) benzotriazole is used at a concentration of 0·15 g/litre but in a monobath using a higher concentration of developing agents benzotriazole is used at a concentration of up to 10 g/litre (C. Orlando, 1958). In conventional developers benzotriazole is generally used at concentrations up to 0·2 g/litre but a more active antifoggant such as 6-nitrobenzimidazole nitrate must be used at a considerably lower concentration or excessive loss in emulsion speed will result. Trivelli and Jensen (1931) have shown that 6-nitrobenzimidazole nitrate is effective at a concentration of $1:25,000$, causing only a slight loss in emulsion speed, though it is unstable in warm developer.

The common feature of these organic anti-fogging agents is that they contain weakly acidic —NH or —SH groups which can react with silver ions to form sparingly soluble silver salts (G. P. Faerman, 1967). Thus like bromide or iodide they can reduce the free silver ion concentration of the developer and thereby inhibit fog formation. Many organic anti-foggants are strongly adsorbed to silver halides and silver (E. J. Birr, 1952-61, H. W. Wood, 1966, and Birr, 1961) has suggested that they may act by selective adsorption to the catalytic nuclei (fog centres) and thus decrease their activity towards developing agents, but the exact mechanism by which antifoggants act is not known at present.

557. The Distribution of the Image in the Thickness of the Emulsion Layer. The same workers who made microscopical studies of the individual grains of a dilute emulsion have also studied the distribution of the grains of the image in the thickness of the emulsion layer. This distribution is affected by a number of factors among which are (a) the transparency of the emulsion layer with respect to the actinic light (b) the direction of the exposure, whether direct or through the support, (c) the ratio between the speeds of development and of penetration of the developer, (d) various treatments which can prevent the development of the latent image in the surface layer of the emulsion.

After partial development, the depth to which the image extends into the emulsion is almost independent of the exposure. On increasing the degree of development, the thickness of the image approaches a maximum for each degree of exposure. The density continues to grow after the maximum thickness is reached. This maximum thickness increases as the exposure is increased, providing that the exposure does not become great enough to cause solarization to appear. S. E. Sheppard and C. E. K. Mees (1904) found that the thickness of the image on a step-wedge ranged from $15\cdot8\mu$ at a density of $0\cdot20$, to $26\cdot5\mu$ at a density of $0\cdot76$. Using a developer that is effective throughout the thickness of the emulsion layer, it was often found that some isolated large grains at a level deeper than the others, had been affected by an exposure that was too small to cause the neighbouring grains to develop.

The distribution of the image in the thickness of the emulsion has a bearing on the action of bleaching, or photographic reducing solutions, particularly on those which act most on the surface layers of the emulsion (§691). The same density can be obtained on two similarly exposed pieces of the same film, one piece being developed for a long time in a dilute developer and the other for a short time in a concentrated developer. In the first case the image is formed by the incomplete development of all the developable grains, and in the second case by the complete development of the grains in the surface layers of the emulsion. The average diameter of the grains, and thus the granularity, is less in the first case than in the second.

When an emulsion layer is exposed to X-rays, the latent image is uniformly distributed through the depth of the emulsion because of the high penetrating power of the radiation. In this case the distribution of the fully developed image does not depend upon the conditions of development.

Since gelatine strongly absorbs light in the far ultra-violet region of the spectrum, this radiation does not penetrate very deeply into the emulsion thickness. The degree of absorption increases as the wavelength decreases. Thus the maximum contrast obtainable on a given emulsion (at γ_∞) decreases with the wavelength of the light used.

In order to reduce the contrastiness of an emulsion, especially when making duplicates in the motion picture industry, a blue-sensitive emulsion is used that is dyed yellow to limit the penetration of actinic light (J. G. Capstaff, 1924). Suitable dyes for this process, which will readily wash out, are tartrazine or naphthol yellow. The dye is applied by bathing the film in a 1 per cent solution of the dye, briefly rinsing and drying. Using such films, a further reduction in the contrast can be obtained by using ultra-violet light.

In the case of a plate or film that has been exposed through the support, the layers of the emulsion close to the support, and which received the greater exposures, are reached by developer that is already partially exhausted and loaded with bromide as a result of development of the surface grains. After an equal time of development in the same developer, a plate exposed through the support is less dense than a plate that is exposed directly, through a sheet of glass of the same thickness as the support, and the developed grains occupy a smaller thickness of the layer. The number of grains developed per unit area of the emulsion is less in the case of the emulsion exposed through the support. The image exposed through the support appears on the outer surface of the emulsion only in the most dense parts (S. E. Sheppard and C. E. K. Mees, 1904).

558. Effect of Dilution of the Developer. An extremely short development cannot be controlled and a developer must be the more dilute, the lower the gamma at which development is to be stopped. In a rapid developer, the value of the gamma increases very rapidly, especially at the start, and it is very difficult to stop development at a given gamma. Moreover, the development would continue to an appreciable extent even though the film or plate were placed in an acid stop bath after removal from the developer.

A. H. Nietz and R. A. Whitaker (1926) found that on diluting a highly concentrated developer, and increasing the time of development in proportion to the degree of dilution, the gamma values that were obtained first of all increased, passed through a maximum, and then steadily decreased.

In some developers the reduction of emulsion speed caused by bromide depends more upon the absolute concentration of the bromide rather than upon its proportion relative to the other constituents of the solution. Thus the dilution of a bromided developer often tends to limit the loss in emulsion speed.

K. Chibisov and V. Cheltzov (1929) found that, on developing in each case to the same gamma, the emulsion speed was not affected by dilution. The drawbacks associated with the use of a very dilute developer are on the one hand an increased tendency of the bath to give development fog, and, on the other hand a rapid exhaustion. This exhaustion is, moreover, manifested locally in a very dilute, fresh bath by a depression of the higher densities. This results in a modification of the characteristic curve so that what would be the upper part of the straight-line portion in the case of normal development becomes rounded off into part of the shoulder. This effect of dilution is sometimes used with advantage in order to reduce the overall density range of the negative without adversely affecting the shadow details. The exhaustion of a diluted bath is particularly rapid when the bath is agitated vigorously in contact with air, or when the dilution is carried out using air-saturated water. When diluting solutions containing the usual organic developing agents, it is better to use a plain sulphite solution rather

than water (McIntosh, 1899). In this way the salt concentration is not unduly diminished and this prevents the over-swelling of the gelatine that leads to reticulation.

P. C. Smethurst (1939) found that a developer containing a high concentration of sulphite, and made alkaline with trisodium phosphate, needed to be diluted between 5 to 10 times before the time of development was doubled. The ionization of the phosphate was depressed by the high concentration of sulphite and on dilution the pH of the solution would remain steady, or might even increase, before ultimately falling.

A simple linear relationship between the developer activity and the concentration of the developing agent is rarely obtained. In these measurements it is not the actual concentration of the developing agent, but the concentration of the active species that should be used. Thus in a metol developer the concentration of the negatively charged (ionized) metol ion should be used in the relationship between activity and concentration. The concentration of the active species of metol depends not only on the concentration of metol but on the pH and the constituents of the developer under investigation.

Where two developing agents are present in a superadditive developer it is not only their concentrations with respect to the solution but their relative concentrations with respect to one another that are important (see Fig. 29.26 § 548).

Developers containing a low concentration of developing agents are used as high definition (acutance) developers (§617). For their action these developers depend upon local developer exhaustion in the high density regions of the negative (see §563 on border effects). Accordingly they contain approximately 0·5 g/litre of developing agent and are discarded after use.

559. Depth Development. A method of *depth development*, that can be used in developing overexposed negatives, has been described by G. Balagny (1903). A solution of amidol with sodium sulphite will develop normally, but on adding bisulphite to such a solution the image appears first in the layers of the emulsion close to the support and development spreads slowly towards the free surface of the emulsion but without reaching it. As the amidol solution diffuses through the emulsion, the gelatine, by virtue of its amphoteric character, reacts with some of the bisulphite ions, reducing the acidity of the solution sufficiently to allow it to develop in the depth of the layer.

A similar result was obtained in a different way by W. Kleist (1936) by saturating a caustic hydroquinone developer with acetylene. A small concentration of acetone was used to increase the solubility of the acetylene. When this solution was used, the silver bromide in the surface layers of the emulsion was rendered non-developable by conversion into silver acetylide.

S. E. Sheppard and C. E. K. Mees (1907) noted that development by solutions of organic developing agents is slowed down by the addition of small quantities of thiosulphate, and they attributed this finding to development being confined chiefly to the depths of the emulsion. H. D. Murray and D. A. Spencer (1937) confirmed this view by comparing under the microscope the results obtained on yellow-dyed plates (§ 557) some of which were exposed normally, the others being exposed through the support. The silver bromide in the surface layers had been transformed into a non-developable complex. The same authors obtained analogous results by adding to the developer other salts that transformed the silver bromide into a difficultly developable form, for example potassium iodide or potassium cyanide. The effect of potassium iodide in this connexion provides an explanation of the influence of iodide in minimizing the appearance of abrasion marks (Lüppo-Cramer, 1914) since such marks are confined to the surface of the emulsion. Sodium thiosulphate, at a concentration of about 0·1 per cent, has been used for the same purpose.

560. The Sterry Effect. The treatment of a plate or film, after exposure and before development by a very dilute solution of potassium dichromate, weakens the latent image and reduces the maximum gamma value (γ_∞) that can be obtained (J. Sterry, 1904). This phenomenon, which is known as the *Sterry effect*, is sometimes applied when making copies with a material that is too contrasty for convenience. If the dichromate solution is acidified or is used at a greater concentration, and is allowed to act for only a very short time, the latent image on the grain surfaces is entirely destroyed on the grains in the surface layers of the emulsion. The results are similar to those that would be obtained by using a surface-acting reducer on the developed image (S. E. Sheppard and C. E. K. Mees, 1907).

561. The Effect of Waste Products of Development. When the developer that has been partially exhausted by the reduction of the

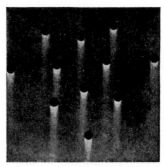

FIG. 29.35. EFFECT OF BROMIDE GENERATED BY THE DEVELOPMENT PROCESS ON MOVING FILM
(Streamers.)

silver halide in an exposed part of the emulsion diffuses out of the gelatine, it is denser than the surrounding solution and tends to descend vertically if it is not prevented from doing so by the agitation of the bath. These descending currents have been observed by following the movements of cotton fibres suspended in the solution (E. R. Bullock, 1922) and have been photographed directly (A. Haelsig and F. Luft, 1933). A simple experiment (J. I. Crabtree and C. E. Ives, 1926) shows the troublesome consequences of the streaming of partially exhausted developer. A plate was given a low, uniform exposure and was then heavily exposed behind a mask having a number of circular holes. The plate was then developed in a vertical position without agitation. The resulting image is shown in Fig. 29.35. The background density is reduced below each dense patch by the streaming of waste products which reduce the rate of development. An upwards streaming can be produced when the emulsion has been soaked in water prior to immersion in the developer. In this case the exhaustion products will be carried upwards by the convection caused at the surface of the plate by the dilution of the developer by the water in the emulsion.

The streaming effect is greatest on emulsions that are rich in iodide. On the other hand, it is least on silver chloride emulsions (E. R. Bullock, 1922).

A used developer contains gelatine and gelatine degradation products formed by alkaline hydrolysis which give rise to foam when the bath is agitated. Furthermore, the presence of the gelatine, etc., may result in the infection of the bath by moulds and by bacteria which attack sulphite, converting it into sulphide which gives an intense fog.

562. Defects in Machine Processing. When motion picture films were developed after being wound on a rectangular frame that was immersed, vertically, in the developer tank, various *rack marks* appeared on the developed film. The density was a maximum where the film passed over the top lateral member of the rack and decreased from the top to the bottom of each strand, being a minimum where the film passed under the bottom lateral of the rack.

Other irregularities due to the same cause are found on films developed on continuous processing machines in spite of the fact that the film moves through the bath at speeds of 25 to 200 feet per minute. The sensitometric strips, which usually consist of stepped exposures varying along the length of the film, and which are interposed between the rolls of film in order to assess the behaviour of the developer, give different characteristic curves according to whether the heaviest exposure precedes or follows the rest of the wedge (J. Crabtree and J. H. Waddel, 1933). On uniformly exposed films, a steady decrease in density can occur from the leading end of the film to the following end. These *directional effects* are particularly troublesome in the development of sound tracks for sound films by reason of the sound distortions to which they give rise.

Finally, the local turbulence, caused by the passage of developer through the perforation holes, tends to sweep away the partially used developer that is in contact with the emulsion, and thus accelerates development, resulting in a small region of increased density. Since the sound track lies very close to the perforation holes, this local non-uniformity of development will be superimposed upon it and the defect emerges as an audible note when the processed track is finally run through the projector. This defect is called *perforation*, or *sprocket-hole modulation*.

These defects are avoided, or reduced to the point where they are negligible, by a sufficient agitation of the developer bath.

563. Border Effects. Other irregularities appear on images developed horizontally in a developer that is not agitated. Lateral diffusion within the emulsion layer of comparatively exhausted developer from a region of high density to an adjacent one of lower density, and of comparatively fresh developer in the reverse direction, results in the formation at the boundary between the two densities of two degraded borders (cf. Fig. 29.28, § 549). The border at the edge of the denser patch is even denser and the border at the edge of the lighter region is less dense than the average for that region (*Mackie Line*). The phenomenon, observed by R. Colson (1898) in studying the development by a thin film of solution, has been studied by G. Eberhard (1912) in so far as it concerns the application of photography to scientific purposes. It is generally known as the *Eberhard Effect* or the *edge* or *neighbourhood effect*. When two small light patches on a dark ground (or two dark patches on a light ground) are very close together the concentration of developer exhaustion products is a minimum (or a maximum) between them. This produces a lack of symmetry of their edges that causes an apparent shift in the distance between their centres. This *Kostinsky Effect* is particularly troublesome in making measurements on neighbouring spectral lines, or on double stars, and in motion picture sound tracks.

564. Infectious Development. Usually, the neighbourhood effect manifests itself as a retarding of development of low densities that are contiguous with high densities. However, a case is known in which the partially used developer is more active than the fresh developer and development is accelerated in regions of low density that border on regions of high density.

This phenomenon, called *infectious development* (J. A. C. Yule, 1945) has been found in the case of fine-grain, high-contrast emulsions of the type used for photomechanical reproduction when development is carried out using a hydroquinone developer having a low (0·1 per cent) concentration of sulphite. Thus the gamma is considerably increased without appreciably increasing the fog but the foot of the characteristic curve is underdeveloped and some loss in emulsion speed results. This effect was studied by ingenious experiments involving the mixing and superposition of emulsions of differing colour sensitivity. The catalytic agent that induces the acceleration of development by the hydroquinone was thought to be the semiquinone radical whose prolonged existence is impossible in the presence of the normal concentration of sulphite (§ 570). The semiquinone is formed by the equation given below where the benzoquinone results from the oxidation of two silver ions according to the equation given previously (§ 537).

At low sulphite concentrations benzoquinone is not removed by reaction with sulphite and the above reaction leads to a build up of the semiquinone which is able to reduce more silver ions and the benzoquinone thus formed auto-catalyses the development reaction by forming the semiquinone.

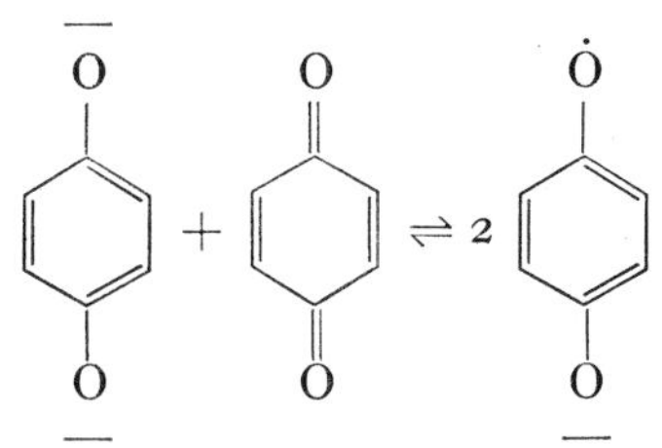

This build up of semiquinone is also thought to occur in superadditive Phenidone-hydro-quinone developers (§ 548) of low Phenidone and sulphite concentration and gives rise to "explosive superadditivity" (J. Q. Umberger, 1966), in which the semiquinone is able to reduce silver ions.

Recently T. H. James (1968) has suggested that the importance of the semiquinone in lithographic developers has been overstated and the increase in development of the more heavily exposed areas has been attributed to the formation of a diaminohydroquinone (Fig. 29.36) formed by reaction of the quinone with gelatine. This diaminohydroquinone is a reducing agent which forms a superadditive developer with hydroquinone.

The application of such a developer to a pen-drawing blocks up the image of fine lines by inducing development of those grains which received by irradiation an exposure that would be too small to cause development under other conditions. The oxidation products that cause development react rapidly with the sulphite of the fresh developer into which they diffuse and the effect of the infection is only manifested over a distance of about 0·1 mm.

A rather similar effect known as *contagious development* was observed on emulsions of the same type as those above when developed in a developer made strongly alkaline with sodium hydroxide and containing traces of hydrazine

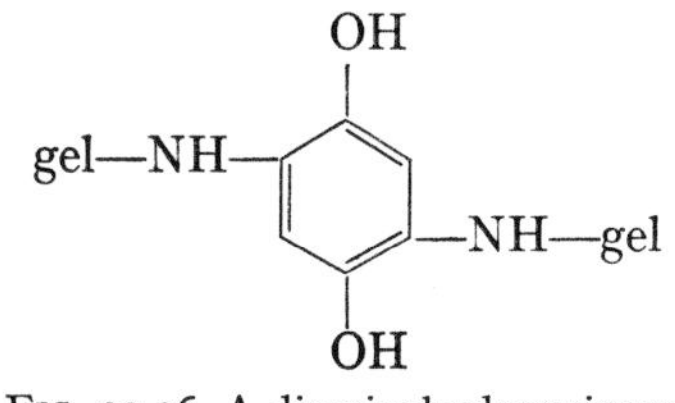

Fig. 29.36. A diaminohydroquinone

(e.g. 0·03 to 0·05 g of hydrazine hydrochloride per litre to the first of the developers). The inertia speed and the gamma are approximately trebled without an appreciable increase in fog (R. E. Stauffer, W. F. Smith, and A. P. H. Trivelli, 1944). This effect has been attributed to the fogging of unexposed grains by an unstable compound of hydrazine and a quinonoid oxidation product of the developer formed in the development of exposed grains in the immediate vicinity. The granularity of the image does not allow practical use to be made of this method of intensifying the image by local fogging during development.

The term *infectious development* is used when development spreads to feebly exposed grains, while *contagious development* refers to development spreading to unexposed grains.

565. The Effect of Agitation. The agitation of the bath does not only serve to reduce local irregularities in development such as those mentioned above. When it is sufficient to renew rapidly the developer in contact with the emulsion, and thus to accelerate the diffusion of waste products from the layer, it speeds up development.

In the case of developers that are very susceptible to the influence of bromide, agitation reduces the loss in emulsion speed. In a hydroquinone developer without bromide, the absence of all agitation causes the same regression of the inertia speed that is found in the same developer when containing bromide and when agitated, the regression being the less as the developer is more violently agitated (S. E. Sheppard and F. A. Elliot, 1923). Some analogous, though less well marked, effects have been found in the case of the other developing agents. In other experiments the same authors (1924) found that the speed of development remained almost constant until the velocity of the solution in contact with the emulsion reached 0·8 metres per second. It reached a maximum when the velocity reached 2·5 metres per second and then decreased until at 10 metres per second, especially in the commencement of development, it reached a value scarcely greater than that found in the static bath.

The agitation must be more efficient as the time of development is decreased, as in developing to a low gamma in a developer of normal concentration, or in developing to a high gamma value in a concentrated developer. The local irregularities in an image developed to a low gamma are exaggerated in the print which is usually developed to a high gamma.

One cannot consider as efficacious the agitation produced by rocking a dish, nor the simple motion of film through the solution in continuous processing machines. In the first case the velocity of the solution relative to the emulsion is insufficient, and in the second case the moving film carries with it a sheath of developer that moves at almost the same speed as the film.

In all cases where the time of development is chosen after previously developing a sensitometric strip in the same developer, the degree of agitation must be taken into account, and, if possible, the test strip should receive the same degree of agitation as it is proposed to use with the material to be developed. For example, the time of development of a particular film, in D76 developer, to $\gamma = 1 \cdot 0$ varied from 9 to 18 minutes (at 18°C) according to the degree of agitation. It should be noted that since the growth of fog depends upon the time of development and not upon the agitation, a film developed to a given gamma is less fogged when the developer is vigorously agitated.

Various methods for obtaining uniform development are described in § 595.

566. The Influence of Temperature. In all developers the rate of development becomes greater as the temperature is raised, but the effect of an increase in temperature varies considerably from one developer to another. On the one hand, all reactions are accelerated by an increase in temperature, and on the other hand the diffusion of ions into and out of the emulsion is greater at higher temperatures, although this latter effect is somewhat offset by the increased swelling of the gelatine.

Besides accelerating development, a rise in the temperature of the developer sometimes causes an increase in the emulsion speed and always causes an increase in the fog density, the development being carried to the same gamma value for comparison in all cases.

It has been found that, in the case of a metol developer, the emulsion speed of the experimental material increased by about 30 per cent on raising the temperature of the solution from 15° to 25°C (K. Chibisov and V. Chel'tsov, 1929). It should be noted, however, that in many cases claims of a marked increase of emulsion speed on warming the developer have been discounted when a careful sensitometric examination has been made, the authors having mistaken an increase in the general density of the image for an increase in speed.

The increase in fog density that occurs when the temperature of the developer considerably exceeds 20°C (as, for example, in tropical conditions, or on warming the bath to accelerate development) necessitates the use of an increased concentration of bromide.

If, in the case of a given developer and sensitive material, the times of development that are required to reach a given gamma at two different temperatures are known, the times of development for the same gamma can easily be calculated for other temperatures, because the logarithm of the time of development is proportional to the temperature (W. B. Ferguson, 1906). For example if the same gamma was obtained by 4·9 minutes' development at 10°C and 3·5 minutes at 18°C, the coefficient of proportionality K is given by—

$$K = \frac{\log t - \log t'}{T' - T} = \frac{\log 4 \cdot 9 - \log 3 \cdot 5}{8}$$

$$= \frac{0 \cdot 6903 - 0 \cdot 544}{8} = 0 \cdot 0182$$

where t, t' represent the times of development and T, T' indicate the temperatures.

The *temperature coefficient*, C, of a developer, for a given emulsion relating to the times of development necessary to reach a given gamma at two temperatures differing by 10°C, is given by—

$$\log C = 10 \, K$$

In the above example $\log C = 0 \cdot 182$, and $C = 1 \cdot 52$.

These calculations may be avoided by using the abacus, shown in Fig. 29.37 after W. Heydecker, 1925. To use the abacus, measure on the time scale the *distance* (e.g. with a pair of dividers) between the times of development that were needed to reach the desired gamma value at the two temperatures. Then, starting from the point of the temperature scale corresponding to the difference between the two temperatures under consideration, erect a perpendicular line equal to the measured length. Draw a straight line from the zero of the temperature scale through the end of this perpendicular line and continue it to cut the temperature coefficient scale, on which it will indicate the required value.

In order to find how much the time of development needs to be increased on lowering the temperature of the developer in the above example from 18° to 15°C, draw a straight, oblique line from the zero on the abacus to 1·52 on the temperature coefficient scale. Then measure the *distance* from the 3° mark on the temperature

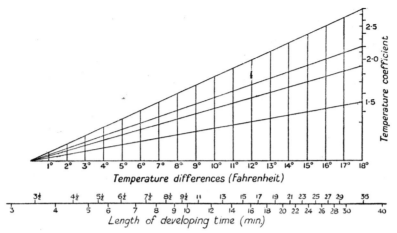

FIG. 29.37. GRAPH FOR THE CALCULATION OF EQUIVALENT DEVELOPMENT
TIMES FOR DIFFERENT TEMPERATURES

difference scale to this oblique line. Then, starting from the 3·5 minute mark on the time scale measure off (towards higher times) the distance found on the abacus and this will terminate at the required time, in the present example, 4·0 minutes.

Since the time of appearance of the image varies proportionally with the total time of development, the Watkins Factor (§ 547) retains its value unchanged.

The temperature coefficient of a developer varies slightly from one emulsion to another. It does not vary much on changing the concentration of the developer, nor does it vary very much for various developer solutions compounded from the same developing agent. The following table shows most usually found values for the various developing agents.

Developing Agent				C
Metol .	.	.	.	. 1·25
p-Aminophenol	.	.	. 1·5
Ferrous oxalate	.	.	. 1·7
Pyrogallol	.	.	. 1·9
Metol-hydroquinone	.	. 1·9
Hydroquinone	.	.	. 2·2 to 2·8
Catechol	.	.	. 2·8

In a developer containing two developing agents of different character, the notion of temperature coefficient loses all significance as soon as the temperature departs far from the optimum. For example, in a metol-hydroquinone developer, the metol alone has any considerable activity at temperatures of about 10°C, while hydroquinone is the more active at temperatures about 20°C.

In order to obtain consistent results, it is necessary to maintain the temperature constant. Failing this, the temperature should be measured and account must be taken of its influence on the time of development.

Most manufacturers publish simplified charts from which it is possible to read the appropriate development times at various temperatures. A typical time-temperature chart for the development of negative materials is given in Fig. 29.38 (Ilford Ltd.).

In order to use this chart the diagonal line from the recommended time at 20°C (68°F) is followed until it cuts the horizontal line representing the actual temperature to be used. The development time at this temperature is then read from the bottom line vertically below the intersection. Thus if the recommended time is 9 minutes at 20°C, at 24°C the required development time will be 6 minutes and at 17°C it will be 12 minutes.

567. Normal Constituents of a Developer.
Although it is possible to obtain faint traces of an image (L. P. Clerc, 1909; E. Cousin, 1912) by treating a sensitive film in a very dilute pure aqueous solution of some developers (diaminophenol, p-phenylene-diamine, and its derivatives, etc.), it is usually necessary, in order to obtain a vigorous image in a reasonable time, to render the developing solution alkaline, so that the hydrobromic acid resulting from the reduction of the silver bromide may be neutralized as it is formed. A pure aqueous solution of

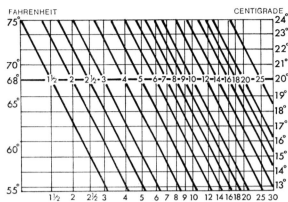

FAHRENHEIT   CENTIGRADE

FIG. 29.38. TIME-TEMPERATURE CHART

hydroquinone does not develop, but a solution containing 5 per cent of hydroquinone and 5 per cent of caustic soda develops a satisfactory image in about three minutes, without fog or appreciable stain (C. E. K. Mees and C. W, Piper, 1911). The caustic alkali may, moreover. be replaced by the salt of a weak acid, easily displaced by the hydrobromic acid and not itself preventing development, provided that the solution has a pH that is sufficiently high for the developing agent under consideration. This is the case with the carbonates and various other salts, among which are the sulphites. With the latter, development is exceedingly slow, except with the developers capable of developing an image in an aqueous solution (about one hour is required to develop a complete image in a very concentrated sulphite solution of pyro). Development is completed in a normal time by adding a carbonate (of sodium or of potassium) to the pure aqueous solution of a developer substance, but these solutions (like nearly all others compounded with a caustic alkali) oxidize in the air with very great rapidity, thus giving rise, during the time necessary for development, to brown oxidation products, which strongly stain the gelatine.

In 1882 H. B. Berkeley observed that the addition of a sulphite to the alkaline solution of a developer considerably delays this oxidation and opposes the formation of the highly-coloured products obtained in the absence of this *preservative*. While sulphite must be considered a necessary constituent of all developing solutions compounded with organic developers, it is not entirely advantageous. While it increases the energy of a solution of p-aminophenol and carbonate (M. Andresen, 1898), it retards development with a solution of hydroquinone and carbonate (J. Desalme, 1921), and furthermore, as a solvent of silver bromide (with which it forms a soluble double sulphite) it favours the formation of fog.

Other substances have been suggested for use instead of sulphite to protect the developing agents from being oxidized by atmospheric oxygen. Greater protection is afforded by substances containing an —SH (thiol) group, such as cysteine and thioglycolic acid (T. H. James and A. Weissberger, 1939). The protection appears to be due, as with sulphite, to the destruction of quinonoid oxidation products which catalyse the oxidation of hydroquinone.

Finally, in many cases a bromide, added in small quantities to the developing bath, must be used as a *restrainer* of chemical fog (§ 552 to § 556). Organic antifoggants (§ 556) are also added to developers to supplement the restraining action of bromide or to replace bromide altogether.

We have seen that a typical developer contains:

1. A developing agent or agents,
2. an alkali or accelerator,
3. a preservative,
4. a restrainer or antifoggant.

The nature of the actual chemicals used as well as their relative concentrations govern the properties of a developer to such an extent that it is important to understand the role of each constituent.

As, however, varying the concentration of the other constituents can, with the same developing agent, produce slow acting and weak or rapid and contrasty results we shall consider their functions first.

568. The Role of the Alkalis in Development. Besides neutralizing the hydrobromic acid which is liberated in development (in the case of silver bromide), the alkali must liberate the free base of those developing agents that are usually supplied in the form of a salt for greater stability in storage, e.g. metol. The alkali facilitates the dissociation of acidic hydroxyl (—OH) groups by forming phenolates. Finally, the pH of the developer is one of the factors that influences the reduction potential, which increases with the alkalinity of the developer solution (§ 527).

If the activity of a developing agent is the same in various fresh developer solutions at the

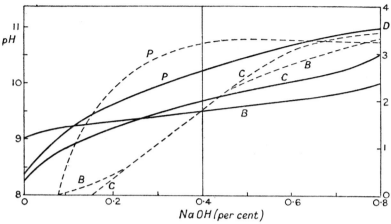

FIG. 29.39. BUFFERING EFFECT OF BORAX, SODIUM BICARBONATE AND DISODIUM PHOSPHATE

same pH, these solutions may behave very differently after some use, or after storing in contact with air. In both cases the pH of the developer solution would have changed, and not necessarily in the same direction. As will be described below, the pH of hydroquinone-sulphite solutions increases on aerial oxidation, while oxidation by a silver halide decreases the pH. The extent of the change in pH depends upon the buffering capacity of the other constituents of the developer (§ 513). A mixture of sulphite and carbonate gives quite good buffering at pH 10, while salts such as borate and phosphate are very useful buffers at pH levels about 9·4 and 10·5 respectively and may be used with advantage in developers at about these pH values. However, borates should be avoided when using developing agents, such as catechol and pyrogallol, containing hydroxyl groups in *ortho* positions because of the formation of complexes.

The behaviour of three buffers is shown by the full curves in Fig. 29.39 (W. Reinders and M. C. F. Beukers, 1931). Three developers were prepared, each containing 11 grammes of hydroquinone and 38 grammes of sulphite, per litre. The first was buffered with 19·05 grammes of borax (B), the second with 8·4 grammes of sodium bicarbonate (C), and the third with 35·8 grammes of disodium hydrogen phosphate (P). The course of the change in pH is shown as sodium hydroxide was added. The vertical line at 0·4 per cent NaOH indicates sufficient sodium hydroxide to make an equivalent amount of metaborate, carbonate, and trisodium phosphate from the respective buffers. The broken

curves show the densities obtained in 10 minutes' development (right-hand scale) on plates that had all received the same exposure.

The full curves show that, in the pH range 9 to 10, the borax buffer was the best, the bicarbonate was acceptable, while the phosphate was mediocre.

The optimum value of the pH varies from one developing agent to another. The following table shows the approximate pH range within which some developing agents can be effectively used (W. Reinders and M. C. F. Beukers, 1931).

Developing Agent	pH Range
Metol . . .	. 6–9·5
p-Aminophenol .	. 7·5–12
Pyrogallol . .	. 8–9·5
Glycin . . .	. 8·5–11·5
Hydroquinone .	. 9·5–11
p-Phenylenediamine .	. 10–13

The rate of oxidation of the developer by atmospheric oxygen is greater as the alkalinity of the solution is increased. For this reason the pH of the developer should not be increased beyond the minimum value necessary. Besides, high alkalinity promotes a detrimental swelling of the gelatine.

Ammonium hydroxide and ammonium carbonate can serve as alkalis in developers, but their use is limited to certain special cases. By virtue of their solvent power for silver chloride and bromide, they favour the formation of *dichroic fog* (§ 552). In a slow-acting developer, ammonium hydroxide limits the values of gamma and maximum density that can be reached. Some of the silver, reduced from the silver halide dissolved from the emulsion, is deposited on the walls of the dish (J. Vidal, 1931). In some cases a derivative of ammonia may be used. Triethanolamine, for example, is more strongly alkaline than ammonium hydroxide and has less solvent action on silver halides.

The addition of acetone or formaldehyde to a sulphite solution results in the formation of an acetone-, or formaldehyde-bisulphite with the consequent liberation of an equivalent amount of sodium hydroxide (Lumière and Seyewetz, 1896). Developers have been used consisting of a solution of sulphite and pyrogallol to which acetone is added. In such developers, if the quantity of sulphite was not in excess of the acetone, the concentration of sulphite is greatly reduced and the image obtained is brown as a result of the formation in the gelatine of a *secondary image* (§ 573) by the oxidation products of the pyrogallol.

Thus, in order to obtain images of high contrast by infectious development (§ 564), hydroquinone developers are made alkaline by the addition of formaldehyde, used in the form of a solution or as the solid polymer, trioxymethylene which depolymerizes when dissolved in a sulphite solution (Lumière and Seyewetz, 1902).

569. The Role of Sulphite. The quantity of sulphite to be used in a developing solution depends on the nature of the developer and of the substances used to render it alkaline, on the dilution of the bath, on the degree of keeping quality desired in partly emptied bottles or in developing tanks, and on the prevailing temperature.

For instance, very little sulphite is required with glycin (the spontaneous oxidation of which is negligible) and with paraphenylenediamine (the oxidation products of which are then almost colourless), while a relatively large quantity is required with pyro solutions to avoid staining the image.

Developing solutions made alkaline with caustic alkalis tend to oxidize more rapidly than those containing carbonates; for this reason the sulphite content should be somewhat increased with the former. All other conditions being equal, the proportion of sulphite to developer must be greater in a dilute solution than in a concentrated one.

With most developers, if the developing solution is prepared shortly before use and is used once only, a sulphite content of about 1 per cent of the anhydrous salt is sufficient. It is, moreover, at this strength that the solubility of silver bromide in solutions of sulphite reaches its minimum; thus chemical fog is markedly reduced (C. E. K. Mees and C. W. Piper, 1912). The amount of sulphite must be increased when a developing solution has to be kept long in a partly empty container, especially when there is a large surface in contact with air (solution left in a developing tank without a floating cover) and in all cases where air has free access to the emulsion during its development (development of film on continuous machines or drums, and development in tanks where the developer is kept in motion by a stream of air).

Finally, as an appreciable rise in temperature always accelerates the atmospheric oxidation of the developing solution, it is necessary in hot climates to counteract this effect by increasing the quantity of sulphite specified for use in temperate countries.

The fact that a small quantity of the silver halide dissolves in the sodium sulphite used as a preservative of the developing solution against oxidation results in the solution behaving, to a certain extent, like a physical developer; the dissolved silver salt is reduced by the developer and deposits itself, partly in the liquid and on the walls of the tanks, and partly on the image.

570. Reactions of Sulphite with Organic Developing Agents. The mechanism of the mutual protection that sulphite and certain developing agents afford to each other against aerial oxidation (autoxidation) has not yet been worked out, but it has been studied in the case of hydroxyphenols and especially in the case of hydroquinone.

Whereas the oxidation of hydroquinone in an acid or feebly alkaline solution yields quinone, this product is not found as a result of oxidation in the presence of an excess of sulphite. Quinone is instantaneously transformed into hydroquinone monosulphonate when added to an alkaline sulphite solution. It is this substance which constitutes the first end-product of the oxidation of hydroquinone in the presence of sulphite (J. Pinnow, 1913). In the case of autoxidation the reaction proceeds—

$$\underset{\text{hydroquinone}}{C_6H_4(OH)_2} + \underset{\text{sodium sulphite}}{2Na_2SO_3} + \underset{\text{oxygen}}{O_2}$$

$$\rightarrow \underset{\text{hydroquinone sulphonate}}{C_6H_3(OH)_2SO_3Na} + \underset{\substack{\text{sodium}\\\text{sulphate}}}{Na_2SO_4} + \underset{\substack{\text{sodium}\\\text{hydroxide}}}{NaOH}$$

In the case of development the reaction is—

$$\underset{\text{hydroquinone}}{C_6H_4(OH)_2} + \underset{\substack{\text{sodium}\\\text{sulphite}}}{Na_2SO_3} + \underset{\substack{\text{silver}\\\text{bromide}}}{2AgBr} + \underset{\substack{\text{sodium}\\\text{hydroxide}}}{NaOH}$$

$$\rightarrow \underset{\text{hydroquinone sulphonate}}{C_6H_3(OH)_2SO_3Na} + \underset{\substack{\text{sodium}\\\text{bromide}}}{2NaBr} + \underset{\text{water}}{H_2O} + \underset{\text{silver}}{2Ag}$$

It will be seen that, whereas in the second case some of the available alkali is neutralized, in the first case sodium hydroxide is formed by the autoxidation. This explains the observation (H. Luppo-Cramer, 1931) that a sulphite solution of hydroquinone that does not develop when freshly compounded, becomes quite active after storing it for several days in a partly filled bottle. It should be noted, moreover, that when the constituents of a developer are put up in two solutions to be mixed just before use (the developing agent in one and the alkali in the other), the oxidation of the developing agent is not avoided merely by adding sulphite to that part. It is necessary to acidify the solution, for example, by adding bisulphite.

The hydroquinone monosulphonate that is formed by the oxidation of hydroquinone is itself a feeble developer, and if the oxidation of the solution is continued, by development or by exposure to air, hydroquinonedisulphonate is formed, whose presence in solution is marked by an intense blue fluorescence.

The protective action of sulphite is the result of its preventing the formation of quinone or quinonoid products which, in the absence of sulphite, energetically catalyse the autoxidation of hydroquinone (T. H. James and A. Weissberger, 1939).

Whereas the oxidation products of metol and p-phenylenediamine are also converted to sulphonates, the oxidation products of Phenidone (1-phenyl-3-pyrazolidinone) will not react in a similar manner with sulphite (A. J. Axford and J. D. Kendall, 1954) and this accounts for the higher activity of Phenidone in a Phenidone-hydroquinone developer than metol in a metol-hydroquinone developer (§ 548).

571. The Effect of Soluble Bromide on Development. In the early days of the gelatine-bromide emulsions the developers always needed a comparatively high concentration of bromide in order to retard the growth of fog. The subsequent improvements that have been made in the manufacture of these emulsions which are stabilized by the inclusion of a small amount of bromide, and the appearance of better developing agents, make it often useless to add bromide to the developer. It is important to keep the bromide concentration down to the minimum because of the loss in sensitivity that it causes. The full lines in Fig. 29.40 show the characteristic curves of a sensitive material developed for 2 and 8 minutes in a developer without bromide. The broken lines show the characteristic curves

for similarly exposed samples of the material developed for the same times in a part of the same developer after adding a moderate concentration of bromide. The dotted curves similarly show the effect of a high concentration of bromide. For each time of development the slope of the curve, determining the contrast, has not been altered by the addition of bromide. The depression of the curves by the addition of bromide means that shadow detail that would be recorded on development in the bromide-free developer becomes lost, to a greater extent as the concentration of bromide is increased. Moreover, as the point (A, B, and C) about which the straight-line portions of the curves pivot, becomes further depressed, a greater loss of shadow detail will be suffered as the gamma at which development is terminated is lowered (*regression of the inertia*).

A. H. Nietz (1920) claimed that the depression of the points of intersection (A, B, C in Fig. 29.40) was proportional to the logarithm of the bromide concentration, and that the point of intersection was depressed perpendicularly. A. P. H. Trivelli and E. C. Jensen (1931) found that the depression was greater for X-ray exposures. This fact has been attributed to the more uniform distribution of the X-ray image through the depth of the emulsion, the deeper parts of the image being reached only by partially exhausted (more bromided) developer.

The induction period is usually increased on adding bromide to the developer.

If the development of a negative is started in a non-bromided developer and is continued in a bromided developer, or conversely, the results are intermediate between those which would

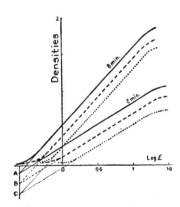

FIG. 29.40. ACTION OF BROMIDE
IN DEVELOPMENT

have been obtained had similarly exposed negatives been developed throughout, to the same gamma, in the bromided and non-bromided developers respectively. Thus, the effect of bromide is not permanent, as it would be if bromide partially destroyed the latent image (J. I. Crabtree, H. Parker, and H. D. Russell, 1933).

The use of a bromided developer often extends the range over which the brightnesses of the subject can be correctly reproduced by the sensitive material (W. Romer, 1934).

By preventing, or considerably retarding, the growth of fog, a comparatively high concentration of bromide in an energetic developer allows development to be pushed further than in a non-bromided developer, thus enabling the maximum contrast to be obtained when it is possible to sacrifice some emulsion speed, as, for example, in copying.

The various developing agents react differently towards the influence of soluble bromide. In the same way that the power of a vehicle can be judged by the effect of a rising gradient on its speed, so can the reduction potential of a developer be evaluated with sufficient accuracy for practical needs by the effect of a given concentration of bromide on its rate of development (R. Abegg, 1899; A. H. Nietz, 1922).

The influence of bromide has been attributed to a reversibility of the development reaction, a reversibility which, under the usual conditions of use, is only found in the case of ferrous solutions.

At the time when it was believed that chemical development proceeded by a reduction of silver bromide that had previously passed into solution in the developer, it was thought that soluble bromide acted by reducing the solubility of silver bromide in the developer. Later this theory became confined to the reduction of fog by bromide in the case in which the fog is due to physical development in addition to chemical development. The influence of soluble bromide is readily explained by the theory of development based upon the idea of oxidation-reduction potentials (§§ 525–7) and upon the adsorption of the developer to the silver bromide grains. On the one hand, by decreasing the reduction potential of the developer, the bromide increases the minimum size of the developable latent image, preventing the development of the less exposed grains (a mechanism suspected by G. Bredig in 1895), and on the other hand it inhibits the adsorption of the developing agent (at least, if a negative ion) to the silver bromide grains.

Contrary to an opinion that is sometimes expressed, soluble chloride, no matter in what concentration, cannot be substituted for soluble bromide, even in the case of the development of silver chloride emulsions in the normal developers (E. Weyde, 1933).

All the effects found on adding soluble bromide to a developer are, obviously, also to be observed in a used developer because its bromide concentration would be increased while the developing agent concentration would be decreased. The effect of organic antifoggants has been given in a previous section (§ 556).

572. The Formation of Sulphide in Used Developers. Used developers that are kept for long periods away from air, as in stoppered bottles and deep tanks, may, when used, give a fog due to the formation of sulphide as a result of bacterial decomposition of the sulphite (M. L. Dundon and J. I. Crabtree). This occurrence is encountered mostly in summer, the optimum temperature for the growth of the anaerobic bacteria, whose presence is made possible by the gelatine dissolved from the developed emulsions, lying between 25° and 40°C.

When the concentration of sulphide is very small, the bath is cleared by the first few films or plates that are developed, and no fog appears on those developed immediately afterwards. However, the fog reappears on recommencing development after a suspension of work. When the concentration of sulphide is appreciable the bath gives off the odour of rotten eggs especially when stirred. In such a case the bath can only be used after adding lead acetate, agitating, and allowing the insoluble lead salts (sulphide, etc.) to settle or filtering them off. When the system becomes infected in this way it is necessary to disinfect the whole system, tanks, baths, pumps, and pipes. Strong disinfectants such as sodium hypochlorite, permanganate, or pentachlorphenate (Santobrite) may be used, the choice depending upon the materials of which the system is constructed.

Disinfectants that can be added to the developer without adverse effect include—alkaline fluorides and fluosilicates, sodium salicylate (2 g per litre), parachlormetacresol (1 g per litre), Sunoxol (ortho-oxyquinoline sulphate, 0·1 g per litre), and various derivatives of acridine yellow.

573. Oxidation Products of Developers; Tanning; Secondary Images. The quinonoid oxidation products of developers that are formed in the absence of sulphite, or in the presence of a very low concentration of sulphite, are deposited in the gelatine at the site of development, and in a quantity proportional to the amount of silver halide reduced. Usually they polymerize, giving rise to coloured, tanning substances of the nature of the humic acids, whose exact constitution is unknown.

After removing the silver image by bleaching with a weak oxidizing solution, such as ferricyanide-thiosulphate (Farmer's Reducer), a yellow or brown *secondary image* remains, which, though it may not appear very intense to the eye, can give acceptable prints on high contrast paper, because of its absorption of actinic light. The following table (Lumière and Seyewetz, 1928) shows the colour of the secondary image obtained in various developers, its relative intensity and the concentration of sulphite necessary to prevent its formation.

Developer	Colour	Relative Intensity	Sulphite (grammes per litre)
Pyrogallol	Yellow-orange	10	11
Catechol	Black	10	6
Hydroquinone	Yellow-brown	10	2
Chlorhydroquinone	Yellow-brown	10	2
Amidol	Reddish-brown	8	2
p-Aminophenol	Brownish-black	3	2
Metol	Brownish-black	2	1
p-Phenylenediamine	Grey	1	–
Glycin	None	0	–

The secondary image is destroyed or weakened by acid stop baths and acid fixers.

Of the usual developing agents, pyrogallol and catechol give the most effective tanning.

574. Tanning Developers. The *tanning developers* are sometimes inconvenient, but, on the other hand, they lend themselves to interesting practical applications.

To quote the disadvantages first, the tanning of the gelatine that takes place during development in proportion to density of the image already formed, slows down the process of diffusion of fresh and exhausted developer, particularly in the high densities, thus depressing that part of the characteristic curve which would otherwise be the straight line portion (K. Jacobsohn, 1928). Again the differential tanning between contiguous areas of different density causes, on drying, local deformation of the image (F. E. Ross, 1921) that is especially harmful when the image is to be used for exact measurements.

Among the applications of differential tanning to be noted are relief images, particularly for

collotype matrices, on thin films exposed through the support, the unhardened gelatine being washed away in warm water after development; also for transferring to metal, resists are copied on paper, coated with an emulsion which is dyed to limit the penetration of the light (§ 557), the paper being stripped in warm water after the image has adhered to the support.

According to A. G. Tull (1963) the mechanism of tanning involves a cross-linking of gelatine by the oxidation product of the developing agent (hydroquinone, p-phenylenediamine) to give a diaminohydroquinone or a diamino-p-phenylenediamine derivative (see § 564).

575. Applications of Secondary Images. The formation of stain images by the oxidation products of the developing agent in a developer having a zero or a low concentration of sulphite, has found practical application. A process of intensification, based on the formation of stain, will be described later (§ 689).

The secondary image acts as a mordant, fixing basic dyes (A. and L. Lumière and A. Seyewetz, 1928), thus giving rise to the possibility of intensifying the image by immersion in a suitable solution of such dyes.

The stain image possesses marked reducing properties towards various metallic salts or complexes (F. Leiber, 1932). It may be intensified by immersion in the copper ferrocyanide toner, or in an ammoniacal solution of silver nitrate. This last reaction has served as the basis for a reversal process (§ 672). The humic acids of the stain image that are formed from polyphenolic developing agents can still, by virtue of their phenolic nature, couple with diazonium compounds to give azo dyes (R. Jodl, 1938).

Some developing agents, of no practical interest, give vividly coloured, insoluble oxidation products. In this way, after removing the silver, one can obtain a blue image after developing by indoxyl, or red after developing with thioindoxyl (B. Homolka, 1906).

576. Colour Development; Chromogenic Development. Intensely coloured images are obtained using aminophenols or diamines (with one unsubstituted amino group) as developing agents when the developer contains a *coupler* which participates in the reduction of the silver halide. The oxidation products of the developing agent and the coupler yield an insoluble and non-wandering dye at the site of reduction of the silver halide grains, the quantity of dye formed being proportional to the amount of silver reduced (R. Fischer, 1912).

Since the coupling reaction increases the reduction potential, developing agents can be used which, in the absence of the coupler would need to be used at a pH level higher than the gelatine would tolerate (A. G. Tull, 1939). For example, a developer containing N, N— dimethyl-p-phenylenediamine gives, in the presence of a substance such as an acetoacetic ester or dibenzoylmethane a yellow or red azomethine dye image duplicating the silver image.

$$(CH_3)_2.N.C_6H_4.NH_2 + X.CH_2Y$$
$$+ 4AgBr \rightarrow 4Ag + 4HBr$$
$$+(CH_3)_2.N.C_6H_4.N:CXY$$

(where X, Y' contain electron withdrawing groups, such as CO or CN, so that the H atoms of the CH_2 group are labile).

Under the same conditions, an aminophenol yields an indophenol in the presence of a phenol, whereas a diamine gives an indoaniline or an oxazine in the presence of a phenol, and an indamine in the presence of an amine.

Because they react with the coupler, the concentration of the oxidation products of the developing agent is always very low. In this sense the coupler behaves in the same way as sulphite. The presence of sulphite is often necessary and the ratio between the quantity of dye formed and the quantity of silver reduced varies to a large extent with the sulphite

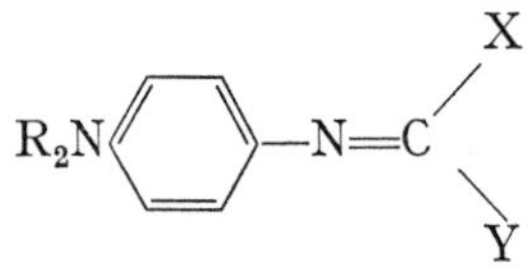

FIG 29.41. An azomethine dye

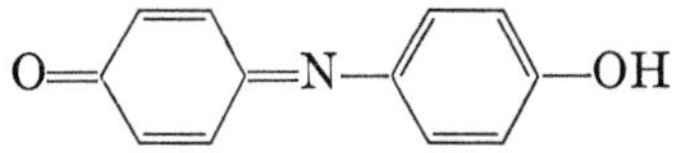

FIG. 29.42. An indophenol dye

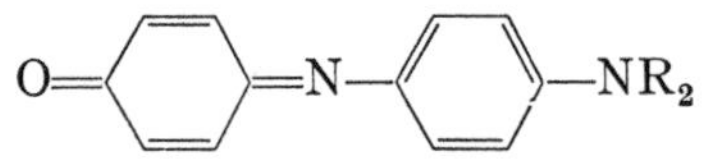

FIG. 29.43. An indoaniline dye

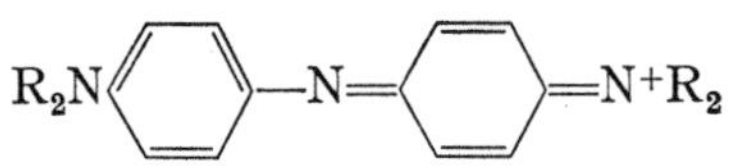

FIG. 29.44. An indamine dye

concentration (R. M. Evans and W. T. Hanson, 1937).

When the silver image and the residual silver bromide are removed (simultaneously by Farmer's reducer) the granularity of the image is very low.

For an experimental test, a deep blue image can be obtained in a developer containing asymmetric dimethyl-p-phenylenediamine, potassium carbonate, and about 1 per cent 1 : 4 naphtholsulphonic acid, prepared immediately before use. Fix in a plain hypo solution because the blue colour is destroyed in an acid bath.

The colour developers usually require an increase in exposure. Some of them tend to give fog, though this can sometimes be avoided by applying the colour development to an image that has been developed, fixed, washed, and rehalogenated, usually to the chloride.

The use of dye development for the production of black-and-white prints has been suggested (J. Kleine and G. Willmanns, 1936) so that all the silver could be recovered.

Sometimes undesirable reactions take place between the colour developer and the dyes in certain antihalation layers.

577. The Effect of Various Substances added to Developers. *Iodides.* The addition of iodide at a concentration (0·02 to 0·2 per cent) much lower than that needed to bring about depth development, considerably reduces the induction period of developing agents having a low reduction potential. In the case of hydroquinone the Watkins Factor is quadrupled. This acceleration of the early stages of development was noted by A. Lainer (1891) and is often called the *Lainer Effect.* A close study of this effect (S. E. Sheppard and G. Meyer, 1920) showed that, on adding iodide, silver bromide precipitated in the absence of gelatine adsorbed a greater quantity of safranine. It is thus possible that iodizing favours the adsorption of the oxidation products of the developing agents, in this way accelerating the start of development.

Thiocarbamide (thiourea). The addition, to a hydroquinone developer, of a small concentration (about 0·04 per cent) of thiocarbamide (§ 647) causes a dense positive image of a somewhat violet hue to form after the neutral-grey negative image has started to appear (J. Waterhouse, 1890). This effect can also be obtained with thiosinamine (allylthiourea) and phenylthiocarbamide. It is most marked in a strongly alkaline developer having a low bromide concentration and used at about 15°C. It does not occur in a strongly bromided developer (A. H. Nietz, 1922), nor in an acid developer. An explanation of the effect was given by S. O. Rawling (1926). The thiocarbamides are adsorbed by the silver bromide with which they form insoluble complexes which, in an alkaline medium, decompose to form silver sulphide. This decomposition is considerably retarded by soluble bromide. The development of the negative image commences before the grains are thus infected (similarly when the emulsion is treated with the thiocarbamide before development) and the reversal appears only when the negative image is visible, the positive image being formed as the result of local variations in the bromide concentration in the emulsion. The sulphided grains, which are more numerous where the negative image is less dense, are rapidly developable.

Urea. It has been claimed that in developers containing 10% urea the development time can be reduced by approximately 30% to give the same results as a developer containing no urea (F. Dersch, 1945). This acceleration of development is thought to be due to the softening action of urea on the gelatine which results in more rapid penetration of the developing agent.

Alcohols. The addition of alcohols has been recommended in the case of developers which are prepared in very concentrated form, in order to avoid the precipitation of the base of aminophenolic developing agents or their addition products with hydroquinone. Sometimes alcohols (from methyl to butyl) are added to developers in order to limit their penetration into the emulsion so as to obtain a surface image.

In the case of developers containing hydroquinone and made alkaline by a carbonate, the addition of ethyl or methyl alcohol in appreciable quantity gives rise to fog.

Neutral Salts. The degree of swelling of gelatine in an aqueous solution is reduced by increasing the salt concentration. If a developer cannot be maintained at a temperature below 25°C, excessive swelling can be avoided by adding a neutral salt having a negligible effect on development (L. J. Brunel, 1910). Of the various salts that may be used (sulphates, nitrates, phosphates, oxalates), sodium sulphate is usually chosen on account of cheapness. Sodium sulphate is sometimes used, also, to limit the penetration of the developer, reducing the depth of the image in the emulsion layer and reducing the gamma.

In a developer having a very low salt concentration, as in the case of amidol developers, the addition of sodium sulphate at a moderate concentration helps to coagulate the colloidal silver that tends to accumulate in the bath, especially when developing fine-grain positive emulsions, thus avoiding the danger of dirtying the whites of the image (L. Lobel, 1920).

The addition of citrates and tartrates, or their acids, to developers causes, in the case of developing agents of low reduction potential, a depression of density and a regression of the speed comparable, in some degree, to the effect of bromide (L. Lobel and J. Lefevre, 1927). This effect seems to be due to a limitation of the dissociation of the carbonate by these salts. A. von Hübl showed, in fact, that the addition of citrate and tartrate (as well as the addition of glycerine) reduced the electrical conductivity of a developer, and probably also the dissociation of the alkali.

Silver Bromide Solvents. The addition, even in very small concentration, of a silver halide solvent to a hydroquinone developer tends to give dichroic fog (§ 552). In the case of metol developers the addition of a small concentration of a solvent tends to dissolve the surface of the grains, reducing their diameter, and helping to obtain images of low granularity (§ 615). Increasing the sulphite concentration increases the solvent power, though this can be achieved by adding a small quantity of a solvent such as a thiocyanate to a developer containing a normal sulphite concentration.

Various. Development can be slowed down by adding to the developer various substances such as glycerine, sugars, etc., which, by increasing the viscosity of the solution, limit its penetration in the gelatine and slow down the exchanges between the emulsion and the solution in which it is bathed (W. de Abney, 1897; L. Baekeland, 1899). These measures tend to give a superficial image of reduced contrast.

Glucose has been recommended as a stabilizer in concentrated developers containing caustic alkali (E. Fournes and H. Diamant-Eerde, 1935). Many non-ionic polymeric compounds such as polyethylene glycols, have been patented as development accelerators and it has been suggested that they act by reducing the activation energy of the development reaction by adsorption to the development centres and so increasing their size (A. M. Churaeva and V. I. Sheberstov, 1963).

According to James (1945) cationic dyes such

as phenosafranine can accelerate development of negatively charged developing agents by lowering of the charge barrier (§ 540) but the increase in development rate may be due to the formation of a superadditive mixture of the developing agent and the reduced (leuco) form of the dye (L. F. A. Mason, 1966).

Wetting Agents. The wetting of the emulsion layer is facilitated, and the risk of the adherence of air-bells is reduced, by the addition to the developer of about 1 g per litre of one of a number of substances that reduce the interfacial tension between water and solid surfaces: alkaline sulphoricinates, the sulphonates of higher fatty alcohols (known under trade names such as Alkanol, Igepon, Teepol, etc.) which are an-ionic and saponin, which is non-ionic. The same substance may also be used in a pre-bath. These wetting agents must be used in higher concentration in acid or neutral solutions than in alkaline solutions. It should be remembered that these substances will give rise to foam in developers that are violently agitated.

Cationic wetting agents such as cetyl-pyridinium bromide give a large accelerating effect on the development reaction, generally with an increase in fog. Their effect on development has been attributed to a reduction in the induction period by lowering the charge barrier (§540 T. H. James, 1951).

Wetting agents may be usefully added to all baths and to dyes or pigments for tinting or spotting. Their presence in the last wash-water facilitates flowing during draining and avoids the adherence of drops which may give rise to drying marks.

THE USUAL COMPONENTS OF DEVELOPERS

578. Organic Developing Agents. The more important organic developing agents are discussed in the following paragraphs, classified for convenience according to their chemical nature. The properties of each group are indicated, then the properties of each particular substance. Most of the developing agents are known commercially under a number of synonymous trade names.

579. Hydroxyphenols. The hydroxyphenols are substances of a weakly acid nature which give phenolates with alkalis, the metal replacing the atom of hydrogen in one or more of the hydroxyl (—OH) groups. With alkaline carbonate solutions the formation of phenolates is always very incomplete and most of the polyphenol can be extracted from the solution on shaking it with ether. The *para* phenols show the acid properties to a more marked degree than the *ortho* compounds, but the latter form strongly acid complexes with the salts of boric acid, e.g. borax.

Hydroquinone. Hydroquinone, *p*-dihydroxy-benzene, quinol, $1:4$—$C_6H_4(OH)_2$, molecular weight 110, was proposed as a developing agent by W. de Abney in 1880. It usually appears as small, colourless, needle-like crystals, melting at 170°C without decomposition. It is odourless when pure. It is very soluble in alcohol (40 per cent), somewhat less so in ether and acetone (15 per cent), and is slightly soluble in water (5·7 per cent at 15°C, more when warmer). It is insoluble in benzene. Hydroquinone gives the diphenolate with caustic alkalis, and principally the monophenolate with alkali carbonates and other alkaline salts. At one time a crystalline substance containing hydroquinone and sulphur dioxide $3 C_6H_4(OH)_2 . SO_2$ was obtainable under the name *hydroquinone yellow.*

Hydroquinone is stable in dry air. When dissolved in an alkaline solution (without sulphite) in contact with air, the solution rapidly turns yellow and then brown, and gives off the sharp odour of quinone. A peroxide is formed as an oxidation intermediate (T. H. James, I. M. Snell, and A. Weissberger, 1938). At equal pH values, the oxidation of hydroquinone may be 13 times as rapid in a borate buffer than a phosphate buffer (A. St. Maxen, 1935), the latter inhibiting the catalysis of the oxidation by traces of copper salts. It has been mentioned above (§ 570) that, in the presence of sulphite, the autoxidation of hydroquinone yields the monosulphonate, then the disulphonate. Further oxidation yields the same humic acids as are found in oxidation in the absence of sulphite. The oxidation of hydroquinone is considerably accelerated by magnesia (A. St. Maxen, 1932).

Hydroquinone is used, with strong alkalis and with a high concentration of potassium bromide, for the development of slow, high-contrast emulsions in the copying of documents, eliminating tones intermediate between black and white. Used with carbonates, it gives warm tones on fine-grain positive emulsions.

For the development of continuous-tone negatives, hydroquinone is almost always used together with metol or Phenidone (§ 583).

By varying the relative quantities of metol and hydroquinone and adjusting the quantities of sulphite and carbonate, almost any desired contrast or rate of development can be obtained.

This developer combination can also be used as a fine-grain developer (§ 614) by suitable adjustment of the formulation.

Chlorhydroquinone. Chlorhydroquinone, or chlorquinol, $C_6H_3Cl(OH)_2$, molecular weight = 144·5, known also as Adurol or Quinotol, was proposed as a developer by Lüppo-Cramer in 1899. It occurs as almost colourless needles, melting at 106°C. It is more soluble than hydroquinone in water (about 50 per cent at 15°C). Unlike hydroquinone it is soluble in warm benzene. Its reduction potential is higher than that of hydroquinone, and under normal conditions it gives a blacker image, but offers no advantages over metol-hydroquinone as a developer for negative materials.

Catechol. Catechol, pyrocatechine, *o*-dihydroxybenzene, $1 : 2 \text{—} C_6H_4(OH)_2$, molecular weight = 110, was introduced as a developer by J. M. Eder and Tôth in 1880. It forms plate-like crystals which are colourless when completely pure but which usually have a pink or greyish tinge. It has a strong coal-tar odour and melts at 105°C. It is very soluble in alcohol, ether, acetone, in water (30 per cent at 15°C), and in warm benzene. A solution containing catechol and borax is strongly acid and will turn litmus red and liberate carbon dioxide from carbonates.

Catechol is used chiefly in the preparation of tanning developers (§ 622) and high definition developers (§ 617) containing a very low sulphite concentration.

Pyrogallol. Pyrogallol, $1 : 2 : 3$-trihydroxybenzene, "pyro," $C_6H_3(OH)_3$, molecular weight = 126, improperly called pyrogallic acid, was introduced by V. Regnault in 1851. It appears both as a very light, white powder, or as small colourless crystals (sometimes called *Pyral*). It melts at 133°C, and is very soluble in alcohol, ether, acetone, water (almost 40 per cent at 15°C), and is slightly soluble in warm benzene. The aqueous solution rapidly turns brown when exposed to air, the oxidation being accelerated by the addition of alkali. The oxidation products stain the skin and nails brown.

Since pyrogallol solutions are stable only when acid, they are usually prepared by mixing two stock solutions, one containing the pyrogallol with bisulphite, and the other the alkali. The maximum energy is achieved by using a caustic alkali in quantity sufficient to form the monophenolate (E. Valenta, 1902), i.e. 32 g of sodium hydroxide per 100 g of pyrogallol beyond the quantity required to neutralize the bisulphite.

Further addition of alkali gives rise to a dense fog and discoloration of the bath.

While pyrogallol has long been used for the development of plates and films, its poor keeping qualities make it unsuitable for large-scale industrial use. It has been suggested that its monomethyl ether (Rubinol), or its monoethyl ether, should be used instead because they are less readily autoxidized. They do not stain the fingers, and their reduction potentials are only slightly inferior to that of pyrogallol itself. Pyrogallol and its derivatives are infrequently used for development of negative materials but are used in tanning developers (§ 622).

580. Aminophenols. The aminophenols are *amphoteric* substances, acids by virtue of being phenols and bases by virtue of their amino group or groups. The acid properties are manifested chiefly when they contain two hydroxyl (—OH) groups. Thus, while in all cases the monophenolate is formed in the presence of caustic alkalis, the carbonate alkalis only give the phenolate in the case of the aminodiphenols, e.g. diaminoresorcinol. The aminophenols are only stable in the form of a salt (hydrochloride, sulphate, oxalate) the free base being rapidly oxidized in air. It is these salts which usually comprise the commercially available developing agents. The following table shows the weights of various alkalis necessary to neutralize the acid and form the free base of the aminophenol. For convenience, the diamine paraphenylenediamine hydrochloride is included in this table. The quantities of carbonate, borax, and trisodium phosphate correspond to the amounts required to form the bicarbonate, boric acid, and disodium hydrogen phosphate respectively.

Weight of the Various Alkalis needed to liberate 100 g of Free Base

	p-Aminophenol Hydrochloride Oxalate		Metol sulphate	*p*-Phenylenediamine hydrochloride
Weight of Developer Salt used	133·5	142	140	167·7
Sodium hydroxide	36·8		32·6	37·2
Potassium hydroxide	51·4		46·6	51·9
Sodium carbonate, anhydrous	97·2		86·2	98·2
Potassium carbonate anhydrous	126·5		112·2	127·7
Borax	174·7		154·6	176·6
Trisodium phosphate	174·3		155	177

p-Aminophenol. The hydrochloride of *p*-aminophenol $1 : 4 \text{—} C_6H_4(OH)(NH_2,HCl)$, molecular weight 145·6, was recommended as a developing agent by A. and L. Lumière and by M. Andresen in 1891. It appears in the form of white, or grey, crystalline needles, which decompose before melting. It is very soluble in water (about 25 per cent at 15°C), less soluble in alcohol, and insoluble in ether. The free base is much less soluble in water (about 1 per cent at 15°C) and in solutions of sulphite and carbonate. It is very soluble as the phenolate in the presence of caustic alkalis, and this property is made use of in the preparation of very concentrated developers which are diluted 20 to 100 times for use. The addition of an alkali carbonate to a solution of the hydrochloride is accompanied by effervescence and the precipitation of the free base. Hence stronger alkalies are required in preparing developers containing p-aminophenol. Particularly in the United States, p-aminophenol is sometimes sold as the oxalate (Kodelon). J. Desalme, 1924, has suggested that the tartrate should be used, in which case the free base is not precipitated on adding carbonate.

p-Aminophenol developers are rapid working free from fogging properties and do not stain. They can however cause excessive swelling of the gelatine because of the high pH and low concentration. Diluted solutions of this developer are suitable for use as high-definition developers.

Metol. Metol, also known as Genol, Rhodol, Viterol, Elon, Monol, Scatol, Satrapol, Pictol, Atolo, etc., is the sulphate of N-methyl-p-aminophenol, $CH_3NH . C_6H_4 . OH, \frac{1}{2}H_2SO_4$, molecular weight = 172. It was first prepared and recommended by A. Bogisch in 1891. It takes the form of small colourless plates which decompose before melting, and which are soluble in water (4.5 per cent at 15°C) and in alcohol, and insoluble in ether.

On adding carbonate to a concentrated solution of metol, the free base is precipitated, as it also is when sodium sulphite is added. The free base melts at 85°C. It is soluble in alcohol, ether, and acetone, and in strongly alkaline aqueous solutions.

After considerable aerial oxidation a sulphite solution of metol appears brown with a blue fluorescence. On exposure to air, an alkaline solution of metol (without sulphite) turns rapidly, through yellow, to a dark brownish-violet colour as the result of the formation of polymerized oxidation products.

Metol can develop when dissolved in a plain sulphite solution, but it is made much more active on adding alkali. At high pH values, when a caustic alkali is used, the reduction potential is very high and the tendency to give fog necessitates the use of bromide. Contrary to a widely held opinion, metol developers (without hydroquinone) will give gamma values as high as other developers, providing that the development is sufficiently prolonged. Metol is often used in association with hydroquinone (§ 579).

The dermatitis which metol developers cause on the skin of allergic users is occasioned by traces of N, N— dimethyl-p-phenylenediamine sometimes present as an impurity in the metol.

Glycin. Glycin, which differs from the aminophenols referred to above in that it is an amino-acid and exists without added acid as an internal salt, is p-hydroxyphenylaminoacetic acid, p-hydroxyphenyl glycine, $C_6H_4(OH)NH . CH_2COOH$, molecular weight = 167. It is known also as Iconyl, Glyconiol, Kodurol, Monazol, or Athenon. Glycin, which was introduced by Bogisch (1891) appears in the form of colourless brilliant plates which decompose at about 200°C. It is almost insoluble in water (0.23 per cent at 15°C). It is insoluble in alcohol and in ether, while it is soluble in dilute inorganic acids, and in mildly alkaline solutions of carbonate and sulphite. It is very soluble in solutions of caustic alkalis.

An important characteristic of glycin is that it is only very slowly oxidized by air, either in the dry state, or in even very dilute alkaline solution. It is well suited for prolonged developments. It has been used for the development of motion picture films on continuous processing machines in which the developer is agitated by bubbles of compressed air, and in development on a rotating partially immersed drum.

Potassium carbonate is better than sodium carbonate as the alkali for glycin developers because it allows the preparation of more concentrated stock solutions.

Glycin is very sensitive to bromide and with alkali carbonates affords a slow-working developer which gives low contrast and has good keeping properties.

581. Diaminophenol. By virtue of its two amino groups, diaminophenol can develop rapidly in a plain sulphite solution. The developer thus obtained has a very high reduction potential.

The *dihydrochloride of 2 : 4-diaminophenol*, $C_6H_3(OH)(NH_2)_2, 2HCl$, molecular weight = 197, known also as Amidol, Diamol, Dolmi, Acrol, etc., was introduced by A. Bogisch in 1891. It appears usually as light or dark grey needles, which, on heating, decompose before melting. It is very soluble in water (25 per cent at 15°C), and it is precipitated from its concentrated aqueous solution by an excess of hydrochloric acid. It is almost insoluble in alcohol and in ether. It is very soluble in sulphite solutions, the sulphite being transformed in part into bisulphite. These solutions have the interesting property of acting as developers without the necessity of adding alkali. This developer oxidizes fairly rapidly in air and, for this reason, should be prepared immediately before use. On adding alkalis to this solution the oxidation is greatly accelerated and a deep violet discoloration appears. If, on the other hand, a weak acid is added (bisulphite, or boric, lactic or glycolic acids) the solution becomes much more stable and the developer can be held for several days in a dish.

It has been suggested that amidol developers can be stabilized by the addition of 1 to 2 g per litre of metol or hydroquinone, which do not affect the photographic behaviour at this low level of alkalinity. Again Desalme found (1921) that amidol developers could be stabilized by the addition of tin salts, e.g. sodium stannotartrate.

When an amidol developer is acidified to the point where there is no longer any neutral sulphite in solution, it acts as a depth developer, the development commencing at the bottom of the emulsion layer (§ 559). Amidol developers give a neutral grey image. The solution tends to stain the skin and nails.

582. Phenylenediamines. *p-Phenylenediamine* or 1 : 4-diaminobenzene, which was first proposed by M. Andresen in 1888, is marketed either as the free base or the dihydrochloride, $C_6H_4(NH_2)_2$, 2HCl, molecular weight = 181. The base appears as crystalline platelets which, though colourless when very pure, are usually light grey in colour. The base melts at 140°C, is slightly soluble (3·7 per cent at 15°C) in water, and is soluble in ether and alcohol. The aqueous solutions have a definite solvent action on silver bromide. The dihydrochloride appears as fine, grey (colourless when pure) crystalline tablets which decompose before melting. It is soluble in water, slightly soluble in alcohol, and insoluble in ether and in concentrated hydrochloric acid.

In plain sulphite solution, *p-phenylenediamine* develops very slowly, only reducing a part of each grain, thus giving images of low contrast with very low granularity. Materials destined for development in such *p-phenylenediamine* solutions should be considerably over-exposed, judged by normal standards. Better contrast can be obtained by adding borax or an alkaline carbonate to the developer, but development is still very slow and tends, often, to give rise to some dichroic fog. If, however, the sulphite solution of *p-phenylenediamine* is made alkaline by a caustic alkali, a rapid developer of high reduction potential is obtained. Even with a low concentration of sulphite this developer keeps quite well. Its oxidation products are colourless.

The rate of development is increased by all circumstances which decrease the concentration of the oxidation products. In the present case this can be brought about by an increase in the alkalinity, which accelerates the spontaneous decomposition of the oxidation products of *p*-phenylenediamine, and by the presence of agents which couple with the oxidized phenylenediamine (T. H. James, 1939).

The activity of phenylenediamine developers is considerably enhanced by the addition of thiocyanates (or sulphocyanides) in a concentration of about 1 g per litre (L. D. Mannes and L. Godowski, 1935) or in combination with hydroquinone (J. F. Williams and G. F. Van Veelen, 1962).

The dimethyl- and diethylparaphenylenediamines and particularly *p*-aminodimethylaniline, $C_6H_4 . NH_2 . N(CH_3)_2$, 2HCl, which are more soluble than the non-alkylated compound, and less readily oxidized in air, give energetic and stable developers on being made alkaline by sodium carbonate. These developing agents are much used in colour development. However, these agents are very harmful to the skin.

A very soluble derivative which does not attack the skin is N-β-methylsulphonamido-ethyl-4-aminoaniline $(NH_2)C_6H_4(NH . C_2H_4 . NH . SO_2CH_3)$. This and some homologues have been proposed for colour development in the presence of sulphite and carbonate (A. Weissberger, 1939).

o-Phenylenediamine, or 1 : 2-diaminobenzene, $C_6H_4(NH_2)_2$, molecular weight = 108, is similar to the para isomer in its properties. However, it is less harmful to the skin and is used in a number of proprietary fine-grain developers.

583. Phenidone. *Phenidone* (registered trade mark, Ilford Ltd.), 1-phenyl-3-pyrazolidone, 1-phenyl-3-pyrazolidinone, $C_6H_5 . N . CH_2 . CH_2 . CO . NH$, molecular weight 162, was first recommended as a developing agent by J. D. Kendall in 1941 and since 1945 it has become one of the most important developing agents especially in superadditive mixtures with hydroquinone. It is moderately soluble in hot water (up to 10%) and sparingly soluble in cold water but, because of its amphoteric nature dissolves readily in aqueous acids or alkalies, including alkali bisulphites and carbonates. Phenidone is, however, hydrolysed slowly by alkalies to form phenylhydrazinopropionic acid according to the following equation (G. C. Alletag, 1958).

$$C_6H_5.N.CH_2.CH_2.CO.NH + H_2O$$
$$\rightleftharpoons C_6H_5.N(NH_2).CH_2.CH_2.CO.OH$$

As this hydrolysis is slow it does not represent a serious objection to the use of Phenidone but obviously will effect the keeping properties of developers containing it. For developers of high pH value Phenidone may be replaced by more stable derivatives such as Phenidone Z or Dimezone.

Phenidone is more efficient than metol in a superadditive developer with hydroquinone and considerably less Phenidone than metol is required to form a developer of the same activity (§ 548). Consequently Phenidone permits the formulation of highly concentrated developers with little tendency for the developing agents to crystallise out. Also an increased quantity of Phenidone produces the highly active developer required by monobaths (§ 621).

Because of the high activity of Phenidone-hydroquinone developers benzotriazole is generally added to supplement the restraining action of bromide.

Phenidone has low oral toxicity and is unlikely to cause dermatitis. Sufferers from "metol poisoning" are generally able to use developers containing Phenidone without any ill effects. Kodak recommend that sufferers from "metol poisoning" should substitute metol by one tenth of its weight of Phenidone in Kodak formulae together with an antifoggant.

584. Summary of the Properties of Developing agents. The important properties of the developing agents are summarised in the table given below (C. I. Jacobson, 1966). Properties of staining and of fog formation, sensitivity to temperature, sensitivity to bromide, speed of development, gradation, and keeping properties have been considered in alkaline carbonate solution, caustic alkali solution, and as a fine grain developer. These are the relevant properties upon which the use of a particular developing agent for a specific purpose, may be decided.

585. Developer Dermatitis. While the impurities found in metol are present only in sufficient concentration to cause dermatitis in allergic subjects, whose susceptibility is greatly increased after a first attack, the continual handling of p-phenylenediamines, especially the dimethyl- and diethyl-homologues, results invariably in dermatitis unless suitable precautions are taken.

It is usually recommended that the hands should be rinsed in dilute hydrochloric acid after handling the developing agents in the dry state or in solution. The acid (2 ml of concentrated acid per 100 ml) should be situated permanently in a bowl near to the developing dishes. The effectiveness of this precautionary measure is probably due to the phenylenediamines being innocuous in the form of the hydrochloride (J. Southworth, 1938). This treatment is advantageous also in that it helps to avoid staining of the hands.

The wearing of rubber gloves is recommended when handling the alkylated phenylenediamines, especially for operators who have had a previous attack of dermatitis. However, the wearing of rubber gloves induces sweating and some skin troubles can arise if the gloves are not frequently washed and dried.

Various ointments have been suggested to protect the skin while handling developers, but they are often too greasy and fluid. The following mixture, which is solid below 90°C has been devised by G. D. Hiatt (1939). A mixture of 33 parts of olive oil and 22 parts butyl stearate is heated to 130°C. Eleven parts of cellulose butyrate (56 per cent butyryl) are added and dissolved by raising the temperature to 170°C. After cooling to 150°C, 33 parts of zinc oxide are added. The cold mixture can be rubbed easily on the skin.

In the event of an outbreak of dermatitis it is best to consult a medical practitioner.

586. Alkalis. *Sodium hydroxide*, or caustic soda, NaOH, molecular weight = 40, is usually obtainable in the form of waxy-white flakes, pellets, or small sticks, and as a concentrated solution or *lye*. It is available in various grades of purity, though most of the grades, if clean and white, will serve for photographic solutions. The ordinary grade usually contains from 2 to 7 per cent of sodium carbonate, the actual proportion depending upon the degree to which it has been exposed to the atmosphere. It also contains a small proportion of sodium chloride.

Characteristics of Developer Substances

A In alkaline carbonate solution; B In caustic alkali solution; C As a fine-grain developer

Developer		(1) Fog Formation and staining	(2) Sensitivity to Temperature	(3) Sensitivity to Bromide	(4) Speed of Development	(5) Gradation	(6) Keeping properties: (a) separately (b) mixed
Metol (Elon)	A	None	Slight	Slight	Normal-rapid	Soft	a and b good
	B	Appreciable	Slight	Slight	Rapid	Soft	a good, b bad
	C	None	Moderate	Moderate	Slow	Soft	a and b good
Hydroquinone	A	None	Strong	Strong	Slow	Contrasty	a and b good
	B	None	Moderate	Moderate	Rapid	Contrasty	a good, b bad
	C		Not suitable	—	—	—	—
Pyrocatechine (Catechol)	A	None	Strong	Strong	Normal	Normal	a and b good
	B	None	Slight	Slight	Rapid	Contrasty	a good, b bad
	C		Not suitable	—	—	—	—
Pyrogallol	A	Stains	Moderate	Moderate	Normal	Soft	a good, b bad
	B		Not suitable	—	—	—	—
	C		Not suitable	—	—	—	—
Amidol	A	None	Moderate	Moderate	Normal	Normal	Solutions do not keep
	B		Not suitable	—	—	—	—
	C		Not suitable	—	—	—	—
Phenidone	A	None	Slight	Slight	Normal	Soft	a and b good
Glycin	A	None	Very strong	Very strong	Slow	Normal-soft	a and b good
	B	None	Strong	Strong	Rapid	Normal	a good, b bad
	C		Not suitable	—	—	—	—
p-Aminophenol	A		Not suitable	—	—	—	—
	B	None	Slight	Slight	Normal-rapid	Normal-soft	a good, b bad
	C		Not suitable	—	—	—	—
Chlorquinol	A	None	Moderate	Moderate	Normal	Normal	a and b good
	B	None	Slight	Slight	Rapid	Contrasty	a good, b bad
	C		Not suitable	—	—	—	—
p-Phenylenediamine	C	Strong staining properties	Moderate	Moderate	Slow	Soft	Varies with formula
o-Phenylenediamine	C	None	Moderate	Moderate	Slow	Soft	Good

Since sodium hydroxide is strongly deliquescent, the solid usually contains a small quantity of absorbed water.

Sodium hydroxide solutions are extremely caustic, especially when warm or hot, and care should be taken when handling them to protect the skin and eyes. Protective goggles should be worn and any splashes on the skin or clothing should be washed immediately with plenty of water.

To prevent the absorption of moisture and carbon dioxide from the atmosphere, solid sodium hydroxide should be stored in tins or plain iron drums with well fitting lids. Neither the solid nor its solutions should ever be stored in glass containers with ground-glass stoppers because these inevitably become jammed in use.

A considerable quantity of heat is evolved when sodium hydroxide is dissolved in water. For this reason, cold water should always be used and the sodium hydroxide introduced slowly, while the solution is constantly stirred and cooled. Without these precautions the solution may boil with explosive violence, and the intense local heating may fracture a glass or ceramic container.

Sodium hydroxide solutions rapidly dissolve aluminium, zinc, and tin and should not be allowed to come into contact with these metals or tinned and galvanized iron.

Potassium hydroxide, or caustic potash, KOH, molecular weight = 56, is very similar in its properties and appearance, etc., to sodium hydroxide and all the above remarks on sodium hydroxide apply equally well to the potassium compound.

Lithium hydroxide is only infrequently used in photography because of its comparative rarity. It appears in commerce usually as the crystalline hydrate $LiOH, H_2O$, molecular weight = 42, which has the advantage of being non-deliquescent and is, therefore, sometimes used as the alkali in powder developers. While the sodium and potassium hydroxides are soluble in water in all proportions, lithium hydroxide is only soluble to the extent of about 15 per cent.

Ammonium hydroxide, or "ammonia," is considerably less basic than the alkali metal hydroxides. It is formed on dissolving ammonia gas, NH_3, molecular weight = 17, in water. The gas tends to leave the solution and some is lost each time the bottle is opened. The alkaline properties of the solution result from the presence of ammonium hydroxide, NH_4OH, molecular weight = 35. The following table gives the specific gravity of various ammonia solutions. The concentrated solution usually obtainable should have a specific gravity of 0·88.

Specific Gravity at 15°C	0·958	0·924	0·895	0·882
Percentage of NH_3	10	20	30	35

Crude solutions of ammonia are contaminated by various salts (carbonate, chlorides, sulphates, sulphides) and nitrogenous organic bases, particularly pyridine.

Care should be exercised when handling concentrated ammonia solutions, especially when opening bottles, to prevent accidents through inhaling the concentrated vapour. Ammonium hydroxide dissolves silver chloride and bromide freely but will dissolve only a trace of silver iodide.

Dilute (3 per cent NH_3) ammonium hydroxide dissolves silver chloride to the extent of about 1·3 per cent. A stronger solution (15 per cent NH_3) will support up to 7·5 per cent silver chloride and 0·1 per cent silver bromide.

Triethanolamine. Triethanolamine $N(CH_2 . CH_2OH)_3$, molecular weight = 149, was suggested for use as an alkali in fine-grain developers by M. L. Dundon in 1932, and in colour developers by E. E. Jelley in 1938. The commercial liquid is yellowish and viscous, with a very faint ammoniacal odour, and usually consists of a mixture of 80–85 per cent triethanolamine, the remainder being di- and monoethanolamine. This liquid, of specific gravity 1·12 at 20°C, is more basic than ammonia but is neither caustic nor irritant. It has no action on gelatine nor on the support of films. It has a lower solvent action in silver halides.

It should be stored in well-stoppered bottles, because it absorbs moisture and carbon dioxide, and slowly turns brown in contact with air.

587. Alkaline Carbonates. *Sodium carbonate* is supplied in several forms. *Anhydrous sodium carbonate,* Na_2CO_3, molecular weight = 106, appears as a white powder in either a dense or a light form, the light form being more common. The monohydrate, Na_2CO_3, H_2O, molecular weight = 124, takes the form of stable, colourless crystals similar in appearance to granulated sugar. It is sold in various grades, the crystals varying from about 1 to 5 mm across. The monohydrate is known also as *crystal carbonate* (not to be confused with sodium carbonate, crystalline, below). This form is more common in photographic work in the United States, although it is manufactured in Great Britain, too. The last, and most common, of the carbonates that are used in photography is the decahydrate, $Na_2CO_3, 10H_2O$, molecular weight = 286, which is the usual *sodium carbonate, crystalline* which, in its crude form, is known as *washing soda.*

When fresh, the anhydrous salt contains 98 per cent of sodium carbonate, but it slowly absorbs moisture and carbon dioxide forming the bicarbonate. If anhydrous sodium carbonate is spread in a thin layer in moist air, it will, after 15 days, contain 20 to 25 per cent of bicarbonate.

The monohydrate is the stable form. Anhydrous sodium carbonate tends to pick up moisture and the decahydrate to lose water of crystallization, to form the monohydrate. When fresh it contains no bicarbonate and has little tendency to absorb carbon dioxide.

The decahydrate is efflorescent. Of the two forms, the anhydrous and the decahydrate, the anhydrous is to be preferred because the efflorescent decahydrate loses moisture more rapidly than the anhydrous tends to gain it, and so is more likely to cause errors.

The pure, anhydrous, monohydrated, and decahydrated forms may be interchanged in the proportions shown in the following table.

	Anhydrous	*Monohydrate*	*Decahydrate*
Anhydrous	1·00	0·85	0·37
Monohydrate	1·17	1·00	0·43
Decahydrate	2·70	2·25	1·00

Sodium carbonate is quite soluble in water. At 15°C the saturated solution contains about 16 per cent of the anhydrous salt, the concentration reaching 36 per cent at 30°C.

Potassium carbonate is usually obtained in the anhydrous form, K_2CO_3, molecular weight = 138, as a white deliquescent powder which should be stored in a well-sealed container. It absorbs moisture and carbon dioxide very readily to form the bicarbonate and, unless a specially purified sample is obtained, most specimens contain a considerable proportion of the bicarbonate. At 15°C the saturated solution contains 81 g of potassium carbonate per 100 cc. At equal concentrations potassium carbonate renders a developer more alkaline than does sodium carbonate.

Ammonium carbonate. The ammonium carbonate used in some developers for warm-tone prints is not the normal carbonate $(NH_4)_2CO_3$ but the sesquicarbonate $(NH_4)_2CO_3$, $2(NH_4)H . CO_3, H_2O$, molecular weight = 272. Ammonium sesquicarbonate appears as fibrous lumps having an ammoniacal odour. It usually contains a considerable proportion of ammonium carbonate. It should be stored in tightly stoppered containers. If the crystals of ammonium sesquicarbonate are covered with a white crust, it should be removed by rinsing briefly, and then blotting off the moisture before weighing. This salt, which is very soluble in cold water (about 25 per cent) is decomposed on heating.

588. Various Alkaline Salts. *Sodium phosphates.* Sodium orthophosphate, Na_3PO_4, $12H_2O$, molecular weight = 380, also known as tribasic sodium phosphate, appears usually as white, efflorescent crystals. It is very soluble in water (20 per cent at 15°C), and is more basic than the carbonate, at equal concentrations. The industrial product usually contains an excess of sodium hydroxide.

Sodium pyrophosphate, $Na_4P_2O_7$, $10H_2O$, molecular weight = 446, has been suggested (H. W. Wood, 1939) as a moderate alkali for fine-grain developers.

Sodium borates. Two sodium borates are used. The *metaborate* is sold as the tetra- and octahydrates, $Na_2B_2O_4$, $4H_2O$, molecular weight = 203·7, and $Na_2B_2O_4$, $8H_2O$, molecular weight = 275·7. Sodium metaborate is fairly basic.

Borax, which is feebly alkaline, is the tetra- or pyroborate, $Na_2B_4O_7$, $10H_2O$, molecular weight = 381.

Sodium metaborate is very soluble in water (33 per cent at 19°C). The crystals are efflorescent, so they should be stored in a closed container to avoid loss of water vapour as well as to limit the absorption of carbon dioxide. The equivalent of 100 g of sodium metaborate ($4H_2O$) can be obtained in solution by adding 14·5 g of sodium hydroxide to a solution containing 69 g of borax, providing that the borax and sodium hydroxide are pure.

This salt, like sodium orthophosphate, has the advantage of yielding developers whose alkalinity is intermediate between that of carbonate and caustic solutions. Unlike sodium carbonate, sodium metaborate does not give rise to bubbles of gas on being carried into an acid solution, so there is no danger of the

occurrence of gas blisters in the emulsion when an acid stop bath or fixer is used directly after development. Again metaborate is to be preferred to orthophosphate because the latter tends to cause a precipitate when carried into fixing baths containing alum (§ 638).

Borax is generally supplied in the form of a fine, white, efflorescent, crystalline powder. It is only moderately soluble in water (2 per cent at 15°C). It should be stored in a well stoppered container to avoid loss of water of crystallization and the errors in weighing that would result.

Borates should not be used in developers containing catechol or pyrogallol because, with boric acid, these form strongly acid complexes of poor developing activity.

Kodalk. Kodalk is a trade name for a mild alkali of the sodium metaborate type, introduced by Kodak. Kodalk is more alkaline and more soluble than borax but less alkaline than carbonate. When used as a substitute for carbonate two parts by weight of Kodalk are equivalent to one part by weight of sodium carbonate. An advantage of replacing carbonate by Kodalk is that if an acid stop bath is used bubbles of carbonate will not be formed in the emulsion.

Various. Of the other alkaline salts that have been used in developers, sodium aluminate (J. R. Allburger, 1939) and sodium metasilicate (H. D. Russell, 1936) may be noted.

589. Practical Equivalence of the Usual Alkalis. At equal concentrations expressed in grammes per litre, sodium and potassium salts are practically interchangeable. It is only in this case that two alkalis can be substituted for each other in proportions that correspond to the same neutralizing capacity. Concerning alkalis, there is no relationship between equivalent quantities in a developer and quantities equivalent in the sense that they liberate the same amount of heat when they are neutralized by the same acid. It has already been mentioned that in a fresh negative developer there is equivalence between alkalis that bring the bath to the same pH value (§ 512), but without the presence of buffers to ensure constancy of pH, it is impossible to envisage any practical equivalence between, for example, carbonates and caustic alkalis. A sodium carbonate solution containing 21·2 g (anhydrous) per litre has a pH of 11·6, a value which would be reached by a concentration of sodium hydroxide of 0·13 g per litre, a quantity that would very rapidly become neutralized and would thus become useless in facilitating development. A suitable buffer allows the amount of available alkali to be increased while maintaining the pH of the bath at a relatively low and almost constant level.

The rule that alkalis can be interchanged at equal pH values must not be considered as being absolute. For example, a developer having a high concentration of sodium orthophosphate, because of its high viscosity, will penetrate into the emulsion layer much more slowly than one brought to the same pH by sodium metaborate. For this reason, and because the rates of change of solution at the emulsion surface would be less in the more viscous solution, development would be slower in the phosphated developer.

pH *Ranges of Buffers for use in Developers.* The following table gives some suitable buffer mixtures (§513) and the pH ranges over which they are effective in photographic developers.

Buffer Mixture	pH
Sodium sulphite/sodium metabisulphite	6·5–8·0
Boric acid/borax	6·8–9·2
Sodium carbonate/sodium bicarbonate	9·0–11·0
Borax/sodium hydroxide	9·2–11·0
Sodium carbonate/sodium hydroxide	10·5–12·0
Disodium hydrogen phosphate/sodium hydroxide	11·0–12·0
Trisodium phosphate/sodium hydroxide	12·0–13·0
Sodium hydroxide	above 12·0

590. Sulphites. Many of the properties of the sulphites, as well as of the hydrosulphites (thionites), and thiosulphates, are difficult to explain unless the fact is taken into account that each of these salts has two tautomeric forms which coexist in equilibrium in solution. The various structures are schematized in Fig. 29.45. Formulae (*a*) and (*b*) correspond to sodium sulphite, (*c*) to one of the forms of

bisulphite, (*d*) and (*e*) to sodium hydrosulphite, (*f*) and (*g*) to sodium thiosulphate.

The co-existence of the sulphinic (*a*) and sulphonic (*b*) forms of sodium sulphite is illustrated by the fact that different substances are obtained when sodium bisulphite is neutralized by potassium hydroxide, than when potassium bisulphite is neutralized by sodium hydroxide. Various organic derivatives are known corresponding to the two forms.

Sodium sulphite. Sodium sulphite is the salt that is usually used in developers. The potassium salt is very rarely used. Sodium sulphite is supplied in the anhydrous state, Na_2SO_3, molecular weight = 126, or as the crystalline septahydrate $Na_2SO_3, 7H_2O$, molecular weight = 252. One g of the anhydrous salt is thus equivalent to 2 g of the hydrate, providing both are pure.

The anhydrous salt is a fine, dense, white powder which, by settling down into a close-packed form, protects itself against the action of the air. The hydrate appears as small, colourless, efflorescent crystals which are often covered by a powdery coat of the anhydrous salt. The proportion of sodium sulphite in the anhydrous product is usually greater than 90 per cent. The hydrate contains between 40 and 45 per cent of sodium sulphite (anhydrous). Both products contain small proportions of sulphate and dithionate arising from oxidation, together with some carbonate, chloride, and traces of thiosulphate. Sodium sulphite should be stored in closed containers.

Sodium sulphite is very soluble in water (about 15 per cent anhydrous at 20°C). While the hydrate cools the solution on dissolving, the anhydrous salt causes no change in temperature

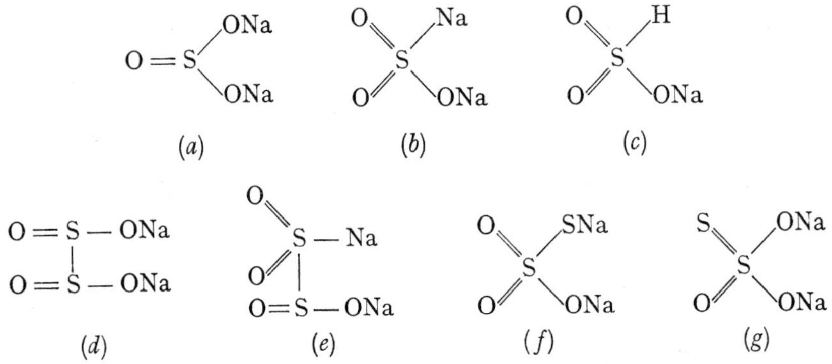

FIG. 29.45. STRUCTURAL FORMULAE FOR SODIUM SULPHO-SALTS
(*a, b*) Sulphite　　　(*c*) Bisulphite　　　(*d, e*) Hydrosulphite　　　(*f, g*) Thiosulphate

and for this reason is to be preferred when the developer is made up immediately before use.

Solutions of sodium sulphite are alkaline towards litmus, which is turned blue. The oxidation of sulphite solutions is very slow at pH greater than 9·6 (T. H. James and A. Weissberger, 1939). The rate of oxidation of the neutral solution is decreased greatly by traces of hydroquinone or p-aminophenol, and by alcohols, glycerine, mannite, or ordinary sugar. Stock solutions of sulphite should not be made up to last for periods greater than one week.

The addition of acids causes the formation of bisulphite and sulphurous acid, and the solution tends to lose sulphur dioxide (SO_2).

The sulphites form complexes with the salts of various heavy metals. Sodium sulphite solutions dissolve silver chloride and bromide, an 8 per cent sulphite solution dissolving 0·08 per cent of silver bromide. The solution slowly deposits colloidal silver and sodium dithionate is formed. Calcium sulphite is insoluble and gives rise to the whitish sludge which slowly settles from developer solutions made up from hard water (§ 508).

591. Bisulphites. *Sodium bisulphite,* or sodium acid sulphite, $NaHSO_3$, molecular weight = 104, does not exist in the solid state but is formed in aqueous solution by hydrolysis of *sodium metabisulphite* which is available as white crystals, $Na_2S_2O_5$, molecular weight 190.

$$Na_2S_2O_5 + H_2O \rightleftharpoons 2NaHSO_3$$

The term sodium bisulphite still occurs in many developer formulae and in some manufacturers catalogues. The solid sodium bisulphite referred to is in fact the metabisulphite. Sulphur dioxide is freely emitted from the solution. In solution sulphur dioxide forms sulphurous acid and it is this that reduces solutions of chromates and permanganates. Bisulphite solutions dissolve silver bromide and chloride in the same way as sulphite solution.

Bisulphite solutions should not be allowed to come into contact with zinc, galvanized iron, or other easily oxidized metals, because, in the presence of these, hydrosulphite is formed which tends to cause a heavy fog or stain.

Bisulphites, which are added to the part of a two-solution developer containing the alkali, will neutralize some of the alkali when the two parts are mixed. Account should be taken of this fact when devising the formulae of the two parts. When a caustic alkali is used, the bisulphite is transformed into sulphite. When an alkali carbonate is used the bisulphite is converted to sulphite with the formation of an equivalent amount of bicarbonate.

Potassium metabisulphite. Potassium metabisulphite, or pyrosulphite, $K_2S_2O_5$, molecular weight = 222, takes the form of large colourless crystals. These are quite stable, but over a long period may become covered with a crust of potassium sulphate and dithionate. Potassium metabisulphite is fairly soluble in water, the resulting solution containing the bisulphite, $KHSO_3$. The solution should be prepared in the cold, all the bisulphite solutions being decomposed, through loss of sulphur dioxide, on heating.

592. Alkali Bromides. *Potassium bromide* forms small anhydrous crystals, KBr, molecular weight = 119, colourless or white, cubical in shape, very soluble in water (over 60 per cent at 60°F), insoluble in alcohol; the chief impurity is potassium chloride, which, however, does not interfere with the action of the bromide. Potassium bromide is a perfectly stable salt.

Sodium Bromide. Sodium bromide is a very deliquescent salt, of very variable composition. It is appreciably cheaper than potassium bromide, but can only be used where sufficient quantities warrant the trouble of ascertaining the quantities to be used, the salt being made up into stock solutions as soon as purchased.

Ammonium Bromide. This occurs in the form of small colourless crystals of anhydrous salt (NH_4Br), which is slightly deliquescent, and turns yellow on long exposure to light. It is even more soluble in water than potassium bromide and is slightly soluble in alcohol. It slowly decomposes at boiling point. It is used in some formulae for warm-tone developers.

PRACTICAL NOTES

593. Qualities Desirable in a Developer. The qualities demanded of a developer vary somewhat according to the results required, and according to the method of use.

In all cases, the developer should cause no more than a moderate degree of swelling of the gelatine emulsion. It should not oxidize rapidly in contact with air, and it should have a low tendency to cause fog or stain on sensitive materials. It is advantageous if the rate of change of gamma with time is slow in the region of the desired gamma value.

According to the work in hand, the developer should be capable of developing the shadow details without it being necessary to proceed to a high gamma value; or, it should be capable of giving images of the finest possible granularity without having to compensate for the incomplete development by giving a considerable over-exposure; or, on the other hand, it should give the maximum contrast so that low exposures are not developed in order that the effects of irradiation or reflections may be eliminated in the copying of subjects containing only black and white tones. It may be necessary to examine the image after the shortest possible delay without sacrificing to any great extent the gradation of the image or the shadow detail.

In an industrial, or semi-industrial establishment, economic considerations are more important than they are in the darkroom of the amateur, the portraitist, or the scientific worker. The cost of development per unit area of processed material should be as low as possible, consistent with a perfect regularity of results, whence it is required to maintain the developer at constant activity for a long period to make the best use of constituents.

The developer should not be used at an unnecessarily high concentration because this leads to waste of chemicals even when the bath is used to the point of complete exhaustion. The sensitive material, even after draining or squeegeeing, carries an appreciable quantity of solution out of the bath, and this is more costly if the bath is more concentrated. The developer carried over will, if more concentrated, more rapidly neutralize the stop bath and make it necessary to re-acidify the fixing bath more frequently.

When working to low gamma values, the developer should be sufficiently dilute to avoid the necessity for very short times of development which often result in local irregularities in development. As a general rule, the concentration of the developer should be adjusted to give a development time of 5 minutes in dish development or 10 minutes in tank development.

On the other hand, too great a dilution of the developer should be avoided because, in this case, the exhaustion is too rapid and it is difficult to maintain the bath at constant activity.

It should be remembered that a very dilute developer gives rise to a greater fog density than would be obtained in a quicker-acting developer.

Formulae for Developers. Some photographers spend most of their time testing successively all the developing formulae that they see, even, when they show but negligible differences from other formulae previously tried. They attribute the success of other workers to the possession of some ideal formula, kept jealously secret, and making good all the failings of the photographer.

Except for some very special purposes, which require the use of developing baths of a composition considerably different from those of the usual type, any good formula is as suitable as another, and the best are generally not the most complicated. The choice between various current formulae should be made more on account of cost than for technical reasons. It has often been said that the best developer is the one with which the photographer is familiar, and it is not by abandoning one formula for another at the moment that its use is becoming familiar that the best results can be hoped for.

Some ridiculous formulae have been published owing to mistakes in converting foreign weights and measures or to typographical errors. Chance coincidences have led some practical workers, with little experience of experimental methods, to recommend the addition of products which are completely useless. Putting such exceptions aside, success depends more on the judicious conduct of the operations than on the choice of a particular formula.

594. The Swelling of Gelatine. The hard gelatines used in the manufacture of emulsions absorb comparatively little water, the amount depending upon the degree to which they were hardened before coating. On an average, at about 15°C, the gelatine of photographic emulsions absorbs about 7 times its own weight of plain water after 10 minutes' immersion.

The swelling of gelatine prepared by an alkaline process is least in a weakly acid medium (pH about 4·6) corresponding to the *isoelectric point* of the gelatine (the gelatines obtained by an acid process usually have a much higher isoelectric point at pH 7 to 8). In an acid solution of pH lower than the isoelectric point, the gelatine, which is an amphoteric substance, combines with acids by virtue of its amino groups. In an alkaline solution, on the other hand, it combines with the alkali through its acid groups. On the acid side, the swelling reaches a maximum between pH 2·5 and 2·7. On the alkaline side, the swelling increases steadily and becomes considerable in dilute solutions of caustic alkalis at about pH 12. The variation

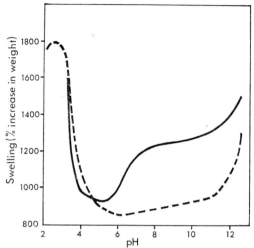

FIG. 29.46. SWELLING OF GELATINE
(—) LIME-PROCESSED GELATINE
(---) ACID-PROCESSED GELATINE

of swelling for an acid-processed and lime-processed gelatines with pH is illustrated in Fig. 29.46. (S. E. Sheppard, R. C. Houck and C. Dittmar, 1942).

The swelling is much limited by the presence in solution of salts at a relatively high concentration. Thus, there is not much swelling in a 15 per cent solution of sodium carbonate, the gelatine absorbing only half its own weight of solution in spite of the high pH value. Even in a 5 per cent sodium carbonate solution it swells to a lesser extent than in plain water. As will be seen below, a swollen emulsion can be dried almost instantaneously by immersing it in a very concentrated salt solution (§664).

The swelling is considerably increased on warming the solution which may cause an irreversible deformation of the gelatine.

The gelatine is attached to a non-stretching support and can only swell in a direction perpendicular to it. When the swelling is excessive, the tangential forces are great and can cause the gelatine to separate from the support or, if the adhesion is sufficiently great, the gelatine *reticulates*.

In the course of the usual processing, a photographic emulsion passes, in succession, through an alkaline developer, the rinse water, an acid fixer, and the final wash water. Thus the gelatine is alternately swollen and contracted, which puts its strength to a severe test (S. E. Sheppard, 1928).

Unless the developer contains a relatively high concentration of salts (sulphite, carbonate, and sometimes sulphate), there is a danger that the swelling will be unlimited and will cause a disintegration of the gelatine.

These conditions tend to be produced, especially at high temperatures, in a very dilute developer by the low salt concentration as well as by the prolonged time of immersion in the bath.

By lowering the salt concentration, rinsing (after development) considerably increases the swelling. The swelling is abated in the acid fixer, but it is increased anew in the final washing. The danger of damage is increased when the various baths are at very different temperatures.

595. Methods of Agitation. The layer of liquid in direct contact with the emulsion, in which the developer oxidation products accumulate after diffusing out of the emulsion, is very adherent and can only be displaced by a sufficiently vigorous agitation. A simple displacement of the sensitive material relative to the solution in the bath only serves to slide this layer along the emulsion surface without removing it.

In the case of dish development, rocking the dish, if it does not achieve uniformity of development, is sufficient to avoid the deleterious effects of exhaustion products (§§ 561-3). Use can be made of rocking devices, moved by clockwork or by an electric motor, to rock the bath automatically during development. If such an arrangement is employed, care must be taken to have a comparatively long period of oscillation. Too rapid rocking may produce stationary waves which can cause the image to show alternate vignetted bands of greater and less development.

In scientific work where perfect uniformity is desirable, the exhaustion products can be removed, as fast as they are formed and diffuse out, by passing a velvet covered roller over the emulsion surface in all directions (O. Bloch, 1921), or a large brush (W. Clark, 1925) that can be made by stretching a piece of chamois leather along the edge of a glass plate, or, finally, by a to-and-fro motion of scraper blades set at an angle of 45° to the direction of travel with a clearance of 0·5 mm between their edges and the emulsion surface.

When developing plates or films in holders in a vertical tank, the agitation can be effected by oscillating the holders vertically by hand or automatically. Furthermore, the bath can be circulated by an external pump or by the rapid rotation of an Archimedean screw inside a tube, open at both ends and shorter by a few centimetres than the depth of the developer.

In development on continuous processing machines, fixed scraper blades can be situated obliquely at a distance of about 1 mm from the surface of the film. The developer solution, drawn from the tank by a pump, can be impinged on the emulsion surface by submerged jets situated in staggered formation along the film path. In continuous processing machines or in machines in which the loops of film are immersed in tubes, the developer can be agitated by bubbles of a relatively inert gas such as nitrogen. The developing tubes should be sufficiently extended to prevent the foam that is created by the bubbling from spilling over. The formation of the foam helps to clarify the bath (C. E. Ives and C. J. Kunz, 1940; C. R. Davies, 1940; A. Lovichi, 1944).

Various types of machine have been devised for the development of sensitometric exposures (L. A. Jones, M. E. Russell, and H. R. Beacham, 1936). Such machines would be well suited to the development of all photometric negatives.

596. Exhaustion of the Developer. When a developer is used continuously, part is carried away by the plates and films that are removed from the tank. The volume thus removed varies from 1 to 5 ml per square decimeter ($\frac{1}{4}$–1$\frac{1}{2}$ oz per sq ft) of emulsion surface, the precise rate depending upon the degree of swelling of the gelatine and on the efficiency of draining or squeegeeing. On an average the rate of carry-over is 2·25 cc per square decimeter ($\frac{1}{2}$ oz per sq ft). A rubber roller squeegee, or a compressed air knife is used to limit the carry-over on continuous motion-picture processing machines.

The concentration of active products in the remaining developer is decreased, while the concentration of bromide is increased. When the sensitive materials are wetted before development, the developer is diluted by the water that is carried in. Cellulose-acetate film supports tend to adsorb a small quantity of the developing agents. Finally, the action of the air converts some of the developing agents to sulphonates both while the bath is being used and in the intervals between use.

When a metol-hydroquinone developer is aerially oxidized, 10 times more hydroquinone than metol is consumed and the pH of the solution is increased. On the other hand, 10 times more metol than hydroquinone is oxidized during development in a developer of low pH, with a decrease in the pH (R. M. Evans and W. T. Hanson, 1938). In consequence of this, it is impossible to assess the degree of exhaustion of the developer just by measuring the pH.

When a large number of exposures are successively developed in a comparatively small volume of developer, it has been found that in order to maintain a constant gamma value it is necessary gradually to increase the time of development. The emulsion speed falls gradually but more rapidly as the exhaustion proceeds, as a result of the sulphite dissolving a greater quantity of silver bromide as the time of development is prolonged.

The loss of speed would be considerable, and intolerable, if the time of development were not increased so as to obtain the same gamma value each time. It is less important when the chosen gamma is high, and this is one reason why a gamma of about 1·1 is recommended for the development of roll-films, other than miniature films. This mode of exhausting a developer is especially suited to the development of radiographs, where development is prolonged sufficiently to obtain almost the maximum gamma ($\gamma\infty$). The effects of exhaustion of the developer are, of course, unimportant when the "one-shot" system of processing is used (§ 498).

597. Replenishment; Maintaining a Developer at Constant Activity. On removing from the tank or machine a volume of developer proportional to the total area of the sensitive material developed, and on topping up the remainder to constant volume by the addition of a suitable solution (replenisher solution), the composition of the bath rapidly tends towards an equilibrium. It would seem that, starting from the moment when this equilibrium is reached, the developer thus maintained might be used indefinitely. In fact, the equilibrium is not a true one and harmful deviations would be produced in the long run. Moreover, various impurities collect in the bath (reduced silver sludge, calcium sulphite sludge, gelatine and its degradation products, dust, coloured oxidation products liable to stain the gelatine, etc.). It is the rule, in large laboratories, to reject the entire bath at the end of each week and to clean and sterilize the installation (§ 572). In a smaller plant the period between installing and rejecting a bath can be considerably increased if, when the bath is not in use, it is covered by a floating lid (§ 498) to protect it from aerial oxidation.

In a vertical tank, the developer is replenished at intervals after developing a given area of material (e.g. a fixed number of spools), and on each addition of replenisher the bath is thoroughly stirred. Since this stirring is liable to disturb the sediment at the bottom of the tank, it has been recommended that the replenishment and stirring should be done at the end of the day's work so that the sediment can settle again overnight (J. I. Crabtree, 1937). In the case of developing machines, the replenishment is generally continuous and automatic. The point in the system at which the replenisher is added is a matter of some importance. In the motion picture industry, the replenisher solution, known as the "boost," is generally added into a reservoir where it is mixed with the developer solution that serves the processing machines, in order to ensure that the developer is of the same composition in all the machines, and to avoid the variations in activity that result from large variations in the average density of the images being developed. In some systems where negative films are developed to a low gamma in slow working developers that are rich in sulphite, the replenisher solution is added at the point of entry of the film into the bath so that development is started in an almost fresh solution, thus reducing the loss of speed that is produced by starting development in the exhausted bath.

In order to maintain the bromide concentration in the bath at a constant level, it is necessary, in spite of the fact that the replenisher solution never contains bromide, to add the replenisher at a greater rate than the solution is carried over by the film leaving the bath. The surplus developer is allowed to overflow, or "bleed," at a suitable point in the system. In order to reduce to a minimum the loss of active chemicals, it is obvious that the developer should not be used at a concentration greater than necessary.

If the sulphite concentration is sufficiently high for its exhaustion to be negligible, the rate of consumption of the developing agents is not proportional to their initial concentration. Thus the proper formula for the replenisher might be quite different from that of the fresh developer. The optimum replenisher formula for a given developer can be found by systematic trial-and-error methods, the behaviour of the developer being frequently assessed by sensitometric tests (§ 600). However, such a method is lengthy, and during the trials some variations in the quality of the work can be expected. A method of systematic investigation involving a calculation of the equilibrium concentrations based on the data from some rapid *analyses* and sensitometric control has been described (R. M. Evans, 1938). The method is lacking in the determination of the alkalinity which, all other concentrations being maintained constant, is controlled by the pH value (as measured by a glass electrode). In order to minimize the variations of activity in a developer until the equilibrium conditions are reached, a very small quantity of iodide and an antifogging agent should be added to the fresh bath (§ 556) in quantities corresponding to those that are formed spontaneously in the course of development.

A developer that is replenished in this way must be controlled by frequent sensitometric tests and, in an industrial laboratory, by rapid analyses carried out alternately on the essential constituents. Such methods of control and analysis have been described by R. M. Evans and W. T. Hanson, 1939; H. L. Baumbach, 1939; S. Bogdanov, 1939; R. B. Atkinson and V. C. Shaner, 1940, etc.

A marked increase in the concentration of sulphate, which is formed only by aerial oxidation, indicates an abnormal degree of aeration due, probably, to a defective pump. A progressive increase in activity indicates the excessive addition of replenisher solution possibly as the result of a leak in some part of the system.

The developers, and particularly the positive developers, should be rejected as soon as they become coloured, lest they stain the gelatine. The bubbling of an inert gas through the developer for about 15 minutes, produces an abundant foam and clarifies the developer, the coloured oxidation products and colloidal silver being carried away in the foam (M. Abribat, 1941).

It is necessary to mention that the rules for the maintenance of a given developer at constant activity fail when the sensitive materials are soaked in water before development, the volume of developer remaining constant. In such a case it is necessary to remove periodically a volume of developer proportional to the area of the film processed, or to the volume of the prebath carried over into the developer. The replenisher solution should be more concentrated than when the sensitive materials are introduced dry into the developer, in order to compensate for the dilution of the bath by the water carried in.

598. Electrolytic Maintenance of a Developer at Constant Activity. The industrial use of an equimolar mixture of sodium anthraquinone -2-sulphonate and of anthraquinone (green), in a solution buffered at pH 4 to 5, has been claimed by J. Rzymkowski (1938). The mixture is formed, and then maintained at constant activity by the cautious electrolysis of a solution of anthraquinonesulphonate. The developer, in which is immersed the cathode, is separated by a porous partition from the anode compartment which contains a solution of sodium hydroxide in which the bromide ions accumulate. The same method would be applicable to other quinones and to indophenols, indamines, etc., by choosing, as far as possible, an agent such that exhaustion would be shown by an appreciable change in colour, thus making it possible to regulate automatically the intensity of the current by a photoelectric cell.

599. Method for the Comparative Testing of Two Developers. The procedure generally adopted by photographers to compare two developers consists in exposing two identical plates or films on the same subject with the same time of exposure; one of these is developed in each developer and the images so obtained are then compared. This method is not very satisfactory because it is not possible to place side by side the parts of the two negatives which have received the same exposure; comparison is therefore difficult.

The test will be found of much more value if it is carried out on a scale of uniform tones obtained by exposing a plate or film in successive bands to intensities which correspond respectively to the shadows, half-tones and high-lights of average subjects; after cutting this negative into several identical strips, each comprising a complete scale of tones, strips are developed for different times in each of the two developers. After fixing and washing, corresponding tones are placed side by side for comparison. The following method was described by J. I. Crabtree, 1922, and does not require the use of a relatively expensive calibrated step-wedge.

Take a plate or film (preferably 7×5 in.) or a piece of sensitized paper, place in a printing frame at such a distance (determined by a preliminary trial) from a weak source of light that after two seconds' exposure a normally developed emulsion just shows a trace of image when compared with a portion which has not been exposed at all. An opaque card held in front of the frame allows different times of exposure to be given to the various parts of the

plate. At the start the card covers a band about half an inch wide and parallel to the longer side. This band will eventually be used for comparing the amount of chemical fog resulting from the various conditions of development. After two seconds' exposure, the card is pushed on about half an inch, and this is repeated after periods of 4, 8, 16, and 32 seconds, counting from the start of the first exposure. When this has been done, cut the plate or film into a certain number of pieces. Fig. 29.47 shows such pieces after different times of development in a metol developer E and in a hydroquinone developer H, and exhibits the characters of the two developers. The image appears very quickly in the metol developer, whilst in the hydroquinone developer it appears very slowly, but the density then increases more quickly, so that the two negatives are almost identical after a sufficiently long time of development. Where many such tests are to be made, a negative should be made once and for all by the same method, and should be developed without being cut up. The darkest band should then be covered with black paper, and the time of exposure adjusted so as to produce, on development, only a faint density under the darkest of the bands next to the one covered by the mask.

The following method (M. L. Dundon, G. H. Brown, and J. G. Capstaff, 1930) is more particularly intended for the control of a tank in which the developer is replaced daily. For these experiments, small pieces of a slow film having a low tendency to fog, e.g. motion-picture positive film, should be used. The film is exposed always under identical conditions, behind a negative carrying several steps of uniform density, obtained as described above, but developed in a dilute bath to a low gamma value. In order to ensure that successive exposures are identical, they should be made in a printer having an automatic timing device and fitted with a lamp reserved for this purpose. To lengthen the life of the lamp it should be run at 10 to 20 volts below its normal rating, the current passing through the lamp being controlled by rheostat and an ammeter. A sufficient number of test strips are exposed at one time to serve the needs of about a week, the strips being used between the second and eighth day after exposure. During the period the change in the latent image is negligible.

Two strips are developed, one in the new bath and one in the old, both developers being at the same temperature. The tests can be carried out on samples of the solutions in glass cylinders of small capacity. The time of development from immersion in the developer to immersion in the stop-bath, is maintained constant and is chosen so that the least exposed step is barely visible on the strip developed in the new bath. Any differences between the stepped images will be readily apparent. The same degree of agitation should be given to both strips. When the strips are fixed and rinsed, they are compared side by side against an opal illuminator. If, each time a new bath is prepared, it is compared in this way with the old one, any mistake in the mixing will be revealed.

A very simple procedure has been described (W. F. Weiland, 1940) that is based on the fact that the time of appearance of a heavily exposed image on a gelatine-bromide paper, depends only on the degree of exhaustion of the developer. The relation between the time of appearance of the image on the test paper and the time of development for a given emulsion can be represented by a straight line.

600. Quality Control. The close control over the activity of the developer, which, since, 1928, has been regarded as indispensable in motion picture processing where the tolerances in the gamma values are very small (± 0.05), is ensured by including a sensitometric strip between every five thousand feet of film.

In normal practice, it is not necessary to draw a complete characteristic curve for each strip, the gamma value being simply read off on a differential densitometer (L. A. Jones and M. E. Russell, 1935; E. Tausch, 1935); various other simple methods have been devised in order to measure the gamma by visual inspection (F. F. Renwick, 1914; J. Eggert, 1930) or by electronic means (H. Brandes and R. Schmidt, 1933). From time to time it is necessary to draw out a complete characteristic curve to determine the effective emulsion speed to find whether this is decreasing as the result of an abnormally high concentration of bromide in the bath.

In cinematography the gamma values are chosen so as to ensure the minimum distortion

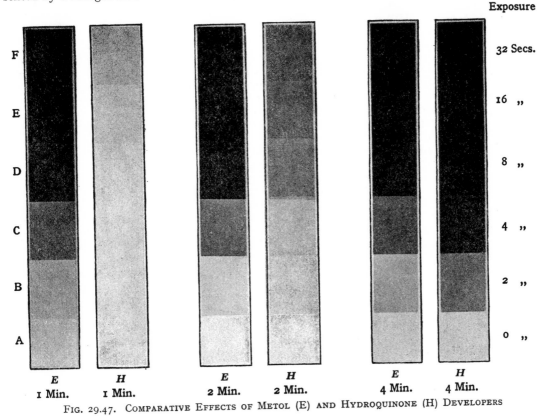

FIG. 29.47. COMPARATIVE EFFECTS OF METOL (E) AND HYDROQUINONE (H) DEVELOPERS

in the sound reproduction. Depending upon the particular recording system used, the gamma values (measured on a diffusing densitometer) lie between 0·55 and 0·80 for the negative and are about 2·0 for the print.

In establishments for the processing of amateur work, a gamma value of 0·7–0·8 is adopted for miniature films in order to avoid excessive graininess on enlargement. To achieve this end, it is necessary to give different times of development for films of different origin. The films are sorted into classes according to their rate of development. Stopping development at a low gamma value calls for perfect constancy of the reduction potential of the developer, and not only constancy in the time of development. It is essential, therefore, that the control of replenishment should be exact.

For the development of films of the usual size it is important that care should be taken to avoid a drop in the emulsion speed. Inquiries by the manufacturers of sensitive materials have shown that this is not always done. Thus, it has been found that in one processing house the gamma values obtained on a succession of rolls from the same batch varied from 0·65 to 1·2, and, for the same gamma there was a range in emulsion speeds of 4 : 1, revealing an absence of proper replenishment (R. F. W. Selman, 1936).

Provided that correct replenishment is employed, or the time of development is appropriately varied, the variations in emulsion speed, as exhaustion proceeds, are negligible when the films are developed to $\gamma = 1·1$, but, on the other hand, they are considerable when development is stopped at $\gamma = 0·7$ (J. I. Crabtree, 1937). The characteristic curves in Fig. 29.48 and 29.49

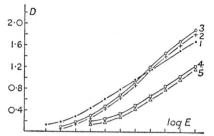

FIG. 29.49. THE EXHAUSTION AND REPLENISHMENT OF A DEVELOPER

correspond to sensitometric strips developed after exhaustion of the number of spools (of 8 exposures $2\frac{1}{4} \times 3\frac{1}{4}$ in.) per litre shown in the following table—

Curve No.	State of developer	Spools per litre	Fig. 29.48 Dev. Time (min.)	γ	Fig. 29.49 Dev. Time (min.)	γ
1	New	0	4	1·08	9	0·66
2	Replenished	105	4	1·15	9	0·93
3	Exhausted	26	18	1·12	40	0·93
4	Exhausted	26	9	0·66	9	0·66
5	Replenished	105	2	—	—	0·66

For the photofinisher it is of primary importance that negatives are uniformly and correctly processed. Unless film development is controlled within carefully defined limits, consistent print quality is not possible. Moreover, uniform negative development is important to operating costs; it reduces the number of reprints and economises in the usage of chemicals. Correct development also helps to retain the usefulness of many underexposed or overexposed negatives, resulting in a greater number of acceptable prints.

Control of development involves time, temperature, agitation and development activity. All of these affect, as we know from previous sections, the overall density and contrast of the negatives. Although the average degree of replenishment recommended for tank development keeps the activity of the solution reasonably constant, variable factors such as considerably different carry-over rates from plant to plant make it necessary to test the activity of the developer at regular intervals throughout its life. For this purpose, test strips are supplied by the major manufacturers. These are pre-exposed strips of film with either two control spots or a number of density steps. They are developed at regular intervals together with negatives and then measured with a densito-

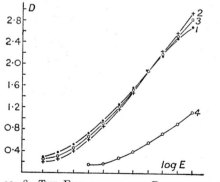

FIG. 29.48. THE EXHAUSTION AND REPLENISHMENT OF A DEVELOPER

meter. The result gives a numerical measure of activity of the developer from which the necessary degree of replenishing can be read from a table.

The test strips should be processed in the middle of a batch of films, if possible in the same position in the tank each time, as this represents the average development conditions for the films. After processing of the strip the densities of the low density spot and the high density spot are measured with a densitometer. Subtraction of the low density value from the high density value gives a figure which must be within the range defined by the manufacturer (0·70–0·85 for the Kodak DN-13 system). This gives an approximate measure of the contrast. The figures obtained from control strips processed at various intervals of time (such as twice a week) are plotted against time to give a *process control chart* (Fig. 29.50). It is of the utmost importance to take remedial action as soon as a discernible upward or downward *trend* is shown in the process control chart. If the process exceeds the control limits (set by the manufacturers) it is too late to take action and the process has got out of control with the result that many negatives are ruined. The accompanying process control chart shows when and where action should be taken.

The dotted lines U.C.L. and L.C.L. represent the upper control limit of 0·85 and the lower control limit of 0·70.

1. Shows that the development activity is increasing and on the 13th of the month remedial action must be taken. The replenisher was therefore diluted and thereafter the process shows an acceptable random scatter.

2. Illustrates a process under control and no action necessary.

3. Shows that the development activity is decreasing and on the 10th the replenisher was made more concentrated and the process once again showed the acceptable random scatter.

601. Interrupting the Course of Development. At a time when only large-size negatives were used, on non-colour sensitive plates which would be considered slow to-day and which were developed by a bright safelight, it was the rule to study the appearance of the image, then its growth, and try to modify its characteristics in any desired direction. Development was started in a dilute bath having a low bromide concentration. The time taken for the first details to appear and the delay between the appearance of the highlights and shadows would indicate to the photographer whether the exposure had been too great, correct, or insufficient, long before the image had attained the desired contrast. The plate was then placed in a dish of water before transferring it to another

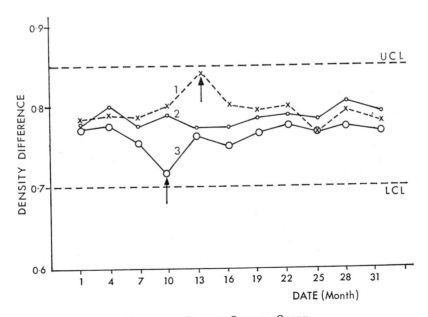

FIG. 29.50. PROCESS CONTROL CHART

dish containing another developer, better suited to its needs. A weakly alkaline, heavily bromided developer provided an ample regression of speed for an over-exposed image; an average developer was used for a normally exposed image, whereas a developer of very high reduction potential, without bromide and strongly alkaline, capable of developing out the weakest exposures, was used for an under-exposed plate. This method of *developing in several baths* was studied particularly by A. von Hübl (1897), director of the Austrian Geographical Service, who had to ensure the correct development of numerous negatives received from field expeditions whose personnel did not always enjoy a photographic competence equal to their skill in topographical matters.

It is sometimes incorrectly stated that changes in the composition of a developer can make no difference to the shape of the characteristic curve corresponding to a given gamma value. Some important variations can be obtained in the lower region of the curve by virtue of the fact that the development of all the grains does not set in at the same value of the difference between the potentials of the silver and of the developer (§ 527), and, as has already been mentioned, some changes (dilution of the developer, use of tanning developers, etc.), can change the shape of the upper region of the curve.

The amateur, to whom the small cost, represented by the quantity of developer, was negligible, and who often worked in a cramped space, would prefer to modify by appropriate additions the developer in use, momentarily transferring it to a glass tumbler.

Frequently the photographer developed his own plates. He knew the characteristics of his subject and would use from the start a developer suited to the range between the extreme brightnesses of his subject in order to obtain a superficial image of low contrast or a deeply developed image of high contrast (§ 559). According to the circumstances, he shortened or lengthened the development, attempting (without always succeeding, because visual judgment is very uncertain in this matter) to reach an optimum density range in the negative, a necessary condition for the production of perfect prints on the limited number of types of paper at his disposal; papers which scarcely differed, one from another, in speed or whose contrast only varied within close limits.

While some adroit workers, possessed of much leisure, obtained remarkable results in this way and found pleasure in thus wrestling with the problem, the tyro or occasional photographer worked sometimes in the wrong direction as a result of frequently confusing the notions of density and contrast.

Such methods of working, obviously, could not be applied to miniature negatives where the details are too small to be studied by safelight and which would no longer be manageable after cutting up the film into individual images. This applies especially to fast panchromatic films developed in almost total darkness. The great exposure latitude in modern negative films and the great variety of papers that are available, can accommodate a wide range of density differences and make the individual control of each negative often unnecessary. Moreover there are not many, even among the most enthusiastic amateurs, who can spare the time.

In the motion-picture industry the working volume of developer in a laboratory is always several thousand litres, a fact which makes it impossible to modify the developer formula. It is difficult even to give a different time of development for each scene and, moreover, there is only one type of positive film available. The results obtained under these circumstances show that very satisfactory, if not always perfect, negatives can be obtained without any visual control over development.

It should be noted that the procedures which will be described below, using in succession two developers of more or less different composition are intended to reduce the consumption of developing solutions when developing to a constant gamma, and are not intended for the control of negatives, neither individually, nor in groups.

602. Factors Influencing the Time of Development. Under any given circumstances (of subject, type of emulsion, composition and temperature of developer), where the exposure has been ample, there is no *one* optimum developing time, but a more or less extended range of times. The particular time chosen would depend on the contrast grade of the paper that is to be used for printing the negative. The shorter times yield negatives of lower granularity and are to be preferred for negatives intended for enlargement and for negatives that need retouching.

When it is desired to bring out the shadow details in an under-exposed image, there is, in general, an optimum time of development (or, to be more precise, an optimum value of gamma) beyond which the shadow details become more and more lost in the background fog (E. R. Bullock, 1926). When the developer has an appreciable induction period (developing agent of low reduction potential, or a partly exhausted, or heavily bromided solution), this optimum time of development often leads to an excessive contrast in the negative (S. O. Rawling, 1932) which necessitates subsequent treatment. In the case of certain emulsions, where the characteristic curve has a long, curved toe, and where a high gamma value can be reached in a non-bromided, high-potential developer, without the appearance of appreciable fog, it is possible to compensate for much under-exposure in the case of low-contrast subjects (when all the exposures are situated on the toe of the curve) by considerably prolonging development (F. F. Renwick, 1913; R. Luther, 1923).

As a result of this characteristic, it is sometimes possible to obtain better images of fast-moving objects on material of average speed than on ultra-rapid emulsions. The density range is not always large enough for the negatives to be used directly, but they give satisfactory prints after *proportional intensification* (§ 682).

The time of development that must be given to obtain a desired gamma value depends upon—

1. The type of emulsion used. The times of development needed to reach a given gamma value can vary as much as 8 : 1 on passing from one negative emulsion to another, and 2 : 1 among successive batches of the same brand.

The more rapid emulsions, having larger grains, develop more slowly than the slow, fine-grain emulsions. Film-pack films, protected from abrasion by a thin layer of gelatine that slows down the diffusion processes, require a somewhat longer time of development than another film employing the same emulsion but without the super-coat.

2. The composition, the concentration, and the temperature of the developer and on the agitation. The influence of all these circumstances on the time of development has been studied. Except in an industrial establishment where the concentration of useful product in each of the constituents of the developer can be found by analysis, the composition of the developer can vary, unknown to the operator, each time a new batch of a chemical is used.

In order to develop to a given gamma value, when the developer is always used fresh (in some scientific applications) or at constant activity, it is necessary to prepare a curve showing the gamma value for each time of development, the developer being at constant temperature. If the temperature cannot be maintained constant, the temperature coefficient for the developer and the emulsion should be known. When the developer is not constantly replenished, it is necessary to draw the curve showing the time of development as a function of the area of the material previously developed in a given volume of developer.

603. Judging the End of Development. The term "visual control of development" implies that development can be stopped at the moment when the density range reaches the optimum for the particular photograph. Unfortunately, there is no means of achieving this condition; the estimation of the density range by inspection, without photometric measurements that are almost impossible during development, results in gross errors, except after long practice on a particular type of work. The coloured light, on the one hand, and the presence in the emulsion of the silver bromide, constituting a weak positive image complementary to the negative image, on the other hand, affect the apparent contrast in opposite ways without compensating each other. Moreover, it is difficult to avoid the mistakes of over-estimating the density range on a negative of low average density, and under-estimating the density range on a negative of high average density. Some professional portrait photographers use a negative comparator, an opal illuminator in front of which are fixed two negatives, suited, respectively, for printing on the most soft, and most contrasty printing papers used in the studio. A space is left between the two negatives to take a negative for comparison. The opal is illuminated with white light for the examination of fixed negatives, and by orange or green light for unfixed negatives, in which case the standard negatives should be stabilized by iodization rather than by fixing.

Various methods have been recommended to beginners to enable them to stop development at a time that is neither too early nor too late, without, however, there being any foundation of facts between the standards of judgment and the desired results.

In particular, it has been suggested that development should be stopped when fog appears on the parts of the negatives that were protected from exposure (by the rebates of the plate-holders, or the back frame of the camera), or at the moment when the dense parts of the image can be seen through the back of the plate or film. This latter recommendation is useless, however, when there is more than one coat of emulsion and, also, when the material carries an antihalation layer of the type that does not disperse in the developer.

The time of appearance of one or other of these two conditions can be influenced by many factors not connected with the rate of development of the image, such as accidental light fogging when loading or in the early stages of development, a poor developer which may also be dilute or too warm, an emulsion more or less rich in silver bromide. Thus, such recommendations are only of a makeshift nature.

When negatives are examined by transmitted light during development, plates should be held by their edges and cut films by the corners, if they are not in holders. The negative should not be held closer to the safelight than is necessary, especially if the safelight is warm. Prolonged examination should be avoided, especially at the commencement of development of non-desensitized materials.

When a normally exposed negative has been developed to a given gamma value, the difference between the extreme densities depends mainly on the ratio between the extreme brightnesses of the subject, and the maximum density upon the degree of exposure. In order to keep the density range constant, the time of development should be varied inversely as the ratio of the extreme brightnesses of the subject. Otherwise, the most regular results are obtained by developing to a constant gamma value. If the gamma value is chosen so as to allow negatives, normally exposed on subjects of a brightness range of 30 : 1, to be printed on normal grade paper (this would be $\gamma = 1 \cdot 1$ for constant printing), then negatives of very contrasty subjects can be printed on soft paper, and negatives of low-contrast subjects can be printed on contrasty paper. Thus, in summer, a greater proportion of soft paper would be used than in winter. The deviations involved in visually judging the end of development would be greater than those found in working to a constant gamma.

It should be recalled that it is possible to develop non-colour-sensitized emulsions to an almost constant gamma value by using a time of development that is a suitable multiple of the time of appearance of the image (§ 547).

Some manufacturers of sensitized materials indicate, for their products, the times of development which will give suitable gamma values ($0 \cdot 8 - 1 \cdot 00 - 1 \cdot 25$) when the recommended developers are used at the stated temperatures. Other manufacturers publish, for some recommended developers, the curves showing the gamma values as a function of the time of development at an average temperature, and the graphs indicating the equivalent times of development at various temperatures. However, it should be added that such publications imply a constancy of the properties of the materials that is not always found in the various batches of a particular brand. In fact, the variations are sometimes such that on developing a large number of batches of the same brand to obtain an average value of $1 \cdot 0$, the values obtained range from $0 \cdot 7$ to $1 \cdot 3$.

604. Rinsing after Development; Stop-baths; Provisional Fixing. The developed negative should be rapidly transferred into a tank or a dish of water, or placed under a jet of water, of moderate pressure, in order to remove the surplus developer and, as much as possible, the developer that is in the emulsion and the gelatine backing layer. In this way one avoids carrying into the fixing bath an appreciable quantity of developer which, on accumulating, can cause spots, dichroic fog, or the precipitation of the alum often employed in fixers in order to harden the gelatine. The hardening property of the fixer reduces the amount of water absorbed in washing and thus increases the rate of drying.

Since development can continue while the negative is being rinsed in water, often causing local irregularities, it is preferable to use as a *stop-bath* a very dilute solution of an acid, or of an acid hardening agent, that stops development rapidly by neutralizing the alkali. The stop-bath can be acidified by adding 2 per cent sodium bisulphite, 2 per cent boric acid, or 2 per cent acetic acid. The stop-bath should be checked from time to time with litmus paper to ensure that it is still acid.

The use of a chrome-alum hardening stop-bath has the advantage that the hardening obtained is more complete than can be obtained by adding potash alum to the fixing bath. The fixer is then more stable and the recovery of silver is made easier.

Chrome-alum, or chromic potassium sulphate, $K_2SO_4, Cr_2(SO_4)_3, 24H_2O$, molecular weight $= 999$, appears usually as large, deep-violet crystals of good purity. The solutions prepared in the cold are grey-violet in colour and become green on warming to 60°C, under which conditions the hardening, or tanning properties are diminished, while the acidity is increased. The salt is quite soluble in water (20 per cent at 15°C). The hardening properties of the solution are rapidly impaired on adding sulphite or bisulphite, or organic acids such as citric, tartaric, and oxalic acids. It is not affected by acetic acid.

The best results are obtained in a 3 per cent solution of chrome alum at $pH = 3.2$. The developer carried over into the stop-bath by the developed plates, etc., rapidly diminishes the efficiency of the stop-bath and this is shown by a change of tint from violet to yellow-green. To prevent this change the bath should be periodically re-acidified by small additions of dilute sulphuric acid. The acidity of the stop-bath is best controlled with the aid of bromphenol blue indicator.

To carry out the test 0.4 g of the bromphenol blue dye is dissolved in 75 ml of a 0.05 per cent solution of sodium hydroxide and the solution is made up to one litre with distilled water. About 2 ml of the stop-bath are diluted by adding 5 ml of distilled water and six drops of the indicator solution. By daylight the resulting colour should be reddish-yellow.

After the negatives are immersed in the stop-bath they should be agitated for not less than 45 seconds to avoid the appearance of blisters, or spots, or the formation of chromium hydroxide in the emulsion layer. The negatives should remain in the stop-bath for about 3 minutes.

When a hardening stop-bath is used, it is essential, after the final washing, to dry carefully the gelatine surfaces to which traces of chromium hydroxide will finally be found to adhere.

The use of a hardening stop-bath is particularly to be recommended when the temperature of the processing solutions is in excess of 25°C. When working at 30°C, after developing in a bath loaded with sodium sulphate (§ 594), a stop-bath of 3 per cent chrome-alum loaded with 10 to 15 per cent of sodium sulphate should be used.

When the volume of work is large, the re-acidifications of the stop-bath can, after preliminary trials, be based on the area of the gelatine surfaces that have passed through the bath.

When working under difficult field conditions where washing after fixing would be difficult,

proper fixing can be postponed, and *provisional fixing* employed. This consists of an acid stop-bath followed by a brief rinse. A weak acid such as boric (5 per cent solution) is to be preferred, because a strong, non-volatile acid will, on keeping, break down the gelatine if it has not been removed. Drying should be carried out away from a bright light.

To enable the negative to be examined in white light as rapidly as possible after development, it can be iodized by bathing for 2 minutes in the following bath (J. G. Capstaff, M. L. Dundon, and G. H. Brown, 1930).

Potassium iodide	.	20 g
Glacial acetic acid	.	20 ml
Potassium alum	.	40 g
Sodium sulphite, anhydrous	.	1 g
Water to make	.	1 litre

After iodizing, the negative should be rinsed in several changes of water, the last containing a little ammonium hydroxide. If it is desired, ultimately, to fix an iodized negative, a new fixing bath or a special fixer (§ 647), should be used, because the silver iodide is less readily soluble than the bromide.

605. Critical Examination of Finished Negatives. Although negatives cannot be usefully examined until after they are fixed, and preferably after they are washed and dried, it does not seem proper to postpone to a later chapter a matter which is so intimately connected with the question of development.

The examination of a negative that does not carry high densities is best made by placing the negative, emulsion side down, on a mat white surface and viewing it by reflected light. A very dense negative is more easily inspected by transmission against an illuminated opal glass, or, failing an opal, a ground-glass, or a sheet of tracing-paper.

In an industrial or scientific establishment, a negative viewer should be used of the type usually used for radiographs which can hold wet or dry films, by means of clips, against a vertical opal glass that forms the front face of a lamp-house.

Mention may be made here of a photo-electric apparatus that shows an enlarged positive image of a negative on a fluorescent screen (F. Biedermann, 1937). This arrangement is chiefly designed for dealers to interest their customers in purchasing enlarged prints of their negatives.

Before making final judgment, account should be taken of the fact that details, particularly in the shadows, that are not clear on the negative may appear in prints made on very contrasty paper (L. A. Jones, 1939). Such a negative is thus very acceptable if the difference between the extreme densities does not exceed the value that can be tolerated when printing on papers of this sort. This does not apply, of course, to negatives that are to be studied without printing or on which it is intended to make measurements (in radiography, photogrammetry, spectrography, etc.), but, if the shadow details would appear in a print, they could be made visible on the negative by strong intensification.

A relatively high density of the image of the shadows (0·5 for example) should not be confused with fog. The fog density will be shown on the parts of the negative that were protected from the action of light in the camera.

A negative is not under-exposed provided that the density in the image of the darkest shadow, in which it is desired to discern details, is very slightly greater than the fog density.

A negative that is well or over-exposed often shows a weak positive image when examined by reflection on the support side, the light falling obliquely on the negative which is held before a dark background. Under the same conditions, a less exposed, or under-exposed negative sometimes shows a positive image when the emulsion side is examined. A normally exposed negative can thus show a positive image on inspecting both sides. These characteristics are not invariable, however.

A negative is not over-exposed provided that when properly printed the image of the highlights is sufficiently detailed. When the range between the extreme brightnesses of the original subject is very extended, the negative may be under-exposed with regard to the image of the shadows and over-exposed with regard to the image of the highlights. A better result would probably be obtained on a negative material able to record a wider brightness range.

If the negative shows details in the shadows and in the highlights, but, as a result of being developed to too high a gamma, the range between the extreme densities is too great to allow printing on the softest paper, and if the negative is sufficiently valuable to justify the trouble, it can be reduced (§ 690), or it can be dealt with by the procedure that allows the compression of the middle tones though these operations are rather delicate.

A systematic under-exposure may be the result of over-estimating the speed of the films or plates, or of the exposure meter being out of

order or used under the wrong conditions, or it may result from the scale of the diaphragm apertures being in error. A systematic over-exposure may be due, among other causes, to an error in the calibration of the shutter.

Photographic beginners, and some experienced workers, easily confuse the notions of density and contrast. Just as it is possible to meet a very steep path at a low altitude and a gentle incline on a high mountain, a negative can be at one and the same time very clear (very low density in the shadows) and very vigorous (great density range), or very dense (relatively high density in the shadows) and very flat (small density range). Thus, there is no correlation between the average density of a negative and the range between the extreme densities.

It is essential to take account of the fact (except when considering granularity) that the characteristics of the image depend only on the range between the extreme densities, the density of the shadow details affecting only the time of exposure when printing. If two similar negatives, made on similar materials, similarly developed, have been exposed under conditions such that corresponding densities differ by one unit (all the opacities of one negative being ten times those of the other), the contact prints obtained on the same paper, using times of exposure in the ratio 10 : 1, would be identical.

The photographic vocabulary is somewhat confusing in regard to negative characteristics, the same term being sometimes used with very different meanings. In the following pages the arbitrary terms shown in the following table will be used. But a negative can only be usefully defined by stating the gamma to which it has been developed and the range between the extreme densities.

Classification of negatives		
According to the density of the shadows	According to the range between the extreme densities	According to the gamma value
Very low—clear	Low—flat	$\gamma < 1$ (contrast low) soft
	Medium—medium contrast	$\gamma = 1$ normal contrast
Great—dense	Great—vigorous	$\gamma > 1$ (contrast high) hard

The rock on which the beginner usually comes to grief is his ignorance of the characters that a negative should possess in order to yield good prints by the usual printing processes. The rational apprenticeship of the photographer should, in our opinion, begin by printing from negatives of suitable quality. For instance, two negatives may be used, one suitable for print-out paper or rapid bromide paper of weak contrast, and the other for a paper of very great contrasts, which negatives must, of course, be supplied with advice as to their correct use. Having acquired experience in printing, the beginner will be in a position to judge what results to expect from his negatives, whereas for lack of a guide, it is usually impossible for him to distinguish between faults in the negative and errors in printing.

Working Procedure

606. Preliminaries. Before beginning the development of a negative it is necessary to see that all solutions and equipment are at hand. The tanks or dishes should be so arranged that the negative being developed may be transferred from one to another in proper sequence. They should be filled with the various baths required, taking care that the temperature of these solutions is about the same as that of the darkroom, which should whenever possible be between 65°F and 70°F (18°C and 21°C). The dishes containing the fixing bath should be placed so that no splashes can reach the developer.

When the various baths, and particularly the developer, are prepared at the time of use by mixture or dilution of stock solutions, the water used for dilution should have been kept for a while in the darkroom in order to acquire its temperature. In all cases be careful not to dilute with water straight from the tap. The tap water is usually colder than the developing solution, and it also contains air which separates in bubbles when the mixture becomes warm; these bubbles may adhere to the gelatine of the negatives, preventing the developer from acting at these points.

To ensure the perfect uniformity of a mixture it is necessary to stir vigorously but not too vigorously or prolonged or air drawn into the solution will cause aerial oxidation. On no account should the various liquids to be mixed be poured separately into a shallow dish, where it is very difficult to obtain a uniform solution even after prolonged agitation. It is still more important to avoid a direct addition to the bath during development of negatives. When developing in a dish, the developers must be poured back into the measure, and any required additions then made. When developing in a tank, the negatives must be removed, and the developer stirred energetically after adding the new solutions.

It is essential that every care be taken to ensure uniformity of treatment during the various manipulations. For this, the emulsion must be wetted almost simultaneously at all points by a perfectly uniform developer, and the plates or films must then be moved several times.

It is specially essential that the solutions used should be perfectly clear, as any suspended matter produces a spot where it settles on the emulsion. All stock solutions and baths previously in use should therefore be poured off from any sediment.

With prolonged use, a sludge of reduced silver and calcium sulphite forms in a tank of developer and, overnight, this settles on the bottom of the tank. However, the sludge is stirred up when the bath is next used and there is a danger of it adhering to the emulsion surfaces. Such a deposit can be easily removed before recommencing work, and without agitating the bulk of the liquid, by use of the following device (C. E. Ives, A. J. Miller, and J. I. Crabtree, 1931). A steel tube, about 3 mm ($\frac{1}{8}$ in.) internal diameter and somewhat longer than the depth of the tank, terminates in a long narrow nozzle, similar to that used on vacuum cleaners. The steel tube is connected by thick-walled rubber tubing to one of two tubes passing through the stopper of a thick-walled glass bottle or demijohn capable of holding about 1/30 of the contents of the tank. The other tube in the stopper is connected by another length of the rubber pressure tubing to a filter pump. By passing the nozzle gently over the bottom of the tank the lower layers of developer containing the sediment are drawn off into the bottle. After the sediment has settled in the bottle the developer is decanted and the sediment is added to the other silver residues for recovery of the silver metal.

The surface of a used bath is often contaminated by a film of scum which will adhere to the emulsion as it is lowered into the solution, and will cause local undeveloped patches. This scum will not adhere if the surface is previously wetted, but it is better to skim the surface of the developer with a piece of filter paper, or butter muslin on a frame, immersed obliquely to a depth of half an inch. This operation should precede the dredging of sediment.

Intense fog has been noticed on non-colour-sensitive materials which had been developed, by the light of an appropriate safelight, in a developer that had been previously used for developing colour-sensitized materials (O. Bloch, 1915).

607. Wetting Plates and Films before Development. In quantity work the adherence of air-bubbles to the gelatine is sometimes avoided by wetting in water containing a little alcohol (industrial spirit). Nowadays it is more usual to use very dilute solutions of the wetting agents used in textile manufacture: saponine, sulphoricinates, and sulphonated fatty alcohols (Ocenol, Lorol, Igepon, Teepol, etc.). These substances can also be added to the developer (§ 577) or to the desensitizing bath (§ 631).

Preliminary wetting accelerates development in a concentrated developer and slows it in a dilute one. With some developers it is possible to ascertain by methodical tests the strength required in order that the duration of development should not be affected by the preliminary wetting. Any tanning of the gelatine reduces the speed of development only very slightly.

In every instance where the emulsion has been wetted before development it is necessary to rock the developing dish energetically for a few moments or to move the plate-holders or film-hangers in the solution so as to ensure the uniform replacement of the water or solution impregnating the gelatine by the developer.

608. Hardening the Emulsion before Development in Warm Solutions. Under tropical, or other warm conditions, the hardening of the gelatine can be deferred until after the development by making suitable additions to the developer (§ 577) but this method of working is only applicable at solution temperatures up to 35°C (95°F), and even at 30°C (86°F) there is some degree of risk.

The usual developers can be used up to 40°C (104°F) if the negative is hardened in a pre-bath according to the technique described below (H. A. Miller, J. I. Crabtree, and H. D. Russell, 1944).

Various attempts had previously been made to harden the gelatine in formalin (§ 662), but the formalin retained in the emulsion often caused the appearance of an intense fog on the developed images. All risk of fog is avoided by the addition of an antifogging agent to the hardening bath (§ 556).

The bath is prepared immediately before use by mixing the two stock solutions. At temperatures above 35°C (95°F) the quantity of antifogging agent is increased up to double, if necessary. The bath will keep for about three weeks at a temperature of 35°C. The negatives are immersed for an average time of 10 minutes,

after which they are drained and rinsed and then placed in the developer. About five square feet (50 square decimeters) of film can be treated per litre of bath. In an industrial establishment, the bath can be maintained at constant activity by adding a replenisher solution to top up the bath to a constant level. In this way 30 to 40 square feet (300 to 400 square decimetres) of film can be treated per litre of the initial bath.

		Normal bath 1 litre	Replenisher 1 litre
(A)	Water . . . . to make	1 litre	1 litre
	6-nitrobenzimidazole nitrate (0·5 per cent solution)	40 ml	55 ml
	Sodium sulphate, anhydrous . .	50 g	50 g
	Sodium carbonate, anhydrous . .	10 g	23 g
(B)	Formalin (commercial strength) .	5 ml	8·5 ml

Pour B into A, while stirring, Final pH = 10·1.

609. Air Bubbles. A small amount of air is sometimes drawn into the solution when the mat surface of the emulsion is plunged into the bath, and this air tends to form adherent, hemispherical air-bubbles, or air-bells. The hemispherical bubbles tend to become spherical, reducing the area in contact with the emulsion. Thus, when air-bells are formed in the developer, the non-developed zone is surrounded by a degraded border. The bubble tends to lengthen in a vertical direction, the tendency being greater the larger the bubble. In a developer that tends to give aerial fog (§ 553), the circumference of the non-developed zone is often more dense, and there is often a descending, denser streamer below the bubble (J. I. Crabtree and C. E. Ives, 1926).

If a gelatine layer is immersed in water or in an aqueous solution and is removed before it is completely swollen, a large number of air-bells tend to adhere on reintroducing the partly swollen gelatine into the liquid.

610. Immersion in the Developing Bath. When developing a plate in a dish, hold it by its edges, emulsion upwards. Large plates must be supported on the four spread fingers of the right hand and held by the thumb placed on the extreme edge. For very large plates the help of an assistant is almost indispensable. The dish is tilted to collect all the developer along one side. An edge of the plate is then rested on the edge of the dish opposite to the one where the developer is lying. The dish is then let down into the horizontal position, and, at the same time, the plate is lowered to the bottom of the dish. The plate is thus swept almost instantaneously by the liquid. The dish is gently rocked, and care is taken to see that the plate is uniformly wetted. Unless the worker is skilled, it is best to avoid developing several plates together in one dish, as there is a risk of damage from one plate sliding over another. However, it is possible to obtain dishes with low dividing ridges on the bottom for the simultaneous development of several stereoscopic plates, and separators of moulded material permitting several plates of small size to be developed together in an ordinary dish.

About 100 ml of developer is required in a dish of half-plate ($6\frac{1}{2} \times 4\frac{3}{4}$ in.) size, and proportionate quantities in dishes of other sizes. It may be well for a beginner to increase these amounts by one-third in order to avoid any irregularity in the wetting of the emulsion by the developer.

When developing cut films in a dish it is best to choose a dish sufficiently large to accommodate two films side by side, and to have plenty of developer in order that the films be well covered in spite of their tendency to curl. The film is slid into the developer, emulsion upwards, and, while held by two adjoining corners, is drawn to the half of the dish farthest from the operator. As soon as this film is well wetted with developer several other films may be introduced in succession, each being drawn to the back of the dish, leaving the front half free, until the last film of the batch has been introduced. The films become very soft, and must be handled with care. They are taken one by one and transferred in reverse order to the front half of the dish, and this transfer from one pile to the other is continued until development is completed.

When single frames or hangers are used with plates or films developed in a tank, care must be taken to see that air-bubbles are not imprisoned in the frame, as such bubbles, when rising, may adhere to the emulsion. To do this, the frames are immersed one corner first, obliquely, and they are gently moved up and down immediately after immersion. The plates or films are introduced with the emulsion facing the operator, and are put in at the back of the tank and then brought to the front so as to leave the back free for the others. By proceeding in this way there is no danger of scratching the emulsion of one negative by the frame containing the next.

After inserting the last frame, the frames are separated as far as possible and moved up and down singly from time to time in order to bring fresh solution in contact with the emulsion. In doing this, each frame must be drawn away from the one behind it so as to avoid scratching the gelatine of the latter.

If the frames are much narrower than the tank they all must be pushed up against one side to avoid retarded development of such parts of the emulsion of a plate or film as would come too close to the vertical side of another frame. Unless the frames are very widely separated from each other it is necessary to avoid developing together negatives of different sizes.

When development is done in vertical, grooved troughs, the developer should be emptied from time to time into a jug, from which it is at once poured back into the tank. Instead, the tank, if fitted with a watertight lid, may be reversed every two minutes.

Owing to the variety of the tanks intended for the development of roll-film, the only reference which can be made is that the instructions issued with them should be followed.

DEVELOPER FORMULAE

611. Introduction. In view of the many hundreds of published developer formulae it is possible to give only a few representative examples which are generally those recommended by the major film manufacturers. This procedure has been adopted so that the reader can refer to the relevant data books or manuals published by the manufacturers for further details on the particular formulae.

Rather than classify the formulae according to the developing agents used, they have been classified according to the use to which the developer is put (e.g. general purpose, fine grain, high contrast etc.), as it has been shown previously (§ 567) that the developing agent is dependent upon the total developer formulation for its particular performance. Where possible, explanations have been given for differences in the constitution of the developers which alter their application. In the formulae given the constituents should be dissolved in the order in which they are written and development times apply to development at 68°F (20°C).

612. General Purpose Developers. These general purpose developers are very versatile and of universal application to plates, cut film, roll film and miniature film where control of graininess is not required. By varying the dilution of the stock solution it is possible to alter the contrast but for extremes in variation it is necessary to vary the proportions of some ingredients of the developer. The following table lists formulae for some typical general purpose metol-hydroquinone (M-Q) developers.

General Purpose M-Q Developers

	soft (ID3)	normal (D61a)	contrasty (ID2)
Metol . . .	6 g	3·1 g	2 g
Sodium sulphite, anhydrous . .	25 g	90 g	75 g
Hydroquinone .	—	5·9 g	8 g
Sodium carbonate, anhydrous .	37·5 g	11·5 g	37·5 g
Potassium bromide	1 g	1·7 g	2 g
Water to . .	1 litre	1 litre	1 litre
Dilution . .	1:3	1:2 (dish) 1:3 (tank)	1:2 (dish) 1:5 (tank)
Development time .	12 min.	7 min. 14 min.	5 min. 9 min.

From the above formulae it can be seen that as the ratio of metol to hydroquinone is increased the developer changes from contrasty to soft-working. Metol is a soft and rapid-working developing agent whereas hydroquinone is contrasty and slow-working. Thus by varying the ratios the desired type of developer may be formulated. The amounts of alkali are such that the activity of the developing agents is appropriate for the developer, i.e. the soft working developer (ID 3) contains sufficient carbonate for metol to act but not too much or the soft working characteristics would be destroyed and the amounts of sulphite are such that the solutions have good keeping properties.

A similar general purpose developer to the M-Q developers given above may be formulated using Phenidone in place of metol and this P-Q developer is recommended for use by sufferers of "metol poisoning" (§§ 583, 585) in place of the M-Q developers.

General Purpose P-Q Developer (ID 67)

Sodium sulphite, anhydrous .	75 g
Hydroquinone . . .	8 g
Sodium carbonate, anhydrous .	37·5 g
Phenidone . . .	0·25 g
Potassium bromide . .	2 g
Benzotriazole . . .	0·15 g
Water to	1 litre
Dilution	1:2 (dish) 1:3 (tank)
Development time . .	4·5 min. 9 min.

The main difference between this formula and the previous M-Q formulae, apart from the developing agents, is that benzotriazole is included to inhibit fog formation from this more active combination of Phenidone and hydroquinone.

613. Fine Grain Developers. The comparisons of the granularity of negatives developed in different developers have no significance unless they refer to equal densities on negatives that were exposed under identical conditions and then developed to the same gamma value. The granularity of a negative varies from one part to another as a function of the density, and from one negative to another (similarly exposed on the same material) as a function of the gamma value. These variations can be easily explained by the fact that the development of different grains sets in after a delay that depends, among other factors, on the degree of exposure, and that the development is not complete at the instant that it is stopped. The necessity of comparing negatives exposed under identical conditions (without the danger of errors caused by capricious shutters) results from the fact that, on the one hand, all developers do not give the same emulsion speed at equal gamma values, and, on the other, that the speed is generally greater when development is carried to a higher gamma value. If development is curtailed to reduce the granularity, it is necessary to increase the exposure, and it is obviously desirable to know what sacrifice in speed must be made.

In modern emulsions the individual grains are not visible on enlargement but unless precautions are taken in the development of negative materials the grains may clump together to form larger groups which are apparent when the negative is enlarged. The clumping or aggregation of the grains is induced by an active developer and accordingly the graininess is reduced if the developer activity is kept to a minimum, generally by developing at a relatively low pH value. The graininess of the image is also reduced considerably if development is carried out using a physical developer and the low pH values generally employed in fine grain developers enables physical development to occur provided a silver halide solvent is present. Physical development by itself leads to the finest possible grain but physical developers (§ 625) are very slow acting, difficult to use in practice and result in considerable reduction in emulsion speed.

The fine-grain developers are, in fact, those slow developers in which the development can be stopped at a gamma value between

0·6 and 0·8, thus making only partial use of the speed of the emulsion. Since the diminished granularity results from the fact that only a fraction of each grain is reduced, it is necessary to increase the exposure so as to affect a larger number of grains (W. Reinders and M. C. F. Beukers, 1938). The best fine-grain developer is that which, for the same low value of gamma, occasions the least increase in exposure. Obviously, to avoid as much as possible the loss in speed, the addition of soluble bromide must be avoided, an addition which, moreover, is pointless because of the low activity of these developers (G. Schwarz, 1935). The best known fine-grain developers require double the exposure that would be needed in the case of the majority of developers for large and average-sized negatives. Some of the developers that have been suggested for miniature negatives require six times the normal exposure, an increase that is inadmissible unless this disadvantage is offset by a great reduction in granularity.

The fine-grain developers are all slow-acting, in order to avoid the irregularities that result when development in an energetic developer is stopped at a low gamma value. Rather than slowing development by dilution, it is preferable to reduce the alkalinity to the minimum necessary for the developer to act. Developers containing hydroquinone need an effective buffer to limit the increase in the alkalinity resulting from the aerial oxidation of the hydroquinone in the presence of sulphite (§ 570). The use of borax is often sufficient with, or without, an excess of boric acid.

In order to reduce the maximum gamma (γ_∞) of the material to a level that is only slightly greater than the desired gamma value, and to reduce the effects of mistakes in working, the fine-grain developers are often doctored with a weak solvent for silver halide. Ammonium chloride (Lumière and Seyewetz, 1904) and ammonium sulphate (F. Burki and L. Jenny, 1943) can be used though, in order to avoid the loss of ammonia gas from the developer, non-volatile amines may be preferred, such as ethylenediamine hydrochloride (P. W. Wittum, 1935). Potassium thiocyanate (P. Strauss, 1937) at about 1 g per litre may be used, or the sulphite concentration can be considerably increased (J. G. Capstaff, 1927).

The neutral, or slightly alkaline, phenylenediamine developers would be perfect if judged only on granularity, but these developers need a considerable increase in exposure. A number of factors lead to the view that development by the phenylenediamines is, to a large extent, physical (Lüppo-Cramer, 1936). It has been observed (F. Baldet, 1943) that in the neighbourhood of gamma 0·9, a sharp increase in the granularity of the image is manifested in these developers. An error of 30 seconds in the time of development or of 0·2°C in the temperature of the bath can cause the gamma to exceed the critical value.

Rather than choose a rapid, coarse-grained emulsion, whose high speed is largely sacrificed by using a fine-grain developer (which is always somewhat capricious), it is better to choose a slightly less rapid, finer-grained emulsion and to obtain its full emulsion speed by developing it in a solution of normal activity.

To summarise: fine grain developers may conveniently be classified into two general types: those of the first type are developers of low pH that contain no solvent other than sulphite and are termed medium fine grain developers. They act by retarded development accompanied by some physical development because the sulphite content is higher than is required for the preservative purpose alone. Those of the second type contain a silver halide solvent in addition to sulphite or bromide. The solvent may be the developing agent itself (p-phenylenediamine) or an additional solvent such as potassium thiocyanate. This type of fine grain developer is sometimes termed a super or ultra fine grain developer.

614. Medium Fine Grain Developers. The following developer (the Kodak D76 formula), has been extensively used for the development of motion-picture negatives and variable-density sound tracks, and, for the development of miniature negatives that often may require to be enlarged 10 to 15 diameters. A better-buffered variant (D76d) has been described (H. C. Carlton and J. I. Crabtree, 1930) which gives identical results when fresh (pH = 8·4) but which changes less rapidly on exposure to air. These developers are very susceptible to the influence of the soluble bromide formed by the reduction of the silver bromide.

	ID11 or D76	D76R (replenisher)	D76d
Metol	2 g	3 g	2 g
Sodium sulphite, anhydrous	100 g	100 g	100 g
Hydroquinone	5 g	7·5 g	5 g
Borax	2 g	20 g	8 g
Boric acid	—	—	8 g
Water to	1 litre	1 litre	1 litre

These developers owe their special properties to their very high sulphite concentration which, in the time necessary to reach a gamma of about 0·8 (being on average 12 minutes in a fresh bath at 18°C), dissolves an appreciable part of the silver bromide from each grain. The silver ions thus brought into solution are reduced and give rise to a silver deposit on the walls of the tank, etc., and to a sediment. The negatives are slightly fogged.

After developing about 20 ft of 35-mm negative per litre of the bath, the time of development should be increased by about 25 per cent.

If the replenisher is used, it should be added in quantities just sufficient to maintain the bath at constant volume. The bath should be rejected after adding a total quantity of replenisher equal to its initial volume.

The very high concentration of sulphite in these developers leads to a very rapid exhaustion of chrome-alum stop baths if the negatives are not briefly rinsed on leaving the developer.

Various methods of large-scale developing in two baths, achieving more economically the results given by D76, are described in § 618.

615. Ultra Fine Grain Developers. The addition of ammonium chloride (40 g/litre) to the Kodak D76 or Ilford ID11 formulae (§ 614) converts these medium fine grain developers of the non-solvent type to ultra fine grain developers of the solvent type but a considerable loss in emulsion speed results and exposures should be increased by approximately 50 per cent. Thiocyanates are much more efficient silver halide solvents and are used at a concentration of about 1 g per litre as in the Kodak DK20 formula:

Metol	5 g
Sodium sulphite, anhydrous	100 g
Sodium metaborate .	2 g
Potassium thiocyanate .	1 g
Potassium bromide .	0·5 g
Water to	1 litre
Development time .	20 min. (dish)
	16 min. (tank)

These solvent developers form finer grain images than those obtained from the non-solvent type of developer but Mason (1966) has summarised some of their disadvantages which are: (a) loss in sensitivity, (b) loss of resolution and sharpness, (c) dichroic fog formation with some fast negative emulsions, and (d) high fog formation with some fast emulsions.

p-Phenylenediamine developers, usually in combination with glycin, are used for obtaining ultra fine grain images. These developers produce the finest possible grain because they act mainly by physical development but require the greatest increase in exposure which limits their usefulness. A typical p-phenylenediamine developer formula is given below (V. B. Sease).

p-Phenylenediamine . .	10 g
Glycin	6–12 g
Sodium sulphite, anhydrous	90 g
Water to	1 litre
Development time . .	15 min.

Although this type of solvent developer produces a very fine grain image the following disadvantages should be noted: (a) considerable loss in sensitivity, exposures should be increased by 1 1/4 to 4 times those used for materials developed in conventional developers, (b) low contrast, (c) toxic developing agent is used, and (d) p-phenylenediamine has strong staining properties.

Attempts have been made to replace p-phenylenediamine by more suitable developing agents such as substituted p-phenylenediamines (Kodak U.S.P. 2,193,015) but these compounds are not quite as good as the parent compound for producing a very fine grain image. However formulae based on hydroxyethyl-o-aminophenol with or without glycin have been used (May and Baker Ltd.) for producing fine grain images similar to those from p-phenylenediamine developers.

616. High Contrast Developers. Developers, higher in contrast than the metol-hydroquinone contrast formula in § 612, are required for certain specialised purposes such as process work, general commercial work and development of aerial or X-ray films. These developers generally employ a high concentration of hydroquinone as the developing agent and are used at high pH values (up to about pH 12·5) to increase the developer activity. The following developer (Ilford ID13 or Kodak D153) is a typical high contrast two solution developer which should be mixed immediately before use.

(A)	Potassium metabisulphite .	25 g
	Hydroquinone . .	25 g
	Potassium bromide .	25 g
	Water to	1 litre

(B)	Potassium hydroxide . .	50 g
	Water to	1 litre
	Dilution	1 vol. A + 1 vol. B
	Development time . .	3 min.

This developer darkens very quickly and should be used once only. A further disadvantage is that it is very caustic and tends to break down gelatine when the temperature exceeds 20°C (68°F). The following developer (Ilford ID19 or Kodak D19b) which keeps better, is often used instead and is suitable for use in a tank for the development of a large number of negatives.

		replenisher
Metol	2·2 g	4 g
Sodium sulphite, anhydrous .	72 g	72 g
Hydroquinone . . .	8·8 g	16 g
Sodium carbonate, anhydrous	48 g	48 g
Potassium bromide . .	4 g	—
Sodium hydroxide . .	—	7·5 g
Water to	1 litre	1 litre
Development time .	5–8 min.	—

A developer giving infectious development (§ 564) is sometimes used for line, and coarse half-tone dot images. In this developer (Ansco AN79 or Kodak D85) most of the sulphite combines with the formalin resulting from the depolymerisation of paraformaldehyde and sodium hydroxide is formed in the reaction (§ 568).

$$(HCHO)n \rightarrow n.HCHO$$
$$HCHO + Na_2SO_3 + H_2O$$
$$\rightarrow CH_2(OH).SO_3Na + NaOH$$

Thus a source of alkali is present which maintains developer activity and the sulphite content is kept at a low level to aid infectious development.

Sodium sulphite, anhydrous	.	30 g
Paraformaldehyde . .	.	7·5 g
Potassium metabisulphite .	.	2·6 g
Boric acid . . .	.	7·5 g
Hydroquinone . . .	.	22·5 g
Potassium bromide . .	.	1·6 g
Water to	.	1 litre
Development time . .	.	2 min.

617. High Acutance Developers. The border effects which were described earlier (§ 563) are employed in high acutance developers. These are developers which are specially formulated to achieve a higher acutance or definition than is obtained in normal developers. The general conditions required for border effects in high acutance developers may be summarised as follows: (a) low concentration of the developing agent which leads to a local exhaustion of the developer in the high density areas, (b) low bromide concentration to enhance the effects of developer exhaustion, (c) low sulphite concentration so that the oxidised developing agent is not rendered innocuous by reaction with sulphite, (d) carefully controlled agitation; too little causes streamers and too much minimises border effects, and (e) thin fine grain emulsions.

A typical acutance developer formula is given below (W. Beutler).

Metol	.	5 g
Sodium sulphite, anhydrous	.	25 g
Sodium carbonate, anhydrous	.	25 g
Water to	.	1 litre
Dilution	.	1:10
Development time . .	.	7–10 min.

The main disadvantage of this type of developer is its susceptibility to aerial oxidation because of the low sulphite and developing agent concentrations. This can, however, be overcome to a certain extent either by mixing a concentrated stock solution and diluting immediately before use, or by making the developer in two solutions, one of which contains the developing agent and the sulphite and the other contains the sodium carbonate, each in half the stated total volume of solution, and mixing equal volumes of the solutions immediately before use.

High acutance developers can be used once only because they depend upon developer exhaustion for their action. It is generally recommended that no more than one 36 exposure 35 mm film should be developed in 600 ml. of the working strength developer.

618. Two-bath Developers. Development in two successive baths may be applied to achieve widely divergent, and opposed, ends.

It was very early applied for the correction of errors in exposure that became apparent at the moment that the image appeared (§ 601). Although this method of development is useful only in a limited field, an example will be described. Consider, as an extreme example, the expedient often recommended for increasing the development of the under-exposed shadows in a negative without making the density of the highlights too great. The negative is transferred to a dish of water that is vigorously rocked to dilute uniformly the developer carried over. The negative continues to develop, by virtue of the developer contained in the emulsion, except in the highlights where the developer is almost instantaneously exhausted. However, it would seem that this method is not always as effective as it is sometimes made out to be. The sensitometric experiments of J. I. Crabtree and H. A. Miller (1939) have indicated that, in a case where the process has been claimed to be efficient, the transferring of the half-developed negative into an inert solution (water, glycerine, alkaline buffer) has given a result that could be exactly equalled by reducing the time of development by 25 per cent.

Two-bath development is employed industrially to obtain a greater uniformity of results than can be achieved in a single replenished bath, and with a more economical use of the developer chemicals. On the one hand the two successive baths may differ only by the state of their exhaustion, but on the other hand they can be of very different composition.

In the extreme case, two baths can be used, neither being, properly speaking, a developer, the complete developer being formed in the emulsion layer by the mixture of the developing agent solution, with which it has been impregnated, and the alkali from the second bath.

The following methods were studied in connexion with the industrial, fine-grain processing of motion-picture, and miniature negatives (J. I. Crabtree, H. Parker, and H. D. Russell, 1933).

The first procedure consists of the use of two successive D76 developers (§ 614). The first bath is fresh and is maintained in practically new condition by topping it up to constant level with fresh developer. The film remains in the developer for a short time only. After 2 minutes in the fresh bath and 18 minutes in the second bath, both at 18°C, the same gamma (0·78) was obtained as resulted after 16 minutes in the fresh bath, the loss in speed being only 25 per cent, while the loss would have been 50 per cent had the film been developed entirely in the second, or used, bath. By rejecting the second bath and replacing it by the first bath, and using a new first bath, the cost of the chemicals was 33 per cent less than that for a single, replenished bath. By limiting the exhaustion of the second bath to 8 metres of cine film per litre (instead of 16 metres, in the above case), the consumption of chemicals was 33 per cent greater than in the case of a single bath, but the emulsion speed was 15 per cent greater.

The same workers studied the successive use of two developers of very different composition, the first (A) being a metol developer of moderate alkalinity ($pH = 9\cdot0$), and the second (B) being D76.

A gamma value of 0·74 was obtained on the experimental film at 18°C after 3 minutes' immersion in A followed by 12 minutes in B. At the

	A	B
Metol	2 g	2 g
Sodium sulphite, anhydrous .	100 g	100 g
Hydroquinone	—	5 g
Borax, crystalline . .	20 g	2 g
Water to . . .	1 litre	1 litre

start, the speed was the same as that in a single, fresh bath of D76. The first bath was maintained at a constant level by topping up with fresh solution. The solution carried over on the film served to replenish the second bath. After developing 16 metres of film per litre of bath, the loss in speed (30 per cent) was the same as that in D76 replenished with a volume of solution equal to that of the initial bath, and used to develop a total of 4·2 metres of film per litre of initial bath. However, the rate of development to the critical gamma was maintained constant.

Various workers have demonstrated the possibility of increasing the development of the shadows, while avoiding an excessive density in the highlights, by impregnating the emulsion with a sulphite solution of the developing agent and then transferring it to an alkaline solution. Sulphite is sometimes added to the alkaline solution to prevent a too-rapid oxidation of the developer diffusing into the bath, and bromide will appear in the solution as exhaustion proceeds (P. Joanovitch, 1907, A. Odencrants, 1922).

The sensitometric study of this method of development (J. I. Crabtree, H. Parker, and H. D. Russell, 1933) has shown an appreciable increase in useful emulsion speed and a sloping-off of the upper part of the characteristic curve. The maximum value of gamma is reached after 3 or 4 minutes in the second bath, this value being increased by a longer immersion in the first bath which allows the emulsion to absorb a greater quantity of developing agent. The development is produced almost entirely in the second bath. The first bath, which is unchanged by the film bathed in it, can be entirely used up.

The same workers studied the application of this method of working to fine-grain development in the case of motion-picture and miniature films. Since a sulphite solution of metol would develop without alkali (a gamma of 0·45 was reached after 16 minutes in the first bath) they slowed down its action, without changing the alkalinity, by adding sugar so that the image appeared in 4 minutes instead of 2 minutes.

The films used in their experiments reached a gamma of 0·52 at 18°C after 4 minutes in the A bath followed by 4 minutes in B. The graininess was the same as that given by D76, the fog being somewhat less than that found in D76, while the emulsion speed was about 40 per cent greater.

(A) Metol . . . . 5 g
Sodium sulphite, anhydrous . 100 g
Hydroquinone . . . 2 g
Sugar . . . . 100 g
Sodium bisulphite . . 5 g
Water to . . . 1 litre

$$pH = 7 \cdot 8$$

(B) Sodium sulphite, anhydrous . 100 g
Sodium carbonate, anhydrous 100 g
Potassium bromide . . 0·5 g
Potassium iodide . . 0·01 g
Water to . . . 1 litre

$$pH = 11 \cdot 4$$

The first and second baths should be replaced after processing 45 metres and 22·5 metres of 35-mm film per litre, respectively. The first bath is affected mainly by the accumulation of bromide washed out of the film, and resulting from the reduction of the silver bromide dissolved by the sulphite. The second bath becomes increasingly charged with developer. Variations in the temperature of the A bath affect the swelling of the emulsion, thus changing the amount of developing agent absorbed. This factor, as well as the time of immersion in the first bath, leads to a variation in the gamma obtained.

619. Tropical Developers. Various special precautions must be taken in hot climates. In the first place, development should not be deferred more than a few days, since the latent image sometimes suffers a gradual fading (regression) under the combined influence of high temperature and atmospheric *moisture*. Films are especially liable to this fading of the image. Next, the gelatine must be prevented from swelling excessively during the process; such swelling might lead to various troubles (melting, frilling, reticulation, etc.). Finally, sudden changes of temperature must be avoided with the swollen gelatine; these only increase the risk of accidents, and it is better to carry out the whole of the operations in baths at the surrounding temperature, even though it be high, than to use chilled baths for some parts of the process and warm water for others. In equatorial regions it is also advisable to carry out the work when the temperature is not so high, generally during the night.

It is well to call attention to the fact that methods which, in temperate and dry climates,

permit the easy handling of plates and films up to 95°F (35°C), often fail when employed in hot and humid climates, producing reticulation at temperatures hardly greater than 80°F(27°C). This anomaly may perhaps be due to the considerable quantity of water vapour absorbed by the gelatine before development.

In order to prevent the swelling of the gelatine without preliminary hardening, addition is made to the developer (and to any baths such as desensitizers used before development) of 10 per cent to 20 per cent of sodium sulphate (§ 594); or alcohol is substituted for a certain proportion of the water.

As the result of a systematic study of a great number of developers used at various temperatures up to 95°F(35°C), J. I. Crabtree (1917) recommended the following developer—

Sodium sulphite, anhydrous . . 50 g
p-Aminophenol hydrochloride . . 7 g
Sodium carbonate, anhydrous . . 50 g
Sodium sulphate, crystals . . 100 to 200 g
Water to . . . . 1 litre

The maximum quantity of sodium sulphate is employed only if the developer is at a temperature of about 95°F(35°C); at about 80°F (27°C) the minimum amount stated is quite enough. A slight reticulation should be produced only after 4 or 5 minutes' immersion in the developer, a time greatly in excess of the normal duration of development, in spite of the retardation due to the sulphate. Development takes twice as long with the lesser quantity of sulphate stated and three times with the larger quantity.

Although this developer has little tendency to give chemical fog, it may be necessary, especially at the higher temperatures, to add to it a small amount of potassium bromide.

A slightly acidified amidol developer without any special addition may be used at temperatures up to 80°F(27°C) and more, by reason of the very slight swelling of gelatine in acid baths, This developer may be adapted to temperatures up to 95°F(35°C) by the addition of sodium sulphate as follows (L. J. Bunel, 1924)—

Sodium sulphite, anhydrous . . 30 g
Potassium metabisulphite . . 10 g
Amidol . . . . . 5 g
Potassium bromide . . . 5 g
Lactic acid (medicinal) . . . 5 ml
Sodium sulphate, cryst. . . . 100 g
Water to . . . . 1 litre

At higher temperatures than 95°F(35°C), sodium sulphate, even in larger amounts, no longer serves to prevent excessive softening of the gelatine, and part of the water normally used for making up the developer must be replaced by alcohol. For temperatures up to about 105°F (41°C) a pre-hardening bath such as Ilford IH5 or the bath previously given (§ 608) is recommended.

Sodium sulphate decahydrate	.	200 g
Formalin	.	25 ml
Sodium carbonate, anhydrous	.	4·6 g
Water to	.	1 litre
Time of immersion . .	.	3 min.

After immersion in the hardening bath the film should be given a short wash prior to development.

The addition of hardening agents to the developer may also be made but the choice of suitable agents is very restricted. Inorganic hardening agents such as chrome alum cannot be used because they only harden gelatine in acidic solutions (pH ca. 4·5), and in alkaline solutions normally used for development the hydroxide is generally precipitated. Formaldehyde also cannot be used because it can causing fogging of the emulsion and in developers it is the the form of the bisulphite and is therefore not available for hardening the gelatine. The most suitable compounds are organic compounds such as dialdehydes or diketones (e.g. diacetyl, glutaraldehyde or acetonyl acetone).

Whatever the developer employed, rinse the developed negative very rapidly, and proceed either with temporary " fixing," according to § 604, or with fixing in a combined hardening and fixing bath (§ 645).

620. Ultra-rapid Development. In some special cases, e.g. in television, aerial photography, race-finish photography, and surgery under radiographic control, it is essential to be able to examine the image with the least possible delay that is compatible with obtaining an acceptable image. Since such results are only obtained to the detriment of the quality of the image, this method of working should be employed only in cases of extreme urgency.

One of the means employed in order to accelerate development is the use of high temperatures. Experiments have been made with special emulsions that can be developed at 50°–60°C. Another way is to use very alkaline developers in which, at 25°C, the emulsion can remain for only a few seconds before it starts to disintegrate. Then there is two-bath development (§ 618) in which one of the factors causing

acceleration is probably the heat released in the emulsion layer by the formation of phenolates.

To develop in 10 seconds, Jaenicke (1937) has suggested plunging the negative for 2 seconds into a 5 per cent solution of hydroquinone containing 2·5 per cent of anhydrous sodium sulphite, and then for 2 seconds into a 30 per cent potassium hydroxide solution containing 0·1 per cent of potassium bromide and 1 part of safranine in 5,000 of the caustic bath to avoid aerial fog.

The negative material can be soaked in a hydroquinone solution, and then dried, before exposing it. In this case, development can be effected by immersing the prepared negative for 1 second in the alkaline solution. By dispensing with an intermediate rinse and proceding directly to an alkaline hypo fixer, the fixing time could be reduced to 5 seconds (W. Jaenicke, 1940).

Better results are obtained by developing for 1 minute in an alkaline-hydroquinone process developer (§ 616) to which 10 ml of a 1/1,000 safranine solution and 10 ml of formalin are added. On the other hand a developer for under-exposed negatives may be used, to which, if it is for use in a continuous-processing machine, 10 g of sodium hydroxide are added per litre (H. Parker and J. I. Crabtree, 1936). The image is developed to a gamma value of about 0·55 and the loss of emulsion speed amounts to 10 to 15 per cent.

J. I. Crabtree and H. D. Russell (1944) particularly recommend the following method. After hardening the emulsion (§ 608) which requires 3 minutes, the image is developed in 15 to 30 seconds at 30°C in—

Methyl alcohol	. .	. 50 ml
Metol	. .	. 14 g
Sodium sulphite, anhydrous	.	50 g
Hydroquinone	. .	. 14 g
Sodium hydroxide	.	. 17·5 g
Potassium bromide	.	. 9 g
Water to	. .	. 1 litre

In cases of extreme urgency, the negatives may be examined after a brief immersion in the stop bath, or after iodizing (§ 604).

When it is necessary to make prints, fixing should be carried out in a warm, agitated bath. After a brief rinse, the wet negative should be enfolded in a sheet of thin cellulose-acetate film so as to avoid contact, during printing, between the paper and the fixing solution. On the other hand the negative can be projection-printed using an enlarger with a carrier, without glass, which can hold the wet negative.

More recently many rapid access systems

have been designed for the ultra-rapid processing of both negative and positive materials. A rapid access system may be defined as a system which gives a total (dry to dry) processing cycle of less than one minute.

By using an active developer at high temperature and pH it is possible to reduce development times of negative materials to less than one second (C. Orlando, 1958, L. S. Fortmiller et al., 1963, and G. E. Duffy, 1962). A typical rapid access developer formula based on metol-hydroquinone at high pH is given below (C. Orlando, 1958).

Metol	.	.	.	.	13 g
Sodium sulphite, anhydrous		.			80 g
Hydroquinone		.		.	26 g
Sodium hydroxide		.		.	26 g
Benzotriazole 1%		.		.	200 ml
Water to .		.		.	1 litre
Development time		.		.	0·2 seconds
					at 185°F (85°C)

To withstand the processing conditions (short time at high temperature) special rapid access films which are thinly coated and specially hardened must be used together with properly designed rapid access equipment that can apply and control the application of the small volumes of solutions in the time available. A few of the basic techniques used in rapid access processing are outlined in succeeding paragraphs, but for further details the more specialised literature on the subject should be consulted.

Cell Processors (K. H. Lohse and M. B. Skolnik, 1961). Small volumes of processing solutions are pumped into a narrow space (0·001–0·003 in.) between the emulsion and the processing device. The film is located over a sealing frame and held in position by a pressure plate. Solutions are metered by a pump into the capillary chamber and remain in the chamber by capillary forces until forced out by other solutions or air, to complete the processing cycle. A dry to dry processing time of approximately 5 seconds is possible with this device: development 1·5 seconds, fixation 0·5 seconds, washing 1 second, and drying 2 seconds.

Viscous Layer Application (P. A. Hermle and H. D. Lowry, 1961). In this system, which is employed in the Kodak Viscomat Processor, a viscous layer of the processing solution is applied to the film surface by a slot applicator or some other coating device (e.g. trough, roller etc.). After processing, the viscous layer is removed from the emulsion surface by a high velocity water spray and dried by a Venturi type air squeegee. Conventional high activity developers and fixers or monobaths may be used for viscous processing provided the solutions are made viscous by the addition of a thickening agent such as carboxymethylcellulose, starch or agar-agar. These thickening agents are generally called *gums*. Apart from the advantage of processing times of less than one minute, viscous processing has many advantages over solution processing, some of which may be briefly summarised as follows (A. Cronig, 1966).

1. Smaller, simpler processing equipment may be designed.

2. Processing is more uniform and requires less supervision.

3. More rigorous environmental parameters can be met, such as processing in aircraft, satellites etc.

4. Incorporated chemistry is possible.

5. Diffusion transfer processing can be carried out (§ 673).

6. Agitation patterns or flow streaks are reduced.

Porous Plate Applicators. The processing solutions are applied to the emulsion surface by pumping through a porous plate such as sintered stainless steel, in contact with the emulsion (R. P. Mason, 1961). Similar porous rollers may also be used for applying solutions. In this method of application hollow rollers have radially distributed holes around their circumference and a meniscus of the solution is formed between the roller and the film surface (E. D. Seymour, 1958).

Spray Applicators. Atomised droplets of the various processing solutions are sprayed onto the emulsion surface at high velocity (R. C. M. Smith and E. R. Townley, 1959). This may be carried out with the film moving past the spray or by spraying successive areas of the film in a discontinuous manner. Because of the fine spray and the likelihood of aerial oxidation, the developers used must contain a high sulphite content. A dry to dry access time of approximately 10 seconds may be obtained by this process.

Roller Applicators. Non-porous rollers may also be used for applying processing solutions. The film is guided over the top half of the roller surface, emulsion side in contact with the roller. The bottom section of the roller dips in and picks up the processing solution (J. C. Barnes and L. J. Fortmiller, 1963).

Normally two rollers are used, the first applies the developer and the second applies the fixer. The film then passes over a spacer roller into a wash tank before drying. Access times of 1 to 10 seconds can be achieved with this system. By the appropriate choice of the number of applicator rollers, their speed and direction of rotation, films may be processed at 100 ft per minute (S. L. Hersh and F. Smith, 1961).

Saturated Web Applicators. Generally this method is not as rapid as those previously discussed but it is very convenient because it does not require pumps, solution containers and complex equipment. In operation the web is pre-soaked with the processing solution such as a monobath and brought into intimate contact with the emulsion surface by winding under tension around a portion of the circumference of a drum. After processing, the web is stripped from the developed film and discarded. In the Kodak Bimat System the web is not discarded after use but is in the form of a gelatin-coated film in which a positive image is formed by diffusion transfer. Thus both a positive and a negative are obtained. The transfer film (web) is pre-soaked with an active developer containing a silver halide solvent and, instead of silver halide, the gelatine contains a nucleating agent such as finely divided silver. On intimate contact of the exposed negative film with the pre-soaked transfer film, the unexposed silver halide of the negative is transferred to the transfer film by the silver solvent where, in the presence of the nuclei, it is reduced to silver. A similar process is employed in the Polaroid system. These processes are of obvious advantage for airborne processing as solutions are not used (i.e. semi-wet processes).

Most of these rapid access systems use the total-loss method of processing i.e. the solutions are used once only and then discarded. This simplifies the apparatus because replenishment is obviously not required. Monobaths (§ 621) are frequently used for further simplification of the equipment but not all the systems are suitable for a monobath process because of the problems associated with deposition of silver in fine slots or capillaries. Where a two-solution technique is necessary a rapid fixer based on ammonium thiosulphate is generally used.

For the visual display of information such as radar or oscillograph traces, a suitable rapid access system may be coupled with a camera and viewer. Using such camera-processor-viewers information can be recorded and displayed in less than one second, when drying the film is not essential before viewing.

621. Monobaths. It is possible to carry out, in a single bath, the development and fixing of a negative plate or film (papers cannot be treated this way without heavy fog resulting). This fact was known to W. D. Richmond (1889). It is, however, only in recent years that it has been possible to obtain satisfactory results this way.

G. Haist (1966) has proposed the following monobath formula which, with some modifications, may be used for the combined development and fixation of a variety of negative materials:

Water	750 ml
Sodium sulphite, anhydrous .	50 g
Phenidone	4 g
Hydroquinone . . .	12 g
Sodium hydroxide . . .	4 g
Sodium thiosulphate, crystalline .	110 g
Glutyraldehyde 25% . .	8 ml
Water to	1 litre
Processing time . . .	7 min.

In preparing this monobath it is recommended that after the Phenidone has been added a portion of the hydroquinone followed by the sodium hydroxide should then be added. After a clear solution has been obtained, the remainder of the hydroquinone should be added followed by the other ingredients, in the order stated. This procedure ensures that the Phenidone dissolves readily in the alkaline solution and the hydroquinone prevents the aerial oxidation of Phenidone in the high pH solution. Glutyraldehyde is included in the formula as a hardening agent.

This monobath was originally formulated for processing Kodak Verichrome Pan film giving almost the same emulsion speed and contrast obtained with conventional processing in Kodak D76 developer, § 614). For processing other films the modifications outlined in the previous section on monobaths (§ 549) may be used. In this formula contrast may be reduced by the addition of glacial acetic acid or increased by increasing the quantity of sodium hydroxide. Contrast may also be varied by altering the thiosulphate content (§ 549).

The monobath can stand for several days after use without ill-effect other than the formation of a sediment of silver.

For the ultra-rapid processing of high speed films (§ 620) a monobath has been formulated which affords a comparable emulsion speed, in

2·5 seconds at 120°F (49°C), with that obtained in conventional Kodak D19 development. A higher fog level and a slightly lower contrast was, however, also obtained (L. Corben, C. Bloom, D. Willoughby and A. Shepp, 1966):

Potassium sulphite, anhydrous	20 g
Antimony potassium tartrate	40 g
Phenidone	3 g
Hydroquinone	60 g
α-Thioglycerol	150 ml
Water to	1 litre
Potassium hydroxide	to pH 12·65
Processing time (120°F)	2·5 seconds

This ultra-rapid monobath employs an organic fixing agent (α-thioglycerol) in place of the more common thiosulphate. Antimony potassium tartrate is included as a stabilizer. It is claimed that this monobath does not form a sludge and may be kept at 120° for at least 7 days with no deterioration.

622. Tanning Developers. Certain developing agents can cause tanning of the gelatine of the emulsion (§§ 573–575). This process is favoured by a low sulphite conent of the developer as it is the developer oxidation products which cause the hardening, accompanied by staining of the gelatine. Under optimum conditions tanning is proportional to the quantity of silver reduced and can be used to obtain relief images by dissolving away the unhardened gelatine in warm water. For the formation of relief images exposure must be made through the back of the negative material to avoid detachment of the image during the washing process. The relief images may be dyed and the dye transferred to a receiving sheet. This process forms the basis of the dye transfer method of making colour prints. Other applications are given in §§ 573–575.

Kodak D175 is a typical tanning developer which uses pyrogallol as the tanning agent.

(A)	Pyrogallol	4 g
	Sodium sulphite, anhydrous	5 g
	Water to	1 litre
(B)	Sodium carbonate, anhydrous	28 g
	Water to	1 litre
	Dilution	1 Vol. A 1 Vol. B

The keeping properties of this developer are not good, the stock solutions A and B should, therefore, be mixed immediately before use.

623. Chromogenic Developers. Although these developers are mainly employed in the processing of modern non-substantive colour films they are also of use in obtaining special effects by re-replacing the silver image of a black and white material by a coloured image. A representative chromogenic developer is:

Developer:

Diethyl-*p*-phenylenediamine hydrochloride	2 g
Sodium carbonate, anhydrous	30 g
Sodium sulphite, anhydrous	1 g
Potassium bromide	1 g
Hydroxylamine hydrochloride	1 g
Water to	1 litre

Magenta Colour Former:

p-nitrophenylacetonitrile	0·5 g
Acetone	12 ml
Industrial methylated spirits (colourless)	100 ml

Cyan Colour Former:

2,4-Dichloro-*β*-naphthol 1% in industrial methylated spirits

Yellow Colour Former:

o-Chloroacetanilide 1% in industrial methylated spirits

Blue Colour Former:

α-Naphthol 0·7% in industrial methylated spirits.

For use 10 mls of the colour former solution are added per 100 mls of developer solution. By mixing the colour former solutions a variety of shades can be obtained. The developer should be discarded after use. After fixing in the normal way, the silver image formed together with the dye image may be removed by a potassium ferricyanide bleach solution e.g. Farmers Reducer (§ 691). It is also possible to use this chromogenic developer on a processed black and white film or print by bleaching the silver image in a potassium ferricyanide bleach containing bromide, washing and then colour developing.

624. Metal Ion Developers. Inorganic developing agents such as ferrous oxalate (§ 535) have been superseded by organic developing agents. However recent inorganic developers employing a metal ion, such as iron or titanium and a modern chelating (sequestering) agent, afford results comparable with conventional organic developers. A formula of this type has been published by G. M. Haist, J. R. King, A. A. Rasch and J. I. Crabtree (1956):

Titanium trichloride (20% solution)	75 ml
EDTA (tetra sodium salt)	100 g
Sodium acetate, anhydrous	20 g
Potassium bromide	4 g
Water to	1 litre
Hydrochloric acid	to pH 4·0

This developer has given good results with cine positive film using a 5 minute development time at 68°F (20°C). It gives higher emulsion speed with a shorter developing time than conventional developers. For the development of negative films it may be advisable to dilute the developer and to increase the concentration of potassium bromide.

These inorganic developers offer the interesting possibility of regeneration by electrolytic methods.

625. Physical Developers. Physical development, which consists in the deposition of nascent silver, formed in the developer, on the nuclei of the latent image, and which is the normal method employed for the development of the image in the wet-collodion process, is also applicable to gelatine-bromide emulsions. As a rule, however, the method has no advantages over ordinary chemical development. The method of physical development is not always applicable to ortho- or panchromatic emulsions, nor to ordinary emulsions after desensitization, because the dyes sometimes prevent development (Lumière and Seyewetz, 1924).

The precipitation of silver may be brought about in solutions which are alkaline, neutral, or acid. One of the most commonly employed methods is that of Lüppo-Cramer (1903, 1923).

The stock solution is prepared as follows—

Metol	.	.	15 to 20 g
Citric acid .	.	.	100 g
Sodium citrate	.	.	15 g
Distilled water to	.	.	1 litre

The formation of mildew in this solution may be prevented by the addition of a small quantity of phenol. When required for use, take 100 ml of this solution and add from 3 to 10 ml of a 10 per cent solution of silver nitrate. Development is very slow. As soon as the developer becomes turbid it must be replaced by a fresh quantity.

Plates of recent manufacture must be used and the exposures given must be large. One condition of success is that all dishes employed must be quite clean; it is best to use a glass dish which has been very carefully cleaned.

It has been proposed (A. Schmidt, 1896) that when a plate has been found to be over-exposed chemical development should be stopped at once by washing in water, the plate being then treated by a physical developer.

Luppo-Cramer (1921) noted that physical development is accelerated, and does not require a heavy over-exposure, when the silver bromide has been superficially iodized, the disturbance of the grain surface allowing access of the developer to the latent-image specks that are formed in the interior of the grains (denudation of the latent-image nuclei). This method has been applied to miniature negatives for physical development before fixing in order to obtain fine-grain images (A. F. Odell, 1933). The negative should be given double the exposure that would be required for normal development. This loss in speed could be largely avoided by prolonging the development, but this would adversely affect the granularity.

The iodization is achieved by immersing the negative for a maximum time of 60 seconds in a solution containing 1 per cent of potassium iodide and 2·5 per cent of anhydrous sodium sulphite. The negative should then be well rinsed.

The developer is prepared immediately before use by dissolving 1·5 g of amidol in 800 ml of water and adding 200 ml of the following stock solution—

Sodium sulphite, anhydrous (20 per cent solution)	400 ml
Silver nitrate (4 per cent solution) . .	500 ml
Sodium thiosulphate (hypo) . . .	150 g

The hypo is added after the precipitate of silver sulphite has redissolved in the excess of sodium sulphite. The pH of the solution should be between 9·2 and 9·3. It may be increased, if necessary, to bring it to the correct value by small additions of very dilute ammonia solution. If the pH cannot be checked, a quantity of borax, equal in weight to the silver nitrate, should be added (F. R. McQuown, 1939).

The development, which is complete in about 30 minutes, is accompanied by some chemical development. The straight-line portion of the characteristic curve is slightly longer than in the case of chemical development (P. V. Turner, 1938). The image has a light grey appearance, so that, after fixing, it appears as a positive when viewed by reflected light against a dark background.

The possibility of developing after fixation was established in 1858 for wet-collodion plates by Young and in 1894 for gelatine-bromide plates by Kogelmann.

The negatives should be well over-exposed, more so for materials of high emulsion speed. The fixing bath should be made alkaline, or sulphite should be added to limit the tendency of the thiosulphate to attack the silver forming the latent image.

The following procedures (A. and L. Lumière, and A. Seyewetz, 1911; 1924) yield silver and mercury images respectively. The negative is fixed in a 30 per cent solution of sodium thiosulphate to which 1 per cent of concentrated (20 per cent solution) ammonia solution has been added. After a maximum of 5 minutes the fixed negative is washed in several changes of ammoniacal water, then, for the last time, in plain water. After the fixing is complete, all operations can be carried out in white light.

The developer is prepared, immediately before use, by mixing 5 volumes of one of the A solutions with 1 volume of the corresponding B solution—

		Silver	Mercury
(A)	Sodium sulphite, anhydrous .	180 g	180 g
	Silver nitrate, 10 per cent solution	75 ml	—
	Mercuric bromide . .	—	9 g
	Distilled water to . .	1 litre	1 litre
(B)	Sodium sulphite, anhydrous .	20 g	20 g
	p-Phenylenediamine (free base)	20 g	—
	Metol	—	20 g
	Distilled water to . .	1 litre	1 litre

The image appears slowly and reaches a printable gamma only after several hours, the bath being renewed every hour. The image is light grey by reflection and grey-violet by transmitted light. After developing for 30 minutes, an image of sufficient contrast for printing can be obtained by intensification.

An old negative, from which the mercury has evaporated, can be restored by developing it again (H. Leffman, 1923).

The "classical" physical developers given above all suffer from the disadvantage that they are unstable and spontaneous precipitation of silver (i.e. precipitation on nuclei in solution) occurs after approximately 1 to 30 minutes. This makes them very difficult to use in practice. A further disadvantage is that the classical physical developers are relatively slow acting and attempts to increase their activity by raising the temperature or increasing the concentration of silver ions makes the spontaneous precipitation of silver occur still more

readily. Recently, however, it has been discovered that the inclusion of a cationic surfactant such as dodecylamine acetate (Armac 12D, Armour Industrial Chemical Co.) to these developers inhibits the spontaneous precipitation of silver (H. Jonker, A. Molenaar and C. Dippel, 1969). The solubility of the cationic surfactant is aided by the addition of a non-ionic surfactant such as Lissapol N (I.C.I. Ltd.).

Metol	.	.	.	.	8·6 g
Silver nitrate	.	.	.	.	1·7 g
Citric acid, crystalline	.	.	21·0 g
Armac 12D, 10% solution	.	.	2 ml
Lissapol N, 10% solution	.	.	2 ml
Distilled water to	.	.	.	1 litre

The inclusion of the surfactants increased the the half-life (the time after which the initial rate of development is reduced by one half) from 12 minutes for the developer containing no surfactants, to 300 minutes. Also it is possible to increase the quantity of silver nitrate in the above formula by a factor of 5 to obtain a higher development rate, and a half-life of 30 minutes, whereas in the corresponding formula with no surfactants present the developer half-life was one minute and was, therefore, impractical.

H. Jonker and co-workers also published formulae for high speed stabilized physical developers based on the ferrous/ferric ion system:

Ferrous ammonium sulphate, crystalline	.	.	.	78·4 g
Ferric nitrate, crystalline	.	.	32·3 g
Silver nitrate	.	.	.	8·5 g
Citric acid, crystalline	.	.	21·0 g
Armac 12D, 10% solution	.	.	2 ml
Lissapol N, 10% solution	.	.	2 ml
Distilled water to	.	.	.	1 litre

By doubling the concentration of silver nitrate it is possible to develop a latent image in a few seconds, but the developer is less stable; the half-life is reduced from 120 days to 8 hours. Apart from the stability of these developers and the resulting ease of use, they may be replenished by the addition of silver nitrate, ferrous ammonium sulphate, and ferrous oxalate.

CHAPTER XXX

DESENSITIZING OF PHOTOGRAPHIC EMULSIONS

626. Use of coloured developers. 627. Loss in sensitivity of emulsions impregnated with developer —effect of developer oxidation products. 628. Desensitizers—phenosafranine—effect of concentration—staining action—latent image destruction—mechanisms of desensitization—aurantia —pina-white—qualitol. 629. Desensitizing practice—properties of ideal desensitizers. 630. Desensitizing power—definition and measurement—variation with: emulsion type, quantity of desensitizer adsorbed and type of desensitizer—effect of anti-halo backing. 631. Desensitization before and during development—pre-baths—addition to developers—increase in rate of development—removal of stain.

626. Use of Coloured Developers. Carey-Lea, as far back as 1877, showed that after immersing a photographic plate in ferrous oxalate developer it was possible, without risk of fog, to illuminate the darkroom much more brightly than would have been possible during the handling of the same plate when dry. This effect was attributed to the orange-red coloration of the developer, and little attention was paid to it, since the emulsions were so insensitive that in all cases a bright illumination could be used.

About 1889 various attempts were made to introduce into photographic practice the use of developers which had been coloured red by the addition of certain dyes, these dyes being subsequently destroyed in an acid fixing bath (coralline, croceine). The method, however, was not successful, since the dyes transmitted both blue and violet light. In 1900 A. and L. Lumière and A. Seyewetz, with the same object in view, recommended the use of an orange-coloured compound, magnesium picrate, which allows the development to be observed at a distance of about 18 in. from a candle or at about 5 ft from a 10-watt lamp, provided development is sufficiently rapid and the plate remains covered by a depth of developer of about ½ in. If these distances are doubled, it is possible to remove the negative from the bath and examine it very quickly by transmitted light. This method of working, although it afforded interesting demonstrations, was not used in practice.

627. Loss in Sensitivity of Emulsions Impregnated with Developer. After the use of organic developing agents had become general, it was frequently pointed out that after the developing bath had thoroughly impregnated the emulsion a considerable lowering of sensitivity took place,

which could not be explained in these cases by any coloration of the bath. In 1901 Lüppo-Cramer carried out some experiments in this direction (using the different developing agents) and discovered that this action occurred with nearly all the most common developers (with the exception of hydroquinone), both in plain and alkaline solutions, and that sulphite tended to reduce the effect. In 1920 the same worker found a very marked reduction in the sensitivity of photographic emulsions (reduced to 1/50th or 1/100th of the original value) after they had been bathed for about 1 minute in a pure solution of diaminophenol-hydrochloride of from 0·02 to 0·05 per cent strength, although no reduction in the latent image resulted from this treatment. An analogous effect may be obtained by the addition of this product to a hydroquinone developer; it was soon recognized that this *desensitizing* was due to traces of oxidation products, which are rapidly formed by the action of the air on dilute solutions of this developer.

It has since been recognized that ferrous oxalate developer is also a very efficient desensitizer.

628. Desensitizers. During further experiments on this phenomenon, Lüppo-Cramer discovered, several months later, the remarkable desensitizing properties of phenosafranine, a violet-red dye of considerable colouring power.

It was soon shown that the desensitizing properties of phenosafranine are possessed by various safranines and, in varying degree, by different substances of similar constitution. The red colour of some of these substances might lead to the supposition that the protection from fog is due to the absorption of the active radiations by the dye impregnating the emulsion. This is not the case, however, for the efficiency of these desensitizers is practically as great with panchromatic as with ordinary emulsions, and, secondly, a sensitive plate exposed behind a cell containing a solution of the dye, even in concentration greater than that used for desensitization, and under a layer of greater thickness than that of the developing bath, develops an intense fog. This is due to the fact that the red safranines absorb very little of the violet radiations. It was discovered not long afterwards that certain violet dyes belonging to the safranine family were capable of acting as efficient desensitizers.

The first experiments were carried out with 1:200 solutions, in which the sensitive plate was bathed for 1 minute. At the end of this time the darkroom may be illuminated as brightly as required, provided the blue and violet radiations are absorbed by a yellow or orange filter. A yellow light source of feeble intensity may be brought quite close to the dish in which the development is taking place, and it is even possible to examine the negative by transmitted light as frequently and for as long as required during the course of development.

Almost immediately it was shown that desensitizing could be brought about even with the much more dilute solutions of 1 : 20,000 and 1 : 50,000, so long as moderate intensity of illumination is observed in the darkroom, either as a bath before development or in the developer itself.

With either of the two methods of desensitizing, safranine prevents or reduces considerably the development fog, so that it is possible, when necessary, to extend development beyond the limits usually fixed by the growth of the fog, and also to use a much more alkaline developer. Finally, hydroquinone developer, which works somewhat slowly in the normal state, acquires almost the properties of a rapid developer, such as metol.

The only defect of safranine is its strong staining action, which causes a considerable coloration of the fingers (more particularly the nails) and of the gelatine, especially if it has been used in the concentrations which were first recommended. The coloration of the gelatine is removed for the most part during the subsequent manipulations and the washing, any defects in this last process being very clearly shown by the unequal coloration of the different parts of the plate. This coloration, however, even when it is fairly intense or irregular, does not affect printing adversely, and may therefore be ignored.

The most useful employment of desensitizing is emphatically with panchromatic plates.

All desensitizers are not, however, suited to all emulsions which are panchromatic, or sensitive to infra-red, probably owing to reactions between the colour sensitizers and the desensitizer. The effect of a given dye on a given emulsion varies greatly from one spectral region to another.

Many contradictions may be noted in publications on the properties of desensitizers owing to the use in experiments of impure or wrongly labelled products. A large number of substances which are energetic desensitizers in plain aqueous solutions are unusable in practice, the desensitization being annulled or decreased during development by the action of one or other of the components of the developer; tests of a desensitizer must therefore include a practical development test in an abundance of yellow light (Miss F. M. Hamer, 1931).

The desensitizers are all weak oxidizers. They can destroy or considerably diminish the latent image in a solution containing also an acid and bromide, the silver formed by light being re-converted to silver bromide. This may be demonstrated (H. Luppo-Cramer, 1924) in the following way. If a uniformly fogged plate is treated with a solution containing a desensitizer and potassium bromide and is then dried without rinsing, it will give, on subsequent exposure, a direct positive image because destruction of the latent image formed in the fogging exposure occurs where the plate receives a second exposure in the presence of the oxidizing desensitizer. This phenomenon is sometimes described as "sensitized Herschel effect".

On the other hand, it has been observed (H. Luppo-Cramer, 1934) that, with certain rapid emulsions, an intensification of the latent image occurs when the desensitized emulsion is exposed to yellow or green light. Desensitization is not effective towards X-ray exposures.

The latent-image destruction that occurs on exposing the desensitized emulsion is brought about most efficiently by red and infra-red radiation, and for this reason it is unwise to use a red light for the inspection of desensitized material. Although a yellow safelight screen usually transmits red and infra-red light, the extension of the transmission into the yellow and green parts of the spectrum, to which the eye is relatively more sensitive, allows the total amount of light to be reduced, without inconvenience, so that the amount of red light transmitted becomes small.

Latent-image destruction occurs if there is a long delay between desensitization of the emulsion and its subsequent development.

The mechanism of desensitization has not yet been completely worked out. Many substances that act as desensitizers for silver bromide emulsions behave as sensitizers for silver-iodide emulsions (these silver-iodide emulsions being only of theoretical interest). Again, a number of cyanine dyes that are used in silver-bromide emulsions as sensitizers towards red light exert on the same emulsion a slight desensitizing action with respect to blue light. Certain substances that act as sensitizers are converted to desensitizers by the inclusion of a nitro ($-NO_2$) group in the molecule. It may be stated, however, that a substance will act as a desensitizer only when it is adsorbed to the silver halide grain.

The investigations of V. Sihvonen (1928) and of E. Bauer (1928) on the mechanism of photochemical reactions lead to the view that the light energy received by the silver bromide is transferred to the desensitizer and that only the desensitizer is reduced i.e. the desensitizer traps photoelectrons and inhibits their combination with silver ions which is required for formation of a latent image. Under normal conditions the reduced desensitizer would be directly regenerated by atmospheric oxidation. This affords an explanation of why a very small quantity of desensitizer can protect a relatively large quantity of silver bromide during a prolonged exposure of low intensity, while the degree of protection is reduced for exposures of high intensity, and no protection at all is afforded in the absence of oxygen (M. Blau and M. Wambacher, 1934, and M. Blau, 1935), as, for example, in a high vacuum or in an inert atmosphere.

Another mechanism that has been suggested is the trapping of *positive holes* by the desensitizer, so assisting their recombination with electrons and inhibiting latent image formation (B. H. Carroll, 1961, V. I. Saunders, R. W. Tyler and W. West, 1963). (Where *positive holes* are formed after excitation and consequent escape of a photoelectron from the conduction band, of the silver halide.) It has also been suggested that the desensitizer is a carrier of photolytic bromine which in the absence of the desensitizer can escape from the grain (W. F. Berg, A. V. Borin, P. I. Logak, V. Sh. Telyakava and M. V. Mishakova, 1962).

The discovery of desensitization led a number of experimenters to seek further desensitizers both among the compounds already known, especially those dyes whose chemical constitutions were similar to those of the safranines, and the desensitizing oxidation products of developers, and among new substances that were specially prepared.

Two inorganic substances have been found to have desensitizing properties, mercuric cyanide (H. Meyer and R. Walter, 1926) and iron nitrososulphide, $NaFe_4$ $(NO)_7S_3$ (J. Duclaux, 1935), but are of little practical interest. Mercuric cyanide causes an appreciable destruction of latent image and often gives rise to an intense fogging.

Besides the safranines, to which reference has already been made, a number of dyes were found to have desensitizing properties, for example, rhoduline red, auramine, chrysoidine, fuchsine (H. Luppo-Cramer), methylene blue, etc. However, the desensitizing action is often accompanied by other, undesirable features which limit the practical value of the substance. The following list includes those desensitizers, which, as well as the safranines, have been found to be of practical use.

Aurantia (A. and L. Lumière and A. Seyewetz, 1921) is one of the few desensitizers which can be added to a hydroquinone developer without precipitation. Its desensitizing action is not very powerful and, used at a concentration of 0·2 per cent, it stains the gelatine an orange-yellow colour. Care should be taken when using this desensitizer not to allow even a dilute solution to come into contact with the skin since it has been found to cause dermatitis.

Pinacryptol Yellow was introduced in 1922 by R. Schuloff and E. Koenig. It consists of the methylsulphate of 1-methyl-2 (3-nitrostyryl) -6-ethoxyquinoline which yields a slightly coloured but non-staining solution. It is very energetic as a desensitizer, particularly when used with panchromatic plates, but it cannot be added to developers containing sulphite since this decomposes it.

Pinacryptol Green (B. Homolka, 1925), or 1:3-diamino-phenyldiazonium hydrochloride, a deep green solution that does not stain. As a desensitizer it is as effective as the safranines with respect to non-colour sensitive emulsions and is slightly better than the safranines for many panchromatic emulsions, but it gives rise to some veil even on developing in total darkness. It is not recommended for use when development is to be carried out in a very alkaline developer, in which case the gelatine becomes irregularly stained a deep grey colour. The solution of pinacryptol green should not be exposed to daylight.

Pina-white (B. Wendt, 1928) is a colourless desensitizer that is used in a concentration of 0·2 to 1 per cent usually together with 4 per cent sodium sulphite and 0·2 per cent potassium bromide. It consists of anthraquinone 1 : 7 disodium sulphonate. It is more active than safranine on panchromatic emulsions, and can be used in the developer without any precipitation. It sometimes gives rise to some veil.

Qualitol (J. D. Kendall, 1937) which is the methyliodide of diquinalylethylene gives a slightly coloured solution that does not stain. It is a very efficient desensitizer for panchromatic emulsions and does not cause fog.

Among other sensitizers which have been described but which do not appear to have been made commercially are the azocyanines (F. M. Hamer, 1924) and the non-staining isophenosafranines (I. G. Farbenindustrie, 1927).

629. Desensitizing Practice. The inspection of an image during development is often considered desirable in order to alter the time of development when the brightness range of the subject is greater (or less) than average, or when doubt exists as to whether the exposure given in the camera was correct. However, the level of illumination permissible during the development of a panchromatic emulsion is quite inadequate to allow any useful examination of the image. Thus, it is only by desensitizing that this inspection can be made possible. Desensitizing offers, moreover, the advantage that the possibility of the incidence of aerial fogging is reduced.

An ideal desensitizer should possess the following properties. It should completely remove the sensitivity of the silver bromide emulsion without attacking the latent image and without causing veil. It should be sufficiently soluble to allow a stock solution to be prepared, preferably without the aid of solvents. It should be stable both in the dry state and in solution, and its *desensitizing power* should not be appreciably reduced by the various chemicals usually found in developers. It should be compatible with the dye in the antihalation backing. The desensitizing solution should allow a large number of plates or films to be treated in succession and, after fixation the desensitizer should be readily removable by washing, hence it should not adsorb to gelatine. It should not be toxic and it should be readily obtainable at a reasonable price.

630. Desensitizing Power. The term *desensitizing power* is applied to the ratio of the sensitivities of an emulsion measured before and after desensitization. This ratio varies according to the type of emulsion used and, for the same type of emulsion, according to the spectral value of the light used in making the measurement. For example, on treating in the same way different non-colour-sensitive plates O. Bloch (1933) found that the degree of desensitization increased as the average diameter of the emulsion grains became larger, the desensitizing power rising from 230 for a fine grain emulsion (average grain diameter 0·2μ) to 3,500 for a rapid, coarse-grained emulsion (average grain diameter 0·94μ). The oxidation products of developers usually have only a negligible influence on the colour sensitivity. Probably as the result of reactions between the colour sensitizing dye and the desensitizer, the effect of a given desensitizer often varies when used on panchromatic and infra-red plates of different manufacture, and the various desensitizers vary considerably in their effect on a given emulsion. The colour sensitivity is usually reduced more than the natural sensitivity. Thus under working conditions where, for a given panchromatic emulsion, the desensitizing power is about 100 for white light, it is possible to reach 1,000 in a particular spectral band.

For the same emulsion and the same desensitizer, the desensitizing power is approximately proportional to the amount of the desensitizer adsorbed per unit area of the emulsion. The adsorption of the desensitizer to the surface of the silver bromide grains is shown by the fact that washing an emulsion after desensitizing decreases the desensitizing power but does not reduce it to unity. It has been found in one series of experiments that the desensitizing power increased from 3,500 to 6,000 when the time of immersion in the desensitizer was prolonged from 2 to 70 minutes. The increase in desensitizing power was very rapid at first and then, after 5 minutes, very slow. The use of a more concentrated solution allows the same result to be obtained in a shorter time of immersion, but it is still necessary for the desensitizer to penetrate right through the emulsion layer. The rate of desensitization is increased on raising the temperature and, on the other hand, it is decreased when the emulsion is strongly hardened.

Irregular results have been frequently obtained in desensitizing plates having an anti-halation underlayer containing manganese dioxide, or "self-screen" orthochromatic plates, by reason of a reaction between the desensitizer and the manganese dioxide or the acid dye constituent of the yellow filter embodied in the "self-screen" emulsion. Again, anomalous results have been found on developing desensitized plates and films when amidol is used for developing.

631. Desensitization Before and During Development. Desensitization may be carried out *before* or *during* development, the desensitizer being used in a pre-bath or added to the developer, providing that the desensitizer is compatible with the developer. It has been noted above that many desensitizers may not be added to developers containing a polyphenolic developing agent because of a more or less rapid precipitation, depending upon the concentrations of developer and desensitizer. The chemical fog that appears on plates, even when developed in total darkness, seems to be connected with the tendency of the desensitizer to precipitate and is, thus, always more intense when desensitizing is carried out during development than when it is effected by means of a pre-bath. At equal concentrations the desensitizing power is greater when the desensitizer is used in the developer than when it is used in a pre-bath, but it should be noted that the concentration should be considerably less in the former case. In many cases desensitization affects the activity of the developer and notably the shape of the curve showing the value of gamma as a function of the time of development. The appearance of the image is usually more rapid, but the total development time is increased. T. H. James (1939) found that safranine and other basic dyes increase the rate of development in solutions containing developing agents whose speed of action is decreased by sulphite (e.g. hydroquinone, chlorhydroquinone, pyrogallol, glycin) and are without appreciable effect on developers whose action is accelerated by the addition of sulphite. In the case where the desensitization is carried out in a pre-bath, the fact that the emulsion is swollen with water tends to retard the appearance of the image.

Desensitization is in general ineffective on emulsions that are physically developed prior to fixation (§ 625). Probably the desensitizer adsorbed to the silver bromide is displaced by the soluble silver salt contained in the physical developer.

Desensitization may be carried out either by a light that is safe for the material being used or, preferably, in total darkness. The light that is to be used for inspecting the desensitized plate should not be turned on for at least two minutes. Five minutes' desensitizing should be given in the case of very rapid panchromatic emulsions. Since these times are the least that may be given when the desensitizer is used in the developer, development in a rapid developer would already be far advanced by the time that the inspection light is turned on and this would reduce the effectiveness of the method in the case of a serious overexposure. The light used for the inspection of the desensitized material should be green, bright yellow, orange, or light red. A green light should be avoided when using a red desensitizer and vice versa because in both cases the desensitized material would appear almost black.

In all cases where, for example, in order to reduce the danger of the formation of airbells, the sensitive material is pre-soaked before development the desensitizer may be added to the pre-bath. It has been suggested (K. Wiebking, 1921) that the desensitizer be incorporated in an anti-halation backing layer which would dissolve in the first solution into which the plate or film is placed.

The desensitizer is dissolved to make a stock solution that may be diluted according to requirements. The formation of moulds in the dye solutions can be avoided by the addition of a very small amount of disinfectant, such as Sunoxol, that would be harmless to the developer or to the emulsion in the very small concentration that is used. For example, a dye desensitizer for use as a preliminary bath at a concentration of 1:5,000 may be made by diluting one part of the following stock solution with 24 parts of water—

Desensitizer	•	•	· 5 g
Sunoxol .	.	.	1–2 ml
Water to	.	.	1 litre

The desensitizing bath may be repeatedly used. It should be filtered to remove any solid matter that accumulates, e.g. dust, deposit from hard water, and, in the case of pinacryptol green, a deposit formed by the coagulation of a part of the dye by potassium bromide dissolved from the desensitized plate. This solid matter, if it is not removed, will cause spots where particles adhere to the emulsion. The bath may be maintained at almost constant activity for quite a long time by topping it up to a constant level with a solution that is slightly more concentrated than the initial bath.

There is no point in rinsing the desensitized plates or films before transferring them to the developer.

Various ways have been suggested for the removal of the red safranine stain that remains in the gelatine after fixing and washing, a step that is usually unnecessary. However, one can bathe the film or plate in dilute (1 per cent) nitric acid or, better, in the coldest possible 1 per cent solution of sodium nitrite containing about 1 per cent hydrochloric acid. In this latter case the safranine is converted to a violet diazonium compound that can be readily washed away. This treatment causes a slight reduction of the image that is, however, usually imperceptible.

CHAPTER XXXI

FIXATION

632. The purpose of fixation. 633. Solvents for silver halides. 634. Sodium thiosulphate—solution preparation—stability—effect of acids—addition of sodium bisulphite. 635. Ammonium thiosulphate. 636. Other fixing agents (stabilizing agents)—potassium or ammonium thiocyanate—potassium cyanide—organic sulphur-containing compounds. 637. The chemistry of fixation—formation of silver thiosulphate complexes. 638. Additions to fixing baths—acids—alum-formalin. 639. Fixation in the presence of alum—reactions of potash alum with thiosulphate—optimum hardening pH—reduction in hardening by organic acids. 640. Fixing capacity of thiosulphate for silver halides—solubilities of silver halides in thiosulphate solutions—solubilities of silver bromide in practical fixing baths. 641. The kinetics of fixation—variation in rates of fixation with temperature and constitution of the fixing bath—effect of exhaustion of the fixing bath—effect of addition of ammonium salts. 642. Fixation in two successive baths—advantages—practical considerations. 643. Choice of the best concentration of fixer. 644. Tests for exhausted silver. 645. Preparation of fixing baths—neutral fixers—non-hardening acid fixers—acid hardening fixers—rapid fixers. 646. Fixation in practice. 647. Fixer for materials rich in silver iodide. 648. Regeneration of fixing baths—maintaining the acidity of a non-hardening fixer—maintaining the acidity of a hardening fixer—electrolytic regeneration of fixing baths—elimination and recovery of iodide from fixers. 649. Recovery of silver from exhausted fixing solutions without regenerating the bath—sulphide precipitation—precipitation by zinc—steel wool method.

632. The Purpose of Fixation. Fixing and washing are necessary in order, firstly, to convert the salts of silver remaining in the image, after its development, into soluble substances, and, secondly, to remove them. Contrary to common opinion, the former of these processes is by far the more important; washing, no matter how prolonged, can only remove soluble substances, and is not effective if the previous process of solution has not been carried to completion by fixing.

It should be mentioned that after as perfect a fixing as possible there always remains, under the greatest densities of the image, a very small amount of silver bromide, which can be developed or dissolved after the silver of the image has been eliminated by a solution of permanganate in sulphuric acid.

633. Solvents of the Silver Halides. It must be said at the outset that there are no true *solvents* of the chloride, bromide, or iodide of silver. When sugar is dissolved in water and the latter is evaporated, spontaneously or by boiling, the sugar is recovered in its original condition; this is really a case of true *solution*. If silver bromide be submitted to the action of one of the saline solutions which are generally considered as its solvents, the evaporation of the liquid so obtained will never leave behind silver bromide; the residue will consist of transformation products of this salt, due to the chemical interaction of the silver salt and the fixing salt. This fine distinction is of great practical importance.

The first practical fixer to be used was sodium thiosulphate (then known as hyposulphite of soda, hence "hypo"[1]) employed for this purpose by Herschel (son of the astronomer) in 1839. Sodium thiosulphate, though it deals effectively with the silver chloride and bromide is only a very mediocre fixing agent for photographic coatings containing mainly silver iodide. It was abandoned on the introduction of the wet collodion process, in which fixing was done by a solution of potassium cyanide. Potassium cyanide is now almost entirely replaced by sodium cyanide. Both of these salts, even in very small amounts, are extremely dangerous poisons, if absorbed by the mouth or through a scratch in the skin. Exposed to the air, their solutions slowly liberate hydrocyanic acid, which by accumulating in a badly ventilated place—as many photographic darkrooms are—may cause

[1] Throughout this chapter "thiosulphate" will be used when making a specifically chemical reference; "hypo" is used when dealing with *sodium* thiosulphate, especially in matters of fixing practice.

indisposition or even serious illness. Sodium thiosulphate returned to favour when the gelatine-bromide plate replaced, except for certain special applications, the collodion processes. It may be considered as being practically the only fixer in common use.

The various other substances capable of converting the halides of silver into soluble substances are considerably more difficult to use. The solutions so obtained are not very stable and are precipitated on dilution, and do not permit of final removal by washing. This is notably the case with ammonia (ineffective for iodide of silver), with sulphites and bisulphites (only slightly active), with sulphocyanides (thiocyanates), with thiourea and its derivatives.

634. Sodium Thiosulphate. Sodium thiosulplate (or hyposulphite) ($Na_2S_2O_3$, $5H_2O$) occurs in crystals of varying size, of specific gravity 1·7, containing 64 per cent of the active substance (anhydrous thiosulphate) and 36 per cent of water. It is deliquescent in moist air and very soluble in water, but insoluble in alcohol. It melts at about 122°F (50°C) in its own water of crystallization, and is completely dehydrated by heating to a temperature above 212°F (100°C) but this leads to partial decomposition unless special precautions are taken, and thus the price of anhydrous thiosulphate is rather higher than that of crystalline.

On dissolving in water, sodium thiosulphate lowers the temperature; for this reason the preparation of solutions should not be left until they are required for use. For making up quantities of sodium thiosulphate on the commercial scale, a Baumé hydrometer should be used, together with the following table, which refers to a temperature of 60°F (15°C)—

Concentration of solution	10%	15%	20%	25%	30%
Degrees Baumé	7°	10°	12·5°	15°	18·5°

Solutions of thiosulphate decompose slowly, even when kept from air and light; sulphur is deposited, whilst a little sulphite is formed in the solution.

With very few exceptions, acids (even the weakest) and acid salts decompose thiosulphate more or less rapidly, according to the concentration and strength of the acid. This decomposition manifests itself by the gradual formation of sulphur, which is set free in such a condition (colloidal sulphur) that it is only seen with difficulty. The particles unite with one another, and at first a bluish opalescence appears, then a white turbidity, and finally a yellow precipitate is formed; at the same time sulphur dioxide

and sometimes hydrogen sulphide are set free, whilst in the solution sodium sulphate and thionates (Seyewetz and Chicandard, 1895) are formed. Once started, this decomposition goes on until the thiosulphate is completely destroyed.

Among the common acids and acid salts, boric acid and sodium bisulphite (§ 591) alone cause no decomposition of thiosulphate solutions; or at any rate, the decomposition is so slow as not to occur during normal times of storage. However, sulphiding of sensitive plates or papers has been noted in a darkroom, where a dish is always kept containing such acidified fixing baths.

This property of sodium bisulphite in relation to thiosulphate causes sodium sulphite to behave as a protector of thiosulphate against acids. The latter are not able to attack the thiosulphate until all the sulphite has been converted into bisulphite.

Neutral or acidified solutions of thiosulphate attack a great many metals, the action being particularly rapid in the case of zinc, so that zinc washing trays are quickly corroded when used continually. Nickel is only slightly attacked, and tanks of this metal may therefore be used for fixing baths, provided that the solutions are removed when fixing has been finished. For commercial use, tanks of wood, glazed earthenware, or even of lead, lapped and self-soldered, are employed. The addition of 1 per cent sodium sulphate to fixing baths prevents or retards considerably the attack of acid fixers on lead (G. Milliani, 1921) without interfering with the normal course of fixing.

Neutral thiosulphate solutions attack metallic silver only very slowly, even when it is in such a finely divided condition as in photographic negatives; even then, free access to the air must be allowed for the action to occur (A. Haddon and F. B. Grundy, 1896). There is no harm in leaving photographic images for several hours in a *neutral* fixing bath, provided that the negatives or prints are fully covered with solution; an appreciable reduction would appear on any portions sticking up from the liquid or lying on the surface.

Acid solutions of sodium thiosulphate, on the other hand, slowly attack metallic silver (A. Lainer, 1890) without the intervention of atmospheric oxygen, the solution of all the silver in a negative sometimes being complete in 48 hours. Leaving negatives or prints for long periods in acid fixing baths is therefore to be avoided.

Alkaline thiosulphate solutions have practically no action on the silver of photographic images. The silver of images fixed with sodium thiosulphate contains traces of some sulphur compound not yet identified. After dissolving away the silver by means of suitable reagents, this substance remains in the coating in the form of silver sulphide (H. Lüppo-Cramer, 1923).

635. Ammonium Thiosulphate. Ammonium thiosulphate is generally obtained as an aqueous solution containing about 60 per cent of the anhydrous $[(NH_4)_2S_2O_3]$. It is somewhat less stable than sodium thiosulphate but more rapid in its action (at equivalent concentration) because ammonium ions are also involved in the formation of complexes with silver (§ 637). It is also available as a solid but should then be stored under controlled conditions because it is thermally unstable. Its stability is, however, increased when it is in the form of mixed crystals containing 20 per cent of sodium thiosulphate (L. F. A. Mason, 1966).

636. Other Fixing Agents (Stabilizing Agents). Potassium or ammonium thiocyanate (KCNS or NH4CNS) are even more rapid in their rates of fixation than ammonium thiosulphate but are more expensive. Thiocyanates soften gelatine and must be used in conjunction with hardening agents or on hardened emulsions. Their use is generally restricted to ultra-rapid fixers and as stabilizers in activator-stabilizer processing.

Potassium cyanide (KCN) is one of the most rapid fixing agents known but cannot be used as a general purpose fixing agent because of its extreme toxicity.

A large number of organic sulphur-containing compounds have been patented as fixing agents (e.g. thiobarbituric acid, ammonium dithiocarbamate, thioacetamide, thioglycollic acid etc.) but because of their high price their use is generally restricted to the stabilization technique in which a relatively insoluble, light insensitive silver complex is formed. This complex remains in the emulsion which should not be washed after processing (§ 650).

637. The Chemistry of Fixation. When a very small quantity of thiosulphate comes in contact with a large excess of a salt of silver it tends to form silver thiosulphate; this salt is unstable, like almost all thiosulphates, and decomposes quickly into brown or black insoluble silver sulphide and sulphuric acid, which remains in solution. This explains the stains formed on sensitive surfaces, particularly on print-out

papers (containing soluble silver salts), when they are touched by fingers soiled with hypo.

It is quite otherwise when the salt of silver comes in contact with a large excess of hypo in sufficiently concentrated solution. Again, silver thiosulphate tends to be formed, but this salt combines at once with excess of sodium thiosulphate, forming *complex thiosulphates of silver and sodium*. These salts are comparatively stable and are sharply differentiated in all their properties from a *mixture* of the two simple thiosulphates For example, these complex thiosulphates have a sweet taste, whilst sodium thiosulphate has a bitter and sulphurous taste, and the salts of silver generally have a disagreeable metallic taste.

The composition of these complex salts appears to vary according to the nature of the salt of silver which is caused to react with sodium thiosulphate (Gaedicke, 1903; L. Lumière and A. Seyewetz, 1907). Whatever the original salt of silver, however, according to the proportions of hypo and of the silver salt, one may always obtain either a soluble complex thiosulphate or an insoluble complex thiosulphate.

The formation of argentothiosulphate complexes may be represented by the following general equation (L. F. A. Mason, 1966):

$$m\ Ag^+ + n(S_2O_3)^{2-} \rightleftharpoons [Ag_m(S_2O_3)_n]^{2n-m}$$

Although many physiochemical studies have demonstrated the existence of a number of complexes from $m = 1$ and $n = 1$ to $m = 3$ and $n = 4$ (H. Bassett and J. T. Lemon, 1933, H. Chateau and J. Pouradier, 1953, H. Baines, 1929). Baines (1955) concluded that only the following two complexes have an essential bearing on fixation:

$m = 1, n = 1$ $\quad Na[Ag\ S_2O_3].H_2O$
$\qquad\qquad\qquad$ (sparingly soluble)
$m = 1, n = 2$ $\quad Na_3[Ag(S_2O_3)_2].2H_2O$
$\qquad\qquad\qquad$ (readily soluble)

Baines (1955) has suggested that adsorption is the first step in the dissolution of silver halides to form a soluble argenthiosulphate and the second step is the formation and desorption of the soluble complex according to the following equations:

$$AgBr + S_2O_3{}^{2-} \rightleftharpoons [Ag\ S_2O_3]^- + Br^-$$
$\text{(solid)} \qquad\qquad\qquad \text{(adsorption complex)}$

$$[Ag\ S_2O_3]^- + S_2O_3{}^{2-} \rightleftharpoons [Ag(S_2O_3)_2]^{3-}$$
$\text{(adsorption complex)} \qquad\qquad \text{(desorbed soluble)}$

It is obvious that it is the formation of the soluble complex thiosulphate which must be aimed at during fixing, because only a soluble salt can be removed by washing. The soluble complex thiosulphates contain, for a given quantity of silver thiosulphate, a higher proportion of sodium thiosulphate than the insoluble thiosulphate; their formation requires the presence of a large excess of *available* sodium thiosulphate, which is not already saturated with salts of silver.

These complex salts decompose spontaneously in the cold, depositing silver sulphide; this decomposition is very rapid in the absence of an excess of hypo and is accelerated by heat and light. The soluble complex salt is decomposed in a pure aqueous solution if its concentration corresponds to more than 3·24 per cent of metallic silver; the greater its concentration the greater the excess of hypo required to render it stable (E. Römmler, 1929). It is well known that used fixing baths deposit in time a black sludge consisting mainly of silver sulphide.

The rules which must be followed in order to ensure the effective fixation of photographic plates, films, and papers follow logically from these facts.

638. Additions to Fixing Baths. At the instant of plunging negatives or prints into the fixing bath, the gelatine (and in the case of papers the base also), in spite of intermediate rinsing, is impregnated with the developing solution, especially in the deeper layers of the film. There is thus danger of development continuing in irregularly-distributed zones. Further, the accumulation of these substances in the fixing bath as more and more negatives are treated tends to produce troubles such as dichroic fog (§ 552) or general coloration of the gelatine by the oxidation products of the developer. Lastly, under these conditions, the fixing bath would become slightly alkaline, and it is in such alkaline media that maximum swelling of gelatine occurs, so that it becomes very tender and tends to reticulate (§ 594). These difficulties may be avoided by acidifying the fixing bath to a slight extent by the addition of sodium bisulphite (J. M. Eder, 1889), or of acetic acid in presence of sodium sulphite, (A. Lainer, 1889) or of boric acid (H. Reeb, 1906; J. I. Crabtree, 1933).

Sheppard, Elliot, and Sweet (1923) showed that whenever considerations of cost do not prohibit the use of acetic acid, the mixture of this acid with sulphite is much the best; in presence of the sodium acetate so formed the free acidity corresponds to only a fraction of the total available acidity, the difference forming a reserve of acidity.

An objection sometimes made to the use of acid baths is that the exhaustion of the solution is masked, and that thus there is a risk that the bath may be used beyond its power, the permanence of the images not being ensured. A neutral bath soon begins to become discoloured by the oxidation products of the developer and to throw down a brown sludge of silver sulphide and reduced silver, changes which suggest the necessity of replacing the old bath by a new one within a reasonable time.

When the temperature of the bath or of the wash water, or of the air in which drying is to be done, rises above 68°F (20°C), it is advisable to harden the gelatine. From every point of view it is best in such cases to combine this operation with that of fixation by adding an alum to the fixing bath. It remains, therefore, to decide which of the two available alums, potash alum (white) or chrome-alum (violet), is preferable. Taking into account only hardening efficiency, chrome-alum should be chosen, and this is, in fact, always used in very hot climates; its price is, however, considerably greater than that of ordinary alum, and also certain printing papers when treated with chrome-alum retain—even after washing—a very slight green tint.

After treatment with alum, the tendency of gelatine to swell is greatly reduced, and its melting point is very considerably raised, sometimes to a temperature above 158°F (70°C).

In a warm and moist atmosphere spontaneous drying is generally slower than the growth of liquefying bacteria. Gelatine which has been suitably treated with alum will resist even the heat of direct sunshine, and drying can then be sufficiently rapid to prevent local liquefaction (L. J. Bunel, 1924). Gelatine may be hardened by solutions of formalin (formaldehyde), but, whilst cases of slow alteration, physical or mechanical, are rare with alum-hardened gelatines, several have occurred in which formalin-treated gelatines have become brittle or even powdery. Formalin is much more effective in a solution rendered alkaline (ammonia must not be used) than in a neutral or acid solution, and may, therefore, then be used at a greater dilution; rinse in water after each immersion in formalin. It may be added that formalin is very irritating to the eyes and the lungs, has a very unpleasant smell, and causes an objectionable hardening of the skin. Very many other substances with an aldehyde character (hydroxyaldehydes, dial-dehydes, etc.), can be employed for hardening gelatine.

639. Fixation in the Presence of Alum. Potash alum $Al_2 (SO_4)_3$, K_2SO_4, $24H_2O$, occurs in large crystals or, more commonly, as a white powder obtained by crushing the crystals. The solubility in water is about 9 per cent at 50°F (10°C), 13 per cent at 68°F (20°C) and 30 per cent at 104°F (40°C). The salt and its solutions are stable. The active substance in it is the aluminium sulphate which may, in fact, be used in place of it in proportion of two parts of aluminium sulphate to three of alum.

Chrome-alum, $Cr_2(SO_4)_3$, K_2SO_4, $24H_2O$, usually occurs in large dark-violet crystals of satisfactory purity. The substance itself and its solutions are very stable; at the most the crystals lose a little water from the surface, becoming covered with a grey powdery layer. Its solution, when prepared cold, is greyish-violet, becoming green when warmed. This change of colour accompanies a modification in the internal structure of the salt, but this leads to no appreciable alteration in its hardening power. Chrome-alum is more soluble than potash alum, especially on warming the mixture so that the change to green occurs; the solubility then becomes more than 50 per cent at 68°F.

The reactions of potash alum with sodium thiosulphate have been studied very completely by Seyewetz and Chicandard (1895); the reactions are almost the same with chrome-alum.

On prolonged boiling, hypo and alum are mutually and completely decomposed; sulphur and alumina are precipitated, sulphur dioxide is liberated, and sodium sulphate is formed in solution.

In the cold the reaction is different; aluminium thiosulphate tends to be formed. This substance is very unstable, and breaks down into aluminium sulphate and hydrogen sulphide. The latter, by reacting with excess of sodium thiosulphate, slowly yields sodium bisulphite and sulphide with precipitation of sulphur. The aluminium sulphate being regenerated, the same reaction is repeated, but always slowly, because of the protective action of the sodium bisulphite, which is formed and which is only very slowly converted into thionates. The acceleration of these reactions on warming the mixture is made use of for the sulphide toning of prints on development papers.

These reactions may be prevented or, at least, very much retarded, by the addition of sodium sulphite or bisulphite (Seyewetz and Chicandard), or of sodium acetate or citrate (P. Mercier, 1894).

Hardening by alums is favoured by neutral or alkaline conditions, but when a mixture of potash alum and hypo is stabilized by sulphite, acid must be added, otherwise a white precipitate of aluminium sulphite will be deposited. This deposition of aluminium sulphite would occur, especially within the gelatine, on account of the alkali of the developer carried over with the negative, and this precipitate would be very difficult to remove.

For the different reasons given in the preceding paragraph and above, an alum fixing bath must be acid (optimum pH, 4·0 to 4·5) to a sufficient extent to prevent precipitation of aluminium sulphate, even after a comparatively large quantity of developing solution has been added to it. It must, however, not be so acid as to decompose the hypo.

Hardening by alum is considerably reduced by the action of oxalic, tartaric, or citric acids, or of their salts, especially at high concentrations. Acetic, formic, and analogous acids and their salts are free from this drawback. Alum-hardened gelatine may even be de-tanned by immersion for some time in a 5 per cent solution of citric acid (Proctor and Wilson, 1916).

640. Fixing Capacity of Thiosulphate for Silver Halides. Sodium thiosulphate does not dissolve with equal facility the different silver salts occurring in an emulsion. Moreover, the power of the same weight of hypo to dissolve the same silver salt increases as its concentration is raised. The following values correspond with saturation of the hypo after long mechanical agitation, gelatine being absent (Richards and Burnells Faber, 1889)—

Concentration of Hypo	Weight of halide dissolved per litre		
	Silver chloride	Silver bromide	Silver iodide
10%	41 g	37 g	3 g
20%	91 g	78 g	10 g
50%	—	213 g	—

Under normal conditions of photographic practice the dissolving power of hypo is considerably less.

Almost all modern negative emulsions contain silver iodide, which is present also in some positive emulsions (notably in positive motion-picture emulsions). This iodide tends to lower considerably the fixing power of hypo. The inactivity of hypo towards silver iodide explains the slow fixation of certain very sensitive

	Weight of silver bromide (mg) dissolved per litre of saturated solution	Weight of silver bromide dissolved in 1 litre of bath without subsequent stain	Weight of silver bromide dissolved in g per g of hypo	Average number of 9 × 12 cm negatives fixed per litre without subsequent stain
Sodium thiosulphate 5%	20	12·5	0·250	33
Sodium thiosulphate 15%	63	38	0·253	100
Sodium thiosulphate 45%	205	50	0·111	133
Sodium thiosulphate 15% and 1·5% bisulphite .	61	16·5	0·110	45
The same with 0·5% chrome-alum . . .	59	22	0·147	60

emulsions, and especially anti-halation plates having a substratum of silver iodide.

It must also be remembered that every plate, film, or print introduced into the fixing bath, brings with it a certain amount of water and takes away with it an approximately equal amount of the fixing solution, when it is transferred to the washing tank. Thus the bath is gradually diluted, and at the same time the total amount of available hypo decreases much more rapidly than it would do merely on account of the reaction of sodium thiosulphate with the silver salts.

By putting more and more negatives or prints into a fixing bath in an attempt to saturate the solution with silver salts, the disappearance of the silver salts would be rendered very slow, and the last samples to be fixed in a reasonable time would certainly become yellowish after some days, due to silver sulphide, formed from the insoluble complex thiosulphate and occurring fairly uniformly throughout the gelatine layer.

The first determinations in this field having an immediate practical bearing on photography were those of Lumière and Seyewetz (1907). These authors did not confine themselves to the determination of the maximum solubilities of silver bromide in pure hypo, hypo with bisulphite, with and without chrome-alum; they also determined the silver content at which any of these baths must be considered as unsuitable for further use, at least when fixation is carried out in a single bath. The above table summarizes the results.

These results show that with single-bath fixation the efficiency of action of the hypo decreases as its concentration increases, and is still further depressed by acidification of the bath, especially in the absence of alum.

It is somewhat curious that, in spite of the fact that silver chloride is more soluble than the bromide in sodium thiosulphate, the practical limit of fixation is more rapidly reached in the case of the chloride; solutions of hypo saturated with silver chloride more easily deposit the insoluble complex thiosulphate.

641. The Kinetics of Fixation. The mechanism of fixation has been studied specially by Sheppard and Mees (1906) and by Warwick (1917). These workers used very different experimental methods, but arrived at identical conclusions, which are in conformity with the general laws of physical chemistry.

A fixing bath dissolves per unit time a constant fraction of the mass of silver bromide existing in the coating at the commencement of the interval of time considered.

The magnitude of this fraction depends on the temperature and on the effective concentration of the bath; it is independent of the silver content of the emulsion, of the quality of the gelatine, of its degree of swelling, and even of previous hardening of the film; it is greater for silver chloride than for the bromide, and for the bromide than for the iodide; for the same silver salt it is greater if the emulsion is one consisting of fine grains.

The disappearance of the milky layer of silver bromide does not indicate that the solution of this substance is complete, but only that the opalescent layer is so much reduced as to be invisible; at this instant there may still be more than 5 per cent of the original silver halide undissolved. Some very ingenious experiments by E. R. Bullock (1922) appear to show that when fixing emulsions consisting of silver iodobromide, the silver bromide is almost totally dissolved when the solution of the iodide is beginning.

In the same way that the best time of development may be determined by multiplying by a suitable factor the time taken for the first details of the image to appear (§ 547), so, by multiplying the time of disappearance of the silver bromide by a factor, the time necessary to give satisfactory fixation may be calculated. The best margin of safety is obtained, when single-bath fixation is employed, by keeping the negative

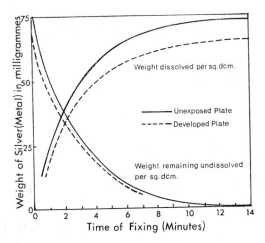

Fig. 31.1. Stages of Fixing
(Warwick)

more than 0·25 per cent of the original quantity of silver bromide, will be partially dissolved in the first of the washing water since the latter soon takes up a sufficient quantity of sodium thiosulphate to behave as a supplementary fixing bath.

The curves in Fig. 31.1, taken from the experiments of Warwick, show, for a surface of 1 sq dm of negative emulsion of average coating weight, the quantities of silver bromide (expressed in weights of metallic silver) to be dissolved and already dissolved at the various stages of fixing in a 20 per cent solution of hypo at 65°F (18°C). The curves shown as heavy lines refer to an undeveloped plate; the finer lines refer to a developed plate. A study of the curves shows the gradual progress of fixation.

The influence of the concentration of the bath and its temperature on the rate of fixation has been very carefully investigated by Welborne Piper (1912–1914); the two graphs (Figs. 31.2 and 31.3) show, for a given emulsion, the nature of the variations which occur when the first phase of fixation (disappearance of the milky film of halide) in pure sodium thiosulphate is considered.

It is seen that whatever the concentration of the fixer, the process is most rapid at the higher temperatures, and the greatest speed is always obtained at a concentration of 40 per cent. At higher concentrations fixation becomes slower as the concentration rises, on account of the increased difficulty with which these solutions diffuse into the gelatine.

in the fixing solution after the apparent disappearance of the silver bromide for a time equal to that taken for the milkiness to disappear. If, for example, at the time of disappearance of the visible silver bromide 95 per cent of this salt has been dissolved, keeping the negative in the bath for another period equal to the first will allow of the solution of 95 per cent of the residual silver bromide, which is no more than 5 per cent of the original amount present. Thus 95 + 4·75 (= 99·75) per cent will be dissolved; the residue, amounting to

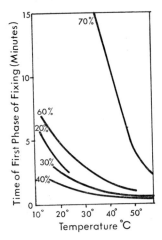

Fig. 31.2. Variation of Fixing Action with Temperature
(Piper)

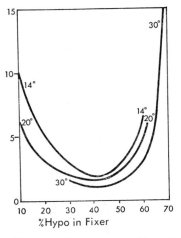

Fig. 31.3. Variation of Fixing Action with Strength of Hypo Bath
(Piper)

The experiments of this author comparing the thiosulphates of sodium, potassium, ammonium, and calcium showed that for each thiosulphate fixation is most rapid at a certain concentration. For the sodium and ammonium thiosulphates the optimum concentrations are respectively 40 per cent and 15 per cent; the duration of fixation is the same for both at a concentration of 33 per cent; at lower concentrations than this the sodium salt acts more slowly, but more rapidly at higher concentrations. For example, at 20 per cent concentration the ammonium salt fixes five times more quickly than the sodium salt.

The rate of fixation is reduced as the bath becomes charged with more silver; the following table (P. Strauss, 1925) shows the influence of silver salts on the time of disappearance of silver bromide in a 25 per cent solution of hypo.

Silver salt dissolved per 100 ml of bath	Silver bromide	Silver chloride
0	73 sec	73 sec
1 g	92 ,,	92 ,,
2 g	101 ,,	94 ,,
4 g	121 ,,	112 ,,
6 g	239 ,,	204 ,,

Silver chloride retards fixation less than an equal weight of the bromide, despite the fact that the chloride contains 75 per cent of silver and the bromide only 57 per cent. From this it is evident that the exhaustion of the bath, caused by the formation of silver thiosulphate, is not the only factor to be considered, but that the rate of fixation must be influenced by other salts arising from the reactions occurring. As a matter of fact, the addition of sodium bromide to the bath retards fixation, whilst sodium chloride accelerates it.

By reason of the very small solubility of silver iodide, the presence of a very little iodide in a solution of hypo is sufficient to retard fixation considerably; the following table shows the retarding influence of this salt on a 25 per cent solution of hypo.

Potassium iodide in 100 ml of
the bath . . . . 0·00   0·02   0·08   0·32 g
Time of fixation . . . 73   91   147   558 sec

Sodium sulphate slightly retards fixation, and all the salts of the heavy metals (copper, lead, etc.) behave in the same way. The nitrates of sodium or potassium accelerate fixation when

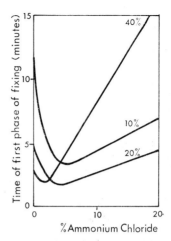

FIG. 31.4. EFFECT OF AMMONIUM CHLORIDE ON RATE OF FIXING
(Piper)

present in small quantities, but at concentrations of 4 per cent or above they retard it. The salts of ammonia, particularly the chloride (ammonium chloride, or sal ammoniac), have a very strong accelerating action, which is, however, not so great with emulsions containing silver iodide (Agfa, 1906; Lumière and Seyewetz, 1908 and 1924), in spite of the fact that the addition of ammonium chloride to a solution of hypo allows it to dissolve more silver iodide.

The accompanying graph (Fig. 31.4) summarizes the observations of Welborne Piper (1914) on this subject. It is seen that for each concentration of hypo there is an optimum concentration of ammonium chloride. This optimum becomes smaller as the concentration of hypo is increased.

The acceleration of fixation by the addition of ammonium salts is, however, counterbalanced by a disadvantage (Lumière and Seyewetz, 1908). The complex thiosulphates of silver and ammonia formed under these circumstances are much less stable than the complex thiosulphates of sodium and silver; the practical limit of use is only about half, and the risks of discoloration of the image are increased. This acceleration, although advantageous in cases of extreme urgency, has no practical application in ordinary work, particularly when negatives are to be kept.

The work of Welborne Piper on the rates of fixation at various thiosulphate concentrations (Fig. 31.3) was carried out using dry films. Alnutt

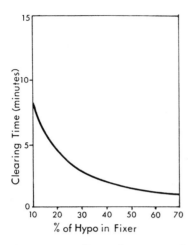

FIG. 31.5. VARIATION OF FIXING ACTION WITH STRENGTH
OF HYPO BATH FOR PRESOAKED FILM
(Alnutt)

(1943) found that presoaking the film for 5 minutes in water changed the shape of the curves given in Fig. 31.3 to those given in Fig. 31.5. The results for the presoaked film are obviously more representative of the conditions under which fixation is carried out in practice. There was no optimum concentration for which the clearing time of the presoaked film was a minimum and the clearing time of the presoaked film did not increase at high thiosulphate concentrations. These discrepancies were explained by Alnutt in terms of the penetrability and the swelling of the emulsion layer. Thus for the dry film the rate and extent of swelling decreases at high thiosulphate concentrations beyond an optimum concentration. Whereas in the presoaked film the water present in the layer dilutes the thiosulphate as it diffuses through the layer to a concentration of greater efficiency, i.e. with presoaked film the rate of fixation is controlled mainly by the diffusion of the thiosulphate but with dry film it is controlled both by the rate and extent of swelling and diffusion.

642. Fixation in Two Successive Baths. In all industrial operations involving the extraction of a substance by a solvent, the mass to be treated is at first extracted with solvent already almost saturated in previous operations, fresh solvent being used only to extract from material which is almost exhausted. Often, indeed, the process is made continuous by causing the solvent to circulate in the opposite direction to that of the material to be treated. This method of systematic extraction, which allows a solvent to be used most efficiently, may be applied with advantage to photographic fixation; it permits of making the most of a solution of hypo whilst giving perfect fixation and permanence of the images. Furthermore, it has the advantage that the residual silver salts are left at higher concentration, and therefore may be recovered more economically, such recovery being always carried out more easily when the substances are in concentrated solution.

In 1894 A. Miethe, on the basis of the experimental results of Haddon and Grundy, recommended fixation in two successive baths, separated by a brief rinsing. Under these conditions the first bath may be used well beyond the normal limit possible when fixation is carried out by the single-bath method. In fact, this bath will not be discarded until the first phase of fixation, indicated by the disappearance of the milky layer of silver halides, occupies an abnormally long time. It is true a portion of the silver will remain in the form of the insoluble thiosulphate, but during the second stage of fixation carried out in a solution of hypo which is almost fresh, the complete solution of the silver salts will be effected. Negatives treated by this process will be fixed as well as if a fresh bath of hypo had been used from the start.

Since the negatives reach the second bath almost completely fixed, there is little more to be done, and thus the practical limit of safety is not attained. When the first bath has to be abandoned, the second is made the first and is itself replaced by a new one.

Negatives are taken from the first bath when there appears to be no more silver bromide to dissolve; they are then placed in the second bath and allowed to remain for about the same time as in the first bath.

643. Choice of the Best Concentration of Fixer. The amateur, having to develop only one or two negatives, and not wishing to keep the bath for subsequent use, will preferably use a fairly dilute bath, for example, 15 per cent hypo (150 g in 1 litre of water).

The professional or commercial worker, working almost continuously and using the two-bath method, will be well-advised to use much more concentrated solutions, which may be used until almost completely exhausted.

If speed of fixation only be considered, it would appear best to use a 40 per cent solution

(§ 641), but other factors lead to the use of a less concentrated bath.

For one thing, the sudden change of concentration on passing from a too-concentrated fixing solution to the washing water, especially if the water is comparatively warm, may cause frilling or reticulation with plates and films, or blisters with papers. For another, if white light falls on the sensitive coatings during fixation, and if the concentration of the fixer be more than 30 per cent, there may occur in the film a slight insoluble residue which will not disappear, however long the negative or print be left in the fixing bath; at concentrations above 50 per cent, this insoluble residue may form even in the dark (Welborne Piper).

For these different reasons fixing baths are usually employed at concentrations between 20 per cent and 30 per cent, i.e. 200 g to 300 g of sodium thiosulphate (hydrate) per litre of bath.

644. Tests for Exhausted Fixer. When fixation is carried out by the single-bath method it is obviously only possible to calculate the area of sensitive material which has been fixed by a given volume of the bath. This calculation is, however, not likely to be of any value, unless data are available concerning the amount of silver in the emulsions used and the volume of the solution removed by the plates, etc., already fixed.

It is sometimes considered that a fixing bath has reached its limit of safety when the time of fixation of a given emulsion becomes double that required with a fresh bath at the same temperature. As a matter of fact, this method of testing results in carrying the use of a fixing bath considerably beyond reasonable limits, and would be more suitable for deciding the exhaustion point of the first bath in the case of two-stage fixation.

More accurate indication is obtained by employing a method of direct control suggested by Gaedicke in 1906, and recommended by Lumière and Seyewetz as being satisfactory. A fixing bath should be considered as exhausted (as a single bath or as the second bath in the two-stage method) when a drop of it, placed on blotting or filter paper, turns brown on exposure for some time to moist air and sunlight.

A more direct method (Bayer, 1921) is to withdraw 100 ml of the bath and to add to this quantity of solution 10 ml of a 4 per cent solution of potassium iodide; the bath may be considered as exhausted, so far as the single-solution method is concerned, when a permanent yellow precipitate is formed.

In an industrial installation, the silver content of the fixing baths is best determined colorimetrically by precipitating colloidal silver sulphide. The estimation is made using a photoelectric absorptiometer (W. J. Weyerts and K. C. D. Hickman, 1935, K. Iino, 1958). The estimation as silver selenide has been described by M. Abribat (1936).

In a professional installation, the silver content of the baths can be estimated approximately by dipping into the solutions test-papers coated with zinc or cadmium sulphide in gelatine. The brown tint obtained is compared with control papers that have been immersed in solutions of known silver content and then preserved, wet, in transparent sachets (H. Arens and H. Berger, 1937). Silver estimating papers are commercially available.

The silver content of the fixing baths should not exceed 4 g per litre for negatives, and 1·5 g per litre for papers. When continuous electrolytic regeneration of the fixer is applied the concentrations should be kept, respectively, to 1·5 g and 0·5 g per litre.

645. Preparation of Fixing Baths. Workers cannot be too strongly recommended to mix correctly the substances used in the preparation of fixing baths. These solutions are sufficiently stable to allow of being prepared beforehand in fairly large quantities. In order to reduce the bulk due to large quantities of stock solution it is a simple matter to prepare the actual baths when needed for use from more concentrated solutions.

We have seen (§ 641) that a very cold or very concentrated solution fixes very slowly, and also that a newly prepared solution of hypo is very cold (§ 634); it is therefore not surprising that a fixing bath prepared just before it is needed by throwing haphazardly, and often liberally, some handfuls of thiosulphate into a dish of water, does not fix. If, weary with waiting for fixation to be completed, one throws the negative into a dish of water, fixation will be very rapid, but in the absence of excess of thiosulphate it will not be complete.

The presence of particles of rust in the water used for preparing solutions (water distributed in iron pipes), or in the hypo (stored in sheet-iron containers), may cause solution of the silver in the image at the points where these particles settle, the iron oxide being slowly converted into ferric bromide by contact with the bromide dissolved in a partly-used fixing bath. (W. F. A. Ermen, 1923).

"Neutral" Fixers. "Neutral" fixers, comprising a plain 25 per cent solution of hydrated sodium thiosulphate (*p*H about 9) are only infrequently used.

Non-hardening Acid Fixers. A fixer rendered acid only by the addition of sodium bisulphite (*p*H about 5 increasing to 6, on exposing the fixer to the atmosphere, as sulphur dioxide is given off) is very rapidly neutralized by the alkali carried over from the developer, especially when no rinse is given. Such a fixing bath should only be used after a stop bath, under which circumstances some sodium sulphite should be added to protect the hypo from the action of the acid carried over.

Sodium thiosulphate (hydrated) .	250 g
Sodium sulphite (anhydrous) . .	10 g
Sodium bisulphite	25 g
Water to	1 litre

Acid Hardening Fixer. The following fixer (H. D. Russell and J. I. Crabtree, 1933) has the advantage of retaining its hardening properties over a greater range of *p*H than other hardening fixers do. When fresh, the *p*H is nearly 4·5.

The sodium thiosulphate is first dissolved in about 300 ml of water. The other ingredients, dissolved separately in small quantities of water, are added in the order given.

	Fixing bath	Acidifying Solution
Sodium thiosulphate, hydrated .	300 g	—
Sodium sulphite, anhydrous .	15 g	30 g
Acetic acid, glacial . . .	10 ml	20 ml
Boric acid, crystalline .	7·5 g	15 g
Potassium aluminium sulphate (alum)	15 g	30 g
Water to	1 litre	1 litre

The re-acidification of this fixing bath under the conditions described in § 648 below, is best carried out using the above solution.

Rapid Fixers. In all these fixing solutions ammonium thiosulphate can be used instead of the sodium compound or a mixture of hypo with ammonium chloride (§ 641). A formula for a typical rapid fixing bath based on ammonium thiosulphate is given below (L. F. A. Mason, 1966):

Ammonium thiosulphate . .	135 g
Boric acid	7 g
Sodium acetate, anhydrous . .	10 g
Sodium metabisulphite . .	5 g
Sodium sulphite, anhydrous .	6 g
Water to	1 litre

This fixer should contain sufficient acid to keep the solution clear and about 5 g/litre of aluminium chloride (as anhydrous).

When fixation has to be completed in 20 seconds or less, sodium or ammonium thiosulphate is not suitable. Satisfactory fixing agents for this purpose are potassium or ammonium thiocyanates. Ammonium thiocyanate has its quickest action at a concentration of 40–50 per cent. If fixing has to be carried out in a matter of a few seconds, the temperature of the solution can be raised to about 50°C (122°F). As solutions of ammonium thiocyanate have a softening effect on gelatine, 5 per cent formalin may have to be added, even when fixing is carried out at normal temperatures. Fixing with ammonium thiocyanate is especially suitable for high speed processing materials having thin and highly hardened emulsion coatings.

Solutions of ammonium thiocyanate are also suitable when the fixing process has to be carried out at very low temperatures, as they do not freeze above —18°C. At —7°C for instance, fixing takes only about 4 minutes, whereas it would take about 1 hour in ordinary hypo.

Another formula for a rapid fixing bath of this type is:

Potassium thiocyanate . .	100 g
Potassium alum . . .	50 g
Water to	1 litre

Dissolve and then add acetic acid 35 ml.

646. Fixation in Practice. Inasmuch as the ill effects of faulty working are not immediately evident, fixation and the washing processes which precede and follow it are not always carried out so carefully as is the case with development.

It is essential to realize that no visible sign shows that fixation is perfect; a negative may be quite clear after fixing and drying and yet may not have been properly fixed; it may not have been allowed to remain long enough in the fixer, or the fixing bath itself may have been exhausted. Images (negatives or positive prints) which are required to be kept for a long time must be fixed in a manner which conforms minutely to the following directions; these directions are much less important in the case of images which have merely passing interest.

The negatives, after being rinsed free of developer are placed in one of the fixing baths already prescribed, generally an acid fixing bath, or, in warm weather, in a fixing-hardening bath compounded with alum.

A safelight should be used, at any rate when putting materials in the fixer; in the case of neutral fixing solutions, negatives should be allowed to remain in the bath for at least three minutes before being exposed to white light; this period may, if necessary, be reduced to one minute in the case of acid fixing baths.

On account of the injurious action of the least trace of thiosulphate on certain developers, the various dishes employed must be so arranged that no splashes or drops of it can fall into the developer. The fingers should be rinsed in water after every time they have come into contact with hypo.

It will be found best to arrange dishes in the order in which they are to be used, those containing fixing solutions being placed at a lower level than those in which development is carried out. No drops of hypo solution must be allowed to fall on the floor, etc.; for on drying, these would give rise to dust of a very harmful nature towards negatives subsequently handled in the room. For the same reason those negatives which in course of treatment are found to be useless should be at least rinsed before being thrown away.

Fixation being generally slower than development, it is advisable, in the case of continuous working, to provide larger dishes or tanks for this purpose than for development. For example, when working with dishes, one would use for fixation those of a size capable of taking two or four of the negatives under treatment.

During fixation, negatives must be well covered by the solution.

After some minutes in the fixing bath, an examination of the back of the negative shows that the milky coating of the silver halides under the developed image is beginning to dissolve, the disappearance of the milkiness occurring as a rule more quickly under the denser parts of the image where least silver bromide remains.

From the time when the last traces of milkiness have disappeared the negatives are kept in the bath for a time equal to that already taken, or, preferably, when two-bath fixation (§ 642) is employed, they are transferred to the fresh bath and allowed to remain there for an equal time. When fixation is complete, negatives are washed.

If fixation is effected by the single-bath method, the solution must be frequently renewed so as not to pass the safety limit. In case of doubt, any of the tests described earlier (§ 644) may be used. In a very acid bath ($pH < 4.9$) the total fixing time should be at least four times as long as the clearing time (J. I. Crabtree, G. T. Eaton, and L. E. Muehler, 1943).

647. Fixer for Materials rich in Silver Iodide. Emulsions which have been more or less completely iodized (§ 604) fix very slowly in a fresh fixer of normal composition. Fixing can be accelerated by adding ammonium chloride, or sulphate (or, for industrial use, potassium cyanide to a solution of sodium thiosulphate.

On adding 4 per cent of thiourea (thiocarbamide) to a 20 per cent solution of sodium thiosulphate, the fixing time of a silver iodide emulsion is reduced from about 35 minutes to 3 minutes (J. Rzymkowski, 1926). The fixing bath should be sufficiently acid to avoid the formation of silver sulphide that would take place in the presence of alkali carried over from the developer. The fixer should be compounded as follows: 58 g of crystalline borax are dissolved in about 800 ml of water. A few drops of an alcoholic solution of methyl red are added, then about 18·6 ml of glacial acetic acid until a bright yellow tint is obtained ($pH = 6.4$); 200 g of sodium thiosulphate (hydrated) and 40 g of thiourea are dissolved in turn in the acid solution. The volume is then made up to 1 litre.

After being fixed in the thiourea bath, the material should be further treated in a plain, or slightly acid hypo solution, otherwise a dense white opalescence will be produced in the emulsion when it is washed.

Silver iodide emulsions can also be fixed in a 40 per cent hypo solution at 30°C. As a result of the high hypo concentration, the gelatine is unharmed (H. Lüppo-Cramer, 1925).

648. Regeneration of Fixing Baths. The following items will be discussed—(a) the maintenance of constant acidity and (b) hardening power, (c) the electrolytic regeneration of fixing baths by removing the silver, the life of the bath then being limited by the concentration of soluble iodide that accumulates, (d) the elimination of soluble iodide, which is not much practised, but which leads to a more economical use of the hypo.

(a) *Maintaining the Acidity of a Non-hardening Fixer.* The acidity is progressively reduced when developer is carried into the bath by negatives that are not rinsed, or which are only briefly rinsed. On the other hand the acidity is increased when an acid stop-bath is used between the development and fixation.

Sulphite is formed when the bisulphite in the fixer is neutralized by alkali, and the bisulphite can be regenerated by the cautious addition of dilute sulphuric acid. This operation should only be carried out by a chemist because an excess of sulphuric acid will cause the decomposition of the thiosulphate. For this reason it is usually preferable to re-acidify the bath by adding sodium bisulphite in concentrated solution. Each time the pH of the bath rises above 6·5, as shown by the change from yellow to blue of bromthymol blue indicator, a quantity of bisulphite should be added equal to half the quantity used when making up the fresh bath. The indicator solution can be prepared by dissolving 0·4 g of bromthymol blue in 75 ml of a 0·05 per cent solution of sodium hydroxide and then diluting to 1 litre with distilled water. Other indicators, mentioned below, are prepared in the same way.

The carry-over of a very acid stop-bath solution into the fixer may result in the decomposition of the sodium thiosulphate (hypo).

$$Na_2S_2O_3 + 2H^+ \rightarrow 2Na^+ + SO_2 + S + H_2O$$

Under these conditions it is necessary to prevent the pH from falling below 4·0 as shown by the change of the colour of bromphenol blue indicator from blue to yellow. This can be accomplished by adding sulphite and, if necessary, a small amount of sodium carbonate.

When a chrome-alum stop-bath is used, it is especially necessary to ensure that the pH of the fixer is not greater than 6·5 because a pH value greater than this may cause the precipitation of chromium hydroxide on the emulsion.

(b) *Maintaining the Acidity of a Hardening Fixer.* Hardening fixers which contain alum, and which are stabilized with boric acid, retain their hardening properties over a wide range (4·5 to 6·3) of pH. They can, therefore, be used without re-acidification to fix a larger area of negative emulsion than ordinary fixers can. Such fixers take (per litre) as much as 100 ft of 35-mm film before requiring re-acidification, whereas a fixer employing only acetic acid needs re-acidifying after 12 ft of film. When no electrolytic recovery of silver is employed, a boric-acid fixer can be exhausted to the extent of two or three re-acidifications. The bath should be re-acidified when 1 ml of bromcresol purple indicator added to 10 ml of the bath shows a reddish colour ($pH = 5·6$). It shows a yellow colour in the fresh fixing solution.

At each re-acidification, about 7·5 ml of acetic acid per litre are added, after the acid has been diluted with about 70 ml of water. The

fixing bath is vigorously stirred while the diluted acid is added.

(c) *Electrolytic Regeneration of Fixing Baths.* Several of the chemical processes for the recovery of the silver from used fixing baths can be used to regenerate the bath providing that the quantity of reagent used is insufficient to precipitate all the silver. These processes have been replaced, in industry, by the electrolytic deposition of the silver from the fixing bath in current use, the silver content of the bath always being maintained at a very low level, and the bath is only rejected when the increased concentration of iodide makes the fixing rate become slow. It has been suggested (P. Strauss, 1925) that the poisoning effect of the iodide could be offset, under these conditions, by adding a small quantity of sodium cyanide to the bath.

The electrolytic regeneration of fixing-baths, suggested by W. M. Schultz (1928) and by F. E. Garbutt and T. M. Ingman (1929) has been very thoroughly studied by K. C. D. Hickman and W. J. Weyerts (1931).

In the electrolytic separation of the metal from the aqueous solution of a simple salt, the metal ion travels towards the cathode (the negative electrode) where it is discharged and becomes an atom of the metal. The acid ion (anion) travels to the anode which it attacks, or it liberates oxygen by reacting with water. In the electrolysis of the complex salt, sodium argentothiosulphate, sodium ions migrate to the cathode and argentothiosulphate ions move towards the anode. The sodium atoms formed at the cathode react with neighbouring ions in solutions, including the argentothiosulphate ions. If there are sufficient argentothiosulphate ions, the sodium atoms react with these, liberating silver. In the absence of these ions the sodium reacts with the thiosulphate (hypo) ions giving, among other things, sulphide ions which, in turn, react with argentothiosulphate ions to form silver sulphide, discolouring the solution.

Thus it will be seen that the metallic silver is produced by a *secondary reaction* on ions which are tending to move away from the electrode on which the metal is deposited. In order to ensure a sufficient concentration of argentothiosulphate ions at the cathode it is necessary either to stir the solution very vigorously so that high current densities may be used, or to limit the current density to a few milliamperes per square decimetre (H. G. Doffin, 1935). The second course would occasion the use of a very large electrode surface in order to achieve an industrially practicable rate of recovery.

In order to recover 1 g of silver, without any loss of current, it would be necessary to use 0·33 ampere-hours.

The anodes employed are always of graphite, and while the cathodes may be also of graphite, stainless steel is usually preferred.

The electrolytic deposition of silver, without the formation of sulphite, is practicable only in an acid bath. The maximum current density that can be used, while obtaining a smooth, shiny deposit, increases, within certain limits, with the degree of agitation, the temperature, the silver content, the acidity, and the sulphite concentration. It decreases as the bromide ion concentration is increased.

With a degree of agitation sufficient to produce a solution velocity of 30 centimetres per second relative to the electrodes, a current density of 0·15 ampere per square decimetre of cathode may be used in a bath containing 1 g of silver per litre. The current density can be increased to 0·5 ampere per square decimetre if the solution velocity relative to the electrodes reaches 75 centimetres per second or, without increasing the agitation, to 0·9 ampere per square decimetre if the silver concentration is 6 g per litre.

At low current densities the silver deposit is white. On raising the current density, the deposit becomes cream, then yellow, and finally dark brown with the formation of a silver sulphide sludge. If this stage is reached, it is necessary to empty and thoroughly clean the installation.

When the silver deposit reaches a thickness of 0·5 millimetre it often acquires a coarse crystalline structure. The immobilization of the solution in the crevices makes it necessary to reduce the current density in order to avoid the formation of silver sulphide. The presence of gelatine and its degradation products in the used fixers favours the formation of a brilliant deposit. However, in the usual concentration, it has an adverse effect on the process, in that the gelatine is attracted towards the cathodes where it is to some extent deposited with the silver, forming a layer of high viscosity around the electrode and thus hindering the access of argentothiosulphate ions to the cathode. This difficulty can be overcome by the addition of thiourea.

Because the perfect clarity of the bath is necessary, as well as agitation, it is necessary to filter it before, as well as during, the electrolysis, otherwise the suspended particles may lead to pitting of the silver deposit with the consequent formation of silver sulphide.

When continuously regenerating the fixing bath, it is necessary to reject part from time to time, replacing it with suitably compounded, fresh solution. An industrial installation should thus include cells in which the silver content of the circulating bath is kept between 0·5 and 1·0 g per litre and at least one "tailing" cell in which the silver is entirely removed, the contents of the cell being then rejected.

The good operation of such an installation consists in the close control over the current density, though means have been suggested by K. C. D. Hickman for automatically estimating the silver content and adjusting the current density.

(d) *The Elimination and Recovery of the Iodide from Fixers.* The fact that the life of a regenerated fixing bath is limited by the accumulation of iodide, and the comparatively high price of iodine, make the recovery of the iodide a practical proposition at least in an industrial establishment (K. Kieser, 1934–7). A 5 per cent (saturated) solution of thallous sulphate (*poisonous*) is added to the bath. The first additions precipitate yellow-orange thallous iodide which soon settled to the bottom of the vessel. The additions are continued until light-yellow thallous bromide is predominantly formed. The thallous bromide is converted to the iodide by adding it to the next batch of fixer to be treated before making additions of thallous sulphate. On an average, the sodium iodide content of an exhausted fixer is about 0·4 g per litre.

After washing it with water, the thallous iodide is reconverted to thallous sulphate by warming with concentrated sulphuric acid to liberate the iodine.

649. Recovery of Silver from Exhausted Fixing Solutions without Regenerating the Bath.

On the average, about three-quarters of the silver contained in sensitive materials pass into the fixing baths. Negatives contain about 10 g and papers about 2 g of pure silver per square metre. A litre of exhausted fixer usually contains 4 to 5 g of silver, or from 10 to 12 g of silver when it is the first of two successive fixing baths. Assuming that the necessarily imperfect process of recovery in a small works only permits a yield of 75 per cent of these quantities, one can estimate the value of this recovery, allowing for the cost of precipitation (never very high) and for the cost of extracting the silver by the smelters.

The silver in fixing baths is generally precipitated in the form of sulphide. Under these conditions, and provided that the silver is not completely precipitated, fixing baths may be used again, at least once, though not indefinitely, because the accumulation of soluble bromides and particularly of iodides in the solution considerably retards fixation in solutions so regenerated.

The silver may also be recovered in the metallic state by precipitation on plates or scraps of zinc, iron, or copper. In this case the silver is contaminated with various impurities and needs to be refined.

To the residues thus collected are added the ashes of clippings from prints and films stripped from waste negatives.

Sulphide Precipitation. When the silver is precipitated as sulphide, the exhausted baths must be stored and treated in a yard or shed which is far enough from darkrooms, storerooms, etc., to avoid any risk of hydrogen sulphide coming in contact with sensitive material.

The used fixing baths are thrown into a large open vessel constructed of wood or plastic. This should be mounted on bricks; it must be provided at about a quarter of the way from the bottom with an outlet or tap, so that the greater part of the liquid may be run off, and at the bottom with a bung-hole, from which the sludge of silver sulphide may be periodically run off. Old developing solutions may also be poured into the same vessel, since they contain a little silver. These solutions will reduce a small quantity of the silver in the fixing solutions to the metallic state, and they will also tend to neutralize the residual acidity of the fixing baths. When the vessel is about three-quarters full, about 45 g of sodium sulphide is added for every gallon of liquid to be treated (10 g of the sulphide for every litre of liquid). This sulphide should be previously dissolved in a little boiling water. The mixture is stirred with a stick and left to settle. The next day a little of the clear supernatant liquid is taken in a test-tube (if the liquid is turbid it must be filtered) and a few drops of a solution of sodium sulphide are added; if no black precipitate forms, the silver has been completely precipitated; if, on the contrary, a black precipitate forms, add to the liquid in the barrel about half as much of the sodium sulphide

as before and repeat this process if necessary until all the silver has been precipitated. After a final settling, the liquid is run off by the tap through a filter-bag of close felt placed so as to trap any silver sulphide which might be lost.

After the vessel has been emptied in this way several times, as successive lots of fixing bath are treated, the black sludge is run off through the lower bung-hole and is collected in a tray. After drying, this mud is stored in a box until a sufficient quantity has been collected for sending to the smelter.

Pure dry silver sulphide contains 87 per cent of its weight of fine silver. On account of numerous impurities which accompany it, silver sulphide obtained in the manner described works out at about 60 per cent if it is precipitated from baths free from alum, and at about 40 per cent when it is contaminated with alumina or chromium hydroxide resulting from the interaction of sulphide with alums.

Precipitation by Zinc. To recover the silver from old fixing solutions by another method, a vessel of 5 to 10 gallons capacity, and equipped as in the previous case, may be used. Before starting the recovery process, the liquid must be neutralized, by means of sodium hydroxide (caustic soda) or milk of lime (lime first wetted with a little water and then left to slake) if it is acidic, or with sulphuric acid if it is alkaline. Then the liquid is acidified by adding sulphuric acid. After stirring, about 1 kg of granulated or scrap zinc for every gallon of liquid (200 g per litre) are thrown into the barrel; this quantity causes rapid precipitation (in about 24 hours, if the mixture is stirred from time to time) of silver (partially in the form of sulphide), which forms a black deposit on the zinc and in the bottom of the barrel.

An appreciable economy of zinc may be effected by enclosing the latter in a bag of coarse cloth suspended in the liquid.

On the next day, in order to find whether or not the liquid still contains any dissolved silver, proceed as follows. In a test-tube take a little of the clear, reddish, supernatant liquid, acidify with a few drops of sulphuric acid, shake (make sure that the liquid reddens blue litmus paper), and add about one-fifth of its volume of a 10 per cent solution of sodium sulphide; if no black precipitate forms, the silver is completely precipitated (a black precipitate obtained without the liquid being acidified has no significance); if silver still is present, keep the zinc in contact with the liquid for another day. As soon as all the silver is deposited, decant the liquid by the side opening.

One charge of zinc suffices for seven or eight such recovery processes without any appreciable slowing of the action. When the precipitation needs from two to three days, it may be accelerated by adding about 85 g of zinc per gallon of liquid (20 g per litre). Under these conditions, 1 g of zinc allows the recovery of about 1 g of silver.

From time to time the black deposit is collected and dried.

These various operations should be carried out in a well-ventilated place, as far as is convenient from darkrooms and any sensitive materials. As well as zinc, copper turnings, and iron, in the form of steel wool, can be used to recover the silver.

Steel Wool Method. It has been found that silver may be efficiently recovered from used fixer by passage through a column packed with steel wool (G. I. P. Levenson, 1963). Theoretically one part by weight of iron (steel wool) should displace approximately four parts by weight of silver from used fixer solutions, but in practice only two to two and one half parts by weight are displaced. In this method used fixer solution is slowly passed upwards through a column packed with steel wool when iron passes into solution and displaces the silver which is held in the steel wool. Almost any vessel from a plastic dustbin to a porcelain vat can be used. Only exhausted fixer should be employed in this method as the effluent from the column, being contaminated with iron, cannot be re-used as fixer. It is recommended that fixer should take about 24 hours to pass through the column to allow sufficient time for the exchange to take place. The size of the vessel required is, therefore, governed by the rate of use of fixer. The recovery unit may be connected directly to the outlet of an automatic processing machine. The exhaustion of the steel wool may be determined by measuring the high silver content of the effluent, or more simply by the visual appearance of grey flecks of silver in the upper layers of the steel wool. When this point has been reached, the used steel wool consisting mainly of silver, is removed from the apparatus and left to dry before sending to the refiners. It is important to ensure that the steel wool with which the apparatus is recharged, should not become rusty by leaving it in a moist condition in the presence of air prior to its use. Once submerged in fixer it is protected from rusting and all operations should, therefore, aim at keeping the steel wool dry before it becomes submerged in the fixer solution.

CHAPTER XXXII

WASHING AND DRYING

650. The function of washing. 651. The mechanism of washing in several changes of water—diffusion of ions—number of changes—optimum volumes and times. 652. The mechanism of washing in running water—conditions for washing—means of finding flow-rate. 653. The washing powers of water—hard water—effect of added ions. 654. Apparatus for washing—design of wash tanks—automatic apparatus—cascade washers. 655. Control of washing—tests for residual thiosulphate—conductivity measurements. 656. Washing in practice—optimum conditions—size of wash tanks—water conservation—speed of washing—washing in hard water. 657. Hypo eliminators. 658. The purpose of drying. 659. The physics of drying—effect of relative humidity. 660. The practice of drying—preliminary removal of surface water—drying rooms and cabinets. 661. Distortion of the image during drying. 662. Acceleration of drying by heat—maximum temperatures—hardening for drying at high temperatures. 663. Rapid drying with a volatile liquid—alcohol-acetone. 664. Instantaneous drying by dehydration of gelatine—saturated solutions of potassium carbonate.

650. The Function of Washing. Photographic materials are washed to remove all the soluble salts formed during fixation, also the constituents of the fixing bath which may be absorbed in the emulsion layer or adhering superficially to the prints or negatives.

According to circumstances, it may be necessary to carry out the washing either in the minimum time or with the minimum quantity of water.

If fixation is complete, so that the emulsion contains nothing but the silver of the image and soluble salts, then the salts are readily washed out, provided the washing is systematic. If fixation is incomplete, the remaining insoluble salts cannot be eliminated, no matter how long the washing is continued. It is probably with a view to establishing a mean between these two experimental facts that photographers generally state the "hypo is strongly retained by gelatine." This is true of the insoluble thiosulphates which result from bad fixation, but it is not so for the soluble salts, which are the only ones remaining after complete fixation.

This chapter will deal with the following subjects: (*a*) The mechanism of washing in changes of water and in running water, and it will be shown that washing in running water in the manner generally employed is a means of consuming the greatest amount of water with the smallest effect. (*b*) The conditions which must be fulfilled in order to wash negatives or prints in the most rational manner. (*c*) The use of *hypo-eliminators*, from which it will be

seen that there is only one perfect eliminator applicable to all cases, viz. plain water.

It may be useful to re-state here an evident truth: an object cannot be cleaner, after washing and drying, than the water used for washing it.

In the activation-stabilization technique of processing, the processed material should *never* be washed unless it is first fixed in the normal manner. This is because, in this technique, relatively insoluble, light insensitive silver complexes are formed in the stabilizer bath and their stability depends upon the presence of an excess of the complexing agent remaining in the material. If the excess of the complexing agent is removed by washing, the silver complexes will decompose and cause either a yellowing or bleaching of the image.

651. The Mechanism of Washing in Several Changes of Water. Thorough investigations of washing in successive baths were made by A. V. Elsden and A. W. Warwick (1919). The methods followed by these two experimenters were almost identical. Plates or films, developed or undeveloped, were fixed in baths of known strength. They were then successively placed into accurately measured quantities of water for known periods of time. The quantities of thiosulphate and soluble silver in each of these washing waters were determined. Finally, after completing the washings, the amount of thiosulphate remaining in the film was also determined.

These experiments, and many others (A. Haddon and F. B. Grundy, 1893–96; Gaedicke,

1897; L. Lumière and A. Seyewetz, 1902), established the fact that, the elimination of soluble thiosulphates by washing with water is easily carried out; this is in accordance with the general law of the diffusion of ions through permeable membranes. It is necessary to wash photographic materials on a paper base for a considerably greater time than those on a glass or celluloid base, as the paper tends to retain the thiosulphates. The thiosulphates are automatically expelled from the gelatine providing their concentration in the gelatine is not equal to the concentration in the liquid in which the material is washed. If a film of gelatine, impregnated with fixing solution of normal concentration, is placed in pure water at a temperature of about 60°F (15°C), the "osmotic pressure" of the thiosulphate, that is to say the pressure which the salt exerts in leaving the gelatine, is considerably greater than 5 lb per square inch.

As soon as a negative, impregnated with any salt which does not react with gelatine (as does alum, for example), is placed in pure water, the salt in the solution adhering superficially to the negative becomes distributed in the water, and the salt absorbed in the gelatine diffuses out, at first very quickly and then more and more slowly, until finally the concentrations in the gelatine and the water are equal.

If the negative has been placed at the bottom of a dish or tank full of still water, the salt solution which diffuses out of the negative, and which is denser than the water, accumulates above the plate; this solution soon becomes equal in concentration to the solution which impregnates the gelatine. The movement of salt is then arrested, since the uniform diffusion of the salt throughout the liquid in the tank takes a very considerable time. If, however, the water is stirred mechanically, or if the negative is placed so that the salt solution can leave it and be replaced by pure water, the diffusion proceeds much farther, each separate washing having a much greater effect. This is the case if the negative is supported emulsion downwards in the upper part of the tank, or is placed vertically in the tank with a sufficient depth of water below it to allow for the accumulation of the denser solution.

When a 13 × 18 cm (7 × 5 in.) plate is removed from a fixing solution it takes with it about 5 ml of solution (the total liquid adhering superficially to the plate and impregnating the emulsion). If the fixing bath contains 20 per cent of hypo the plate will have removed 1 g of it from the bath. If now the plate be placed in a dish containing 95 ml of water, the total volume of liquid will be 100 ml. By rocking the dish, equilibrium will be attained between the internal and external concentrations of hypo, which will become 1 per cent, that is to say, a concentration of one-twentieth the initial concentration. By repeating this process, the concentration becomes one-twentieth the previous concentration, and so on—

Number of washings	1	2	3	4	5
Concentration %	1	0·05	0·0025	0·000125	0·000006

It can be assumed (K. Hickman and D. A. Spencer, 1922) that a residual amount of hypo equal to 0·0016 g per square decimetre has no adverse influence on the permanence of silver images. By taking a quantity ten times as small (to ensure absolute safety), viz. 0·00016 g per square decimetre, or 0·00036 g for a 13 × 18 cm plate, it will be seen that if this quantity is regarded as being distributed in 3 ml, which is approximately the volume of water absorbed by the emulsion, the washing may be considered effective as soon as the concentration in the washing water has been reduced to 0·00036 × 100/3, or about 0·01 per cent. This stage will be reached after a very small number of separate washings, provided each one is carried out to completion in a sufficient volume of water.

Equilibrium between the concentrations inside and outside the gelatine is generally reached after 5 minutes' rocking of the dish, but 99 per cent of the amount which will diffuse from the gelatine has usually come out in about 2 minutes. It is thus seen that, for rapid washing, each separate washing need not be longer than 2 minutes provided sufficient agitation is used.

As a general rule, when washing, it is not essential to rock the dish or to wait until equilibrium has been reached: it is only when the amount of water available is restricted that these considerations become important, and then special methods are employed (§ 656). In general, then, each washing withdraws only a fraction of the amount of hypo which could be removed if equilibrium were attained, and this fraction, which varies according to the mode of working, is to some extent a measure of the effectiveness of the washing. It was shown that washing is more effective if the negatives are held vertically than if they are placed emulsion upwards at the bottom of the tank; the efficiency can be still further increased if the surface liquid is allowed to drain from the negatives before transferring them to the clean bath.

Most experimenters agree that there is nothing to be gained by prolonging the duration of each washing beyond 5 minutes, and that if 15 ml of water per square inch of emulsion is used, 5 or 6 washings are quite sufficient to ensure that the permanence of negatives on film or glass supports will be as great as the efficiency of the fixation permits.

652. The Mechanism of Washing in Running Water. Washing tanks are frequently so badly adapted to the object in view that the water flows directly from the tap to the sink without flowing *through* the tank, and therefore does not remove more than an extremely small proportion of the hypo which it should remove. The effectiveness of washing depends neither on the amount of water used nor on the time during which the water flows, but on the volume of water which comes into effective contact with the plate and on the rapidity with which the water charged with hypo is replaced by fresh water. Unless a scientifically constructed apparatus which permits the frequent renewal of the water in contact with the negatives is employed, running-water washing is slower than washing in separate changes of water, its only advantage being an economy in labour.

The proportional reduction in concentration of the liquid in the emulsion, in a fixed period of time, will always be in the same ratio providing the washing conditions remain constant. The magnitude of this ratio, which is to some extent a measure of the effectiveness of a washing apparatus varies from one apparatus to another.

The best method of washing a single plate in running water is to allow water to flow directly across the plate (this method is not applicable to papers or films); the elimination of hypo is then about twice as fast as it is when the plate is placed in a washing tank through which water passes much more violently.

The worst conditions are obtained by using a large dish, or a tank without an outlet at the bottom, and a thin stream of water. Then, owing to the presence of eddies in the water, the speed of washing varies considerably from one part to another.

Experience shows that in the case of a tank, with vertical grooves for the plates and fed by a constant stream of water which is removed by a siphon, the elimination of hypo is more rapid when the tank is fully loaded with plates; it would seem that when there are no plates in the tank the incoming water dilutes the salt solution instead of displacing it.

The very accurate work of K. C. D. Hickman and D. A. Spencer (1922–25), to whose work we are indebted for much of the data in this paragraph, has shown that washing in running water may be considered as taking place in two stages: the total replacement of the water in the tank, and the attainment of equilibrium between the liquid in the emulsion and the water in the tank. The time necessary for equilibrium varies, according to the type of plate or film used, from 5 to 10 minutes; obviously no time can be set down for the complete renewal of the water in the tank, but it often requires more than an hour. It is easy to determine experimentally the time required for this phase of washing, by the following method.

Place in the dish or tank (in the case of a vertical tank, the place normally occupied by plates to be washed should be filled with plain glass) about 2 ml of a 2 per cent solution of safranine, or of a saturated solution of permanganate (permanganate solution should be employed only in tanks constructed of glass, earthenware, or slate; safranine only should be used with tanks of wood or metal) for each square inch of surface to be washed (25 ml for a $4\frac{1}{4} \times 3\frac{1}{4}$ in. plate). The time is noted, under normal conditions of washing, for the water in the tank to become completely decolorized. The end-point can be judged by comparing water from the tank and pure water, using two identical glass vessels against a white ground for the purpose.

If, for example, it is usual to use six $4\frac{1}{4} \times 3\frac{1}{4}$ in. plates, then about 150 ml of the coloured solution would be required. If an interval of 35 minutes is necessary for complete decolorization of the solution, then for normal washing with the same water supply the time should be 35 minutes plus the 10 minutes necessary for obtaining equilibrium between the solution in the gelatine and that in the tank; the washing time, therefore, under the conditions of the test, will be 45 minutes.

Since the gelatine backing of films holds as much hypo as the emulsion, their area must be doubled in order to calculate the amount of coloured liquid required for the test. The back of a film should be washed as carefully as the front; the spots of silver sulphide, arising from the decomposition of the silver thiosulphate absorbed in the fixing bath, are liable to occur also on the back.

653. The Washing Powers of Water. G. I. P. Levenson (1967, 1970) investigated the efficiency of washing of thiosulphate from emulsion layers, by water containing different ions and of differing hardness (§509). From measurements of the quantities of hypo remaining in the film after washing in various types of water (Fig. 32.1), Levenson found that washing of hardened emulsions was most efficient in hard water and very inefficient in distilled water. The efficiency of distilled water could be made to match that of a hard water by the addition of sodium bicarbonate to achieve the same hardness. The washing efficiency for various added ions at concentration of M/250 was found to be in the following order: hydrochloric acid < sodium thiosulphate < distilled water < sodium chloride < sodium bisulphite ≪ sodium sulphate ≪ sodium bicarbonate ≪ sodium sulphite < sodium hydroxide. The increase in pH on moving along the series increases the washing efficiency although the effect reached a limit at pH 9.

Levenson also showed that the washing efficiency decreased with increase in hardening

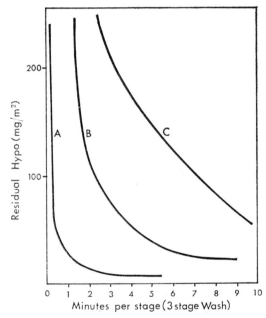

FIG. 32.1 RESIDUAL HYPO PLOTTED AGAINST WASHING TIME FOR A HARDENED MOTION PICTURE POSITIVE FILM FIXED IN THE PRESENCE OF ALUMINIUM ION. CURVE A. TAP WATER TOTAL HARDNESS 196 PPM, $CaCO_3$, CURVE B. TAP WATER TOTAL HARDNESS 25 PPM. $CaCO_3$. CURVE C, DISTILLED WATER.

(Levenson)

of the emulsion, the time of washing (the time required to reduce the residual hypo concentration to a particular value) was roughly proportional to the concentration of hardener when an aluminium-based hardener was used.

Levenson's studies explain why washing is relatively inefficient in areas where pure (soft) water is available and considerably more efficient in hard water areas; the main contribution to washing efficiency being the bicarbonate anion.

654. Apparatus for Washing. The washing of a small number of plates is frequently carried out in dishes, but for continuous work vertical tanks (tanks with grooves, or tanks, without grooves, into which the plates are placed in developing racks) are generally preferred. To ensure efficient washing it is essential that the tank be effectively traversed by the current of water. For this, two arrangements are used concurrently; water can be led in at the bottom of the tank and out over the top or through an overflow pipe, or it can flow directly from the tap into the tank and then out through a tube which communicates with the bottom of the tank and empties at a level slightly lower than the rim of the tank. The type of tank commonly used by amateurs, viz. one with an outlet only in the bottom, can easily be converted by fitting to the tap a rubber tube which is tied to the tank by string; or by soldering to the interior of the outlet a lead tube bent into the form of a swan's neck.

Various washing devices are available in which the water is kept in turbulent movement either by entering through obliquely-set nozzles, or by the plates or films being mounted on a drum which is kept rotating by a very simple water motor (paddle-wheel or simple turbine).

As it has long been realized that washing in running water is slower than washing in changes of water, many inventors have attempted to construct an automatic apparatus for changing the water so that the handling, which is the only objection to this method of washing, may be eliminated. These machines are usually either tanks operated by a large emptying siphon, which is self-priming directly the tank is full, as with the tantalus cup, or ordinary tanks fed intermittently from a flush tank, or tanks with automatic flushing controlled by the outlet plug, or finally, for small sizes of plates, dishes which empty by tilting when full, and then immediately return to the filling position under the tap.

For economy in water, several washing tanks are sometimes arranged in *cascade form*; it is then necessary to place the plates to be washed in the lowest tank first and then to transfer them successively from tank to tank, so that the final washing takes place in the upper tank containing pure water. Unless this counter-current movement of the plates is adhered to, plates in the lowest tank will not be in contact with water of a sufficient purity and hence will not be completely washed until after the washing of all the other plates in the tanks higher up in the series.

To ensure that the washing is done under the best possible conditions, the tanks should be smooth inside and should not be larger than necessary; a plate can be washed more quickly in a small than in a large tank.

655. Control of Washing. Since the completion of the washing process is not accompanied by any indication that all the salts have been eliminated, various methods have been suggested for ascertaining when washing is complete.

It is possible, for example, to discover that the water which drips from a plate or print does not contain enough hypo to be detected by the usual methods, i.e. does not decolorize a starch solution which has been made blue with a trace of iodine, or a solution of permanganate, both solutions having been made of a suitable strength.

Dissolve 1 g of potassium permanganate and 1 to 2 g of sodium carbonate in 1 litre of water. This solution has an intense violet colour. Collect the drainings from several plates or prints in one glass vessel, and an equal quantity of the water used for washing (taken straight from the tap) in another. Add to each one drop of the above permanganate solution. If the colour persists in the drainings for as long as it does in the fresh water, the washing may be considered to be complete.

Should the single drop of permanganate be instantly decolorized by the water used in the blank test (owing to the presence of organic matter), further drops should be added until a permanent pink colour has been obtained. The same number of drops should be added to the drainings.

A much more sensitive reaction, in which the traces of thiosulphate catalyze the discoloration by sodium azide (NaN_3) of the iodine coloured by starch, has been described by E. E. Jelley and W. Clark (1929), but its application is more delicate.

Finally, attention should be drawn to a check method invaluable in experimental work, but the practical use of which is restricted as it involves the loss of the images tested, and is therefore suitable only for cinematographic films of which it is always possible to cut off a strip of a few inches. Pour into a test-tube 10 ml of a solution containing 25 g mercuric chloride and 25 g of potassium bromide per litre. Then put in 10–15 sq cm of image (film, or layer of emulsion scraped off a plate). The liquid becomes opalescent when thiosulphate is present; the concentration can be ascertained by comparison with samples prepared with known quantities of thiosulphate (J. I. Crabtree and F. E. Ross, 1930).

In commercial establishments the control of washing may be effected by comparing the electrical conductivities of the feed and waste waters of the tanks (K. C. D. Hickman, 1923).

These tests are very good in their way, but it is essential that their exact significance be understood. The fact of finding no thiosulphate in the drippings certainly indicates that the soluble thiosulphates have been removed and that, as a consequence, the washing is complete. But it gives no information as to the completeness of the fixation, and hence of the permanence of the image, the test giving no indication of insoluble complex thiosulphate of silver and sodium which may be in the film. This control of fixation may be made, after washing, by placing on the clear part of a plate or print a drop of a 10 per cent solution of sodium sulphide. If fixation is not complete, a brown spot, more or less dark, will appear. As a spot of this sort is indelible, it is obvious that the test is applicable only to waste plates or papers, unless the material is deliberately sacrificed for the purpose of the test.

656. Washing in Practice. As far as the amateur photographer is concerned, the choice between washing in running water and washing in changes of water will be settled by personal convenience; for the professional, or on the industrial scale, the choice will depend on the relative costs of water and manual labour.

It must be remembered that washing in running water is less effective when it is carried out in baths of large size, and that the hypo should be removed from the tank directly it diffuses out of the emulsion. It may be said that on the average *the first seven minutes are taken up with washing the plates and the rest of the time with washing the tank* (K. C. D. Hickman, 1925). It is therefore necessary to use tanks of suitable size and design so that the washing of the tank is almost as rapid as that of the negatives.

In a case of extreme urgency, water may be allowed to flow directly over the plate to be washed, or three successive washings each of 2 minutes may be given, but plenty of water must be used and the dish must be rocked continuously for the whole period; the interrupted washing should be subsequently completed.

In ordinary work, when washing in changes of water, five or six washings of about 5 minutes each in plenty of water are given. With running water, at least an hour should be allowed when using a tank which is effectively flushed with a rapid current of water; or, better, the time required for complete washing should be determined for the particular tank with a given consumption of water (§ 655).

When the supply of water is very limited, the best results are obtained by employing for each washing only just enough water to cover the plates, draining the plates between each washing and increasing slightly the number of washings. For washing in running water the *capillary flow method* (L. Lumière, 1922) may be used. The complete washing of a plate $4\frac{1}{4} \times 3\frac{1}{4}$ in. may thus be done in 12 to 15 minutes with only about 30 ml of water. For this purpose, the slow and regular capillary flow of water in an almost vertical ribbon of cotton twill is used. The water is fed from above by a tank, from which, so to speak, it is siphoned; the plate is placed on the twill, which has been previously wetted, care being taken to avoid air bells. The flow of water may be regulated by the height of the fall measured from the level of the water in the reservoir to the free end of the ribbon.

Plates and prints can be washed in sea-water, except that at least two washes in soft water are necessary to remove the salts of the sea-water, and particularly the deliquescent magnesium chloride. The use of distilled water or of slightly acid water does not result in the complete elimination of hypo owing to the impossibility of converting the "gelatine thiosulphate" formed during fixation in the acid fixing bath, into "calcium gelatinate."

When a plate is taken from the fixing bath and placed in the washing-tank, the concentrated fixing salt diffuses out from the emulsion and is partly absorbed by any other negatives in the tank which may have been partially washed. Therefore whenever plates are introduced one after the other into a bath to be washed together, the time of washing or the number of changes of water must be counted *from the insertion of the last negative.*

In the case of films or prints left to themselves in a dish or tank, washing in running water is liable to be ineffective if the surfaces to be washed cover each other and thus afford mutual protection against free contact with the current of water. Washing in several changes of water is therefore the only possible way, but the films or prints must not settle in a stationary heap at the bottom of the dish but must be kept moving. This can be done by making two piles in the dish and transferring the prints or films one by one from one heap to the other: also by transferring them singly from one tank to another.

In view of the increased consumption of water and the limits and cost of present water supplies, it is becoming increasingly necessary to use the minimum quantity of water for washing of photographic materials. This can be achieved, to some extent, by the use of wash tanks of the correct size for the quantity and size of materials to be washed. However, it should be borne in mind that an automatic processing machine can use more water in one hour than a domestic household uses in one week.

In automatic processing machines, the consumption of water can be substantially reduced by using a 2 stage counter-current wash in which the water flows through 2 wash tanks in the opposite direction to the film travel (L. E. West, 1969). A washing system of this type is shown in Fig. 32.2.

Pumps can be eliminated by the use of sufficiently large pipes and by having the overflow of the weir to the first tank below the weir to the second tank (Fig. 32.2). Counter-current wash conversion units are now being made commercially available to reduce the water consumption to as low as one eighth of the water originally required. In a multi-stage process economies in water consumption can be effected by leading the waste from the first tank to a wash tank used for an earlier stage in the process.

Economies in water usage can also be made by the use of flow control devices and automatic switches. These ensure that the optimum flow is used and that the water flow is stopped when the machine is not in use. Still further economies can be made by the substitution of ammonium thiosulphate for sodium thiosulphate as the

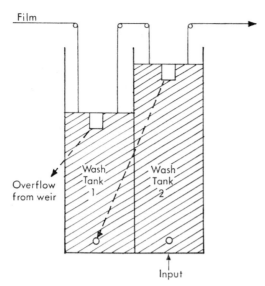

Film

Overflow
from weir

Wash
Tank
1

Wash
Tank
2

Input

FIG. 32.2. A TWO-TANK COUNTER-CURRENT
WASH
(L. E. West)

fixing agent. The former is used at about one half the molar concentration of the latter and, in addition washes out more easily from photographic film (J. I. Crabtree, G. T. Eaton and L. E. Muehler, 1943, L. E. West, 1969).

Contradictory opinions have been expressed on many occasions regarding various circumstances which are capable of affecting the speed of washing. It has been stated, for example, that the washing of plates which have been fixed in an acid bath is slower than the washing of plates fixed in a neutral bath, when, on the contrary, the swelling of the gelatine in a neutral bath prolongs washing considerably. It is often stated that washing is accelerated by increasing the temperature of the water but many experiments show that the speed of washing is independent of the temperature of the bath (more rapid diffusion is compensated by the swelling of the gelatine in the warmer water).

If, in certain circumstances, it is necessary to keep a plate in water for an unusually long time, it is advisable to add (to the water) a little sodium bisulphite (about 5 per cent) to stop the gelatine swelling excessively and thus becoming very tender. An emulsion, which has not been hardened with alum, if kept for a long time in polluted water is liable to be attacked by bacteria, which will cause liquefaction of the gelatine in patches. For this reason plates should never be left in water overnight.

When the only water available for washing contains a large quantity of chalk, which tends to form a superficial fog on drying, it is advisable, to ensure that the negatives shall have a perfectly clear surface, to follow the washing with a few minutes' immersion in a 1 per cent solution of hydrochloric or acetic acid. This precaution is particularly to be recommended for the very small negatives intended for large scale enlargement. In this case lime deposits, even imperceptible to the naked eye, increase graininess of the enlarged image. It is also advisable for all negatives when alcohol is used for rapid drying, since it avoids the formation of an opaque white fog, which would appear chiefly on those portions of the plate which had dried most rapidly (L. P. Clerc, 1917).

It is as well always to complete the washing of plates under a spray of perfectly filtered water, to free them from foreign bodies which may adhere to the gelatine during drying.

It is sometimes recommended that film negatives should be rinsed in water containing a little glycerine in order to give a greater suppleness to the dry film. But all photographic images which have been treated with glycerine remain permanently damp, and atmospheric action on the silver is thus facilitated; many cases have been cited of slow changes in images thus treated.

657. Hypo Eliminators. The idea of attempting to destroy hypo instead of eliminating it is almost as old as photography. This idea is unfortunately opposed to common sense, and to a sufficiently large number of experimental facts. To begin with, a chemical action never " destroys "; it can only transform; and those who have commended such practice have usually not tried to discover whether the products of this transformation are any less liable to damage the image than is the hypo from which they have been obtained. On the other hand, the substance which actively alters images is not so much the sodium thiosulphate as the insoluble complex thiosulphate of silver and sodium. It is therefore necessary to find out the form in which this salt of silver exists after the action of the eliminator.

All the substances which have been recommended as hypo eliminators are oxidizers; we may mention sodium hypochlorite (F. W. Hart, 1864), hydrogen peroxide (A. Smith, 1866), iodine (H. Vogel, 1872), potassium persulphate (Schering, 1894), sodium hypoiodite (P. Mercier, 1897), potassium percarbonate (G. Meyer, 1901), alkaline ammonium persulphate (L. Lumière and A. Seyewetz, 1902), alkaline perborates (G. F. Jaubert, 1903), and the sodium compound of p-toluene-chloro-amide-sulfonate (E. F. Shelberg, 1922), which, in aqueous solution, slowly decomposes to give hypochlorite.

As early as 1889, Traill Taylor stated that " if one wishes to take all the precautions which are necessary in order to apply the would-be hypo eliminators without danger to the photographic images, the operation will be found to be longer and more complicated than the washing itself."

Many experimenters who have studied the reactions involved in the oxidation of thiosulphates (notably Chapman Jones, 1899, and E. Sedlaczek, 1904) have shown that most of the oxidizers used attack the silver of the photographic image, and that in reacting with the thiosulphate they form tetrathionate and dithionate (as well as inert sulphate), which appear to be as dangerous to the image as is the thiosulphate itself; they also resemble thiosulphate in interfering with subsequent treatment, such as intensification.

Experiments made by A. E. Amor (1925) to determine the effectiveness of various eliminators, in which the residual hypo of plates at various stages of washing (with and without eliminator) was measured, show that the efficiency of oxidizers is less than that of a single washing in a 0·2 per cent solution of caustic soda, and that after one extra wash (the duration of each wash being 2 minutes) the elimination of hypo is more complete than it would be were an eliminator used for the same time, and much less risk of damage to the image is incurred.

Sodium hypochlorite is the most dangerous of all the eliminators, yet, in France, it is also the one most frequently employed. The resulting image contains silver chloride, which is liable to change on exposure to light, giving irregular violet-coloured patches; and, in fairly strong solution, sodium hypochlorite attacks both silver and gelatine.

The best method, then, is to leave these various reagents severely alone, and to use the only perfect eliminator, pure water, constantly applied to the surface to be washed.

658. The Purpose of Drying. Photographic plates and films which have been washed at temperatures between 60°F (15°C) and 68°F (20°C) and have been wiped free of water clinging to the surface, contain an amount of water which is about six to ten times the weight of the gelatine in the emulsion, so that it may be as much as 0·05 to 0·15 ml of water per square inch of emulsion surface. In the case of films coated on the back with gelatine, an approximately equal quantity of water will be contained in this backing layer. The amount of water absorbed is considerably greater at higher temperatures.

In the process of drying, this water has to be evaporated without injury to the image (partial or complete melting, markings, reticulation, etc.); at the same time, the adhesion of dust to the moist emulsion must, as far as possible, be prevented.

Obviously, drying will be more rapid if superficial water is wiped off at the start.

It must be noted that even after long and effective washing, the water held by the negative still contains traces of sodium thiosulphate too small indeed to be detected even by the most delicate means. As drying proceeds, however, adhering water collects in drops, which grow smaller and smaller, so that the whole of the thiosulphate in this water becomes concentrated in small areas which may then show up as defects due to insufficient washing (K. C. D. Hickman, 1926).

659. The Physics of Drying. The air always contains a certain amount of water in the form of vapour, this quantity varying greatly according to circumstances. Comparatively dry air, when kept in the presence of water or moist bodies, or into which water vapour is introduced by a boiler, will take up moisture to a certain maximum, which increases according to the temperature of the air. When this limit has been reached, the air is said to be *saturated* with moisture. The ratio of the quantity of water vapour present in a given volume of air to the quantity which would be present in the same volume of saturated air is called the *hygrometric condition*, the *fraction of saturation*, or the *relative humidity*. On cooling the air, its relative humidity is increased, and it may become saturated (condensation of mist or deposition of dew). Conversely, the relative humidity of air is decreased when the temperature is raised.

Air of 50 per cent relative humidity is considered as being very dry. In cold, damp weather the almost saturated outside air has its relative humidity lowered to 30 per cent or even less when it is warmed to the normal temperature of a workshop or dwelling house.

Dry gelatine absorbs water in a moist atmosphere, whilst moist gelatine loses moisture in a dry atmosphere. In saturated air, which is unable to take up any more moisture, all evaporation is prevented, and as a consequence moist gelatine cannot be dried in it, even though the amount of moisture to be removed be very small. The rate of drying is very nearly inversely proportional to the relative humidity of the air. Air which is warmed to reduce the relative humidity has its capacity for drying increased to a greater extent when the rise of temperature is large. The practical limits of drying by this system are, however, quickly reached because of the risk of melting the gelatine. Since the air becomes loaded with moisture as evaporation proceeds, it soon becomes saturated, so preventing further drying, unless it is continually renewed at the surfaces of the materal that is to be dried.

Gelatine should never be completely desiccated; it is considered to be dry when it contains no more than about 10 to 15 per cent of moisture. Further drying renders it very brittle, a fault which would be specially evident with film negatives, and might also cause injurious effects in the case of glass negatives.

Drying in an atmosphere of less than 60 per cent relative humidity tends to dry the surface layer before the underlying portions; the evaporation of the imprisoned moisture is thus retarded. Injury may occur to negatives which are stored, or to films which are rolled, in this condition when the imprisoned water becomes re-distributed through the whole thickness of the coating.

The drying of films in motion-picture laboratories is carried out as a rule in a current of air at 70 per cent or 80 per cent relative humidity, at temperatures between 78°F (25°C) and 87°F (30°C).

The evaporation of water is accompanied by the absorption of heat, which, in the case of spontaneous evaporation, results in a lowering of temperature. Since, at the same relative humidity, the rate of evaporation of water decreases as the temperature of the water to be evaporated is lowered, it is seen that drying tends to become progressively slower. This retardation is all the more marked when evaporation takes place simultaneously from both sides of a negative; a drop of water adhering to the back of a negative often results in retarding the drying of the portion of the gelatine layer immediately opposite to it.

660. The Practice of Drying. Before drying, the plates or films should be given a final rinse in a bath containing a few drops of wetting agent and both sides should be wiped gently but firmly with a piece of moist viscose sponge or similar material, to remove all superfluous water. For lengths of film, use may be made of a pair of squeegees, hinged at one end and elongated to form handles. Not only does this preliminary procedure accelerate drying, but it removes any spots or flecks of gelatine which may have settled on the film and it also removes the possibility of small areas of irregular density due to drops of water remaining on the film.

Glass plates should be placed on a rack for drying. The plates should not be placed too close together or there will be insufficient air circulation between the plates. Under extreme conditions it is possible for water that has evaporated from one plate to condense on the back of the neighbouring plate.

Cut films, if they have been processed in hangers, are generally kept in these hangers until drying has been completed. The hangers may be suspended from special racks or placed in ordinary plate racks.

Lengths of film which are not more than about 3 or 4 ft long are suspended vertically from clips; the lower ends of the films are weighted with special clips of sufficient size to prevent the films from curling.

Drying should be carried out in premises that are well ventilated, dry, dust free, and at a moderate temperature. In commercial installations drying is carried out in specially constructed rooms or cabinets into which warm, filtered air is passed. Modern automatic processors normally include a drying section and air squeegees or squeegee rollers to remove the excess moisture prior to the films entering the drying section. In these drying units the air may be passed through a de-humidifying unit to remove the water vapour from the air which varies from day to day. The air is partially dehydrated by a refrigeration unit and re-recirculated, making the control of drying independent of external atmospheric conditions.

If a drying cabinet is not available for drying plates or films it is important that there should be no sudden change in ambient temperature, relative humidity, or speed of air currents. Every negative which is subjected to great changes in drying conditions shows a distinct mark between the portions dried under different conditions. Those parts which have dried most slowly may be more or less dense than the other areas. In particular, negatives should never be allowed to stand in the sun during drying. It follows, therefore, that once the drying process has started, the negative should not be disturbed no matter how great the impatience to examine them. This also applies to drying in a drying cabinet where opening the door can lead to a considerable change in the drying conditions.

For the amateur rapid film dryers are available. These dryers blow filtered air upwards through the film which remains on the spiral. It is claimed that drying time is considerably reduced and the possibility of dust settling on the films is eliminated.

In a humid atmosphere, a high drying temperature leads to an increase of density and contrast. Evaporation in a moist atmosphere is slow and consequently cooling of the gelatine is negligible so that the gelatine can become softened by the high temperature. This allows the silver grains to be rearranged to a certain degree. In a dry atmosphere the evaporation of water is rapid; this cools the gelatine and keeps the emulsion fairly firm in even comparatively warm air. Variations of 25 per cent have been noted, after drying in various conditions, in densities that were equal before drying (J. Crabtree; D. R. White, 1922).

Drying should never be undertaken in a place where there is a risk of the temperature falling low enough to freeze the water with which the negatives are impregnated; "ice flowers," which would be formed under such conditions, would leave their distinct impression in the gelatine.

661. Distortion of the Image during Drying. Very slight deformations, quite negligible in the common applications of photography, occur in the emulsion during drying, especially near the edges. They may need to be taken into account in high-precision measurements (cartography, astronomy, etc.).

These deformations are mainly due to local inequalities of drying. They occur chiefly on negatives developed with a tanning developer (pyrogallol), as the denser portions of the image, which are tanned, contain less water than the surrounding gelatine. The presence of drops of water adhering to the gelatine surface, or even to the glass, causes similar deformations due to local retardation of drying. Every negative has a margin of about half an inch in which these deformations are fairly considerable. Distortion, which is due to inequality of drying, may be considered as temporary if the gelatine has not been hardened with alum, and with this exception it is possible to remedy the defect by allowing the negative to swell in water and to dry again with all necessary precautions, particularly by hastening drying by treatment with alcohol (§ 663).

662. Acceleration of Drying by Heat. The drying of glass negatives or paper prints may be greatly hastened by a current of warm air, or by placing the material to be dried near a source of heat, provided that the gelatine has been hardened to raise its melting-point to withstand the rise in temperature. The heating of the emulsion on a glass plate on which a current of warm air is directed can be limited by blowing a current of cold air on to the back (glass) surface at the same time. If heating, in this way, is excessive when applied to films, it often causes a permanent deformation of the film base (notably curling at the edges), which may be an obstacle to perfect sharpness of prints.

Negatives fixed in solutions containing alum, and especially in a fixing solution containing a large quantity of chrome-alum (§ 638), will generally stand a temperature of 120°F (49°C) to 140°F (60°C). They may be dried in full sunlight, provided that no shadow falls on them, since shadows would cause local inequalities of drying. Drying in the sun is indeed often the only possible method in very warm and humid climates.

In the case of negatives which have only a passing interest and from which prints are urgently required, the gelatine may be rendered proof against melting, even at the temperature of boiling water, by bathing the negative for about 10 minutes in a solution of formalin or formaldehyde. (The liquid sold under the name of formalin is an aqueous solution of about 40 per cent of formaldehyde, a gas. It will sometimes be found to change on standing, a white precipitate of trioxymethylene being formed. When this happens, it loses its effectiveness wholly or partly.) A suitable dilution for this purpose is 5 parts in 100 parts of water, which is ample to give the desired hardening (J. McIntosh, 1900), and the low concentration has the advantage that a small amount of formaldehyde is liberated from the negatives during drying. When frequent recourse to this method of drying is necessary, it is best to obtain a sheet-iron drying box, through which air can be circulated and led to the outside, and in which the temperature can be raised to about 212°F (100°C). Drying by heat after treatment with formalin may be accelerated still more if alcohol is used in place of part of the water for diluting the formalin.

663. Rapid Drying with a Volatile Liquid. Many liquids evaporate much more rapidly than water, owing to their vapours not being commonly present in the air, and to the fact that their boiling points are lower than that of water, and also because their heat of vaporization is much lower than that of water (half for methyl and ethyl alcohols, quarter for acetone). Any of these liquids that are miscible in all proportions with water may be employed to hasten the drying of the gelatine of photographic negatives and prints; in the case of films there is, of course, the additional requirement that they must not dissolve the film base. After some minutes' soaking in the selected liquid the latter will have almost completely displaced the water and drying will then be very rapid.

Considerations only of cost suggest the use of denatured alcohol (methylated spirit), which has the added advantage that it causes the gelatine to contract. It may almost be said that alcohol does not penetrate the gelatine but merely extracts the water, the attraction of gelatine for water being very small or non-existent (H. R. Proctor, 1909). The alcohol, by gradually taking up water, becomes useless for this purpose after it has dealt with a number of negatives, and requires regeneration. Too rapid dilution of the alcohol should be prevented by draining or wiping the negatives before placing them in it, and after the alcohol treatment is finished, the alcohol clinging to the negatives is allowed to drain into the bath before completely removing the negative. These precautions almost double the amount of material which can be dealt with by a given amount of alcohol (L. P. Clerc, 1917). Negatives of which some parts have already dried spontaneously should not be treated by this method on account of the risk of marks. Denatured alcohol diluted with water may be regenerated by shaking it with dehydrating agents which take up water with great avidity and are not soluble in alcohol or water-alcohol mixtures, e.g. anhydrous sodium carbonate or silica gel.

The extra speed of drying is obviously greater when concentrated alcohol is used, but the use of methylated spirit at its maximum concentration presents various difficulties. In addition to the precipitation of lime salts from hard water in the form of a white opaque fog (§ 656), it sometimes produces a dulling effect on the surface of the gelatine, which has been attributed to the dehydration of the gelatine mycelles (H. Lüppo-Cramer, 1915). Concentrated alcohol can be utilized by employing two successive baths, of which the first contains a hygroscopic substance, for instance, crystallized calcium chloride (2 g per litre) (Schering and Kahlbaum, 1928), or a non-hygroscopic substance conferring pliancy, as for instance, urea (1 g per litre), or salicylic acid (10 g per litre) (Zeiss-Ikon, 1930). Also, the use of concentrated alcohol, by softening the base of film negatives and dissolving an appreciable proportion of the plasticizers, may cause frilling of the gelatine or permanent deformation of the film.

The following table shows the time required for drying negatives (7 × 5 in.) after 10 minutes' treatment in denatured alcohol to which water has been added in different proportions. These times are of course only relative, for they must depend also on the thickness of the gelatine and on the atmospheric conditions—

	Pure denatured alcohol					Pure water
Water (added) %	0	20	40	60	80	100
Time of drying	40 min	80 min	115 min	175 min	210 min	270 min

It will be seen that whilst the effectiveness of alcohol decreases very quickly with dilution, alcohol diluted with water to a moderate extent (up to 20 per cent) is still considerably more rapid than spontaneous drying, and yet avoids the various troubles which may result from the use of too highly concentrated alcohol. Methylated spirit becomes turbid on adding water because of the precipitation of lime salts from the water and of resinous or tarry substances present in the denaturing agent. Very clear dilutions of alcohol may be obtained by adding a small amount of ammonia (1 ml per litre), shaking with several changes of animal charcoal (about 20 g per litre) and filtering or decanting the clear liquid (A. Ninck, 1926).

Negatives which have been passed through alcohol may, during drying, be subjected without harm to a higher temperature than would be safe for negatives heavily charged with water.

After treatment by the alcohol method of drying, there is a temptation to consider negatives to be dry which are really only dry on the surface and in which the deeper parts of the gelatine are still wet. If such negatives are piled together in this condition it may be impossible to separate them afterwards.

664. Instantaneous Drying by Dehydration of the Gelatine. Certain salts which are very soluble in water may be employed in very concentrated aqueous solutions in order to bring about the rapid dehydration of gelatine impregnated with water without causing any ill effects on the gelatine itself (L. Lumiere and A. Seyewetz, 1912). Among the salts which may be used (aluminium sulphate, sodium sulphate, sodium thiosulphate, etc.), potassium carbonate in saturated solution gives the best results without harming the negatives, even in the case of prolonged contact.

This method of drying should be considered as suitable for the *temporary drying* of negatives, permitting of their immediate use for periods up to several weeks. They must be given a further washing in order to get rid of traces of potassium carbonate from the gelatine. The washing of a plate or film impregnated with a very concentrated solution of salts should, preferably, be begun in a dish, using repeatedly just sufficient water to cover it, in order to avoid too sudden a change in concentration which might cause reticulation of the gelatine.

Potassium carbonate after a time, may give rise to stains, or, in certain cases, to the separation of the film from its support. Since the washing of the negatives must be repeated later on, the first washing and even fixing may be shortened, these processes being completed later.

The negative containing water is immersed for 4 or 5 minutes in a saturated solution of potassium carbonate (about 53 per cent at 60°F, 15°C) or 110 parts of the salt to 100 parts of water. The negative is rapidly wiped between blotting paper to remove the bulk of the adhering solution, and drying is completed by wiping the film with a soft cloth. The surface, which is very hard, is of glossy appearance. The negative may be used at once for printing.

The solution of potassium carbonate may be regenerated from time to time by dissolving more of the salt in it.

CHAPTER XXXIII

THE CHIEF FAILURES IN NEGATIVE-MAKING

665. Introduction. The enumeration of the faults which may occur during the various phases of the process of negative-making may be sufficient to discourage the novice in photography; it has, however, no other purpose than to allow the cause of a failure to be discovered. It must be admitted that any list of possible defects is never complete, unexpected failures sometimes occurring which cannot be traced to their causes.

When a beginner (and sometimes even an experienced photographer) meets with a failure he immediately blames the camera, the plates, the chemicals and their respective purveyors; almost always he forgets to ask himself what blunder he has committed.

Nobody is infallible, and, in spite of strict control, a manufacturer (of whom one cannot ask that he should test all his plates and films before issuing them for sale) will send out—but very seldom—a plate or film showing some slight defect. Long experience shows, however, that the great majority of failures are due to faulty working of which the photographer is often unconscious, and which he will not hesitate in good faith to deny.

If, after careful investigation, a fault appears to be due to manufacture, and is repeated on several plates from the same box or from the same emulsion, replacement may be demanded from the manufacturer. This will always be courteously furnished if it be courteously asked. In addition to the faulty negatives, some other plates (exposed or otherwise) which have not been developed should be returned, packed in their original wrappings.

666. Faults Appearing During Development.[1]

[1] Some of these defects, especially if they are not very marked, will not be found until later, sometimes not until after drying. For the characteristics of negatives which have been under-exposed or over exposed.

The Image Does Not Develop. Anti-halation plate exposed through the back; plate not exposed; absence of one of the essential ingredients from the developing solution. Put the plate aside for the time being in pure water, and then try to develop it later in another bath. A slow appearance of the image may be due simply to putting the plate in the developer upside down.

The Image Lacks Density. Lack of density generally results from under-exposure or under-development or both. Under-development may be distinguished from under-exposure by the appearance of detail in the highlights and faint detail in the shadows; if the shadows are free from veil, i.e. almost clear when viewed through the negative laid face downwards on a sheet of white paper, then the cause is under-development. Intensification treatment for under-developed negatives is described in Chapter XXXV (§§ 682–689). Under-development may be caused by: too short development time, too low a development temperature, the use of a partially exhausted developer, or incorrect composition of the developer (insufficient developing agent or alkali).

The Image Appears very Dense. Excessive density generally results from over-development and/or over-exposure. Over-development of negatives which have received a correct exposure generally leads to an increase in contrast. Correction of over-developed negatives may be achieved by the use of photographic reducers (§§ 690–695). The causes of over-development are the converse of the causes of under-development (see above), i.e. too long development etc.

The Emulsion Darkens Before any Image Appears. The sensitive surface has been exposed to light outside the camera or has been affected by X-rays or other penetrating radiation.

The Image Appears Almost Lost by Uniform Fog. If those parts of the sensitive emulsion which were protected by the rebates, etc., of the dark slide are not fogged, the trouble is probably due to excessive exposure; to sunlight on the lens during exposure (absence of lens hood); or to the use of a lens of which some parts are dirty or covered with mist.

If the fog also covers the protected parts of the surface, several causes may be suspected: long storage of the plate or film under unfavourable conditions; wrongly-mixed developer (excess of alkali, insufficient bromide), or developer contaminated with thiosulphate or metallic salts from the materials of which dishes and accessories are made, or with sulphide formed by bacterial action in old developing solutions which have been kept for a long time. In either of these cases of fogging the cause may be the action of certain materials used in the construction of the dark slide (resinous wood, varnish, drying oils, or of paper used for re-packing the plates or films between exposure and development). Prolong development as for a normal negative adding a fairly large amount of bromide or antifoggant. In spite of being very dense, the negative will yield passable prints.

Fog Appears After the Image is Distinctly Visible. Development is being done too close to a darkroom lamp which is fitted with an unsuitable safelight filter; or a very little diffused light is penetrating to the inside of the darkroom. In these cases the sensitive surface in the shadow cast by the sides of the dish remains clear of fog. In the case of a developer containing hydroquinone, the fog may be due to aerial oxidation of the developer as a result of too prolonged withdrawals of the negative for examination (§ 553). These failures may be avoided by desensitizing.

Intense Ray-like Fog. Fog starting as a rule from one corner or edge and throwing rays in different directions indicates leakage of light in the dark slide or its junction with the camera. Similar directed fog on roll-films is due to leakage of light between turns too loosely wound when the film is removed from the camera. Such light at grazing incidence can be recognized by the long shadows cast by any small protuberance, which are recorded in the fog.

Marginal Fog. Fog forming a black or dark grey border and falling off towards the centre sometimes occurs on plates or films which are very old or which have been kept under bad conditions. This may occur on two edges only.

Parts of the Emulsion do not Develop, or Develop only Slowly. The surface of the emulsion has not been fully covered by the developer, probably because too little solution has been used and this has not been well stirred; possibly, also, to the dish or tank not being level. In tank development access of developer may be obstructed by improper contact of the emulsion with another piece of sensitized material, or with the rack or other device for holding the material.

Black Lines Covering the Whole or Part of the Plate. During the preparation for taking a photograph, or when carrying the camera, an image of the sun is formed on the sensitive surface by a tiny hole in the camera itself. This acts like a pinhole, and moves in all directions according to the movements of the camera. Parts of these lines may be reversed by solarization. Similar tracks of the images of electric-light bulbs may show striations due to the supply current alternations.

Black Spots Irregularly Distributed over the Image. Black spots of various shapes and sizes may be due to specks of some substance which causes fog or accelerates development. These may fall on the surface as dust or as particles from the developer itself. Dust may arise from the friction of the slide in an aluminium film or plate holder. They may also be due to undissolved particles of the ingredients in an unfiltered developing solution; crystallization may also occur in a concentrated developer when the temperature falls too low. These spots sometimes have tails, which are usually vertical, when tank development has been employed. When dust has fallen on the surfaces before exposure to light, the black spots may have a transparent centre.

Black or white spots may be due, in exceptional cases, to a local increase or decrease of sensitivity during manufacture, owing to the acidity or oxidation-reduction equilibrium of the emulsion being modified by microscopic foreign inclusions or bacterial growths.

Pseudo-reticulation. Dark lines somewhat like the meshes of a net have been caused in many cases by development in a bath which is not rocked or in a dish which contains only a small quantity of developer.

Edge and Streamer Markings. When development is done in a very shallow layer of solution in an unrocked dish, there are sometimes produced dark margins on the dense regions of the image and light margins on the adjacent lighter regions. This is due to diffusion exchanges between the active developing agent and the products of reaction. For the same reason, when vertical tank development is employed, light streamer markings, extending below the denser parts of the image, are produced.

Irregular Stream-lines, Darker or Lighter than the Rest of the Image. The developer was not perfectly mixed when plates or films were placed in it. It may not have been sufficiently mixed when a concentrated developer has been diluted, or when the solution has been prepared from various stock solutions. Stream-lines spreading from the clips of hangers or other holding device may be due to an unsuitable metal or solder used in its construction, or to its previous contamination with hypo. In the latter case a lighter band with a glossy surface may have darker edges. In very low concentration hypo accelerates development, giving the dark edges, while in slightly higher concentration it retards development and may even dissolve the surface grains giving the glossy finish when dry.

Mottling. This defect is usually the result of curtailed development of a much over-exposed negative, the developer being dilute or exhausted and insufficiently rocked.

White Spots. Several cases must be considered. Tiny areas bare of emulsion would result in completely transparent areas *before fixation*, and would be recognized after drying by the depressions in the film. This defect is extremely rare. White spots, which on great enlargement are found to have sharply-defined irregular edges, usually angular, are the shadows of dust deposited on the emulsion before exposure to light. Little white spots with no foreign speck in the centre, circular or oval in shape, are generally due to air bubbles preventing the developer from coming in contact with the emulsion; they frequently occur when the developer has been diluted with water taken from a high-pressure supply, or with water at a lower temperature than that of the darkroom and which, on being warmed, liberates some dissolved air. Air-bells adhering to the emulsion when the developer has not been poured uniformly on to the plate are usually of a sharply-defined rounded shape, but irregular. Lines of air bubbles are sometimes formed when development hangers or holders of films are used and are introduced suddenly into the developer.

White or Clear Spots, Round or Irregular, with Graded Edges. These spots are generally due to

splashes of water on the emulsion, or to condensation of moisture when camera or slides have been in a very cold atmosphere, and are brought into a warm place. Similar circumstances sometimes produce mottled markings, or marks with a light marginal fringe. In tropical climates, spots arising from splashes sometimes have either a dark centre or a dark ring. Very rarely such spots are due to dust contamination of the gelatine layer during manufacture. In such cases a central speck may be visible under a magnifier.

Finger-markings. Finger-markings appear white after contact of dry fingers with the surface of the emulsion (and even with the backs of the plates if the latter are piled together after contact). The slightest quantity of grease deposited on the emulsion prevents the penetration of the developer. Finger-markings will appear black if the surface of the emulsion has been touched with fingers soiled with developer, fixer, etc.

Black or White Lines. Lines, generally very fine and straight, are due to friction on the emulsion. The slide of the film or plate holder may be bent; there may be abnormal resistance to the pulling over of films in a bent film pack; the guide rollers may be working badly in a roll-film camera, or it may be winding too tightly. Lines from these various causes are usually light on a dark ground and dark on a clear ground.

These lines are not to be confused with the broad and very opaque bands with diffused edges which are due to the passage of light between the sections of the curtain shutter of a dark slide, nor with the broad black lines with shaded edges which start perpendicularly to one edge of the plate and end in a black disc (or vice versa). These latter are caused by the movement and subsequent stopping in front of the plate of a hole in the blind of a focal-plane shutter. (Such holes are often caused by burning of the rubber of the blind occasioned by the focused image of the sun.)

Dark Tree-like Markings. Static electric discharges on an emulsion leave black brush- or tree-like markings. This trouble is hardly ever met with except on films, and then only in very dry weather (especially in frosty weather). It may be due to friction or merely to the unrolling of the spool.

The Image Appears as a Positive. An image which has been considerably over-exposed may appear as a positive, altogether or partially; in such cases it is usually fogged. An image which at first appeared as a negative may during development be converted into a positive by the action of light (white light or unsafe darkroom lighting); it seems in this case that the first negative image protects the underlying emulsion against fog; at the same time the sensitivity of the emulsion is decreased by the soluble bromide already set free by development. Delayed reversal may also result from very long development in an extremely dilute developer; the chemical fog of the unexposed regions becomes denser than the image itself.

Double Images : Ghosts. The superposition of two entirely different images is obviously caused by two exposures on the same plate or on the same part of a film. Very curious effects are sometimes caused, however, by the superposition of two exposures without moving the camera; the shutter may have been opened twice or it may have rebounded, or it may be that the sensitive surface has remained uncovered for some time, and a second image has been projected by means of a hole in the front of the camera; one of these images is always so faint that only persons dressed in light colours standing near during or after the exposure appear in it; such figures then appear as transparent ghosts. These effects are often attributed to supernatural causes!

Broad Transparent Shaded Mark, Starting from One Edge. A very large out-of-focus image of a finger, held in front of the lens during exposure, so that it obscures part of the field.

Broad Light Bands Parallel to One Side of the Film. When a focal-plane shutter is used, the rapid passage of an opaque body in front of the lens cuts out the image (or reduces its density if only a portion of the lens aperture is masked) on the parts of the film which happen at that instant to be uncovered by the slit of the shutter.

667. Defects Appearing After Fixing. *Milky Markings with Diffused Edges, visible on the Back of the Negative or by Transmitted Light.* Fixation has been stopped too soon, and has left patches of silver bromide between the image and the support.

Transparent Marks of Irregular Shape and with Diffused Edges. Local solution of metallic silver in an old fixing bath, which contains particles of rust, or in any fixing solution containing particles of potassium ferricyanide or other reagents capable of attacking silver. A clear mark may be produced by the prolonged action of a crystal of undissolved thiosulphate on a part of the emulsion.

A uniform opalescence of the gelatine is sometimes observed on removing a negative from a strong fixing bath. It is due to dehydration and disappears on washing.

Blisters. Blisters may be caused, particularly on films and papers, by bubbles of gas, which, instead of being liberated at the surface, are formed within the gelatine itself or between the latter and the support (immediate use of water delivered at too great a pressure; transference without intermediate rinsing from a developing solution containing carbonate to a very acid, non-hardening, tepid fixing bath).

Yellow or Brown Stain, Local or General. General stain may be due to the staining action of products of development on the gelatine. This occurs if the developer is old and highly-coloured, or if it contains insufficient sulphite. Stains in patches may be caused, especially with films and papers, on portions of the surface which during the first few moments of fixation have not been immersed in the solution. Solutions of alum, sometimes proposed for the removal of these stains, are quite useless, but the stains may be destroyed as follows. After washing the negative, immerse it for about 5 minutes in a solution of 5 per cent chrome-alum, in order to complete the hardening of the gelatine and to avoid any softening during the further treatment, and then rinse it rapidly. The image is then bleached in a mixture of equal volumes of the following solutions (A) and (B), which should be mixed fresh when required.

(A) Potassium permanganate	. .	5 g
Water to . . .	.	1 litre
(B) Hydrochloric acid	.	50 ml
Water to . . .	.	1 litre

After the image has been bleached it has a general brown coloration due to manganese oxide deposited in the gelatine. The negative is rinsed and is placed in a 5 or 10 per cent solution of sodium bisulphite until the brown colour has disappeared. The image is then blackened by treating it in an ordinary developer in full white light until no more white silver chloride remains visible through the back. Finally, wash the negative in two or three changes of water without fixing. The above treatment may be applied to a negative even if it has been dried.

An iridescent yellowish-brown silver stain is sometimes produced by physical development on to nuclei of silver sulphide formed in the emulsion surface by traces of sulphide in the developer. Such soluble sulphides are usually due to bacterial growth in the developer. The stain can often be removed from the dry negative by firm wiping under spirit (not anhydrous).

668. Dichroic Fog. The fog generally known as dichroic, although it does not always show two complementary colours, most commonly appears greenish-yellow by reflected light, and pink or purplish by transmitted light. It consists of ultra-microscopic particles of silver (colloidal silver) formed when silver bromide is subjected simultaneously to the action of one of its solvents, and to that of a developer capable of reducing silver salts *in situ* as soon as these salts are dissolved.

The conditions necessary for the formation of dichroic fog may thus prevail during development and also during fixation. The milky appearance (by reflected light) of this fog often leads, in the dim light of the darkroom, to its being mistaken for a residue of undissolved silver bromide.

Dichroic fog hardly ever occurs during development, except in the under-exposed portions of a negative where there is no silver reduced in its ordinary black condition,[1] and when development is prolonged in the empty hope of bringing up detail which the light has not registered or when slow-acting developers like hydroquinone or glycin are used. The solvent causing its formation may be hypo accidentally introduced into the developer, or it may be ammonia added as such or as an ammonium salt, or it may be sodium sulphite used in excessive amount. H. Lüppo-Cramer (1905), however, obtained dichroic fog in a developer containing only sodium carbonate and an amino developing agent, substances of this latter class behaving as feeble solvents of silver bromide.

If formed during fixation, dichroic fog may extend over the whole or part of the negative without any relation between its distribution and that of the image; its formation is due to developer carried over into the fixing bath by the gelatine of the negatives. A neutral fixing bath favours its formation because in such a solution the developer retains its activity until it has become diffused into the bulk of the solution; a very old fixing bath also favours its production, because of the accumulation of

---

[1] Where the silver is already reduced it plays the part of a nucleus on which is deposited silver, which, in the clear parts, forms in the colloidal condition.

developer in it. Dichroic fog can, however, be formed in a fresh acid fixing solution if two film negatives or paper prints adhere to one another during fixation, because in this way the free access of the fixer is prevented; the developer is thus in excess of the fixer, and so the ideal condition for the formation of colloidal silver is provided. In all cases the presence of ammonia or of ammonium salts, and the exposure of the plate to light before fixation is complete are circumstances favourable to the appearance of dichroic fog.

The occurrence of dichroic fog during fixation is almost certainly avoided by rinsing negatives between development and fixation, especially if the rinsing is done in slightly acidulated water.

The only practical reagent known to dissolve this colloidal silver without attacking the image was, for several years that recommended by J. Hauff in 1894—

Thiourea (thiocarbamide) . . .	1 g
Citric acid	1 g
Water to	100 ml

As the outcome of an experimental study of this trouble, Lumière and Seyewetz (1903) recommended bathing the negative for 5 minutes in a 0·1 per cent neutral solution of potassium permanganate; after rinsing, the negative is placed in a solution of 5 per cent to 10 per cent sodium bisulphite in which the silver oxide formed by action of the permanganate and also the brown colour of manganese dioxide formed in the gelatine disappear. The process is finished by washing in two or three changes of water. A dilute solution of potassium cyanide (0·5–1·0 per cent) slowly dissolves the colloidal silver in the presence of air.

669. Defects Occurring During Washing. *Reticulation.* The reticulation of gelatine, giving it the appearance of grained leather or crocodile skin, is due to the excessive swelling which may arise from various causes. One is transfer from a very concentrated or warm fixing bath into cold water, especially if the fixing bath contains no alum. Another is a considerable difference in temperature, one way or the other, between the developer and the fixing bath. In general, reticulation is liable to be caused by any circumstance tending to cause very rapid swelling or shrinkage of the gelatine, such as transfer from a very alkaline bath to one which is strongly acid, or inversely. When the reticulation is not very marked, it is sometimes possible to remedy it by placing the negative in alcohol (with films, at least 20 per cent of water must be added to the alcohol), and then hardening it with alum, if necessary, before proceeding to any other operation.

Frilling of the Gelatine at the Edges. This defect, which starts as a kind of curling along the edges of the support, is due to the same causes as reticulation ; the same methods may be tried in order to prevent it.

Transparent or Clear Spots of Irregular Shape. Local attack of the gelatine by liquefying bacteria during prolonged washing, particularly in warm weather.

670. Defects Appearing During or After Drying. *Partial Melting of the Gelatine leading to Irregular Deformation of the Image.* The negatives have been subjected to a temperature above the melting point of gelatine whilst in a wet and insufficiently hardened condition. They may have been placed too near a fire or in the direct rays of the sun.

Patches of Uneven Density. Local variations in the rate of drying due to changes of temperature, humidity, or speed of air currents. These patches may sometimes be got rid of by converting the image into silver chloride and re-developing as described in § 667 for removing developer stains.

Light Spots or Marks with Dark Edges. These marks are caused by drops of water left on the face of the gelatine during drying, or which have been splashed on to its surface after it has already dried. In course of drying these splashes dry first at the edges of the moist region and cause the particles of silver to be dragged from the centre towards the edge. Re-wetting of the negative, followed by normal drying, does not always provide a remedy for this.

Clear Spots of Bare Glass or Film. Local liquefaction of the gelatine by colonies of bacteria during very slow drying in a warm, moist atmosphere. Clear, irregular spots may be due to the attack of various insects on the gelatine.

Metallic Stains on the Edges of the Negative. Opaque fog of a lustrous metallic appearance, generally seen only on the edges of the negative, may be due to the use of an exhausted developer with old emulsions, or to a superficial sulphiding of the silver by hydrogen sulphide (often present in the atmosphere of industrial towns). It may usually be removed by dry rubbing with chamois leather ; in obstinate cases, moisten the leather with methylated spirit in order to

increase the friction, but in any case rub very lightly.

Traces of Foreign Matter Embedded in the Gelatine. Dust, particles of fibre, etc., deposited by the washing water and not removed by a final rinse in filtered water, or deposited during drying.

Distorted Films. A film which has been dried too rapidly (in too dry and warm air), under excessive tension, is often waved at the edges. The remedy consists in washing until the gelatine is uniformly swollen, and then drying under normal conditions.

White, Granular Deposit. This deposit, which is quite distinctly rough to the touch, is caused by the deposition of lime salts from a very hard water when no final rinsing in soft water has been employed. It may be removed by washing in slightly acidified water (1 per cent hydrochloric or acetic acid is suitable, but non-volatile acids must not be used) and again drying. Negatives should be gently wiped with the fingertips under the tap before they are put to dry.

White, Powdery Deposit. This is usually caused by aluminium sulphite deposited in or on the gelatine from an acid-alum fixing bath in which too much of the acid has been neutralized. It may be removed by wiping under the surface of a solution of sodium carbonate (about 10 per cent) followed by washing in clean water.

Yellowish-white Opalescence. This veil is generally due to the deposition of sulphur in the gelatine caused by the acidification of a fixing bath containing insufficient sulphite, or by the use of an acid fixing bath at too high a temperature, or by treating the negative with alum before or after fixation without intermediate rinsing. The only possibility of dissolving this sulphur without affecting the image is, after thoroughly hardening the gelatine, to try to convert it into sodium thiosulphate in a warm solution of sulphite (10 per cent solution of anhydrous sulphite of soda, warmed to about 110°F, 43°C), in which it is allowed to remain for some minutes. The process is finished by washing in several changes of water. The treatment is not successful with old negatives.

Silvery-white Opalescence which is Yellow by Transmitted Light. This variety of white deposit, covering all or part of the image, and particularly parts which have been dried too rapidly (edges), is caused by too rapid dehydration of the gelatine by concentrated alcohol (neat methylated spirit), especially if the negative has been washed in very hard water. It may be removed by washing in slightly acidified water (see "White Granular Deposit"), which method may also be employed as a preventive.

671. Defects Occurring in a Negative After Drying. *Ink Marks or Stains of Aniline Dyes.* Black ink stains (indian ink excepted) or coloured stains arising from dyes or any coloured substance (including dust from a copying pencil) disappear entirely under the treatment described in § 667 for developer stain.

Brown Stains. Brown stains may appear on a negative after a lapse of time ranging from some weeks to several years (more rapidly in a moist atmosphere). This is due to the slow conversion into silver sulphide of silver thiosulphate left in the negative after incomplete fixation or washing (in the latter case there is often a general weakening of the image in the region of the stain). There is no certain method of removing this kind of stain; it is often better to make a new negative from a print taken before the defect arose, or to make, first, a positive transparency on a panchromatic plate through a deep orange filter and then a fresh negative from that. The effect of the stain is thus greatly reduced.

Scratches. The effect of various fine markings, produced by friction, may be reduced by varnishing the negative (§ 709).

Cracked Plate. A cracked plate, of which the gelatine film is intact may be saved by stripping the film to another support (§ 713), provided that the broken glass is supported during manipulation. This may be carried out very simply as follows. Take an old, unexposed and fixed plate, and dip it in water for a very short time, so that the gelatine does not swell appreciably, then slide the back of the cracked negative gently on to the moist gelatine so prepared. The very thin film of water interposed is absorbed by the gelatine and perfect adhesion of the two negatives is then assured on account of atmospheric pressure.

CHAPTER XXXIV

REVERSAL PROCESSES: METHODS FOR OBTAINING DIRECT POSITIVES

672. General considerations—solarization—reversal by destruction of a negative image—diffusion transfer reversal. 673. Diffusion transfer reversal (DTR)—Polaroid and Bimat processes. 674. The production of autopositive contact prints by destroying a latent fog. 675. Reversal by means of a second controlled exposure—the Albert effect. 676. The sensitometry of reversal emulsions—reversal of the emulsion residue—total black and density of solarization—exposure latitude—control of tone reproduction—variation in first development time—use of silver halide solvents. 677. Reversal of the residue after controlled dissolution of the silver halide. 678. Methods of dissolving the first negative image—permanganate bleaches—dichromate bleaches—etch-bleach process. 679. Development of the reversal image. 680. Reversal methods for paper.

672. General Considerations. We will first mention a method which cannot, properly, be considered as a reversal process, but which is sometimes employed for obtaining positive images directly. By developing so as to obtain silver, which is whitish by reflected light, and employing plates in which the emulsion is coated on a black or very dark support, the image appears as a positive. This method was chiefly used for making "ferrotypes," also known as tintypes. A variation of this method has been used by the American Army Air Force (1925) for the rapid examination of negatives taken during urgent reconnaissances. The support in this case is of blue-violet celluloid, appearing almost black by reflected light, but through which positive prints may be made. The image is negative for transmitted light although positive by reflection. An ordinary negative image on a transparent support may also be made to appear as a positive if the black reduced silver is converted into a white salt of silver, and the plate is then given a black backing. This method is sometimes employed for printing from a very flat negative. The negative is bleached with mercuric chloride, rinsed, dried, and mounted against a black ground. A copy can then be taken.

The methods of reversal, properly called, may be classified as follows—

(*a*) By considerable over-exposure; the image is *solarized* and develops directly as a positive.

(*b*) A sensitive material is uniformly fogged to a high density and is then exposed to the image under such conditions that on normal development the fog density is reduced in proportion to the image exposure. As a rule radiations of different qualities are used for the fogging and the image exposures.

(*c*) After normal development of a negative which has been normally exposed and has not been desensitized, only a part of the thickness of the emulsion will have been employed in obtaining the negative image; the remainder is still sensitive to light (although its sensitivity may have been reduced). It is therefore possible, by exposing the negative to light, to produce in this residue a latent positive image which will remain, although weakened, after dissolving out the silver of the negative image and may be developed so as to give the final positive image (C. Drouillard, 1901).

It is possible to obtain a positive image by a similar procedure without dissolving the negative silver image first (F. Leiber, 1932). The positive image is developed in a developer which produces a stain image as well as a silver one (§ 573). All the remaining silver bromide and silver are then bleached away and the stain image is intensified.

(*d*) It has been noticed (J. G. Capstaff, 1921) that, after the negative image is dissolved, the speed of the remaining silver bromide varies considerably from one point to another, being the less at each point the more the quantity of silver dissolved there. As a matter of fact, the various grains of silver each have different speeds, and in each spot it is the fastest grains which, during the first exposure, are brought first into developable condition; thus there remains in the image of the shadows the majority of the most rapid grains, while the slowest grains alone remain in the image of the high-lights. A uniform, and properly controlled, second exposure can therefore produce an effect practically identical to that of exposures, variable from one point to another, corresponding to printing a positive under a negative; what happens is almost as if the second exposure to light were made under the first (negative) image, although the latter has been removed. Development and fixation then follow, just as with an image obtained under ordinary conditions.

(e) In a negative which has been developed but not fixed there exist two images. These are complementary to one another, but generally of very unequal quality; one is the negative image, consisting of reduced silver, and the other is a positive image, consisting of the residual silver bromide. Whilst dissolving the silver bromide (fixation) only leaves the negative image, the removal of the silver by a solvent having no action on the bromide leaves the positive image. All that is then needed is development of the silver bromide to the state of metallic silver or of some compound of suitable colour (C. Russell, 1862). This method was applied in practice for the first time by Lumière for the production of colour photographs on Autochrome plates, and is now used in the *Etch-bleach* process for obtaining positive relief images (§ 678), and in other reversal processes.

(f) Lastly, the production of positives by a diffusion transfer method should be considered. This is often referred to as *diffusion transfer reversal* (DTR) or *silver diffusion transfer* (SDT) and currently available materials include the *Polaroid* process, the Kodak *Bimat* process, and the *Gevacopy*, Agfa *Copyrapid* and Kodak *CT* (chemical transfer) document copying systems.

The basic principle of diffusion transfer processes is the simultaneous production by physical development of a positive image in an absorbent layer in contact with a developing negative image (A. Rott, 1945). During the development of the negative image in the exposed layer, the developer dissolves the unexposed silver halide which diffuses into the receiving layer where a positive image is formed as the dissolved silver halide is reduced by the developing agent in the presence of catalytic nuclei present in the receiving layer. The chemistry of the process is given below in a much simplified form:

In the emulsion layer:

$$AgCl + developer$$
$$\rightarrow Ag + oxidized\ developer + Cl^-$$
(exposed)   (negative image remaining in emulsion layer)

$$AgCl + 2S_2O_3^{2-} \rightarrow [Ag(S_2O_3)_2]^{3-} + Cl^-$$
(unexposed)   (soluble complex diffuses to receiving layer)

In the receiving layer:

$$[Ag(S_2O_3)_2]^{3-} + developer + catalytic\ nuclei$$
$$\rightarrow Ag + oxidized\ developer + 2S_2O_3^{2-}$$
(positive image)

In view of the very heavy exposures necessary in order to produce a solarized image, method (a) is quite impracticable for camera photography and is even difficult to apply for copying work, largely because the results are often not reproducible or are non-uniform.

There are numerous versions of method (b); one may utilize the effects described earlier under the name of *Herschel, Clayden* or *Villard* effect, or, better still, a procedure already mentioned in connexion with infra-red spectroscopy. According to a technique described by Lüppo-Cramer (1923), this method is applied for the production of auto-positive emulsions. Special emulsions for the production of auto-positives by an analogous process, have been worked out by H. Arens, J. Eggert, and E. Heisenberg (1931). With these, a laterally reversed duplicate of a negative or positive can be obtained by exposing the material in contact with the original for a time from 10 to 500 seconds at a distance of three feet from a 40-watt tungsten lamp.

In its original form, method (c) is difficult to apply, since all silver-solvents will attack the finely divided latent-image silver. The version suggested by Leiber has found numerous applications. Another version is applied commercially for the production of positives in multi-layer colour films. After the negative development, the film is exposed uniformly to light, and development is continued in a colour-forming developer. (§ 576). Finally, all the silver and silver halide is removed in a "reducing" solution to be described below under the name of Farmer's reducer (§ 691).

For many years method (d) has given perfect results in amateur black and white cinematography. It allows errors in exposure to be compensated for within wide limits, but requires a very accurately controlled second exposure. This is best done by preliminary tests on pictures taken under the same conditions as those to be treated. The method is only practicable in cinematography, since here it is always possible to sacrifice for testing a few frames from each scene. It was formerly used for amateur films processed on continuous machines with a device for automatic adjustment of the exposing light according to the average amount of silver bromide remaining after the dissolution of the first image. This adjustment is effected by means of a thermo-electric couple sensitive to a beam of infra-red light transmitted by an image without affecting its emulsion; a relay postpones this adjustment until the image that has been measured appears in the exposing window.

Reversal by the "residue" method is better suited for treating individual images. Various means of augmenting its flexibility will be described.

It is obvious that reversal cannot be applied to plates or films coated with several superposed emulsions; the best results are generally obtained with sensitive material specially prepared for this treatment.

Whatever the working method employed in procedures (c) to (e), it is essential that the first development be thorough, for the undeveloped latent negative image would be superimposed on the positive image, being able even to cause a re-reversal in the image of the high-lights.

673. Diffusion Transfer Reversal (DTR). Reversal by diffusion transfer appears very simple (§ 672) and in principle has been known for over 100 years (B. Lefevre, 1857), but it is not easy to obtain good results in practice. It is difficult to achieve the correct balance between development and dissolution of the silver halide in the emulsion (negative) layer. In current practice this is usually achieved by the use of a highly active developer, such as a Phenidone-hydroquinone developer at high pH, and sodium thiosulphate as the silver halide solvent. Secondly, unless a toning agent, such as 1-phenyl-5-mercapto-1,2,3,4-tetrazole (E. Weyde, 1955), is incorporated in the receiving layer or processing solution the positive image appears yellow-brown. Thirdly, the catalytic nuclei must be very active or diffusion within the receiving layer would occur and the image would be unsharp.

Fortunately for the user, diffusion transfer materials are sold as complete systems and these major difficulties have been overcome by the manufacturers. The *Polaroid* and *Bimat* processes are typical in camera DTR systems for which the user has no control over the sensitometric characteristics which are fixed by the composition of the emulsions and processing chemicals (c.f. monobaths, § 549). In both the *Polaroid* and *Bimat* systems material is exposed and immediately thereafter DTR processed in specially designed cameras to yield a positive

image within one minute of taking the photograph.

In the *Polaroid* process, the exposed material is mechanically squeegeed in contact with a receiving sheet of white paper containing the catalytic nuclei. During the squeegeeing operation a pod containing the developer and silver halide solvent is broken and the viscous processing solution spread between the layers. The soluble silver complexes formed from the unexposed silver halide diffuse from the negative layer to the paper receiving layer where they react with the catalytic nuclei to form the positive image. After a few seconds the layers are peeled apart to yield the print. It is possible to keep the negative for subsequent transfer operations but these are of decreasing maximum density and increasing processing times. Alternatively, the negative can be kept for conventional printing, after removal of the antihalation backing and processing chemicals in an alkaline bath. The positive may be stabilized by treatment with a polyhydric alcohol and zinc acetate or by washing and drying in the conventional manner.

The Polaroid black and white process gives speeds up to about 3000 ASA which is greater than the speed of a fast negative material. The high speed has been ascribed to the high amplification of the process (i.e. the image is dense but contains little silver) and the very active catalytic nuclei (G. F. Duffin, 1966). Both these factors lead to use of the toe region of the characteristic curve and hence a very high speed.

The Kodak *Bimat* system is essentially similar except that the exposed negative layer is wound in intimate contact with a receiving film, containing the catalytic nuclei, which has been presoaked in a monobath solution. After the required contact time, 10 seconds to 20 minutes depending on the type of Bimat film used, the layers are peeled apart to yield both positive and negative images. For complete permanence of Bimat film it is recommended that the film is washed and dried in the conventional manner, although the untreated film is stable for several months provided it is kept dry.

DTR semi-dry processes are of obvious importance in aerial reconnaissance work, where rapid access is essential, space is limited and conventional processing using solutions is not possible. A dry diffusion transfer process has recently been patented (R. Wendt, 1957,

W. Zindler, 1965). The receiving layer contains a polyvinyl alcohol and the processing chemicals, which on heating in contact with the negative layer to 70°–80°F (21°–27°C) gives off water and causes the formation of the positive image.

674. The Production of Autopositive Contact Prints by destroying a Latent Fog. A fine-grain silver-chloride emulsion is uniformly fogged so as to obtain on processing the maximum density required afterwards in the positive image. It is then bathed for two minutes in a solution containing 0·01 per cent of safranine and 1 per cent of potassium bromide. The material is dried without washing.

The emulsion layer so treated is then exposed in contact with the negative or positive one wants to duplicate. According to the density of the original, the exposure should be some 30 to 50 times as heavy as that needed to produce the fog. If the intensity is kept low and time of exposure long, the tone range of the process is considerably longer than for short exposure times and high intensities; in a certain instance, an exposure of 36 minutes allowed four times the range to be reproduced as an exposure of one minute with a correspondingly adjusted intensity (Lüppo-Cramer, 1927). The only difficulty in preliminary tests is to establish the most favourable conditions of the two times of exposure which give the optimum results. A sensitometric step tablet is almost essential for this work.

Any developer is suitable for this process. One should avoid, however, developers which act very slowly, and those containing a silver-halide solvent. These latter are liable to develop the internal latent image of the first exposure, since it is only the superficial latent-image specks which are destroyed by the second exposure.

675. Reversal by Means of a Second Controlled Exposure. Since this method is not practicable except in automatic processing machines, there is little point in discussing technical details, but the principles of the method are of some fundamental interest.

V. B. Sease (1931) has, however, described a method which does not require automatic compensation or the preliminary testing of samples. A second exposure is given which is so adjusted as to be definitely too weak. This is followed by brief development and a further exposure is estimated from the character of the developed image. Further exposures are given as necessary, each followed by development, until a satisfactory positive is obtained. These operations are facilitated by the fact that the reversal bath destroys the dye sensitizers and reduces the sensitivity. According to F. Leiber (1932) the gamma of the resulting positive is reduced if the second exposure or exposures are applied from the back.

In the high-light portions of a negative, all the fastest grains of an emulsion have been used; in the half-tones or shadows, the fast grains remain unused to a smaller or greater extent. It is thus easily seen that the average sensitivity of the remaining emulsion varies considerably from point to point.

The local differences in sensitivity are accentuated by yet another factor (H. Baines, 1936). In the course of the first development, the iodide always present in fast emulsions is released and reacts with the neighbouring grains, which are thereby coated with a superficial layer of iodide and consequently reduced in sensitivity. This effect is more pronounced the larger the amount of silver produced during the first development.

The *Albert effect* also comes under the present method of reversal; it has been explained by G. W. W. Stevens (1939) in the following fashion. The superficial latent image is easily destroyed by the oxidizing treatment used to destroy the negative latent image. The internal latent image specks are not destroyed and act as condensation nuclei for any further latent-image silver produced during the second exposure. For grains which have received no first exposure, the latent image will be formed on the surface as usual. The second development thus acts only on the grains carrying superficial latent image specks; it cannot react with the internal latent image, unless the internal specks are laid bare by dissolving the outer layers of the silver halide grains.

The average sensitivity of the remaining emulsion is the greater the shorter the first exposure, i.e. the smaller the number of grains affected by the first development. By arranging the two exposures properly, practically identical positives can be obtained for first exposures varying as much as 16 to 1, if the tone range (ratio of the extreme brightnesses in the subject) does not exceed 30 : 1.

676. The Sensitometry of Reversal Emulsions. By contrast to the negative photographic images, reversed images are built up essentially from the finest grains in the emulsion, some medium-sized grains occurring in the middle tones, and a few large grains in the shadows. The graininess of the reversed image is thus considerably less than that in a negative obtained with the same emulsion or in a positive obtained by printing. Furthermore, if two samples of the same emulsion are developed to a negative and a positive respectively, the threshold sensitivity is often considerably greater for the positive than for the negative (H. Staude, 1938).

An ideal reversal emulsion should therefore contain a sufficient number of large grains to give it sensitivity, and of small grains to produce a brilliant picture of low graininess. An ordinary negative emulsion yields a reversal image of rather low contrast; a positive emulsion would be too insensitive.

For the method of reversal of the residue of an emulsion, whether with or without the application of a silver-bromide solvent, the two concepts of total black and density of solarization are of importance (L. Lobel and J. Lefevre, 1927). The total black is the density that would be obtained if all the silver-halide grains throughout the depth of the emulsion were reduced to silver. The solarization density is the maximum density that can be obtained in a given developer for a certain exposure, called the solarization exposure. Beyond the solarization exposure, the density stays constant for some while and then decreases; it is always less than the total black.

Let us consider the characteristic curve N of a negative, represented diagrammatically in Fig. 34.1. The total black of the emulsion is represented by the horizontal line T. When the silver developed as a negative has been removed, and the remaining silver bromide reduced to silver, the resulting positive is represented by the line P. The lowest density of P is d_0; this must be considered as being much too high to represent the high-lights of the scene.

The lowest positive density would be higher than d_0, if the exposure were less than a critical value, which is determined by the maximum brightness of the scene and not by the minimum shadow brightness as in negative work. If the exposure exceeds but slightly the critical value, several half-tones would merge with the highlights. Thus it is clear that the method of reversal of the residue of an emulsion has no exposure latitude whatever.

If a suitable silver-halide solvent is used, which is as a rule added to the developer, the maximum black is reduced. In practice, it is reduced to a new value T' which should be as close as possible to the maximum solarization density. The resulting positive curve P' is obtained by moving the curve P downwards bodily, so that the minimum density d'_0 can be made as small as desired, by arranging a suitable concentration and time of treatment in the silver-halide solvent. By this method the effect of a reduced exposure can be compensated for by increasing the time of development, an effect which has no parallel in negative-positive work. The use of a silver-halide solvent in the developer thus introduces a certain degree of exposure latitude, although this is much less than can be obtained by using a controlled second exposure.

In order to ensure correct tone reproduction the gamma of the positive curve should be as near unity as possible. In other words, the gamma of the positive should be equal to that of the negative, but, of course, of opposite sign. On the one hand, one would like to push development to the maximum in order to ensure that the value of the solarization density s is high; on the other hand, the gamma of the final positive should not differ materially from unity. These conditions are not always realized in practice.

The curves in Fig. 34.3 represent positives obtained on a reversal cinematograph film for different times of the first development, indicated on the left or on top of the individual curves (W. Rahts and W. Schulz, 1931). Fig. 34.3 shows similar curves obtained in a developer containing a silver halide solvent and also shows the negative curve N obtained for 8 minutes development. The negative curve shows a high fog level caused by dichroic fog which is dissolved with the negative silver and thus causes no trouble.

The use of a developer containing a silver-halide solvent allows a thick emulsion layer

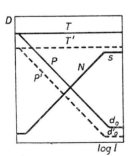

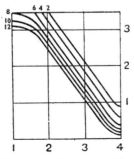

FIG. 34.1. SENSITOMETRY OF A REVERSAL MATERIAL FIG. 34.2. POSITIVES OBTAINED BY VARYING THE TIME OF FIRST DEVELOPMENT

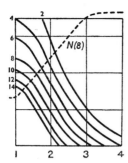

FIG. 34.3. POSITIVES OBTAINED
IN A DEVELOPER CONTAINING
SILVER HALIDE SOLVENT, AND
CHARACTERISTIC CURVE OF
NEGATIVE MATERIAL DE-
VELOPED FOR EIGHT MINUTES
IN THE SAME DEVELOPER

to be used and in this way the exposure latitude is increased considerably. An appreciable under-exposure, however, reduces both the maximum density and the tone range that can be reproduced.

By allowing a developer containing a solvent to act for different times on an unexposed material, which is afterwards blackened in white light, the effect of time of treatment and concentration of the solvent can be readily demonstrated (L. Lobel, M. Dubois, and J. Vidal, 1928). They found, for example, that the addition of 2 per cent of ammonia of strength 28° Baumé decreases the total black of a positive film from 4 to 0·5 within 5 minutes at 65°F (18°C). The silver bromide is completely dissolved in 15 minutes although a solution of ammonia of identical strength but in the absence of the developer requires several hours. No similar anomaly is obtained with hypo which gives otherwise similar results. The ammonia effect is caused by the fact that the ammoniacal silver complex is continuously reformed as the silver is precipitated on the latent image and the walls of the vessel; in this way, the solvent is regenerated all the time and does not decrease in concentration.

677. Reversal of the Residue after Controlled Dissolution of the Silver Halide. It has already been pointed out that the method of reversal of the residue is not practicable except for special thinly coated emulsions. Films or plates for additive colour photography or amateur cinematograph films are suitable for this method. We shall consider below the production of reversal images on paper.

Certain photographic materials are sold complete with processing rights and the user need not preoccupy himself with the details of the processing, which is carried out by the manufacturer. Detailed instructions are given with other materials, and since emulsions vary widely and display their own special characteristics, we can only recommend the user to follow in detail the processing instructions, in particular in respect to the first development.

678. Methods of Dissolving the First Negative Image. From the various possible silver solvents, as a rule an acid permanganate solution is recommended but frequently also an acid dichromate solution is used. The latent image which is not developed in the first developer is completely destroyed by acid permanganate at the usual times of treatment and concentration. With acid dichromate, on the other hand, a very feeble image persists even after several hours' treatment (G. W. W. Stevens, 1939). Acid permanganate is thus superior for the purpose, since it stops any residual negative image from interfering with the reversed positive image.

Reversal using a sulphuric acid-dichromate bath causes an appreciable tanning of the gelatine layer, whereas acid permanganate softens the gelatine. It should not be used at temperature above 77°F (25°C) and above 68°F (20°C) the concentration should be halved, in order to avoid the gelatine being dissolved or stripped from the support.

Some workers maintain that the use of a dichromate bleach decreases the contrast whereas others report the opposite result. One would conclude that this effect cannot be very great. It has been suggested that the advantages of both bleaching agents may be combined if used together. A bleach-bath often used is mixed immediately before use from stock solutions of 0·4 per cent potassium permanganate and a 1 in 50 solution of concentrated sulphuric acid in water (20 ml or 35 g of acid, and water to make 1 litre). The individual stock solutions keep indefinitely.

After the first development, the material is briefly rinsed and put into the bleach-bath. With the method of reversal of the residue, all operations bar the first can be carried out in white light. When all the silver has been dissolved, the material is briefly rinsed and transferred to a solution of 5 or 10 per cent bisulphite, which acts as a clearing bath by dissolving the manganese dioxide formed in the gelatine and the silver chloride formed from the chloride ions introduced with the wash-water. The clearing bath also restores some of the sensitivity of the silver halide lost in the bleach-bath. If at this stage any traces of the original negative image should be noticed, the procedure of rinsing, bleaching, rinsing, and clearing should be repeated.

If an appreciable quantity of silver bromide is found to persist in the high-lights, it is feasible to treat the negative in a very dilute hypo solution (approximately 1 per cent), stopping the treatment by passing the negative into a large volume of water just before the high-lights become completely transparent.

The following details on the chemical treatments may be useful. Potassium permanganate occurs in the form of small dark violet crystals with reddish brown reflections. It is sparingly soluble in cold water (6 per cent at 15°C). The solutions are also dark violet in colour, and it is therefore difficult to ascertain whether the salt is completely dissolved. It is better to use lukewarm water to dissolve the salt. Both the dry substance and its solution keep well. Permanganate causes a brown stain with organic substances by the precipitation of manganese hydroxide [$Mn(OH)_4$]. The stain can be removed easily by sodium bisulphite or oxalic acid. In the preparation of sulphuric acid solutions of permanganate, one must never pour concentrated acid into the permanganate solution or on to the dry salt, since this would cause a reaction of explosive violence. K. C. D. Hickman (1930) has recommended that the sulphuric acid be replaced by an equal volume of a syrupy solution of concentrated phosphoric acid; the mixture is said to be stable.

Where the negative image is bleached in an acid dichromate solution, the clearing bath should be a neutral sulphite solution.

In *Etch-bleach* reversal processing the silver image formed after the first development is removed together with gelatine, leaving the unexposed emulsion in relief. The unexposed emulsion is then developed to produce a positive relief image which requires no fixing. This process is used for making direct positives from line or half-tone images without making an intermediate negative and has advantages in the preparation of reversals for photoengraving, positive-working lithographic plates, and drop-out masks for colour reproduction.

The combined removal of the negative silver image and its gelatine may be carried out in the following solutions (Kodak EB-3).

A	Water, 86°–95°F (30°–35°C)	.	750 ml
	Cupric chloride	. . .	10 g
	Citric acid	. . .	10 g
	Water to	. . . .	1 litre
B	Hydrogen peroxide 10 volume solution.		

For use mix equal volumes of solutions A and B. Hydrogen peroxide solutions tend to decompose on storage and this may result in incomplete removal of the gelatine although the cupric chloride will still bleach the silver image. If this occurs it is recommended that the proportion of hydrogen peroxide be increased.

679. Development of the Reversal Image. When the original negative has been bleached, cleared, and briefly rinsed, the residual silver bromide can be developed in any developer in room light, or after a uniform exposure to light, or finally, after treatment in a fogging agent. In order to avoid the risk of physical damage to the gelatine which might result from the alternate use of acid and alkaline solutions, an acid hydrosulphite developer might be used (§ 534). The rate of development will then be highest in the highlight regions (M. Abribat, 1930).

As a fogging agent, a dilute solution of thiourea might be used (§ 647); this chemical can be added to the clearing bath, thus reducing the number of operations necessary.

Development should be carried on until examination from the back shows that all the silver bromide present has been reduced. This is followed by a brief wash, no fixation being required.

Development of the residual silver bromide may be replaced by transformation to a coloured substance, such as the brown silver sulphide, under conditions to be described below.

When examining critically the resulting reversal image, one should take into account that any changes in the operations will produce very different effects on a negative and on the positive obtained from it by the reversal technique. Thus a patch of fog in the negative causes a clear patch in the positive; a thin positive results from over-exposure or negative development which was too much prolonged; and a very dense image even in the highlights is the consequence of under-exposure or under-development of the negative.

680. Reversal Methods for Paper. There are on the market several kinds of silver bromide papers specially manufactured to yield reversed pictures, especially for automatic portrait machinery, or for document copying. The processing instructions of the manufacturers should be strictly followed.

Excellent results can be obtained, however, on papers designed for negative-positive work, especially for the production of enlarged negatives without an intermediate positive. The procedures are not widely different, whether the picture is to be viewed by reflection (positive) or by transmission (negative).

When positive images to be viewed by reflection are to be produced, certain sensitometric peculiarities have to be taken into account. The tone range for a picture viewed by reflection is much reduced compared with that for a transparency. From the moment when the image viewed by reflection reaches its maximum gamma, which happens very quickly, the characteristic curve maintains its shape and merely moves bodily along the exposure axis towards smaller values of the exposure. Thus, viewed by reflection, the gamma of a reversed image is practically identical with that of a non-reversed image on the same paper.

With most positive papers carrying emulsions which are not too heavily hardened, satisfactory results are in general obtained by adopting an exposure which is two or three times as heavy as for ordinary printing. Development might be 15 to 30 times as long as for normal use. There is no need for agitation, except for the first few seconds, as long as the paper is covered by at least a quarter of an inch of solution. The picture will then be black all over, the less dense regions appearing dark grey.

After washing in several changes of water, the sheet is treated in acid permanganate until the silver is just dissolved, rinsed, cleared, and washed again until all traces of stain disappear.

If a wet sheet of paper is exposed uniformly to light, a patchy result is obtained, since the local variations in the thickness of the water layer causes the light to be refracted. It is thus necessary for the second exposure to be carried out on dry paper. Development or blackening (sulphiding, etc.) may then be carried out.

This method, described by G. Schweitzer (1935) has found very widespread application. We recommend that a sensitometric step tablet be used, when first setting up the method, with the material it is proposed to adopt.

CHAPTER XXXV

METHODS OF AFTER-TREATMENT: INTENSIFICATION, REDUCTION, RETOUCHING, CLASSIFICATION AND STORAGE

681. General Considerations. Of the various corrective operations described in this chapter, intensification and reduction are purely chemical manipulations, whilst the others, retouching, etc. (including the local application of intensifiers and reducers), are processes requiring manual skill, and presuppose some artistic knowledge (ideas of values and ability to draw, knowledge of anatomy for those who are concerned with portrait retouching) and the mastery of a special technique (reversal of tone values). We propose to deal chiefly with chemical methods here, because retouching, properly called, cannot very well be taught from a book.

Intensification and reduction were operations of great importance in former days when, in the absence of the great variety of printing papers available at the present time, all negatives had to have almost the same density range. In addition the shadow portions of the negative were almost completely transparent so that printing exposure times, to daylight, already long, should not become excessive. Intensification and reduction are now the exception and not the rule.

Whilst intensification, as suitably carried out on a negative which has been properly fixed and washed is an operation which does not entail much risk, the same cannot be said for reduction, in which there is always an element of uncertainty, especially when it is applied to an already dried negative. Moreover, in the case of very dense negatives, such as result from long exposure and normal development, it is often better to confine oneself to using a more intense light for printing, or a longer time of exposure, rather than to risk the destruction of the scale of tones by reduction.

The intensification or reduction of film negatives which have a coating of gelatine on the back often leads to local stains, which occur in the gelatine backing. They are due to insufficient washing. When this occurs the gelatine backing may be removed (§ 716).

In the case of a negative having a very great scientific or documentary value, it is usual to refrain, even in the most extreme cases, from all attempts at direct improvement. Instead, a positive transparency is made from the negative under the best possible conditions; on this positive any intensification or reducing which may be necessary is carried out, and then a reproduction, forming an improved duplicate of the original negative, is printed. By taking the precautions necessary to preserve the sharpness of the image in the course of successive printings, and by choosing for each one of the printings an appropriate method, it is possible to obtain from a very mediocre negative, without any corrective operation whatever, a very satisfactory reproduction, in which the contrast is increased or diminished to the desired degree.

INTENSIFICATION

682. Action of Intensifiers. Intensification is the name given to all processes, which after the negative has been developed, are used to increase the densities of the image. Intensification may be carried out in various ways:

1. By altering the covering power of the silver image.

2. By adding organic dyes to the silver image (e.g. re-developing in a staining developer such as pyrogallol or a chromogenic developer after bleaching).

3. By adding metal atoms such as silver or mercury, or metallic compounds to the image.

4. By converting the silver image to a silver compound which absorbs light more strongly (e.g. the silver salt of quinone thiosulphuric acid).

All such methods of intensification increase the light-stopping power of the original negative, but some methods of intensification lead to the formation of a coloured image (frequently yellow-brown) together with or instead of the original image, which appears less dense. On printing this intensified negative its effective opacity is increased because its colour has changed to yellow-brown which absorbs blue light to which the printing paper is sensitive (L. P. Clerc, 1912). This type of intensification is known as *optical intensification*.

Although this process involving the formation of the stained images is termed optical intensification, a variety of methods of "true" optical intensification are known which require no chemical treatment of the negative, its density being effectively increased by such methods as printing the negative with its emulsion side in close contact with white paper or opal glass, or by printing in contact with a positive transparency made from the original negative (unsharp masks).

Intensification, however, carried out, may conveniently be classified into the following three types:

Proportional Intensification (Fig. 35.1) in which the densities are increased by an amount that is proportional to the densities of the original image resulting in a slight increase in contrast.

Super-proportional Intensification (Fig. 35.2) in which the higher densities of the image are increased by a greater amount than the lower densities so greatly increasing the contrast.

Sub-proportional Intensification (Fig. 35.3) in which the lower densities are increased by a greater amount than the higher densities resulting in a reduction in contrast.

683. Choice of Method of Intensification. The method which, unfortunately, is generally employed (bleaching the image in mercuric chloride and blackening with ammonia) has contributed not a little to the discredit of intensification; it destroys the details of the shadows and blocks up the highlights; in addition, a negative intensified by this method is very unstable, the image gradually fading without the possibility of renewing it by any method whatever. Fortunately, it is very far from true to say that *all* methods of intensification merit this discredit.

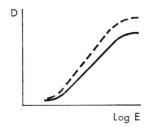

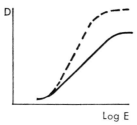

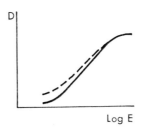

FIG. 35.1. CHARACTERISTIC CURVE SHOWING THE ACTION OF A PROPORTIONAL INTENSIFIER

(Contrast Slightly Increased)

FIG. 35.2. CHARACTERISTIC CURVE SHOWING THE ACTION OF A SUPER-PROPORTIONAL INTENSIFIER

(Contrast Greatly Increased)

FIG. 35.3. CHARACTERISTIC CURVE SHOWING THE ACTION OF A SUB-PROPORTIONAL INTENSIFIER

(Contrast Reduced)

Properly conducted intensification may be made to give the same results as would have been obtained by prolonging development; it can even give better results, for example, when it is feared that, after a certain stage of development, fog may develop more rapidly than the image itself. As would be expected nearly all processes of intensification give increased granularity of the image.

In general, intensification should increase the densities of a negative proportionally. In certain circumstances, as with under-exposed negatives, it may be desirable to intensify the lowest densities to a greater extent. This can be done by means of a silver intensifier (§ 689). One should mistrust intensifiers which yield negatives which are "too clean"; the extreme clearness of the intensified negative shows that the fog has not been intensified and consequently the shadow tones also have not been increased, in spite of the fact that it is precisely these parts of the image which generally are in greatest need of intensification. The use of such an intensifier should therefore be confined solely to black and white subjects, that is to say, to copies of pen-and-ink drawings or similar originals.

It is essential that the intensified image should be as stable as the original negative. Finally, it is an advantage if the intensified image can be further intensified or reduced at pleasure, if the optimum condition has been passed.

In spite of the great variety in the methods of intensification, there are fairly narrow limits in the choice of a method giving the best result in a given case.

The amateur photographer will, as a rule, prefer methods by which intensification is brought about in a single operation (mercuric iodide intensifier), which makes control easier, or those methods which do not require the use of poisonous materials (chromium intensifier).

The photographer using miniature negatives is limited to those methods of intensification which give no increase in granularity.

The physicist will prefer, in certain cases, the only method yielding exact proportionality between densities before and after intensification together with perfect stability of the image (negative bleached with mercuric chloride and then blackened with ferrous oxalate).

The maker of black-and-white line reproductions has often no interest, indeed sometimes just the opposite, in preserving the tones of the negative, especially when these tones are only due to slight spots or to inequalities of illumination of the original and are frequently removed before intensification by means of superficial reduction. He is therefore only concerned with the increase of contrast. The negative, bleached in mercuric chloride, is blackened by ammonia if only moderate intensification is required and if the negative need not be preserved; or in silver cyanide, if considerable intensification is sought.

Lastly, those methods which give great intensification are specially useful in saving negatives which have only a faint trace of image and which cannot be replaced under better conditions.

The use of mercury intensifiers is to be avoided for very small negatives which require considerable enlargement, because the graininess is often very much increased. A negative or positive which is to be preserved should not be treated with a salt of mercury unless subsequent treatment is given, which reduces the mercury to the metallic state, or to the state of sulphide; in any other case the image is certain to be destroyed after a more or less prolonged period.

The intensifiers described in the following

sections have been classified according to their action (J. I. Crabtree and L. E. Muehler, 1931, H. W. Bennett, 1904):

Proportional Intensifiers. Chromium intensifier, § 686 (potassium dichromate-hydrochloric acid bleach followed by re-development in a non-staining developer). Mercury intensification in two successive baths, § 683 (mercuric chloride-bromide bleach followed by a silver-potassium cyanide developer: known as Monckhoven's Intensifier).

Silver Intensifier, § 689 (physical development after partial bleaching in potassium permanganate-sulphuric acid).

Super-proportional Intensifiers. Copper-silver intensifier, § 687 (cupric bromide bleach followed by treatment with a silver salt solution).

Mercury intensification in two successive baths, § 684 (mercuric chloride-bromide bleach followed by darkening with sulphite solution or a normal developer).

Sub-proportional Intensifiers. Single solution mercuric iodide intensifier, § 685. Quinone thiosulphate intensifier, § 688. Chromium intensifier, § 686 (with incomplete bleaching or redevelopment).

It should be emphasised that these classifications are approximate as they depend a great deal on the exact conditions employed. For example chromium intensifier is generally considered to be proportional in its action but where the negative is incompletely bleached or incompletely redeveloped it tends towards sub-proportionality. It is, therefore, recommended that the user finds for himself the type of intensifier that suits his purpose best. This may be done by intensifying half of a spare negative, and printing *separately* on the same paper the best possible print of each half, comparison being made on the prints.

684. Mercury Intensification in Two Successive Baths.
When a negative, in which the image is almost wholly metallic silver, is treated in a solution of mercuric chloride,[1] the silver is converted into a double mercurous-silver

chloride, a complex white salt having properties which are slightly different from those of a simple mixture of silver chloride and mercurous chloride or calomel. The chemical reaction is represented by the equation

$$\underset{\text{Silver}}{Ag} + \underset{\substack{\text{Mercuric} \\ \text{chloride}}}{HgCl_2} \rightarrow \underset{\substack{\text{Mercurous-silver} \\ \text{chloride}}}{AgHgCl_2}$$

In this way the silver adds to itself about double its weight of mercury (200 parts of mercury to 108 parts of silver). At this stage of the operation there is exact proportionality between the original density and the new density, the latter being considerably less than the original density.

More recently it has been suggested that mercurous-silver chloride is not formed but the total reaction between silver and mercuric chloride may be represented by the following equation (B. H. Tavernier, 1970) involving an oxidation-reduction reaction:

$$\underset{\text{silver}}{4Ag} + \underset{\substack{\text{mercuric} \\ \text{chloride}}}{4HgCl_2} \rightarrow \underset{\substack{\text{silver} \\ \text{chloride}}}{4AgCl} + \underset{\substack{\text{mercurous} \\ \text{chloride}}}{2Hg_2Cl_2}$$

As a rule, a solution is used containing about 30 g mercuric chloride and 5 ml hydrochloric or nitric acid in 1,000 ml. Such a solution hardly deteriorates at all on keeping; used solutions may be kept for further use until the active substance is exhausted.

The presence of traces of sodium or silver thiosulphate in the negative due to incomplete washing causes the formation of opalescent patches or spots.

During the first few moments in the bath the image darkens, and by transmitted light shows a violet tint; it then gradually becomes white. For proportional intensification the treatment is continued until the image, when viewed from the back, is seen to be completely whitened. In the case of a hard negative in which it is desired to intensify the parts of least density (sub-proportional intensification) the

---

[1] Mercuric chloride, is a colourless salt, crystallizing in needles, though it is generally sold in pieces of fibrous appearance. It is very dense (specific gravity 5·4), and is not very soluble in pure water (about 7 per cent at 15°C); in warm water its solubility is greater. It is volatile and is carried over in the steam from a boiling solution. Its solubility is increased by the presence of acid or of ammonium chloride. It is very soluble in alcohol. Mercuric chloride, like all other salts of mercury, is a poison which may be sold over the counter by registered dispensing chemists only; its solutions should not be allowed to touch the

skin if the latter is broken. Mercury salts as a group attack many metals (gold, silver, copper, etc.), which are thus amalgamated. Aluminium is strongly attacked by it, yielding thread-like deposits of alumina. Solutions of mercury salts must not be allowed to touch any metals, especially jewellery, and for this reason rings must be taken off, and watches must not be touched by fingers moistened with these solutions. In the case of a neutral solution, a small amount of mercuric chloride is uniformly retained by the gelatine of negatives which have been bathed in it.

action of the mercuric chloride may be interrupted before the heavier densities are completely bleached.

After it has been removed from the bleaching bath the negative must be washed in several changes of water before being darkened. This washing should preferably be done with water slightly acidified with hydrochloric acid, in order to dissolve the mercuric chloride retained by the gelatine.

The layer of gelatine being often very rough after treatment with mercuric chloride, any abrasion on the image, or a strong jet of water, can cause tears that after blackening show as pin-holes. Similar careful washing must also be carried out after darkening by any of the processes now to be described.

Darkening with Ammonia. The image, bleached and washed as described above, turns brown and then black almost instantly when it is placed in a very dilute solution of ammonia (30 ml per litre). The greater part of the silver chloride in the image is dissolved by the ammonia and takes with it an appreciable amount of the mercury, whilst the residual mercuric salt is converted into a black substance which is very opaque but not very stable. The mercurous chloramide thus formed has the formula $Hg_2Cl.NH_2$.

The optical density is multiplied by a factor varying from 1·4 to 1·7 in the denser parts of the image, the higher values of this factor corresponding generally with the use of a dilute solution of ammonia in which the negative has been allowed to remain for a time only sufficient just to blacken the image throughout its thickness. If the image fades after such intensification it cannot be regenerated.

The ammonia solution employed for blackening each negative must be thrown away after use.

As we have already noted, this method of intensification, which is not suitable for negatives with grey tones nor for those to be kept, reduces the clear tones (or at any rate does not intensify them) whilst it strengthens the heavy densities.

Transfer from a very acid bath to an alkaline bath often causes numerous markings and sometimes reticulation of the gelatine; it has been recommended, in order to diminish the liability to these defects, to avoid all rubbing of the film during and after its treatment with ammonia, and to add alum (about 3 per cent) to the solution of mercuric chloride.

Darkening with Sodium Sulphite. A considerable improvement in the mercury intensification process is made by using sodium sulphite (C. Scolik, 1884) instead of ammonia for darkening the image.

The image darkens almost instantly in a solution of sodium sulphite. Half of the silver is found in the darkened image, together with a quarter of the mercury which was associated with it, both metals being for the most part reduced to the metallic condition (Chapman Jones, 1894), whilst the other half of the silver and three-quarters of the mercury go into solution as complex sulphites. Secondary reactions also slowly occur between the metals in the image and in the solution, if the contact is maintained; there is a deposition of silver, which is to some extent added to the image, and to some extent replaces part of the mercury. The presence of a small amount of silver chloride in the image can be demonstrated (as also in the case of images darkened by ammonia) by the fact that the densities are slightly decreased when the negative is placed in a solution of sodium thiosulphate.

As a rule, a solution of about 5 per cent of anhydrous sodium sulphite (or 10 per cent of crystalline sulphite) is employed in a slightly acid condition; the acidification is effected by the addition of sodium bisulphite or of an acid. Solutions which have been used must be thrown away after treatment of each negative.

The intensification becomes a little more energetic if, instead of converting the image into the mercurous-silver chloride, it is converted into the corresponding bromide. This may be done by bleaching in a solution containing equal weights of mercuric chloride and potassium bromide (30 g of each, dissolved separately in 500 ml of water, then mixed). In addition, some of the irregularities of intensification are diminished, due to the fact that silver bromide is much less soluble than the chloride in solutions of sodium sulphite.

Whilst, after bleaching in mercuric chloride, the factor of the increase of densities for an image darkened in sulphite ranges from 1·0 to 1·2 when one goes from low densities to high, these values increase to between 1·2 and 1·6 when the negative is bleached with mercuric *bromide* or in a mixture of equivalent amounts of mercuric chloride and potassium bromide such as the Kodak IN-1 mercury intensifier which contains 22·5 g of potassium bromide and 22·5 g of mercuric chloride in one litre of water.

In either case the intensified image is quite stable.

Darkening with Ferrous Oxalate. By means of a ferrous oxalate developer (§ 535), an image which has been bleached in mercuric chloride is reduced completely to the metallic condition without exposure to light being necessary. This process is so exact that satisfactory photometric measurements may be made of the lower densities after intensification, the proportional factor for the increase of density being applied. If the gelatine is hardened and other suitable precautions are taken, including intermediate washing, the whole set of operations (bleaching and blackening) may be repeated as many times as desired, the densities and contrast increasing each time with exact proportionality. The factor for growth of density is 1·45 for each intensification. The developer may be used several times over.

This method of intensification is only to be recommended for certain scientific applications of photography.

Darkening with an Organic Developer. Common developing solutions are capable of darkening images which have been bleached in mercuric chloride or bromide. Due to the chemical reducing action of the developer, the greater part of the metals which would be dissolved in solution of pure sulphite is reduced to the metallic condition, though the reduction is never complete. As mentioned previously and for the reasons already given, it is advantageous to use mercuric bromide for bleaching. Amidol, whilst it is far from giving the greatest intensification, gives very satisfactory proportionality between the densities before and after intensification. The value of the proportionality factor is about 1·18.

Whatever the developing agent, each portion of the solution should be used once only.

Various Other Methods of Darkening. A great number of reagents have been suggested for darkening images bleached in mercuric chloride; sodium thiosulphate gives only a negligible intensification, except for the accidental formation of sulphide which generally occurs as stains in the lighter parts of the image. Other solutions which may be mentioned as capable of giving strong intensification are as follows: a very dilute solution of caustic soda, to which formalin has been added (Blake-Smith, 1901), a solution of stannous tartrate prepared when required for use by dissolving a little stannous chloride in a dilute solution of tartaric acid

(Hélain, 1901) and many other substances which are reducing agents in the chemical sense.

Special mention should be made of the process of darkening by means of silver cyanide (D. van Monckhoven, 1879), which is frequently used commercially in the copying of originals, since it reduces the lower densities (fog, etc.) at the same time that it increases the higher densities considerably. The darkening solution may be prepared by dissolving 25 g of silver nitrate in about 500 ml of water and adding in small quantities at a time a solution of 20 g of pure sodium or potassium cyanide in about 200 ml of water until the precipitate first formed is almost entirely redissolved. The volume is then made up to 1,000 ml with water. The solution may be used several times over.

685. Single-solution Mercuric Iodide Intensifier. Intensification in a single solution of mercuric iodide was described in 1879 by B. J. Edwards. Since mercuric iodide (or di-iodide of mercury, a very heavy red salt, generally supplied in the form of powder) is insoluble in water, this author proposed dissolving it in a mixture of potassium iodide and of sodium thiosulphate (in each of which it is separately soluble). Later, it was found (L. Lumière and A. Seyewetz, 1899) that the use of sulphite instead of thiosulphate permits a slightly more vigorous intensification. Whilst a negative which has been fixed in a fresh bath may be thus intensified after very brief washing, a yellow fog will result, due to precipitation of silver iodide, if the negative has been fixed in a bath containing much silver salt and is badly washed.

The following baths are used—

	I *Edwards*	II *Lumière and Seyewetz*
Potassium iodide	20 g	—
Sodium sulphite, anhydrous . . .	—	100 g
Mercuric iodide	20 g	10 g
Sodium thiosulphate . . .	20 g	—
Water to	1 litre	1 litre

The first of these solutions contains no oxidizable product, and is more stable than the second. The solutions may be used many times so long as they are kept away from light when not in actual use.

In these baths the image is intensified progressively without changing its appearance; the silver is converted into iodide, whilst at the same time metallic mercury is deposited on it. It seems that the series of reactions occurring in this intensification process may be represented by the equations—

$$2HgI_2 \; + \; 2Ag \; \rightarrow \; Hg_2I_2 \; + \; 2AgI$$
Mercuric iodide   Silver   Mercurous iodide   Silver iodide

$$Hg_2I_2 + 2Na_2SO_3 \rightarrow Hg + HgI_2, 2Na_2SO_3.$$

Mercurous iodide Sodium sulphite Mercury Mercuric iodide dissolved
in the sulphite

The process is stopped when the desired degree of intensification has been obtained; the negative is then thoroughly washed.

The image intensified by the first of these methods is slightly more stable than that intensified by the second.

In moist air, though more slowly in dry, an image intensified in this way becomes yellowish (probably due to the formation of a complex of mercuric oxide and silver iodide). Absolute stability can be conferred on the image by placing the negative, after washing, in an ordinary developing bath, which reduces the silver iodide to metallic silver, or in a 1 per cent solution of sodium sulphide which changes the two metals into sulphide without appreciably modifying the densities of the image.

A negative, which for the lack of these precautions has suffered this alteration of colour, may at any time be brought back to its original condition after intensification by treating it for a sufficient time with a developer or with the sulphide solution.

The action of this intensifier is not proportional (A. H. Nietz and K. Huse, 1918); the action is greatest with the lower densities, which is a considerable advantage in most cases of practical interest, the shadow parts of a negative requiring more energetic intensification than the image of the highlights. The lowest densities are approximately doubled whilst the higher densities are multiplied by about 1·4.

Altogether the mercuric iodide intensifier is one of the most general usefulness. Especially for the purposes of press photographers, wh often need to give a little sparkle to negatives, it has the very great advantage that there is no need for the very long washing for removal of hypo which is required when using most other intensifiers. The possibility of a subsequent change in the negative is often a matter of no importance.

A single solution of mercuric thiocyanate has been suggested as an intensifier (Andresen and Leupold, 1899), but, after intensification, the image tends to bleach if it is allowed to remain in the bath; this can, however, be remedied by treatment with a developer.

686. Chromium Intensification. About 1880 Eder suggested as a possible method of intensification the conversion of the silver of the photographic image into silver chloride by means of a solution of dichromate acidified with a little hydrochloric acid, and its re-development in a pyrogallol developer. In this way, in addition to the black image of the reduced silver, there is superimposed on it the brown image which is formed in the gelatine by the oxidation products of the pyrogallol.

In experimenting with this process, which had been forgotten, C. Welborne Piper and D. J. Carnagie in 1904 found that the intensification was partly due to the deposition of a chromium compound (probably the oxide) in the image, the amount of this deposit being greater if the bleaching solution were only slightly acidified. The active agent in this intensification appeared to them to be a *chlorochromate* (produced by the action of hydrochloric acid on a dichromate), and they found that the silver chloride thus formed was developable without exposure to light, at any rate if the bleaching bath did not contain a great excess of hydrochloric acid; the latter, by being partially converted to chlorine, yielded ordinary silver chloride, which was only developable after exposure to light. For darkening they recommended the use of an amidol developer as lending itself best to the purpose of successive intensifications without causing frilling of the gelatine. The progressive increase of density by repeated intensification has been confirmed by photo-micrographs published in 1916 by W. T. P. Cunningham.

It has been shown that the mixture of dichromate and hydrochloric acid may be replaced by a pure solution of a chlorochromate (L. Lumiere and A. Seyewetz, 1919), or by mixtures of chromic acid with a chloride (C. H. Bothamley, 1918), or of a bromide (L. J. Bunel, 1923).

Lumière and Seyewetz consider that, on bleaching, only half of the silver is converted into developable silver chloride, the other half forming a double chromite of silver and potassium, a brown insoluble compound which would not be acted on by a developer. In this way may be explained the increasing brown coloration of images which have been successively intensified, as also the decreasing magnitude of the effect of re-repeated treatments.

For the practical application of this method of intensification two stock solutions are prepared. These by themselves will keep indefinitely—

(*A*) 10 per cent solution of potassium dichromate.
(*B*) Concentrated hydrochloric acid diluted to ten times its volume with distilled water.

7

If it is required to obtain varying degrees of intensification, heavy, medium or slight, one of the following mixtures must be made up at the time required—

Intensification	Strong	Medium	Slight
Solution A . . .	10	20	20
Solution B . . .	2	10	40
Distilled water to .	100	100	100

The effect of any of these mixtures, given here only as an approximate indication, varies very much with the nature of the emulsion on which the image is obtained. With some plates the solutions recommended for weak intensification give quite a heavy effect, and in such cases the amount of hydrochloric acid must be adjusted. The amount of acid prescribed for strong intensification may be very much too small if the water employed contains much calcium bicarbonate.

The various operations in intensification must be carried out in weak daylight or in artificial light in order to avoid solarization of the silver chloride. The negative is allowed to remain in the bleaching bath until all traces of black image have disappeared when viewed from the back, but it should not be allowed to remain in this bath for a longer time than is necessary, otherwise irregular markings are likely to be produced.

Negatives must be washed in several changes of water until the coloration of the gelatine has almost completely disappeared. The washing process may be considerably shortened by immersing the negatives, after rinsing, in a solution containing about 5 per cent of sodium carbonate.

The image is then re-developed, preferably in a metol-hydroquinone developer. In case the dichromate is incompletely eliminated (which is possible even after prolonged washing) using an amidol developer risks the formation of insoluble oxidation products resulting in the formation of red spots (W. A. Ermen, 1928). In some developers the image comes up very rapidly at first and then appears not to change, though in reality it increases slowly for at least a quarter of an hour.

If the intensification is thought to be insufficient it may be repeated; there is, however, very little to be gained by intensifying more than twice. The factor of proportionality attains successively the following values in the case of several successive intensifications, re-development being effected in a metol-hydroquinone developer which is only very slightly alkaline (P. E. Boucher, 1935)—

Number of intensifications .	1	2	3
Factor	1·4	1·65	1·8

Images intensified in this way are quite permanent; their warm black tone renders the method very suitable for the intensification of lantern slides or paper prints, either for the purpose of intensification as such or, by slightly increasing the amount of acid, to improve the colour. It may be noted that this method of intensification, which, incidentally, does not make use of any poisonous substance, is extremely economical.

The only objection which may be raised against this method of intensification is that it gives to the gelatine of some emulsions a granular structure which makes retouching difficult, though it does not show on printing either by contact or on enlarging.

The sensitometric measurements of Nietz and Huse (1918) have shown that, contrary to conclusions drawn from photometric measurements, the action of this intensifier is not proportional, but is greater in the least dense regions (sub-proportional) a property which we have already seen to be very valuable.

687. Heavy Intensification with Copper and Silver. A method which has been used for a very long time, consists in treating the negative in a solution of cupric bromide in which the silver is converted into bromide and at the same time fixes an equivalent amount of cuprous bromide.

The negative, after rinsing, is transferred to a solution of silver nitrate, some of which is reduced to metallic silver by the cuprous bromide; this silver is thus precipitated with an equivalent amount of silver bromide in the image along with the existing silver bromide according to the following equations:

$$Ag + CuBr_2 \rightarrow AgBr + CuBr$$
$$CuBr + 2AgNO_3 \rightarrow Cu(NO_3)_2 + Ag + AgBr$$

After washing, and reducing the silver bromide, the amount of silver is exactly three times that originally present (W. de Abney, 1877). During washing, the cuprous bromide is partially redissolved or re-oxidized and so escapes reaction.

The method has been improved by Luther and Schreiber (1923), and by G. Zelger (1924), by using in the first operation a solution which deposits in the image not cuprous bromide but a cuprous salt which is absolutely insoluble and non-oxidizable, such as cuprous thiocyanate or cuprous iodide.

As before, the density is exactly trebled by intensification; it may be again trebled by repeating the process, and thus sufficient contrast may be obtained to print an image which exists as a mere ghost, as is sometimes obtained with films in which regression of the latent image has occurred.

Care must be taken to avoid uneven action or reticulation of the gelatine if the process is repeated more than once.

The " bleaching " bath (which, as a matter of fact, gives a yellow image) is prepared by pouring solution (A) into solution (B)—

	Copper sulphate, cryst. .	5 g
A	Acetic acid, glacial .	28 ml
	Water to . . .	500 ml

	Potassium iodide . .	5 g
B	Ammonia 0·880 . .	50 ml
	Water to . .	250 ml

Heat is generated when the solutions are mixed, and the bath must not be used until cool. The mixed solution, which is clear blue in colour, should be slightly acid; if it is not, a little acetic acid must be added until blue litmus paper is faintly reddened by it. This solution is quite stable and may be used until exhausted.

The negative is immersed in it until the image becomes yellow throughout its thickness. After thorough washing it is blackened in a solution containing 0·25 per cent of silver nitrate to which about 1 per cent of sodium acetate has been added (so preventing the copper nitrate formed during the reaction from attacking the silver). Before treatment with silver nitrate, the negative may be immersed in a saturated solution of alum, so preventing combination of silver nitrate with the gelatine.

The silver salts, other than silver iodide (chloride precipitated in the gelatine due to the use of ordinary water and silver nitrate combined with the gelatine), are removed by immersion for about two minutes in a bath containing about 1 per cent of ammonia, which has no action on silver iodide.

The process is completed by reducing the silver iodide to the metallic state by means of a solution of sodium hydrosulphite containing a little sodium bisulphite, or by means of an amidol developer made alkaline with sodium carbonate.

688. Quinone Thiosulphate Intensifier. This is a single solution intensifier specially recommended for under-exposed or excessively thin negatives. It was introduced by Muehler and Crabtree (1945) and produces a greater degree of intensification than any other known single solution intensifier, particularly when used for high-speed materials. The following solutions are required—

A	Distilled Water (70°F, 21°C) .	750 ml
	Sulphuric acid (conc.) . . .	30 ml
	Potassium dichromate . .	22·5 g
	Distilled Water to . .	1 litre
B	Distilled water (70°F, 21°C) .	750 ml
	Sodium metabisulphite . .	3·8 g
	Hydroquinone . . .	15·0 g
	Wetting agent (10 per cent solution)	20 ml
	Distilled water to	1 litre
C	Distilled water (70°F, 21°C) .	750 ml
	Sodium thiosulphate (cryst.) .	22·5 g
	Distilled Water to . .	1 litre

If kept in stoppered bottles Solution A is stable indefinitely while solutions B and C are stable for several months. Solution B should be re-mixed whenever it becomes appreciably coloured as a result of oxidation and solution C should be discarded if a precipitate forms indicating sulphurization.

For Use. To one part of Solution A, with stirring, add two parts of Solution B, then two parts of Solution C. Continue stirring and finally add one part of Solution A. The order of mixing is important and should be adhered to.

Negatives should be washed for 5–10 minutes and hardened in the following alkaline formaldehyde hardener for 5 minutes at 68°F (20°C) and then washed for 5 minutes.

Water	500 ml
Formaldehyde (40 per cent solution)	10 ml
Sodium Carbonate (anhydrous) .	5 g
Water to	1 litre

After hardening, immerse in the intensifier with frequent agitation to avoid streaking. When working in a dish treat only one negative at a time. The intensifier should be freshly mixed and used only once. Maximum intensification is given in about 10 minutes at 68°F (20°C). Then washing for 10 to 20 minutes is followed by drying as usual. Lower degrees of intensification can be obtained by treatment for shorter times.

This intensifier is unique in that the greatest intensification is obtained on the images of relatively coarse-grained emulsions (medium and high speed) while very fine grained materials are intensified to a negligible degree. A maximum photographic intensification of the order of 10 times and a significant increase in apparent emulsion speed can be obtained. Traces of chloride in the water used for preparing the intensifier solutions have a great effect on the course of intensification, causing a progressive decrease in the degree of intensification as the concentration of chloride ion increases upwards from about 15 parts per million. Thus it is advisable to use distilled water. The intensified image has a brown tone and is not indefinitely permanent, but under normal conditions of storage should be stable for at least 5 years. The intensified image is destroyed by acid hypo, so under no circumstances should the intensified negative be placed in fixing baths or wash-water contaminated with fixing bath.

Negatives which have received the maximum degree of intensification are appreciably grainy; this is not unexpected since graininess is known to increase with increase in gamma and also since maximum intensification takes place in the densities where the greater proportion of the too large grains occurs.

According to Muehler and Crabtree (1945) the dichromate and sulphuric acid oxidize hydroquinone to benzoquinone which then reacts with thiosulphate to form a dark brown-silver salt of hydroquinone thiosulphuric acid.

$$O$$

S—SO$_3$.Ag

$$O$$

689. Other Methods of Intensification. The methods of intensification described in the preceding paragraphs are amply sufficient for all practical requirements, so that we shall be content to mention only briefly some others which are sometimes used, or which are in themselves curious because of the means employed.

R. B. Wilsey (1919) showed that intensification by means of pyrogallol provides a means for increasing almost indefinitely the contrast of a negative while preserving very fair proportionality between the effective final and the initial densities. This is done by successive bleachings and re-development of the image, using a pyrogallol developer containing only a small amount of sulphite—

BLEACHING

Potassium ferricyanide	30 g
Potassium bromide	10 g
Water to	1 litre

RE-DEVELOPMENT

Sodium sulphite, anhydrous	10 g
Pyrogallol	5 g
Sodium carbonate, anhydrous	10 g
Water to	1 litre

The bleaching bath keeps for a long time, even if used, but the re-development bath should be made up in small quantities and used only once.

The factor for the increase of density and contrast has the following successive values in the case of a negative developed originally in metol-hydroquinone.

Number of intensifications	1	2	3	4	5
Factor	1·70	2·10	2·40	2·65	2·80

On the other hand, a negative which has been developed in pyrogallol (or intensified by the above method) may be reduced proportionally by bleaching it in a solution of permanganate acidified with hydrochloric acid and re-developing it in any developer which yields a black image.

Intensification by precipitation of silver according to the method already described for physical development before or after fixing (§ 625) is especially suitable for fine-grained images. It is often an advantage to precede this process by immersion in a very dilute solution of permanganate acidified with sulphuric acid (the reversal bath described in § 678 diluted twenty or fifty times with water), and to follow it by treatment with sodium thiosulphate. (This method of intensification may be carried out *before* fixation.)

The granularity of a negative can be reduced without appreciably increasing its contrast by applying a variation of blackening by sodium sulphide suggested by P. Strauss (1940). This is in fact toning the image. The silver image is converted to silver bromide by treatment with a ferricyanide bleach consisting of 3 per cent potassium ferricyanide, 1·5 per cent potassium bromide, and 1 per cent sodium carbonate. After bleaching, wash well and immerse in a 1 per cent sodium sulphide solution containing 0·5 to 1 per cent sodium thiosulphate. (The optimum amount must be determined by trial for each emulsion.) The silver bromide is converted to silver sulphide and a small amount of the silver bromide is dissolved by the hypo from the surface of the grains and reprecipitated as colloidal silver sulphide near the grains. By this means the spaces between the grains are more or less filled thus reducing the apparent granularity.

A method giving great intensification but requiring rather delicate manipulation has been described by K. Hickman and W. Weyerts (1933): a sulphide-toned image is placed in a solution of silver sulphite and, under the action of a strong artificial light, it progressively becomes intensified by deposition of silver. After intensification to the desired degree the image is rinsed, placed in a fixing bath and washed.

It has been suggested that a negative may be intensified by " doubling " the image in " carbon " on the gelatine of the negative by the Carbro process. Finally, intensification may be carried out by bleaching the silver image in a re-halogenizing bleach and re-developing in a colour developer (§ 623). Generally a yellow colour former is used for this method of optical intensification.

REDUCTION

690. Choice of a Reducer. The usual reducers act by gradually dissolving the silver which forms the photographic image, but widely different results are obtained according to the substance (or mixture of substances) which is used for this purpose. Photographic reducers are in effect chemical oxidizing agents and should not be confused with chemical reducing agents (e.g. developers). The general reaction of reducers is to oxidize the image silver to silver ions which are then removed by fixation:

$$Ag + M^{n+} \rightarrow Ag^+ + M^{(n-1)+}$$

here M represents a metal ion of variable valency. The oxidized silver is generally in the form of a sulphate or halide depending on the anions present in the reducer.

Uniformity of action of a reducer is obviously only possible if it can penetrate to all parts of the image at the same speed; in the case of a dry negative, however, and particularly if fixation has been done in a bath containing alum, the permeability of the gelatine is often very different in the various parts of the image,

and thus there is a great risk that the process of reduction will produce markings which cannot be removed. Traces of grease on the negative (finger-marks, etc.), even though they do not prevent the swelling of the gelatine, cause the reducer to penetrate more slowly, and so cause trouble. Where necessary, these traces of grease must be removed by cleaning with pure benzene or petroleum spirit. The addition of wetting agents (§ 607) can facilitate the uniform penetration of the reducer. If, therefore, reduction has not been carried out before drying the negative, the latter should be soaked in water until the gelatine has swollen uniformly, which will sometimes require three or four hours.

The characteristics of a reducer depend largely on the dimensions of the grains forming the image, and on the distribution of these grains in the depth of the layer; hence there are considerable variations in effect according to the type of emulsion, and even with negatives of a given emulsion developed under very different conditions.

Differences have been noticed in a given negative in the reduction of areas of equal density produced by different rays, or corresponding to latent images of different ages at the moment of development (C. Jausseran, 1933).

The various reducers may be schematically classified, like intensifiers (§ 682) into three groups—

1. Subtractive reducers.

2. Proportional reducers.

3. Super-proportional reducers.

Subtractive reducers are very active solvents of silver. They attack the silver almost as fast as they penetrate the film of gelatine, so that the different densities in the image are decreased by approximately the same amount (Fig. 35.4), and if the action is allowed to go on too long some parts of the image may disappear altogether. These reducers are specially suited for the clearing of fogged negatives. They are generally chosen for local reducers in retouching.

A *proportional reducer* decreases every density in the image in the same proportion. This may be brought about by converting the silver of the image into a less absorbing substance or mixture of substances (Fig. 35.5), e.g. by blue toning (L. P. Clerc, 1899) or by iodizing the image. The removal of the same fraction of the

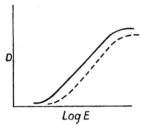 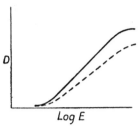 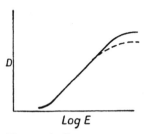

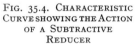

FIG. 35.4. CHARACTERISTIC CURVE SHOWING THE ACTION OF A SUBTRACTIVE REDUCER

FIG. 35.5. CHARACTERISTIC CURVE SHOWING THE ACTION OF A PROPORTIONAL REDUCER

FIG. 35.6. CHARACTERISTIC CURVE SHOWING THE ACTION OF A SUPER-PROPORTIONAL REDUCER

quantity of silver at every point of the image is never realized except, approximately, by the use of solvents whose action is so slow as to be negligible during the time taken to penetrate the film of gelatine. These reducers are most suitable for diminishing the contrasts of negatives which have been over-developed.

A *super-proportional reducer* removes a greater proportion of the silver from the dense parts of a negative than from the lighter parts, as if its action started from the support of the film and moved outwards towards the surface of the gelatine (Fig. 35.6). The only reducer known to belong to this group is ammonium persulphate; it dissolves silver slowly, and its activity is increased by the silver sulphate produced in the course of the reaction (auto-catalytic reaction).

Lastly, in certain cases, it is required to reduce only the dense parts of the negative. This may be done indirectly by allowing the solvent of silver to act only after all the silver contained in the surface layers of the film has been converted into an insoluble compound.

In using any of the reducers of the first three groups, the negative should always be withdrawn from the bath a short time before the desired effect has been produced, because the solution of the silver continues during the first moments of washing.

691. Subtractive Reducers. Whichever of the reducers of this class may be used, its peculiar character is exaggerated by anything which tends to increase the rate of solution of the active silver (increase in concentration of the active substance) or to diminish the velocity of penetration into the gelatine (excessive swelling of the film, thickening of the liquid, etc.). The converse tends to make these reducers behave in a proportional manner.

The concentrations recommended later are averages which may be increased or diminished as desired. It must, however, be borne in mind that the use of comparatively highly-concentrated reducers renders control difficult unless a glass dish, illuminated from below, is employed.

Farmer's Reducer. The oldest known of the subtractive reducers (H. Farmer, 1884) is a mixture (prepared when required for use) of a solution of potassium ferricyanide[1] with a solution of sodium thiosulphate. In this very unstable mixture, which generally loses its activity (recognized by the decoloration) in a time varying from a few minutes (mixture of highly concentrated solutions) to a few hours (mixture of very dilute solutions), the ferricyanide controls the activity of the mixture, the concentration of thiosulphate being always sufficient to give rapid solution of the silver salt which is formed.

The ferricyanide converts the silver to silver ferrocyanide which is dissolved by the thiosulphate if the latter is present in excess

The reaction is as follows—

$$4K_3Fe(CN)_6 + 4Ag \rightarrow Ag_4Fe(CN)_6 + 3K_4Fe(CN)_6$$

If the ferricyanide is in great excess, 15 per cent ferricyanide + 0·5 per cent anhydrous thiosulphate, an unstable solution is formed in which

[1] Potassium ferricyanide, occurs in crystals of intense red colour having the formula $K_3Fe(CN)_6$. The crystals are often covered with an ochre-like layer due to exposure to the air; this should be washed off before a solution is prepared. The salt is very soluble in water (solutions up to 30 per cent may be prepared in the cold); its concentrated solutions have a yellowish brown colour, whilst dilute solutions are greenish yellow. These solutions are unstable, especially in light, becoming partially converted into ferrocyanide. For this reason large quantities should not be dissolved at one time, although for use as a reducer its solutions may be stabilized by means of sodium chloride added in amount double that of the ferricyanide.

intensification by sulphide toning of the image may occur (Kickman and Hecker, 1934).

Practised workers, in judging how to mix the two stock solutions, are guided by the depth of colour of the mixture. At first it will be suitable to mix in equal volumes a 1 per cent solution of potassium ferricyanide and a 10 per cent solution of sodium thiosulphate.

By making the mixture alkaline with a little sodium carbonate (Stürenberg, 1903) or with ammonia (R. Namias, 1910) it will retain its activity considerably longer and its rate of attack on the silver will be retarded a little; at the same time the somewhat persistent coloration of the gelatine by the ferricyanide will be prevented.

In order to avoid irregular action, the dish must be rocked during the whole process of reduction. The negative must be rinsed every time it is taken out of the bath for purposes of examination, otherwise streaks of lighter density may occur.

As a solvent of the silver ferrocyanide, the thiosulphate may be replaced by cyanides (*poisonous*) or by the alkaline thiocyanates the mixtures thus formed are very stable.

Permanganate Reducer. A very dilute, acidified solution of permanganate (R. Namias, 1899) behaves as a reducer. It is very economical and its action is not quite so entirely subtractive as that of Farmer's solution.

The following mixture is made up when required—

Potassium permanganate, 0·4 per
  cent solution . . . 3 to 5 ml
Sulphuric acid, 2 per cent solution 3 to 5 ml
Water to . . . . 100 ml

Instead of the water, a 2 per cent solution of alum may be used in order to avoid the softening of the gelatine in warm weather.

The silver is dissolved in the form of sulphate; (A. Marriage, 1954):

$$10Ag + 2KMnO_4 + 8H_2SO_4$$
$$\rightarrow K_2SO_4 + 2MnSO_4 + 8H_2O + 5Ag_2SO_4$$

A part of the sulphate is precipitated as the chloride by the chlorides present in the water used for making up the solutions or in rinsing the negative. In addition the negative becomes brown due to the manganese dioxide formed in the partial reduction of the permanganate. Both of these substances may be removed by immersing the negative in a solution containing about 10 per cent of sodium bisulphite, followed by washing in several changes of water.

Other Subtractive Reducers. Of the many other reducers that have practically identical properties, mention may be made of those which may be kept ready for use and which can be used several times.

The following may be included in this group: a mixture of ferric oxalate, sodium sulphite, and sodium thiosulphate (L. Belitski, 1883), which is perfectly stable in the dark. A modified formula (J. I. Crabtree and L. E. Muehler, 1932) which remains active for about three days without special precautions, would appear to be the most perfect of superficial reducers, all the densities being decreased by the same value (E. L. Turner and W. J. Smith, 1935)—

Ferric chloride, cryst. . .	25 g
Potassium citrate . . .	75 g
Sodium sulphite, anhydrous .	30 g
Citric acid	30 g
Sodium thiosulphate, cryst. .	200 g
Water to	1 litre

Also a solution of potassium dichromate acidified with sulphuric acid (10 g dichromate and 10 ml acid made up to 1,000 ml), which may be made up as a very concentrated stock solution (E. Gosselin, 1889); a solution obtained by adding to a solution of sodium thiosulphate a solution of cuprammonium sulphate which is prepared by adding ammonia to a solution of copper sulphate until the precipitate first formed is re-dissolved in a *large excess* of ammonia (Prunier and Mathet, 1892); lastly a solution containing about 5 per cent of cerium (ceric) sulphate (*poisonous*) acidified with sulphuric acid (L. Lumière and A. Seyewetz, 1900).

We may also mention, but only to advise the avoidance of its use, the possibility of reducing a negative by a very dilute solution of sodium hypochlorite, which acts mechanically by dissolving the gelatine, so removing the surface layers of silver.

692. Proportional Reducers. *Quinone Reducer.* The addition of sulphuric acid to the extent of about 20 ml to 1,000 ml to a saturated solution (0·5 per cent) of benzoquinone (ordinary quinone) furnishes a reducer (L. Lumière and A. Seyewetz, 1910) which has more recently been found (R. Luther, 1923) to act almost proportionally on the various densities. This solution, which is clear yellow, gradually turns brown, and finally gives a brown deposit. An image which has been reduced in this bath acquires a slightly reddish tint. It is necessary, after reducing and brief rinsing, to bathe the negative for some time in a solution containing about 10 per cent of sodium bisulphite before proceeding to the final washing.

Ferric Sulphate Reducer. A very dilute solution of a ferric salt which is quite free from chlorides and bromides (a condition which is generally satisfied by ferric ammonium alum which is a crystalline salt of pale rose-violet colour), and which is acidified by a little sulphuric acid, forms a reducer which is almost exactly proportional in its action and keeps well (H. Krause, 1919). The solution employed may usefully be a 2 per cent solution of the salt in rain water or distilled water containing about 0·5 per cent of pure sulphuric acid. After rinsing, the negative is bathed for some time in a very dilute solution of sulphuric acid before the final washing.

Permanganate and Persulphate. A mixture in suitable proportions of the subtractive acid-permanganate reducer with the super-proportional persulphate reducer forms a reducing solution of intermediate character, the action of which is almost proportional (N. C. Deck, K. Huse and A. H. Nietz, 1916).

The bath must be prepared when required for use by mixing the following substances in the order given, each one being dissolved separately in a small amount of water—

Potassium permanganate .	0·10 g
Sulphuric acid (1 per cent solution)	60 ml
Ammonium persulphate .	10 g
Water to	1 litre

The time required for reduction is from 2 to 5 minutes. The negative is then rinsed and bathed for 5 minutes in a solution containing about 10 per cent of sodium bisulphite before being washed in several changes of water.

693. Ammonium Persulphate Super-proportional Reducer. The selective action of alkali persulphates on the higher densities of photographic images was discovered in 1901 by A. and L. Lumière and A. Seyewetz, who specially recommended the use of ammonium persulphate.[1] It must, however, be stated that

[1] Ammonium persulphate is obtained in small colourless crystals having the composition $(NH_4)_2S_2O_8$. The substance readily absorbs moisture from the atmosphere and then becomes unstable. The salt should be stored in well-stoppered bottles. When a bottle of persulphate is opened a smell of ozone is often noticeable, this substance being formed together with the inactive sulphate when the salt is partially decomposed. Ammonium persulphate is very soluble in cold water (more than 30 per cent), but the solution is not very

with negatives which have been developed with *p*-aminophenol (and only in this case) ammonium persulphate behaves sometimes as a subtractive reducer.

Various cases have been discovered in which reduction by persulphate is prevented or retarded by certain dyes adsorbed on the silver of the image during previous treatment (H. Lüppo-Cramer, 1928).

Persulphate converts silver into silver sulphate, which, in proportion as it is formed, tends to accelerate the attack on the remaining silver.

$$(NH_4)_2S_2O_8 + 2Ag \rightarrow Ag_2SO_4 + (NH_4)_2SO_4$$
Ammon. persulphate Silver Silver sulphate Ammon. sulphate

This simple equation does not, however, represent the actual reaction because the solution becomes acid during use. Also hydrogen ions and silver ions accelerate the photographic reduction and are thought to be formed in the actual reaction (H. Marshall and J. K. H. Inglis, 1902).

The presence of chlorides, which is practically inevitable, causes trouble (E. Stenger and H. Heller, 1910) if the amount of sodium chloride is as much as 0·01 per cent: this is noticed as an exaggerated superproportionality with a discontinuity in the reducer for a certain density; this value of density is raised by increasing the amount of chloride present (G. Higson; S. E. Sheppard, 1921). It will thus be understood that reduction by persulphate may be impossible with tap water which is relatively rich in chloride, such as may be found in some coastal districts.

Certain reducers which, in the absence of chlorides, hardly ever behave in a way other than subtractively can, when a suitable amount of chloride or bromide is added to them, dissolve the silver of the high densities, whilst that of the low densities is converted into chloride or bromide.

The presence of chloride in a persulphate reducer shows itself by the formation in the bath of a slight white precipitate round the dense parts of the negative.

stable and it is advisable to prepare only a small amount of solution at a time (in the presence of 20 per cent of sodium sulphate these solutions may be kept for several days without alteration); persulphates are at once decomposed by boiling water.

Potassium persulphate is much less soluble (1·7 per cent at 15°C), but for this reason much easier to obtain pure. It may be used instead of ammonium persulphate as a reducer of photographic images.

The rate at which persulphate attacks the silver varies considerably with the acidity of the substance. The action is controlled by the addition of a trace of sulphuric acid or of a very small quantity of a silver salt (even of a small amount of an already-used solution) or of iron alum (S. E. Sheppard, 1918–1921); all these substances slightly diminish the risk of " poisoning " by chlorides.

The reducing bath is prepared when required for use as follows—

Ammonium persulphate	.	2 to 5 g
Sulphuric acid[1]	. .	0·1 g
Water to	. . .	100 ml

The reduction, which is comparatively slow at first, gradually gains in speed and may become too rapid. The action of the bath must be stopped a little before the desired effect has been attained; this is done by plunging the negative, without intermediate rinsing, in a solution of about 10 per cent of anhydrous sodium sulphite, which at the same time dissolves any traces of silver chloride formed in the film. The negative is then washed in several changes of water.

The microscopic observations of J. I. Pigg (1904) and of W. Scheffer (1906), on tests carried out on identical pieces of the same scale of tones before and after reduction with persulphate, showed that the persulphate acts simultaneously throughout the thickness of the film and attacks the large grains first.

694. Reduction of Granularity by Indirect Proportional Reduction. A. Seyewetz (1938) recommended the following method of proportional reduction giving the benefit of the fine grain of negatives developed in paraphenylene diamine.

The silver image is converted into silver thiocyanate by bleaching in a solution containing 10 per cent of potassium ferricyanide and 0·5 per cent potassium thiocyanate. After rinsing, the image is re-developed in a developer containing 6 per cent anhydrous sodium sulphite and 1 per cent *p*-phenylenediamine (free base). By this means the gamma is reduced (0·8 to 0·5 in one treatment) without undue reduction of threshold speed. The image produced on a high-speed emulsion without special precautions in development may thus yield an image with a granularity comparable with that of a fine-grain emulsion.

[1] A solution of about 1 per cent of sulphuric acid may be made up and 10 ml used for 100 ml of the bath.

The fact that no silver can be detected in the developer solution afterwards suggests that the reduction in grain size so apparent in photomicrographs, is due to a change in the structure of the silver resulting in more compact grains than those originally present. It is not certain, however, whether this treatment results in a genuine reduction of graininess in the print, since the negative of lower gamma will have to be printed on harder paper.

695. Indirect Reduction of Heavier Densities. The image is treated in a bath containing about 2 per cent of potassium ferricyanide and 2 per cent of potassium bromide, in which it gradually bleaches. The operation is interrupted by washing in plenty of water a little before the higher densities have been completely bleached; the remaining silver is then dissolved in a solution of potassium permanganate acidified with *acetic* acid (R. Namias, 1911–1925).

After dissolving the residual silver, the negative is washed thoroughly and is transferred to a solution containing about 10 per cent of sodium bisulphite which decolorizes the gelatine and dissolves the acetate and bromide of silver formed; it is then re-developed in any ordinary M.Q. developer whilst exposed to weak light.

It is also possible to protect the greater part of the silver against the action of Farmer's reducer by transforming it into silver sulphide, or by toning it with gold or selenium. The silver can also be converted to bromide or chloride and re-developed superficially, the unreduced silver halide being dissolved in a fixing bath.

RETOUCHING

696. The Purpose of Retouching. As a rule, the term " retouching " (negative retouching) is used to describe any work done on the gelatine of a negative with a brush, pencil or knife. Retouching corrects certain technical faults in negatives and, above all, faults of modelling. It is an almost universal rule in portrait photography to tone down or suppress wrinkles, freckles, and superfluous hair, to accentuate some lights and to lessen shadows which are too deep; often to modify an expression, and sometimes even to change the form of the face.

In professional practice retouching on the negative may be replaced by employing make-up on the model using a similar technique to that employed in film studios where retouching is impossible.

Technical faults requiring correction by retouching include the modification of the relative printing values of certain areas of the image which have a simple outline. This may be done in order to remedy any irregularity arising from faulty working in making the negative; or it may be to improve the rendering, for example, by reducing the contrast, which is sometimes great, between sky and foreground in a landscape or between the lights and shadows of an interior photograph; or to obtain the details of the image of white clothing, or to subdue the too pronounced details of a background on a portrait negative or on the negative of a commercial subject.

No retouching is admissible on negatives whose interest is scientific, historical, or documentary.

As a matter of principle, retouching should never be employed to make up for faults if the opportunity is available to avoid them by making a new negative under better conditions.

The beginner must be patient and should practise as much as possible on waste negatives. He will save a great deal of time if he can arrange to take some lessons from a practised retoucher.

The amateur who wishes, in an exceptional case, to retouch one of his own pictures, will save time by making an enlargement, on which all corrections may be much more easily effected, then making from this enlargement a negative of the size required.

697. Apparatus for Retouching. The retouching desk, large and firm, should be installed for preference near a north-light window, and at such a height that the retoucher may work seated before it without having to lean forward. Blinds must be arranged to screen both desk and worker from light at the sides and back. For work with artificial light it is often advantageous to cover the usual mirror with a sheet of white mat paper.

The folding desks described in many catalogues should, as far as possible, be avoided. They may, however, be considerably improved by replacing the silvered mirror with which they are fitted by a mat opal glass, and the ground glass serving as a support for the negative by a piece of clear glass.

The amateur may construct an illuminated table by placing a strong piece of glass on two boxes. The under side of the glass must be covered with white tracing paper and may be illuminated by means of light diffused from an inclined sheet of white cardboard. The light may be supplied to the latter from a window or lamp which is screened by a blind from the view of the operator.

Brushes used for spotting (§ 705) should be of camelhair or sable in a range of different sizes. Any stray hairs must be removed in order to obtain a perfect point, otherwise the brush will not produce a round spot. This may be done by dipping the brush in water then forming a point by drawing the hairs across a sheet of blotting paper while rotating the brush. Any protruding hairs are burnt off by holding the brush in the flame of a match for a short time.

Air brushes are commonly used in commercial, industrial and advertising photography for removal of unwanted backgrounds or for modification of certain areas of the negative (or print). An air brush consists of a fine nozzle, a reservoir containing the pigment and a button controlling a needle valve to the air supply. The air supply is normally a cylinder of compressed air or a compressor driven by an electric motor. Generally air brushes are used in conjunction with a mask or stencil to protect the areas of the negative that require no retouching. Masks are usually cut from transparent material such as celluloid or tracing paper and are held down by weights to prevent the pressure lifting the mask and the formation of unsharp outlines. Air brushing is usually carried out on the back of the negative and may be done without a mask when sharp outlines are not required.

The knives should be of very good quality and very carefully sharpened; one may use a surgeon's lancet, a vaccinating pen mounted in a solid penholder, or a large tailor's needle of which the point has been hammered and ground so as to obtain an edge formed by two surfaces inclined at about 45°, the needle then being fixed in a wooden handle, or mounted in the handle of an engraver's needle. A small oilstone (Arkansas stone, white and translucent) is used for sharpening the scrapers; the surface of this stone must be kept soaked with mineral oil. Sharpening is finished with a razor strop.

It has also been suggested (R. Demachy, 1905) that engraving tools and the triangular scrapers used by engravers should be used for removing details or undesirable reflections from negatives. Whatever type of retouching knife is used, it must be of such thickness that it does not vibrate when drawn across the negative. For local abrasion of the film, the use of a scraping brush of metal or glass wire has been recommended.

We must also note the use of stippling tools,

which are similar to pencil shells. In the inside of one of these tools is a point which is actuated by a minute electric motor, either with a to-and-fro motion or with an eccentric circular motion.

The pencils for negative retouching are of the best-quality graphite, selected from the groups F, H, HB, and B, or the bare leads of similar grades mounted in the corresponding lead holders, inside which the leads may be completely covered in order to protect them when not in use.

The letters constituting the distinctive marks of the various grades of pencil are the initials of the adjectives *firm, hard,* and *black.* The repetition of the letters H and B correspond to grades which are of increasing hardness or blackness. It must be remembered that the bare leads increase in diameter on passing from the hardest to the blackest, and therefore lead holders marked with the same letters should be used so as to avoid confusion.

For some time past use has been made of lead holders in the interior of which the lead is actuated by longitudinal to-and-fro movements or by eccentric circular motion.

Pencils should have long and very regular points; the wood is cut for a length of 1¼ in. or 2 in., care being taken not to break the lead. A little square of emery paper is then folded in two with the emery inside; this is held between the thumb and first finger of the left hand, and the lead of the pencil is introduced into the fold and turned between the fingers of the right hand, at the same time giving it a to-and-fro movement.

Pencils will not as a rule mark bare gelatine or the varnishes generally employed to protect negatives; the surfaces must first be prepared by means of a special varnish (retouching medium).

In order to allow pencil work without varnishing, the negative may be treated with powdered pumice gently rubbed in by circular movements of the palm of the hand.

Retouching medium may be prepared by dissolving gum dammar in benzene, or, better, in a mixture of equal volumes of benzene and turpentine. The proportions are 0·5 to 1·0 g to 100 ml, and a few drops of oil of lavender or castor oil are added.

The outfit of the retoucher should also include a good lens, and in order to avoid the fatigue resulting from the unequal use of the eyes with ordinary lenses, we cannot too strongly recommend the use of binocular lenses making use of

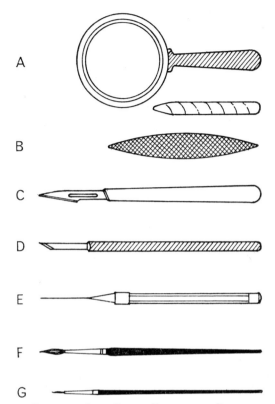

FIG. 35.7. SOME SIMPLE RETOUCHING TOOLS.

both eyes; these lenses are generally fixed to the head by means of a ribbon, or by side pieces as in the case of spectacles, thus leaving both hands free. Some simple retouching tools are illustrated in Fig. 35.7.

698. Technique of Retouching. O. R. Croy (1953) recommends that retouching should be carried out in the following order:

1. *Chemical methods* such as intensification and reduction.

2. *Dye retouching* in which the thinner areas that print too dark are made more dense by tinting the gelatine with water soluble dyestuffs.

3. *Mechanical or frictional reduction* in which the density of the negative is reduced by mechanical abrasion.

4. *Knifing* to lighten details or to remove them completely.

5. *Pencil retouching* is finally carried out after applying a varnish to the negative.

In all the methods of retouching involving the application, with a brush, of an intensifier, a reducer, or a dye, it is an advantage to use liquids which are sufficiently dilute and to carry out the operation by successive applications of the same reagent. In this way the appearance of sharply-defined edges to the areas treated may be avoided; such sharp edges, if they do occur, frequently do not coincide exactly with the outline which is intended to be followed. The edge of partial, successive treatments overlap one another to some extent, and give a graded effect which is much less obvious.

As gelatine always retains a considerable amount of moisture which does not allow the best conditions for working, it is advisable, before commencing retouching by methods 3 to 5) to dry the negatives by placing them for some time in an oven or near a fire, taking care not to melt or soften the gelatine.

699. Local Intensification and Reduction with a Brush. In order to allow for control, it is necessary to choose methods which make use only of a single solution and which do not produce more than temporary coloration of the gelatine; thus the mercuric iodide intensifier and Farmer's reducer, or one of their variants, are suitable.

If the sodium or potassium cyanides (dangerous poisons) are obtainable, they may be used with advantage in 4 per cent solution to replace the solution of sodium thiosulphate in this reducer. A stable mixture is thus obtained which does not leave the slight yellow coloration of ferricyanide; this is useful for dealing with paper prints which are to be locally reduced.

The operation is preferably carried out on the wet negative, which has been well wiped. The negative is mounted horizontally and illuminated from below (for reducing a sky, it may, however, be held almost vertically, with the image of the sky at the bottom). In order to help the liquid to adhere to the gelatine and to prevent its excessive diffusion on to neighbouring regions, its viscosity may be increased by dissolving sugar or by substituting glycerine or glycol for a part of the water in the mixture. In the case of reduction, the negative must be rinsed between each application.

700. Local Tinting of the Gelatine. Working up may be done by the additive method of tinting those parts of the negative which are too clear, or by the subtractive method of uniformly tinting the gelatine and then de-colorizing it in those parts of the negative which are too deep. Which method is preferable depends on the relative areas of the parts to be tinted and to be left plain.

For *additive tinting* one chooses a water solution of a dye which is absorbed by the gelatine but is not fixed by it, and which may therefore be completely removed by washing in cases where it is desired to obtain the negative again in its original condition. Of the substances complying with these conditions are notably *neo coccine*, giving a poppy-red colour (F. Schmidt, 1913), or *naphthalene black A* (G. L. Wakefield, 1938) and *tartrazine*, a lemon-yellow dye. When using coccine the work can be controlled better by placing a blue-green filter behind the negative as the visual density is then little different from the printing density although actually a little higher (H. Cartwright, 1935). The first trial applications should be made very carefully, only experience being able to teach the effect of a given intensity of colouring, red or yellow.

At the start a comparatively concentrated stock solution of one or other of the dyes is prepared, and from this stock solution are made up two solutions for use; one of these is so dilute that a single application by means of a brush on a transparent part of the gelatine produces only a very weak coloration which can hardly be seen; the other is about five times more concentrated. The colour is applied with a sable brush No. 2 or No. 3 for very small surfaces, No. 4 to No. 8 for large surfaces, according to the size of the negatives.

The brush, soaked in the diluted solution and well wiped, is moved over the parts to be tinted without breaking contact between the brush and the gelatine until all the liquid has been absorbed. The brush is re-charged and wiped, and the process continued, returning as often as necessary to the same parts, and, if necessary, allowing the gelatine to dry when it becomes saturated with water. It is only by the super-position of a great number of very thin layers that perfect uniformity is obtained, and slight errors of outline are made negligible. The more concentrated solution is only used when a certain amount of skill has been acquired, and even then only to obtain very intense tints; in any case it is as well to prepare the film by at least one treatment with the diluted solution.

For *subtractive tinting* a uniform yellowish-brown coating is produced by bathing the negative for some time in a solution of potassium permanganate containing 1 g per litre, without any addition of acid. After the negative has been rinsed and dried, local decolorization is carried out by means of a dilute solution of sodium bisulphite (e.g. 5 parts of the commercial solution diluted to 100 parts), thickened with glycerine or gum arabic (R. Namias, 1914). When the work is finished, the negative must be washed in a strong stream of water or shaken vigorously in a large dish of water.

A more recent method of tone control is by the use of *retouching foils*. The foils, consisting of a cellulose sheet coated with red or purple dye, are placed in contact with the negative and held in position by tape. For tone control the dye is decolourized by a bleaching solution in the areas required. Retouching foils are available in different densities and may be superimposed with different areas to give further control. The negative is printed in register with the foil and this method has the advantage that retouching does not affect the negative itself.

701. Local Abrasion of the Negative. In order to diminish the density of small areas of the image, the surface of the gelatine may be rubbed down by means of the finger or a piece of wash-leather with a little powdered pumice or kieselguhr; if a less vigorous treatment is required, the rubbing may be done with a wad of flannel or a skin stump soaked with metal-polish, or merely moistened with alcohol.

Abrasive pencils are sometimes used. These are prepared as follows: melt some hard paraffin wax and thoroughly mix into it some very finely powdered pumice. The amount of the latter should be as great as possible, while allowing the mixture to be poured. Mould in paper cartridges which have been made by rolling paper round a pencil. After the wax has set, the pencils may be peeled for the whole or part of their length, and may be pointed for allowing work to be done on very small surfaces. When a negative has been worked up in this way any grease is removed from it with light petroleum spirit (K. Smith, 1925).

702. Work on the Back of the Negative. A little carmine (moist water-colour) may be applied with the finger to the back of a glass negative, so as to cover uniformly those parts which are to be blocked out; the boundaries of these parts may be overstepped, and in such cases the excess may be removed with a moist duster, followed by a moistened brush. Printing must be carried out in diffused light, so that the thickness of the glass will prevent the outline of the work from showing too clearly in the print.

The back of a glass plate may also be covered with colourless or tinted *matt varnish*. Those parts which are to be clearly printed are then cut away with a scraper or with a wad moistened with alcohol, according to the area of the part to be treated. Parts which need darkening are covered with colour, as above, or are worked up with blacklead (graphite, plumbago), put on with a dry brush or with a soft stump.

An excellent matt varnish of average grain may be prepared according to the formula given below. The resins are dissolved in the ether[1] in a flask fitted with a sound wood cork. When they have dissolved, a process which may take several days in spite of frequent shaking, the benzene is added slowly, and the mixture is allowed to stand at least a week before the clear liquid is decanted—

Ether	700 ml
Sandarac . . .	65 g
Mastic (tears) . .	15 g
Benzene to . . .	1 litre

A finer grain is obtained by increasing considerably the amount of ether; on the other hand, a slight increase in the amount of benzene gives a much coarser grain. The matt varnish may be coloured yellow by dissolving a certain amount of *aurantia* in it.

The precautions necessary for spreading the mat varnish on the glass side of the negative are described later in the paragraph dealing with varnishing (§ 709). The chief thing to avoid is the application of any varnish to a place already dried. A negative on which the varnishing has not been successful may be cleaned by rubbing with a wad of cotton wool moistened with methylated spirit.

None of these methods is suitable for film negatives, but equivalent results may be obtained by working on a thin sheet of mat celluloid or on a piece of tracing paper which is fixed to the back of the film by pieces of cellulose tape.

703. Reduction in Contrast by the Use of a Soft Positive. It has often been suggested (A. Leitner, 1890) that excessive contrast in a negative may be compensated by placing

---

[1] Ether, is a very volatile liquid the vapour of which is very heavy and inflammable. It must be stored in well-corked bottles. The handling of ether, or the preparation of a mixture containing ether, must not be carried on near a fireplace or flame. The matt surface of this varnish is due to the sandarach used being insoluble in benzene, and so being precipitated, during the evaporation of the ether, in minute grains enclosed in a transparent layer of mastic.

against its back a soft positive transparency taken from the same negative. A special "auto-retouching" printing frame was indeed constructed (E. Artigue, 1903) for this purpose; with this apparatus a suitable transparency, which had been previously printed in the same frame, could be interposed in correct register.

This method is frequently used to reduce the contrast of subtractive colour transparencies (Kodachrome, Agfacolor, etc.), for the making of paper prints. The positive is then usually called a mask.

704. Blocking-out. The object of blocking-out is to obliterate all traces of background in a photograph which could not be taken against a white ground; the shadows cast by an object standing on a white ground are also obliterated by this method. The professional worker generally avoids these shadows by arranging the objects on transparent glass and photographing them from above. The glass is supported above a well-illuminated white background and far enough from it to prevent any shadows being projected. For this, one of the following methods may be used. The negative may be worked-up by tinting the gelatine in the way previously described (§ 700), or an opaque paint may be applied, either to the glass side (for a portrait in which the outlines are not usually very clearly marked) or to the gelatine surface (photographs of furniture, machines, etc., in which the outlines are sharply defined). Water colour body-paint or water colours (chrome yellow, vermilion, india red, etc.), or a solution of 20 per cent bitumen in turpentine thickened with a little wax, or special opaque paints may be applied with a brush or pen (at least for the outlines) to a breadth of about half an inch. Areas beyond this band may be masked by covering them with opaque paper. Good water-colour brushes, giving fine points, must be used. Before starting work it is advisable to remove all traces of grease from the surface of the negative by rubbing lightly with a wad of linen or cotton soaked in methylated spirit. In order to dilute the colour to the desired strength and to make sure of rapid drying, alcohol, or a mixture of alcohol and water, may be used.

705. Spotting. Spotting is the process by which the clear spots on a negative (dust, air bubbles, scratches, etc.) are touched out. For this purpose very small sable brushes are used; these, when moist, must give a very fine point. It is usually impossible to match the density of the spot exactly with that of the image, and thus it is usual to try to produce a slightly greater density in the spot than exists in the surrounding image. The work is then finished by retouching the positive prints.

Spotting is carried out on a well-illuminated retouching desk. The ground glass of the desk should be masked with a sheet of black paper having an opening of small diameter. The different parts to be spotted are then brought one by one over this opening, so that attention is concentrated on the spot to be treated.

For this purpose black water-colour, more or less diluted, may be used, or indian ink thickened with gum arabic or strong liquid glue (usually obtained in tubes); or blacklead mixed in a little negative varnish (§ 710). Mistakes may then be cleaned off by means of alcohol, but negatives which have been retouched in this way cannot be varnished unless a varnish is chosen which has no action on the resins of that previously used.

The work is followed through a lens. It is essential not to allow the colour to go so far as to form a ring round the hole to be filled, otherwise the defect is made worse. For very small holes, the colour used must be fairly thick; only a little must be placed on the brush, and the latter must be held perpendicularly to the surface of the negative.

706. Knifing. A series of close parallel strokes should be made until the whole of the area has been scraped. The area is then worked over a second and even a third time changing the direction of the strokes so that each successive scraping runs at an angle with the previous scraping.

The knife is used by its point or its edge, according to the extent of the marks which have to be erased or the outlines to be modified; it must be handled very lightly in the same way that it would be used to remove an ink mark on paper; avoid any heavy cuts which would pierce the gelatine. It must always be remembered that the pencil must be used on the scraped parts in order to finish the work and to equalize the density on the scraped parts with those of the surrounding areas.

707. Pencil Retouching. Before proceeding to retouch with the pencil it will be necessary to cover the portions to be worked on with a very light coat of medium or varnish (§ 710). For this purpose, a very small wad of cotton wrapped neatly in linen is used with a drop of the medium on it, or the end of the finger may

FIG. 35.8. STROKES USED IN PENCILLING A
NEGATIVE

be used. The excess may be removed by rubbing with the palm of the hand.

Local application of medium to an unvarnished negative sometimes leaves a slight halo. This may be avoided by previously cleaning the negative with a wad soaked in a little turpentine.

For preference, the hardest pencil capable of giving the desired effect will be used; thus the B pencil will be kept for those parts of which the density is to be considerably increased. The pencil should be applied very lightly in dots of fine hatching, straight or curved, or in over-lapping circles. Each mark should be so light as to be hardly visible by itself; the direction of the marks should follow the general lines of the subject. Fig. 35.8 shows on an enlarged scale some of the styles commonly adopted for re-touching. The pencil should always be applied very lightly, the pressure being slightly greater in the middle of each mark than at the extremi-ties. If it is required to darken certain parts of the image considerably, they must be worked over several times, each time putting on the marks at 45° to their preceding direction. Any retouching work which is too heavy may be lessened by knifing; moreover, at any time work may be entirely removed with a little turpentine.

During the process of retouching, it is well to examine the negative from time to time by turning it gelatine side downwards on the desk in order to judge the effect better.

Parts which are not dark enough, due to insufficient pencil work, may also be treated by stippling them with a fine brush moistened with crimson lake (water-colour).

After the retouching has been finished a trial print is made and is carefully compared with the original print.

708. Added Backgrounds. Some photo-graphers occasionally pose their models in front of a black background, filling in a background to the negative by subsequent work on the glass side. One of the methods used for this purpose is very old (La Blanchère, 1863), and has even been used by some celebrated painters to make "negative drawings" of pictures and so to furnish an infinite number of prints by means of photographic printing. The negative (or plain glass) is placed on a black ground (velvet, cloth, paper) and the desired design is drawn on the glass by painting with white body-colour; it thus appears as a positive by reflection and a negative by transmitted light.

For very simple backgrounds (draperies, clouds, etc.), a very light and uniform layer of finely-powdered red chalk may also be deposited on the glass; this is worked on by wiping off with a cloth or stump. In this way only very feeble contrasts can be obtained, but the effect may be very agreeable. The work is protected by spraying with a "fixative" or by covering with another sheet of glass.

VARNISHING, STRIPPING, CLASSIFICATION
AND STORAGE

709. Varnishing Negatives. The varnishing of negatives ensures them against numerous accidents. It is advisable for negatives which are required for large numbers of prints, and which in time may become scratched by rubbing. Varnishing is strongly recommended for nega-tives which have been retouched to any extent, but it is essential, in this case, to make sure, by trial on a waste negative, that the varnish to be used will not destroy the pencil retouching by dissolving the film of medium which serves as a substratum. Finally, when enlarging by direct light, varnishing of the negative lessens the effect of minor superficial scratches which are not noticeable in contact prints. Certain varnishes, called *hot negative varnishes*, can be used only if the negative has been previously warmed to a temperature of at least 90°F (32°C). Unless this is done, a matt surface is formed by condensation of the moisture in the atmosphere on the surface of the varnish, which is cooled by the evaporation of the solvents. These hot varnishes are suitable only for plates as the hot solvent may attack the film base.

Warming of the negatives is dispensed with if *cold negative varnishes* are used, the only precaution necessary being thorough drying of the negative beforehand. Varnishing of nega-tives should never be carried out in a damp or cold room.

A number of satisfactory varnishes are sold commercially but, if preferred, any of the formulae in the following paragraphs are suitable.

710. Preparation of Varnishes. Varnishes prepared with alcohol are generally used for glass negatives, and, since they do not dissolve the dammar of the medium, can also be applied to retouched negatives. Ordinary collodion to which a very small quantity of castor oil has been added is occasionally used; and a solution of celluloid or cellulose acetate in amyl acetate is sometimes employed. Alcohol varnishes should never be applied to films (which seldom require varnishing), as the alcohol tends to soften the film base. Instead, a water varnish for retouched negatives, or a benzene varnish in the case of unretouched ones, should be used.

It should be borne in mind that the various solvents usually employed in the preparation of varnishes are inflammable; if it is desired, therefore, to hasten solution of the resins by warming the mixture, the operation should not be carried out near a naked flame. Ether, or any mixture containing ether, should never be heated. All risk of fire can be avoided by the use of non-inflammable solvents, such as carbon tetrachloride and other chloro compounds, in the preparation of varnishes.

Hot Negative Varnish. The following varnish will take retouching quite easily, and is compounded in the cold or over a moderately warm water bath.

Sandarac	. 150 g
Essence of lavender . .	. 15 ml
Alcohol, 96 per cent, to . . .	1 litre

Cold Negative Varnishes. Waste pieces of film can be used in the preparation of the following varnish, after they have been washed and dried—

Cellulose acetate . .	. 15 to 20 g
Amyl acetate to . . .	1 litre

For unretouched negatives, one of the following varnishes, which take work with a pencil easily, can be used—

Sandarac	. 100 g
Acetone	. 400 g
Crystallizable benzene . .	. 400 ml
Denatured alcohol to . .	. 1 litre

or—

Powdered copal resin . . .	. 50 g
Gum dammar	. 20 g
Carbon tetrachloride to . .	1 litre

The latter must be prepared boiling and filtered while hot.

Water Varnish for Films. White gum lac (125 g) is dissolved in 250 ml of alcohol. When dissolved, 200 ml of concentrated ammonia is added. The gum lac is thus precipitated in a finely-divided state, and the whole should be shaken several times to re-dissolve it (to a soapy resinous state). Boiling water is added to bring it to a volume of 1,000 ml, and the whole is kept on a water bath for a while. The liquid is never quite clear and should be used only after it has stood for some time.

Benzene Varnish for Films. A 2 per cent solution of gum dammar in crystallizable benzene is used. The film should be allowed to dry for several days, otherwise it might adhere to anything with which it is pressed in contact.

711. Application of the Varnish. Plates to be varnished should be thoroughly dried by keeping them for some time near a source of heat. A drying cabinet in which hot air circulates is very useful.

For cold varnishing, the plates are first dried in this way and then left to cool. When cold carefully dust the plates just before the application of the varnish. The knack of coating the varnish can be acquired after several trials, but its description is somewhat lengthy; Fig. 35.9 shows the various stages of the operation. The plate is balanced on the fingers of the left hand and kept level under the thumb at the left-hand corner. The varnish is poured on to the centre of the plate until it covers about one-third of the surface. It is then allowed to spread until the liquid reaches the two sides of the corner opposite the thumb. By careful manipulation,

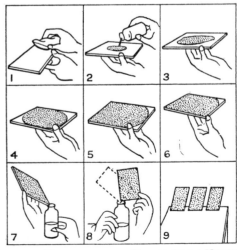

FIG. 35.9. MANIPULATION IN VARNISHING A NEGATIVE

this corner is inclined, then the other corners in succession, care being taken that the varnish does not reach the thumb and run up the arm. When the whole of the plate is covered, it is raised first at an angle of about 45° and then vertically, allowing the excess of varnish to drain into the bottle. While draining, the plate should be rocked from side to side to prevent streakiness. The negatives should then be put to dry, away from dust.

For hot varnishing, both the plates and the varnish are first warmed, and the coating carried out preferably over a hot slab or a stove, observing the same precautions as given for cold varnishing.

Films can be varnished by immersion in a dish which is filled with varnish to such a depth that the film is completely covered. After a few minutes, having ascertained that there are no air bubbles under the film, the latter is slowly lifted out, allowed to drain for a minute or two, and finally hung up by a corner until completely dry.

When using a water varnish, the films can, if required, be varnished as they come from the last wash water. Varnishes, such as the cellulose acetate/amyl acetate varnish, may be applied to the negative by spraying with a small atomizer or spray gun.

712. Removal of Varnish from Negatives. Glass negatives, which have been varnished, and which have been subsequently found to require after-treatment, can be cleaned by allowing them to soak for some time in denatured (industrial) alcohol in which 2 per cent of caustic soda or caustic potash has been dissolved. The varnish very soon becomes milky and can then be easily removed by gentle rubbing with a wad of cotton wool soaked in the alcoholic solution of soda. The negative is then washed in several changes of water and put to dry.

The varnish from a water-varnished film negative may be removed by immersing in a very weak solution of caustic soda (about 1 per cent) to which about 20 per cent of industrial alcohol may be added to avoid excessive swelling of the gelatine. The operation is completed by gentle rubbing with a tuft of cotton wool, and washing in several changes of water.

Gum-dammar varnish can be removed from a film negative by prolonged immersion in rectified benzene (crystallizable benzene would evaporate too quickly). The cleaning is completed by rubbing with a wad of cotton wool impregnated with crystallizable benzene, and the negative put to dry.

713. Stripping Plates. Stripping, that is to say, detaching the emulsion from the glass support, is used for certain methods of printing which require a reversed negative, or to save a negative which is cracked but not broken (§ 671) or, on occasions, to reduce the space occupied by a collection of glass negatives. The emulsion layer can either be preserved as such, or mounted on a fresh support.

To avoid the swelling of the gelatine when removed from its support, it must be well hardened. Preferably the plate should be kept at least one hour in a 3 per cent solution of chrome-alum or ordinary alum, quickly rinsed to avoid crystallization of the alum during drying, wiped down and dried. In the case of emergency formalin may be used (§ 662). Whatever method of stripping is employed, the gelatine film is first cut through to the glass with a scalpel or razor blade, either about a quarter of an inch from the edge of the plate, or as far as may be done without encroaching on the required subject.

Commercially, a 1 per cent solution of hydrofluoric acid, is generally used for the purpose, which frees the gelatine by dissolving the surface of the glass to a slight extent.

Concentrated hydrofluoric acid (solution of about 50 per cent) is very dangerous to handle; a drop falling on the hand causes a blister which takes a long time to heal, and inflammation which spreads up the arm. In dilute solution the acid is not so dangerous. Whatever its concentration, it dissolves glass, stoneware, and all usual metals, and can therefore be stored and used only in containers (bottles, funnels, and dishes) of moulded synthetic resins, or possibly in susceptible materials protected by a thick coating of varnish or paraffin wax. If stripping is carried out only occasionally, the difficulties arising from the use of hydrofluoric acid itself can be avoided by employing alternative methods.

It is possible, for instance, to use a mixture, prepared at the moment of using, of equal volumes of a 5 per cent solution of sodium fluoride, and of a 5 per cent solution of hydrochloric acid or 1 per cent solution of sulphuric acid (measured in volumes).

After a few minutes the emulsion layer becomes detached. To make sure, the margin beyond the cut is tried with the finger-tip. The whole layer may then be lifted off. For this purpose, a sheet of paper (preferably parchmentized, also called sulphurized paper, or, failing this, good quality white paper) larger than the negative, is previously put to soak in a dish of water. This sheet of paper is now placed on the negative, which is laid flat on the table, and, working from the centre outwards, the water is expelled by means of a squeegee or a soft, thick, rubber roller. A corner of the paper is then gently lifted until a corner of the negative is visible. If the emulsion has not come away with the paper, it should be lifted with a blunt point (such as a soft pencil) to make it adhere to the paper and, taking hold of both paper and emulsion with the fingers, it is pulled off with a gentle and even movement. The emulsion thus taken off with the paper can then be transferred to its final support.

The above method, although quite suitable for small and medium sizes, is difficult for the treatment of very large negatives owing to the fragile nature of the gelatine film. In such cases the emulsion should be strengthened, before making the marginal incision, by coating it with a 2 per cent solution of collodion to which a little glycerine is added, and then left to dry.

If the negative emulsion layer is to be kept as such for making prints which require a reversed negative, it should be coated with a syrupy solution of rubber before collodion varnishing, and left until the excess of solution has drained off and the greater part of the benzene evaporated. Prolonged immersion in the bath of fluoride solution is necessary for the liquid to penetrate completely between the film and the glass.

A slower but very certain method (Liesegang, 1892, perfected by H. Drouillard, 1903) consists in placing the negative to be stripped, after it has been cut round the edges, in the following bath for *at least* half an hour (it can be left there all night). This bath can be used repeatedly—

Sodium carbonate, anhydrous	.	30 to 40 g
Formalin .	.	.	.	50 ml
Glycerine .	.	.	.	10 ml
Water to .	.	.	.	1 litre

On removal from this solution, the surface of the negative is blotted off, and, without any rinsing, it is then left to dry completely, hastening the latter process, if necessary, by gentle warming. The drying rack should be placed in a clean dry dish, as the film sometimes comes off while drying. If the emulsion does not then peel off easily the dry negative is placed in a solution containing about 5 per cent of hydrochloric acid. This causes an effervescence, some

of the carbon dioxide gas thus evolved being liberated between the emulsion and the glass. In this way the emulsion becomes detached, or at any rate its adhesion is so reduced as to allow of its being removed on to paper as described above.

Finally, attention should be called to the following rapid procedure, which is very suitable for negatives of small size and which can be used after washing but before drying them (A. Popovitsky, 1900). The negative is immersed for 10 to 15 minutes in a saturated solution of potassium carbonate, in which about 5 per cent of caustic soda or potash has been dissolved. The negative is then dried between blotters, polished with a soft cloth, and a cut made round the part required. One of the corners is then lifted with a penknife and the film detached with a gentle pull.

714. Stripping Films. It is sometimes necessary to strip the gelatine emulsion from film negatives, even though such negatives, being extremely thin, can be printed from either side satisfactorily, provided care is taken to avoid poor contact.

To remove the emulsion it has been proposed (Lumière, 1903) to swell the celluloid base by immersing it in one of its solvents, such as acetone, to which enough water has been added to prevent solution.

Also, the following process has been recommended (Eastman Kodak Co., 1922). The surface of the negative is coated with a 6 per cent solution of gelatine, flowed on at the lowest possible temperature. After drying, the film is placed in a strong solution of formalin (25 to 50 per cent of the commercial liquid) for about ten minutes, and then again dried. A cut is then made with a penknife, and the negative placed in a 15 per cent solution of acetic acid, when, after a few minutes, the emulsion layer can be detached from the support.

715. Transfer of the Emulsion Layer to a New Support. When the emulsion layer is to be transferred to glass or celluloid, the latter should be previously coated with an adhesive, such as a weak solution of gum arabic, or with a solution of gelatine of about 10 per cent strength poured on while hot and allowed to set to a jelly. When the new support is to be celluloid, this gelatine should be dissolved in glacial acetic acid of about 10 per cent strength, after which about a quarter of its volume of alcohol is slowly added, so as to make the gelatine adhere to the celluloid. For the occasional stripping of a negative a fixed-out and well-washed film or plate can be used. The film can also be transferred to a piece of perfectly clean glass which has been polished with French chalk or coated with a solution of wax in ether; after drying the film on this temporary support, it is coated with a syrupy solution of rubber, allowed to dry, and finally given a coat of collodion or celluloid varnish.

Either before or after transferring to the final support, the film should be washed with water to get rid of the salts used in the stripping process; when the washing is done before transferring, a piece of plain glass, larger than the film, is placed on the bottom of the dish on which the film can be lifted out without risk of tearing it.

Care should be taken to put the right side of the film in contact with the support. The side will vary according as the film is placed on a temporary or a final support, or if it is to be used for making direct or reversed prints. If, when the film has been taken off on a piece of paper, the upper surface is not that which must come into contact with the support, it can be transferred to another piece of paper and then applied to the prepared surface of the final support, which has been evenly wetted (or coated with a solution of gum, if this adhesive is used). The excess of liquid is removed with a squeegee or a rubber roller.

716. Removal of the Gelatine Coating from the Back of Film.

When the gelatine coating on the back of a film has been stained or scratched it can be removed fairly easily (J. I. Crabtree and F. E. Ross, 1926). To do this, the emulsion side of the film is applied to an adhesive surface, and perfect contact is ensured by passing a soft rubber roller or squeegee, care being taken that there is no defect in contact at the edges of the film in a width of about $\frac{4}{5}$ in.

The waterproof adhesive surface can be of glass covered with rubber (coated at least 30 minutes previously with a thin layer obtained by evaporating a syrupy solution containing at least 5 per cent amyl acetate), or glass covered with a coating containing vinyl resins, or surgical rubber strapping. The back surface is then moistened with a mixture of equal volumes of water and acetone. When the work is finished the film is separated from the adhesive and cleaned with petrol.

717. Removal of Emulsions from Waste Plates and Films.

In cleaning off the emulsion from old negatives and for recovering the silver contained in the films, the simplest method consists in softening the gelatine by long immersion in water to which a small quantity of caustic soda has been added, and then dissolving it by placing in very hot water. The partly melted gelatine is then scraped off and the cleaning of the support completed by leaving it for a minute or two in a very weak solution of sodium hypochlorite followed by rinsing in cold water.

Commercially, various enzymes are used to remove the gelatine by digestion. Old celluloid films which have been freed from gelatine with caustic soda and insufficiently washed have been known to ignite spontaneously while drying.

Another method is to soak the gelatine in a solution of sodium carbonate of about 10 per cent strength to which a little caustic soda has been added; when dry, the film is stripped off by treating with hydrochloric acid, it being of course unnecessary to take any of the precautions given above for proper stripping.

718. Titles on Negatives.

Numbers, titles, and signatures may be added by cutting out the letters from a dense part of the image with a fine-pointed graver, or by writing with a pen on a lighter part. The latter method is preferable, being quicker, and the work is of better quality. Instead of writing in ink, which requires the use of a retouching desk, it is simpler to use yellow water-colour which has been thinned to a suitable consistency. The writing is then quite visible by reflection, and can be done with the negative flat on an ordinary table. It may be useful to write from left to right, as is the practice of engravers and lithographic draughtsmen, on the negative, turned upside down, making the characters as shown in the accompanying specimen (Fig. 35.10). After a few hours' practice it is possible to write in this fashion quite readily and without using a specimen.

For engraving negatives there have been placed on the market bronze styles fitted in an insulated handle and heated to about 176°F (80°C) and connected to alternating current by a small electric bell transformer. The hot point melts the gelatine, leaving a transparent line with sharp edges. Another more complicated method for transferring an inscription on paper to gelatine has been suggested. The inscription is written on glazed paper, using a glass pen, with a very concentrated solution of potassium ferricyanide thickened with a little glycerine and to which a small quantity of blue dye may be added. The paper is transferred to the gelatine surface which has been previously moistened in

0123456789

abcdefghijklm

nopqrstuvwxyz

ZYXWVUTSROQON

ABCDEFGHIJKLM

0123456789

abcdefghijklm

nopqrstuvwxyz

ZYXWVUTSROQON

ABCDEFGHIJKLM

FIG. 35.10. REVERSED TYPES FOR TITLING NEGATIVES

the required place. When it has been in contact with the gelatine for a few minutes, i.e. when the silver has been attacked, the silver ferrocyanide so formed is dissolved out in a fixing bath. The negative should then be washed.

In the case of negatives made for large numbers of prints, the title is generally set up in type, and printed on to the negative. Special rubber type is sold giving an imprint similar to that shown in the specimen. When the letters have been assembled in the type holder, they are printed on a thin part of the negative with a greasy ink. The density of the imprint is increased by dusting over with a little blacklead, afterwards brushing off the excess: the lead adheres to the greasy ink and not to the dry gelatine.

Another method is as follows. Using a good typewriter, from which the ribbon has been temporarily removed, the title is written on a piece of very thin paper which has been placed between the prepared surfaces of two pieces of unused black carbon paper. In this way the letters are printed on both sides of the paper at the same time, thus obtaining sufficient density. This is then attached to the negative and the two printed together. A clear area for the title may be formed on the negative as follows. A black gummed strip is stuck on the emulsion before exposure, on the side corresponding to the bottom of the picture. This is detached before processing so as to allow free access for the fixing solution (E. J. Kloes, 1925).

Titles to print white on a black ground can also be set up in type and transferred to the negative in various ways. The impression can be made on thin sheets of Cellophane with a very stiff ink and moderate pressure, dusting over with blacklead as above while the ink is still tacky. The titles are then cut out, and the printed side fixed to the gelatine with a very weak solution of gum arabic which has been applied on the part to be covered.

The imprint can also be made on lithographic transfer paper with a good transfer ink. The titles, when cut out, are placed face upwards on a pad of damp blotting paper, and covered with some dry blotting paper to prevent their curling up.

After a few minutes the soluble layer of the transfer paper becomes sufficiently moistened, and the printed surface of each strip can then be applied to the gelatine of the negative in the required position, causing it to adhere by pressure with the fingers. The back of the paper is dried with two applications of dry blotting paper, and the transfer done by pressure with a burnisher. After some time (judging the correct length of time is the beginner's only difficulty; it is therefore advisable to take at least two proofs of each specimen, so that one can be used to experiment with on a waste negative), the back of the paper is moistened with a paint-brush, a corner raised with the point of a penknife, and the paper lifted smoothly off. When the gelatine is dry, the ink impression is strengthened by powdering with blacklead.

Titles which have frequently to be repeated, such as a trade-mark or a signature, can be copied on a contrasty plate or film from the original. The prints can be made on transfer paper or on a very contrasty plate from which the emulsion is stripped, and applied while wet to the gelatine of the negative.

For titles to print black on a light part of the picture, a film negative of the desired text can be transferred to the negative after having scraped off the gelatine from an area to receive it, the title negative being secured with a weak solution of gum-arabic. The text can be made, for instance, with the help of a stencil of the type used by industrial artists or for titling amateur ciné film, and which permits of normal or reversed writing at will.

In the case of a signature which has to appear in black on a white ground, a method of double printing is generally used. A negative of the signature is made on a contrasty film or plate, any small defects being carefully blocked out on the dense portion, and the sides extended with masks of opaque paper. After exposing the sensitive paper under the negative of the subject, it is then exposed under that of the signature, adjusting the latter to a suitably chosen position, or setting it against stops of thin cardboard cemented to the signature negative.

719. Classification of Negatives. A methodical classification is necessary in order that negatives required for any purpose can be found without loss of time. To this end, all negatives should be numbered and arranged in numerical order. Since negatives of different sizes cannot be kept together without risk of accident, it is advisable, in order to avoid mistakes, to adopt a separate series of numbers for each size. Each size then forms a series designated by a letter which precedes the number.

An index of the negatives will naturally be carried out differently by a professional, amateur or research worker, classification being according to commercial importance in the first case, whilst technical information is of primary importance in the last two cases.

Such a file-index, besides containing numerical classification data (negative number, date, type of subject), and particulars of accounts (details of the order, agreed price, amount of deposit, promised date of delivery, amount payable) may also contain any information which is likely to explain the cause of a failure or deterioration, and any facts which will enable one to profit in the future by the experience gained (camera used, lens aperture used, film, light-filter, lighting, exposure, and any further details). The register may also contain any data which might facilitate the future use of the negative (suitable methods of printing, the best conditions for printing or enlarging, the most desirable method of mounting proofs, etc.).

In some cases the index can be usefully supplemented by a complete collection of actual prints contained in an album or card-index file. All or some of the particulars mentioned above (with, of course, the exception of accounts) may then be written at the side or on the back of the print instead of in the register.

720. Storage of Negatives. The most economical method of storing plates, and that which requires the least space, is to keep them in the cardboard boxes in which they were originally packed. Each plate should be protected by a wrapper of some kind, on which the series letter and the number of the negative

is written, to avoid the negative being scratched, or the retouching, working-up, or title on the negative being rubbed off. These wrappers should be, if possible, fairly transparent so as to allow the negative to be identified without removing it from its wrapper. In the case of plates kept in a box it is quite satisfactory just to use interleaving sheets of paper giving the necessary information, instead of a complete wrapper for each plate.

The transparent envelopes usually sold for negative storage are quite suitable for films, but totally unsuitable for plates. The sharp edges of the glass cut the envelope when the plate is slipped in, and after a certain amount of handling, the edges of the envelope which overlap the plate become creased and bent. Again, the film side of the negative should never be allowed to come into contact with the gummed part of such envelopes, since gum of bad quality has been known to cause deterioration of the image.

The boxes should be kept on shelves in the same way that volumes are placed in a bookcase, and labels indicating the lowest and highest numbers of the negatives contained therein should be stuck on the side of the box or lid, exposed to view. Apart from the fact that this arrangement of the boxes on edge allows of their being taken out and replaced without disturbing the others, the boxes of negatives suffer the least possible strain, and are therefore less exposed to accidents.

Similar arrangements could be adopted for storing a small quantity of film negatives, each film being protected by a transparent envelope or in an album containing envelopes of transparent paper for this purpose. For large collections, the negatives may be kept vertically as in a card index, in suitable boxes or drawers. Negatives should be stored in a room which is neither very damp nor very dry.

In Great Britain the storage of celluloid in the form of sensitive film or celluloid negatives is subject to regulations under Section 79 of the Factory and Workshop Act.

As regards sensitive films, kept on premises in a quantity which as a rule does not exceed 14 lb., storage in a drawer or cupboard in a private office or other room in which no handling of celluloid is done, is officially regarded as complying with the requirement for " safe storage."

The regulations with respect to developed negatives will depend to some extent on the amount of such negatives. Where the latter are of considerable weight, they require to be kept in a fire-resisting store, such as a cabinet or cupboard constructed of fireproof material, e.g. sheet metal, asbestos sheeting, or wood effectively treated to resist flame. The store requires to be of sound construction and is to be kept locked. The door or lid needs to be so arranged that there is no naked light or open fire near at hand. The store should not be situated in a workroom where celluloid is handled, nor on a staircase, nor near a door, nor in a passage through which persons might have to pass to escape in the event of a fire. The nature of the contents should be clearly marked on the outside of the store, and a cautionary notice put up prohibiting the use of naked lights. An adequate supply of buckets of water should be kept always available close outside the store, water being the best extinguisher of burning celluloid.

The foregoing recommendations apply mainly to the storage of celluloid films manufactured before 1950. The fire precautions only apply to museums and film archivists who store quantities of celluloid films since modern film base materials are no more inflammable than paper.

Index

The numbers refer always to the paragraph numbers in the text, and *not to the page numbers.*

The numbers refer always to the paragraph numbers in the text, and *not to the page numbers.*

The numbers refer always to the paragraph numbers in the text, and *not to the page numbers.*

The numbers refer always to the paragraph numbers in the text, and *not to the page numbers.*